Three
Invasions

Three German Invasions of France

The Summer Campaigns of 1870, 1914 and 1940

by

Douglas Fermer

Pen & Sword
MILITARY

First published in Great Britain in 2013 by
Pen & Sword Military
an imprint of
Pen & Sword Books Ltd
47 Church Street
Barnsley
South Yorkshire
S70 2AS

ISBN 978-1-78159-354-7

A CIP catalogue record for this book is
available from the British Library.

Typeset in 10/12 Ehrhardt by Concept, Huddersfield, West Yorkshire
Printed and bound in England by CPI Group (UK) Ltd, Croydon, CRO 4YY

Pen & Sword Books Ltd incorporates the imprints of Pen & Sword Archaeology,
Atlas, Aviation, Battleground, Discovery, Family History, History, Maritime,
Military, Naval, Politics, Railways, Select, Social History, Transport, True Crime,
Claymore Press, Frontline Books, Leo Cooper, Praetorian Press, Remember When,
Seaforth Publishing and Wharncliffe.

For a complete list of Pen & Sword titles please contact
PEN & SWORD BOOKS LIMITED
47 Church Street, Barnsley, South Yorkshire, S70 2AS, England
E-mail: enquiries@pen-and-sword.co.uk
Website: www.pen-and-sword.co.uk

Contents

List of Maps

List of Illustrations

1. Emperor Napoleon III (1808–73).
2. Marshal Edmond Le Bœuf (1809–88), Minister of War.
3. Helmuth von Moltke the Elder (1800–91).
4. German troops storm the Chateau of Geissberg during the Battle of Wissembourg, 4 August 1870. From an 1884 painting by Carl Röchling (1855–1920).
5. Defence of Stiring station near Forbach, 6 August 1870. From an 1877 painting by Alphonse de Neuville (1835–85).
6. French troops in retreat, August 1870. Sketch by Alphonse de Neuville.
7. A convoy of French wounded, August 1870. Sketch by Alphonse de Neuville.
8. On the Firing Line: A Memory of 16 August 1870. Engraving after an 1886 painting by Pierre-Georges Jeanniot (1848–1934).
9. Marshal Achille Bazaine (1811–88). Photograph taken during the Mexican campaign.
10. Storming of the Cemetery of Saint-Privat, evening of 18 August 1870. Engraving after an 1881 painting by Alphonse de Neuville.
11. The French retreat towards Metz, 18 August 1870. Engraving after a painting by Richard Knötel (1857–1914).
12. The White Flag at Sedan, 1 September 1870.
13. Proclamation of the German Empire in the Hall of Mirrors at Versailles, 18 January 1871. From an 1885 painting by Anton von Werner (1843–1915). Bismarck is in the white uniform at centre.
14. Kaiser Wilhelm II (1859–1941) and, at right, Helmuth von Moltke the Younger (1848–1916) on manoeuvres before the First World War.
15. A French regiment departs for the front, Paris, August 1914.
16. General Joseph Joffre (1852–1931) at centre with Generals Paul Pau (1848–1932) at right and Edouard de Castelnau (1851–1944) at left. Note Pau's artificial left hand, the result of a wound in 1870.
17. A German infantry column marching through a burning Belgian village, August 1914.
18. Joffre's counteroffensive depended on moving units rapidly by train. Men of the 6th Territorial Infantry Regiment prepare to embark at Dunkirk, August 1914.

Picture sources and credits: *Cassell's Illustrated History of the Franco-German War*, London, 1899, No. 2; Jules Claretie, *Histoire de la Révolution de 1870–71*, Paris, 1872, Nos. 1, 3; *Illustrated London News,* 17 September 1870, No. 12; J.F. Maurice, ed., *The Franco-German War 1870–71, by Generals And Other Officers Who Took Part In The Campaign*, London, 1900, Nos. 4, 11, 13; Quatrelles, *A coups de fusil*, Paris, 1875, Nos. 6, 7; Jules Richard, *En Campagne: Tableaux et Dessins de A. de Neuville*, Paris [n.d.], No. 10; Jules Richard, *En Campagne (deuxième série)*, Paris [n.d., circa 1885], No. 8; L. Rousset, *Histoire Générale de la Guerre Franco-Allemande (1870–1871)*, illustrated edition, 2 vols., Paris, 1910–12, No. 5.

Nos 1–14, photography by Tony Weller; Nos 15–30 courtesy of TopFoto.

Preface

This book tells the story of three pivotal events in the history of modern France – the German invasions of 1870, 1914 and 1940. It focuses on the opening campaigns fought between the French and German armies in three wars, offering in each case a compact account of what happened and how. One justification for such an approach is that on all three occasions the first six weeks of fighting following the crossing of the French frontier by German armies proved crucial in determining France's ability to continue resistance. In each case the force and speed of the German offensive forced the French to abandon their own military plans in order to defend their own territory. The three campaigns saw fighting sometimes over the very same ground, but none was an exact replay of the last, and each had a different outcome. In two cases the military decision went in Germany's favour but in the other, in 1914, German forces were checked by a French counteroffensive.

The lives of three generations of Frenchmen and Germans were shaped by the recurrent clashes between the two powers in their protracted contest for mastery in Europe. The German Empire was created as a result of the Franco-Prussian War, when the Germans achieved a spectacularly rapid victory at Sedan in 1870 over a French imperial army that until that summer had been considered the best in Europe. Although newly mustered French armies fought on for another five months, they proved unable to reverse the verdict of the opening campaign. Learning from the disaster, the next generation of Frenchmen succeeded in turning back the German invasion of 1914 by a victory at the Marne, but they were unable to drive their stronger opponent from French soil for another four years, and then only with the help of allies. Germany was defeated in 1918, but the attempt to restrain her military power by the Treaty of Versailles unravelled within a few years. The revival of German ambitions under Hitler, and his unscrupulous use of force against Germany's neighbours, brought the two countries to war again twenty-one years later. In 1940 German armies achieved victory on a scale that led with breathtaking speed to French capitulation. It was the one occasion when military triumph enabled the victor to impose his political will immediately.

Of course, each of these three wars had a distinctive character. The first involved Germany and France alone, whereas in both the First and Second World Wars the fighting on the French frontier was but one front in a European war that later became global. The theatre of war was much wider than in 1870, and ever larger numbers of men were mobilized. The technology and weapons in use had also developed by leaps and bounds. In 1870 breech-loading rifles and cannon were only beginning to reveal their lethal potential, and whilst commanders could move armies by railway and send orders by telegraph, they also had recourse to sending messages by balloon and carrier pigeon or, more usually, by mounted messenger. By 1940 their successors had radios and telephones, could move at least a portion of their troops by motor transport, and had at their disposal tanks, aircraft, high explosive shells and a whole range of weaponry scarcely dreamt of by their predecessors. Hence these three campaigns are customarily treated not together but as episodes within the history of three distinct conflicts: the Franco-Prussian War, the First World War and the Second World War. The half-century of increasing historical specialization since Alistair Horne wrote his epic trilogy on the Franco-German Wars has perhaps reinforced a tendency to compartmentalize events in which Horne rightly discerned a certain unity.

Within a modest compass, this account invites the reader to consider these three invasions as a connected series rather than in isolation. The narrative therefore includes chapters briefly describing how the outcome of each conflict contributed to the coming of another, and how the strategy and tactics of each war influenced those of the next.

The perspective of time also invites the treatment of these events as a unity. Although the battles of 1870 seem very distant from us, they were separated from those of 1940 by only seventy years, the proverbial lifespan of man. While the lives of hundreds of thousands of young men were brutally cut short by the conflicts described here, others lived through or even served in at least two of them, and some elderly French people alive in 1940 had the misfortune to experience all three invasions. The last veteran of the Franco-Prussian War survived until 1955, the last *poilu* of the Great War until 2008. More time now separates us from the events of 1940 than separated Sedan from Dunkirk, where in 2010 French and British veterans gathered, probably for the last time, to remember their shared ordeal of seventy years earlier.

That commemoration was a reminder of how different the French experience of the 'German Wars' was from that of her British ally. The differences derived not only from geography and diverging strategic priorities, but from the French experience of invasion and defeat. In Britain 1940 is celebrated as the 'Finest Hour', the year of the 'miracle' of Dunkirk and the Battle of Britain, of deliverance and survival. But for France there came no miracle, no salvation: only a catastrophic military defeat that for a few awful weeks seemed to presage the collapse of French society. In France 1940 remains for ever the year of disaster, the nightmarish prelude to the 'dark years' of occupation. Like the defeat of 1870–71 before it, it became the subject of long soul-searching and recrimination over responsibility for the defeat – between generals and politicians, between the friends of the Republic and its enemies, between Right and Left, between capitulators and resisters. The controversies about 1940 are not yet extinct, and probably the French and British views of the campaign can never be fully reconciled, but they can at least be set in their historical context.

Finally, several volumes much thicker than this one would be required to do justice to the Franco-German Wars and their impact, and to explore the many themes touched on only in passing in this narrative. Readers who want to delve deeper into the subject can find a few suggestions for further reading in English at the back of this book. Many of the titles listed contain extensive bibliographies. In the meantime, the present volume may serve as a convenient introduction to events upon which the fate of France turned, and which thrice shook Europe and the world.

Douglas Fermer
2013

Acknowledgements

As for my previous books, my thanks go to the staffs of the British Library, the Institute of Historical Research, King's College Library, Croydon Central Library, and also to Diana Manipud of the Liddell Hart Centre for Military Archives. Thanks, too, to Tony Weller for photography and digital processing of illustrations 1–14, and to Mark Dowd of TopFoto for supplying illustrations 15–30 with permission to reproduce them here. Once again I have the privilege of including maps by John Cook in my text. I owe him a debt of thanks for his creative collaboration, and also his son Matthew for preparing the maps digitally. In matters technical I have been several times narrowly saved from apoplexy provoked by the perversity of computer systems thanks only to the technical proficiency of my son Edward and son-in-law Anthony. Finally, I am as ever grateful to the team at Pen & Sword Books, particularly Rupert Harding and my editor Sarah Cook, for their help and support in producing this book.

The Background

Not so long ago, the only question at issue when discussing the military power of the states of Europe was whether France could hold her own against the rest combined.

Anatole Prévost-Paradol, 1868

Chapter 1

The Era of French Ascendancy

The unity of Western Christendom enforced by the emperor Charlemagne was fractured in the decades following his death in the year 814. In the battles fought by his grandsons for their share of his inheritance in what is now eastern France can be discerned, however dimly, the clash of opposing armies speaking languages recognizable as Old French and Old High German. Yet warfare could alternate with co-operation. At Strasbourg in 842 two of the grandsons, Charles the Bald and Louis the German, swore an oath to aid each other against the other grandson, the emperor Lothar. By a treaty signed at Verdun the following year they forced Lothar to agree to divide the empire in three. That division, it should be emphasized, was made not on the basis of race or language but according to the conveniences of feudal lordship and geography. Charles became King of the West Franks, Louis King of the East Franks, while Lothar was left with a middle kingdom stretching from the North Sea to the Italian plains. When some years later Lothar's son and namesake died without issue, his central portion of that middle kingdom was divided between Charles and Louis, leaving only an echo in the name of the border region called Lothringen in German, Lorraine in French. From these partitions were to develop over succeeding centuries the kingdom of France in the west and to its east the Holy Roman Empire – the first German Reich.

The intermittent struggles of those rival powers with each other, with their other neighbours and with their own rebellious subjects need not detain us. Suffice it to say that by the seventeenth century it was France's turn to be in the ascendant. France by that time had been unified by its kings and was strongly centralized, while the German lands of the Holy Roman Empire were fragmented and ravaged by decades of religious war. Louis XIV could not resist taking advantage of the weakness and disunity of his German neighbours. By the Treaty of Westphalia which restored peace to central Europe in 1648 he took most of Alsace, and capped his gain in 1681 by seizing Strasbourg, the great trading city on the west bank of the Rhine. Lorraine was peacefully acquired by France during the reign of his grandson and successor, Louis XV, in 1766.

By that time a formidable new German power had appeared on the European scene. Little by little the Electors of Brandenburg had added to their disparate territories which straddled the north-eastern boundary of the Holy Roman Empire presided over by the Habsburg Emperors of Austria. Prussia had become a sovereign state in 1660, and by 1701 had achieved such status that its Hohenzollern ruler assumed the title of king. As it expanded, Prussia advertised itself as a refuge for Protestants persecuted in Catholic countries, particularly those expelled from Louis XIV's France, for it needed manpower. Having no natural defensive barriers, it was not so much a country as a state efficiently organized to support a fiercely disciplined army which was disproportionately large in relation to its modest geographical area. In the middle decades of the eighteenth century Frederick the Great showed what could be achieved by bold use of this redoubtable weapon, and a Prussian way of war became recognizable – compensating for being the under-dog by aggressively taking the war to his enemies before they could unite. Although nominally a subject of the Holy Roman Empire for some of his lands, in 1740 Frederick showed how little weight he attached to such obligations by attacking Austria at a period of weakness and seizing Silesia, and then in 1756 attacking neighbouring Saxony. When the Great Powers combined against him in the Seven Years' War he contrived to beat them one by one, thrashing the French at Rossbach in 1757, and by the greatest good luck managed to survive and hang on to his gains from Austria.

The French Revolution of 1789 heralded a new era of French expansion fuelled by ideological fervour. The beleaguered French royal family hoped desperately for help from the European courts, which became rallying points for dispossessed French royalist *émigrés* whose complaints were echoed by German aristocrats whose surviving landholding rights in Alsace had been abolished by the French National Assembly. Threats to the revolutionaries from Austria and Prussia raised the temperature. In France the cause of republicanism and liberty had become inextricably linked with the struggle against monarchist reaction and its sponsors at home and abroad. Under the spell of eloquent promises by its leaders that the war would be short and easy, and that the subject German peoples would soon rise up to throw off the yoke of their despotic rulers, the French Assembly declared war on Austria in April 1792. Henceforth those in France who opposed the revolutionaries could be stigmatized as traitors and foreign agents.

Rather to the surprise of the French, the Prussians made common cause with the Austrians, with whom they had secretly agreed territorial gains in the event of victory. The allied invasion that summer precipitated some of the key events of the revolution. In Paris on 10 August the revolutionaries stormed the Tuileries Palace and took the royal family prisoner. When news came through that the Prussians had captured Longwy and Verdun, fears spread that the foreign armies would carry out their threat to sack Paris. The response from the revolutionaries was not merely the inspired oratory of Danton but terror – the massacre in September of all suspected royalists held in the capital's prisons.

The Prussians, too, had expected an easy victory, believing the tales of the *émigrés* that the French regular army had been weakened by the loss of too many of its aristocratic officers. Yet when they reached Valmy at the southern edge of the Argonne on 20 September they found a larger French army drawn up to face them and not at all inclined to yield. With their army debilitated by sickness and supply difficulties, it took little more than a heavy French cannonade to persuade the Prussian commanders to withdraw. Although it ended in a stand–off, Valmy took on immense mythic importance to the French. That first successful defence of French soil became the lasting symbol of republican triumph over aristocracy and reaction, of patriotic volunteers over foreign enemies, and of peoples over kings. The failure of the Austro-Prussian rescue doomed the deposed Louis XVI and his Austrian queen to the guillotine the following year. During 1793 French armies enlarged by mass conscription went over to the offensive, conquering the left bank of the Rhine which the revolutionaries declared to be France's 'natural frontier'. Prussia, while still winning some victories over the French on western German soil, came to see the war against them as a distraction from the opportunity for major territorial gains at the expense of the Poles, who had been attacked by the Russians. With the Terror in France over, in 1795 Prussia made a pragmatic separate peace with France and turned to secure its share of the second partition of Poland, leaving Austria and Britain to continue the struggle against the revolutionary armies.

Before France had plunged headlong into war with most of Europe, Robespierre had warned his heedless compatriots of its dangers. An invasion of the German states would exasperate the inhabitants, among whom the cruelties perpetrated by Louis XIV's armies remained a byword: 'The most extravagant idea that can take root in a politician's brain is to believe that it is sufficient to mount an armed invasion of a foreign country for its people to adopt your laws and constitution. Nobody loves armed missionaries.'[1]

His words proved prophetic, for although at first there was much enthusiasm for French ideas among middle-class Germans, particularly artists and intellectuals, the realities of liberty, equality and fraternity exported at bayonet-point presented an ugly contrast with the cosmopolitan ideals of the revolution. Short of pay and regular supplies, the French ruthlessly pillaged the countries they occupied – not only the German states but the Low Countries and Italy – occasionally provoking desperate acts of resistance by the inhabitants. Quickly persuaded that foreigners were unworthy of liberty and fraternity, the French mostly showed an arrogant disdain for the people of occupied countries. A German pamphleteer complained in 1793 of their tendency

> To write and speak with indecent contempt about Germans in general, about German customs, intelligence, society and taste – indeed about everything there is under the German sun, and to use the words *tudesque*, *germanique* or *allemand* as synonyms for stupid, ponderous and uncouth.[2]

Robespierre made another prescient prediction about the risks of waging war amid divisions at home: 'In times of troubles and of factions the leaders of armies become the arbiters of the fate of their country ... If they are a Caesar or a Cromwell, they will seize power themselves.'[3]

Napoleon Bonaparte, victorious in his campaigns in Italy, passed from being the saviour of the Directory to presenting himself as the saviour of France, as at once the terminator of the revolution and the guarantor of its gains. First Consul in 1799, he crowned himself Emperor in 1804 in conscious emulation of Charlemagne.

With hindsight, but only with hindsight, we can appreciate the irony that it was Napoleon I who set in motion the reshaping of the German states that would culminate decades later in their unification. Yet that was far from being his objective. The rationalization of the map of Germany carried out by the French from 1803 was driven partly by crusading zeal to sweep away feudalism and replace it with French laws and principles. However, their overriding need was to exploit the German states in their own interests as sources of men, money and supplies. The medieval jigsaw puzzle of more than 300 independent petty sovereignties was eventually reduced to fewer than 40. The middle-sized states were willing partners in this division, which allowed them to appropriate the lands of wealthy bishoprics and abbeys and to expand at the expense of their former neighbours.

Once Napoleon had spectacularly defeated Austria and Russia at Austerlitz in 1805, he was free to create a Confederation of the Rhine east of that river, formed of client states whose foreign policy he controlled. His allies the rulers of Bavaria, Württemberg and later Saxony were made kings, those of Baden and Hesse-Darmstadt grand dukes. With the formation of the Confederation in July 1806 the Holy Roman Empire became a dead letter, and after nearly a thousand years of existence its crown was formally resigned by the emperor of Austria in August.

This expansion of the Napoleonic Empire brought the well-seasoned *Grande Armée* to the borders of Prussia, which could buy Napoleon's alliance only at the price of accepting vassal status. Intending to teach Bonaparte a lesson, Prussia issued him an ultimatum to withdraw beyond the Rhine. Prussian officers made a show of sharpening their sabres on the steps of the French embassy in Berlin. But it was Napoleon who administered the lesson before his enemies were ready. Militarily sclerotic and without allies, Prussia's armies were routed at the twin battles of Jena and Auerstadt on 14 October 1806. The following year, having also defeated the Russians, Napoleon imposed crushing terms on Prussia, including a huge indemnity, the loss of much territory, military occupation and enforced compliance with the French blockade of Great Britain. Prussia's western territories were combined with Hanover to form a new Kingdom of Westphalia for Napoleon's brother Jerome.

Had it not been for Napoleon's hubris, for his pursuit of endless conquest and subjection, who can say how long French domination of the German lands might have endured? When he invaded Russia in 1812 more than a quarter of his huge army of over 600,000 was German-speaking, including the Prussian contingent. After the catastrophic winter retreat from Moscow, the defection to the Russians of General Yorck's Prussian troops undermined French hopes of holding the line of the River Niemen, and with it the Napoleonic Empire in central Europe. Yorck acted in defiance of his hesitant king, who remained fearful of French retaliation but was persuaded to join in a war of liberation in alliance with Russia. Austria, fearful of Russian domination of Germany, offered Napoleon peace on the basis of his withdrawal west of the Rhine. He refused, trusting in his powers as a commander to defeat his divided enemies. Finally Austria too joined in the war against him being waged in Germany. Napoleon was brought to bay by the armies of the coalition around Leipzig in Saxony in October 1813. Although he escaped destruction he received such a mauling that he withdrew from Germany, while the rulers of the lesser German states who had been his allies changed sides on condition that the allies allowed them to retain the lands, titles and sovereignty that he had granted them. The allied invasion of France followed: a long rearguard action that ended with their capture of Paris in March 1814 and Napoleon's abdication.

A year later the allies were still working out the peace settlement in Vienna when news arrived of Napoleon's escape from Elba and his return to power. They immediately declared him an outlaw with whom they would not treat, and marched against him. In Blücher, leading a Prussian army reinvigorated by the reforms of Scharnhorst and Gneisenau, Napoleon met a commander of will and energy equal to his own. Despite defeat at Ligny, Blücher brought his army to Wellington's support at Waterloo, so ensuring a decisive victory.

So ended the Napoleonic epic, the culmination of a quarter-century of warfare. The victorious allies punished France by stripping her of all her gains since the conflict began, by a large war indemnity and by occupation by allied forces until 1818. If the peacemakers of Vienna could not restore the Holy Roman Empire or undo all Napoleon's changes in Germany, they created a new German Confederation of thirty-nine states within the boundaries of the old Empire, once again presided over by Austria. Napoleon's Kingdom of Westphalia disappeared, partly into the hands of Prussia, which also received a large portion of the Rhineland. However, the other allies resisted Prussia's demands for Alsace and Lorraine, having no wish to see her grow too powerful or to undermine further the credibility in France of a Bourbon monarchy twice restored by foreign bayonets. If Prussia and Austria remained rivals for influence over the smaller German states, they presented a united front with Russia in their determination to contain France within her old boundaries and to react immediately to any sign of renewed aggression on her part. That resolution lasted for a generation after Waterloo.

At the popular level a current of mutual mistrust between Frenchmen and Germans ran deep, but there was also much cultural interchange. German liberals pressing their monarchs for constitutional reform drew inspiration partly from French ideas. Socialists and other political exiles from the police of ultra-reactionary German state regimes found a haven among the large German community in Paris, where they could develop their ideas and prepare propaganda for distribution at home. German state governments could all too easily point to France as the source of revolutionary subversion, and use the bogey of the French menace to bolster the established order.

Yet the German state authorities, taking their lead from Austria, were equally fearful of the new spirit of German nationalism ignited by the War of Liberation against Napoleon and kept alive, particularly by student groups, despite political repression. German nationalists drew inspiration from philosophers like Fichte, whose *Addresses to the German Nation* (1807–8) had been delivered in Berlin during the French occupation; to activists like Jahn, propagandist and organizer of rallies and popular activities; and to poets like Arndt, who declared that the French were the hereditary enemy. However limited their impact in the post-war years of reaction, the nationalists made a lasting impression on the generation of young men who came to maturity in mid-century, by which time the growth of railways, roads, canals and the telegraph increasingly made the maintenance of petty sovereignties appear anachronistic and a handicap to commerce.

At times of international crisis the power of German nationalism could be suddenly laid bare, for instance in the wake of the 1830 revolution in France which overthrew the Bourbon monarchy and led to a confrontation with Prussia and Austria over the question of Belgian independence. German popular anger was manifested even more dramatically in the crisis of 1840, when France seemed ready to take on Europe over a Near Eastern quarrel. And when during the revolution of 1848 German liberals called a parliament in the hope of creating a united Germany, the demands of some members for the inclusion of all German-speaking Europe, including Alsace and Lorraine, revealed the extent of nationalist ambitions.

The French were slow to understand the depths of resentment they had left behind them in the regions they had conquered at the zenith of their military power. Amongst French intellectuals indeed there was a fashionable enthusiasm for all things German in the decades following the wars. Inspired by Germaine de Staël's somewhat idealized vision of the lands beyond the Rhine in her book *De l'Allemagne* (1814), a generation of French writers and thinkers made the pilgrimage to Germany, not just to admire and learn from the achievements of German science, philosophy, music, literature and historical writing, but to imbibe the 'mysterious' spiritual atmosphere of its forests and mountains, peopled by supposedly peaceful, pipe-smoking and beer-drinking peasants. 'I have studied Germany and felt that I was entering a temple', wrote the young Ernest Renan, testifying to its hold over the imagination.[4]

Such attitudes hardly percolated beyond a cosmopolitan elite. All French governments, of whatever political stripe, resented the settlement of 1815 and looked forward to the day when it could be modified or overthrown. That attitude was widely shared by the French public, among whom the notion of the 'natural frontier' of the Rhine was equally well-rooted. The French harboured too a pervasive nostalgia for conquest and the days of *la gloire* which military victory had brought them, expressed through the Napoleon cult. Immediately after Waterloo leading Bonapartists had been proscribed, even murdered, and the royalist police were vigilant for the slightest sign of political activity by those loyal to Napoleon, but as the decades passed the cult grew stronger, fed by patriotic histories. In 1840 King Louis-Philippe's bellicose minister, Adolphe Thiers, persuaded him to organize a ceremony in Paris to witness the return of Napoleon's remains from Saint-Helena. Possibly a million people attended. Thus the Orleanist regime capitalized on popular Napoleonic sentiment, even as it imprisoned Louis-Napoleon, the political pretender to the Napoleonic inheritance, after his second attempt to stage a coup.

At the time of the 1840 war-scare French feelings ran quite as high as German, but the strident nationalism on display had strong ideological overtones. For many Frenchmen, not only was the settlement of 1815 perceived as deeply unfair, but the ideals of the revolution seemed to be at stake. They saw France as having a continuing mission to support liberty among oppressed nations and to break the hold of the reactionary autocracies which suppressed it within their domains and had combined to keep France in fetters. The prudent foreign policy pursued by royalist governments could only condemn them as cowardly and contemptible to the heirs of both the Jacobin and Bonapartist traditions. When a revolution in Paris toppled Louis-Philippe in 1848, its leaders declared that 'In the eyes of the Republic the treaties of 1815 no longer exist in law.'[5] Subsequent peaceful professions could not dispel German fears that French armies would soon be on the march, though in the event the revolutionary Left soon lost power.

Foreign governments were again apprehensive when later that year Napoleon's nephew was elected President of the French Republic by a large democratic majority. Louis-Napoleon proved to be a guardian of order at home, but he knew how to exploit the immense popularity his uncle's name brought him in France. On the anniversary of Austerlitz, 2 December 1851, he staged a coup d'état and shortly proclaimed himself Emperor Napoleon III with the overwhelming support of French voters. He reassured them and foreign powers by declaring at Bordeaux in 1852 that 'the Empire means peace'.

Within a decade Napoleon III appeared to have restored France's fortunes both literally, in the years of economic prosperity which the country enjoyed, and on the foreign stage. In the 1850s the alliance which had defeated his uncle broke apart. He joined with Britain to defeat Russia in the Crimea, a conflict which produced a rift between Austria and Russia over their Balkan interests. The peace conference to settle the war was held in Paris, where the emperor of the French could savour the prestige of victory. In 1859 he made successful war on an isolated Austria in Northern Italy, where in his youth he had joined in the struggle for liberation. Although his hopes of creating an Italian client state went unfulfilled, he did achieve the first small but significant reversal of France's former territorial losses. Nice and Savoy were ceded to France by Piedmont as a reward for her aid, and the transfer was ratified by plebiscites in both territories.

This French success raised German hackles, and fears that victory in Italy would be the prologue to an advance to the Rhine. Prussia's partial mobilization of her forces in the west helped persuade Napoleon to make an early peace with Austria. The furore in the German press was immense, and books like Adolf Tellkampf's *The French in Germany: Historical Pictures* (1860) luridly revived the sufferings of the earlier struggle. The excitement died down, and in 1862 France and Prussia signed a commercial treaty. The crisis had been a stark reminder, nevertheless, that whatever the rivalries and mistrust between the German states and the strength of local loyalties to the reigning dynasties, the surest way to unite all German opinion was through confrontation with France, for 'Against the French, all Germans are one.'[6]

Part I

1870:
The Débâcle

Whether the unification of Germany into a single state is accomplished under the nose of a passive France or against the will of a beaten France, in one way or another it means the irrevocable overthrow of French dominance.

Anatole Prévost-Paradol, 1868

Chapter 2

The German Challenge

By 1860 France seemed fully to have recovered her place in the world after her defeat at the hands of the combined powers of Europe a generation earlier. She was prosperous, with a growing empire in Africa and the Far East. Paris was being transformed by an ambitious rebuilding programme. In matters of fashion and culture France was the arbiter of taste, and her language was the currency of courts and diplomats in their relations with each other. Her army was the most respected in Europe, and the campaigns of the first Napoleon were everywhere studied as master classes in the art of modern warfare. Although the past had shown her need to avoid coalitions against her, France seemed still capable of defeating any single power that might challenge her, as she had demonstrated by defeating the armies of Russia and Austria within the last five years.

In the second decade of his reign Napoleon III's fortunes seemed to wane even as his health declined. If the Italian campaign had brought prestige, its outcome displeased the Catholic party at home, who were dismayed by the Pope's loss of his territories. Compelled to maintain a French garrison to protect the Papal City of Rome from Italian nationalists, Napoleon forfeited what little gratitude the Italians felt for his intervention against Austria on their behalf. His attempt to impose French rule on Mexico (1861–7) led to a protracted guerrilla war which was unpopular at home and ended in a fiasco. Once United States forces, victorious in the American Civil War, were free to take threatening positions along the Rio Grande, French troops were withdrawn. The Austrian Archduke Maximilian, installed by the French as Emperor of Mexico, was captured and executed by the Mexicans.

Within Europe, though conspicuously not outside it, Napoleon III professed interest in redrawing the map to reflect the claims of nationality. In practice, this interest was inseparable from a desire for French strategic gains. In 1863 his proposal for an independent state for the rebellious Poles, reflecting widespread public sympathy in France for their cause, only deepened a rift with Russia. His proposal for an international congress to revise the 1815 settlement was rejected by the other powers, which rightly suspected a French scheme for possible acquisitions in the Rhineland or Belgium. The congress idea was privately condemned by Queen Victoria as 'an impertinence', and suspicion of French ambitions played its part in disposing Russia and Britain to view the subsequent enlargement of Prussia as an acceptable counterweight to France.[1]

The rise of Prussia dominated the European scene from 1864. Her Minister President, Otto von Bismarck, had been appointed by King Wilhelm I in 1862 to push through contentious reforms to the conscription system which greatly expanded her army. When a dispute arose between Danish and German nationalists over the succession in the border duchies of Schleswig and Holstein, Bismarck exploited the situation to resume Prussia's traditional policy of territorial expansion, aimed at joining up her separated eastern and western territories. In a short war Prussia and Austria defeated the Danes and jointly annexed the duchies. French sympathy was strongly with the Danes, but Napoleon III initially saw Prussia not as a threat but as a potential ally or client, whose disruptive ambitions might further his own plans. Bismarck encouraged him in this view, while avoiding any formal engagement.

Austria had joined with Prussia in the war against Denmark both to maintain her own claims to primacy in Germany and to keep a rein on Prussian ambitions. But the two victors soon fell out over their spoils. An agreement between them at Gastein in 1865 made French diplomats apprehensive, and to reassure Napoleon Bismarck travelled to the resort of Biarritz that October. There he sounded the emperor on France's attitude in the event that Prussia were to make gains in Germany at Austria's expense, and reported that Napoleon was ready 'to dance the cotillion with us without knowing in advance when it will begin or what figures it will include'.[2] Henceforward Bismarck made ever more exacting demands on Austria, leading to a breach the following summer. Napoleon also encouraged the Italians to make a military alliance with Prussia: an alliance Prussia needed in order to put the larger Austrian army under pressure from the south while Prussia attacked it from the north. The three months time-limit on the agreement set the timetable for war.

When hostilities broke out in June 1866 Napoleon seemed to be in an excellent position. So anxious were the Austrians for his neutrality that they agreed to hand over Venetia, and verbally assented to French gains along the left bank of the Rhine if Austria won. Napoleon had no formal agreement with Prussia, but he had told her ambassador that in the event of Prussian victory he would discuss the matter of the Rhine with King Wilhelm. The war between Austria and Prussia was being fought to decide which would dominate the other German states. A long conflict seemed probable, opening opportunities for French intervention. Whatever the outcome, Napoleon would gain prestige for securing Venetia for the kingdom of Italy, and France seemed poised to make gains on her eastern frontier.

After a lightning campaign into Bohemia, the Prussian armies met and destroyed the main Austrian force at the Battle of Königgrätz or Sadowa on 3 July: a fateful day for the future of Germany, and no less so for the course of Franco-German relations. The shock felt in Paris at this unexpected news was like a thunderclap from a clear sky. Prussia was now master of North Germany. Having connived at the break-up of the German Confederation, how should Napoleon react to this dramatic shift in the Central European balance of power? The cabinet was divided, as was French opinion. The political Right, including the Empress Eugénie, Marshal Randon, commander of the army, and the Duc de Gramont, the French ambassador in Vienna, urged prompt mobilization of the army on the eastern frontier, so that France could act as an armed mediator and set a limit to the ambitions of Protestant Prussia. This was consistent with the traditional foreign policy of using French strength to keep Germany divided and weak. The opposing view, held not only by many liberals and republicans but by powerful cabinet figures like Eugène Rouher, was that the humbling of arch-conservative Austria, pillar of the 1815 settlement, was to be welcomed, that Prussia was a progressive force at the head of German national aspirations, and that it was in French interests to reach an accommodation with her.

Napoleon at first opted for armed intervention, but was soon persuaded that it was better to present himself as a peaceful mediator. French public opinion was at this point strongly opposed to military involvement. There were also reasons to doubt the army's readiness as many of its best regiments were overseas and its infantry was armed with muzzle-loaders, whereas at Sadowa the Prussians had given a sobering demonstration of the power of their breech-loading, bolt-action rifles, the so-called needle gun. In any case, Prussia quickly indicated its acceptance of Napoleon's offer of mediation.

Many condemned Napoleon III's failure to intervene decisively to curb Prussia's designs, first among them the Empress, who was strongly Catholic and pro-Austrian. On returning from a visit to Lorraine to mark the centenary of its accession to France, she proposed on 23 July that her husband should abdicate in her favour. 'We are marching to our ruin,' she told the Austrian ambassador with ill-advised candour, 'and it would be best if the emperor *suddenly disappeared*, at least for some time.'[3] Napoleon was suffering miseries from bladder stones but, much though he might have preferred to devote himself to his project of writing a life of Julius Caesar, he was not inclined to relinquish power. If his options in Germany were limited by the extent of Prussia's victory, he believed that France could exercise an important influence on the final peace treaty between Prussia and Austria. Although Prussia annexed not only Schleswig and Holstein but all the states north of the River Main which had taken Austria's side, including Hanover, Hesse-Cassel, Frankfurt and Nassau, Napoleon insisted that Saxony should retain its separate identity and that the German states south of the Main, principally Bavaria, Württemberg and Baden, should have an independent national existence. He also had a provision inserted in the treaty that a plebiscite should be held in largely Danish northern Schleswig as to its future. On these terms he accepted Austria's exclusion from Germany and Prussia's dominance north of the Main.

As a reward for his benevolent neutrality, Napoleon presented Bismarck with his bill: a brazen request for substantial 'compensation' for France on the left bank of the Rhine. Bismarck kept the French talking while he concluded a settlement with Austria. With every passing week Prussia became less vulnerable to the possibility of French military intervention, which Bismarck soon surmised was unlikely to materialize. Napoleon found himself thwarted by an astute and ruthless opponent who respected only force. Bismarck showed the French plan for compensation, which included a large area of Bavarian territory, to the governments of the South German states, letting them see that Napoleon was not their protector but a predator. They were persuaded that their own safety required alliance with Prussia, particularly as Bismarck offered them the inducement of remitting the heavy war indemnities he had demanded of these recent allies of Austria. The southern states signed offensive-defensive alliances with Prussia even before the peace with Austria was concluded. Seeking to make gains to satisfy French public opinion Napoleon had, instead of making allies of the South German states, driven them into the Prussian camp. Even the French stipulation of a plebiscite in Schleswig was subsequently disregarded by Bismarck.

In a circular that September Napoleon claimed that his German policy had been a great success, helping to reshape Europe on the basis of nationality. In reality, having been hailed at the beginning of July as the liberator of Venetia and the arbiter of Europe, the impotence of his search for compensation had been exposed. Critics complained that he showed more interest in advancing the claims of Poles, Germans and Italians than skill at securing gains for France. Bismarck meanwhile exploited German nationalist anger at French demands for German-speaking territory and pretensions to determine the future of Germany. French public opinion veered round to apprehension of the danger presented by the new Prussian-dominated North German Confederation created by Bismarck in the wake of the victory over Austria. France was seen to have been humiliated, and Napoleon appeared as an importunate cur worrying for scraps at Bismarck's table. From the autumn of 1866 war between France and Prussia was talked of as a probability on both sides.

But Napoleon had not given up the search for compensation. The French ambassador in Berlin, Vincent Benedetti, was instructed to approach Bismarck for a treaty of alliance by which France would support the Prussian absorption of the South German states in return for Prussian support for the French annexation of Luxembourg, and possibly later of Belgium. Bismarck had no wish to enter into a commitment and let the matter drop, though he retained the draft treaty in Benedetti's handwriting. Next spring Napoleon, believing that he had Bismarck's informal encouragement to do so, attempted to purchase Luxembourg from its owner, the king of the Netherlands, who was willing to sell but thought it prudent to inform the king of Prussia. Once word of the transaction got out there was a wave of nationalist anger in Germany at the sale of any 'German' territory. For although Luxembourg was not part of the new North German Confederation, it had belonged to the old German Confederation. The Prussian garrison in its fortress was strengthened, and Prussian troops were deployed menacingly close to the Dutch border. The intimidated Dutch king backed out of the sale. War seemed imminent – 'our swords were fairly jumping out of their scabbards', wrote a French officer[4] – but was averted by an international conference held in London. Although

Luxembourg was neutralized and France obtained the withdrawal of the Prussian garrison, the confrontation had been another public rebuff for Napoleon, who believed that Bismarck had acted in bad faith.

Moreover, Rouher's pretension to the French Chamber that the South German states were genuinely independent was mocked by Bismarck's publication of his military treaties with them, by the progressive assimilation of their armed forces into the Prussian military system and by Bismarck's inclusion of them in the parliament of the German Customs Union, which was essential to their prosperity.

Although courtesies were observed when King Wilhelm and Bismarck visited Paris for the Universal Exhibition in the summer of 1867, Napoleon and his advisers were aware of the danger to the regime of any further loss of face at the hands of the North German Chancellor. In any future confrontation France would need to stand firm and to be in a position of strength. Napoleon initiated army reforms and sought allies. His efforts to secure alliances with Austria and Italy, which continued into the summer of 1870, produced little more than professions of good intentions between the sovereigns concerned. It was unlikely that Italy would embrace an alliance involving her old oppressor Austria, with whom she had so recently been at war and who still occupied regions she coveted. Between France and Italy lay always the obstacle of Rome, which France was committed to defend but which was the goal of Italian ambitions. Austria was even more diffident about an alliance with France, which had prised her Italian provinces from her, acquiesced in her losses in Germany and abandoned a Habsburg prince to his fate in Mexico. The newly powerful Hungarian half of the empire had no interest in a war of revenge in Germany. Even so, Napoleon pursued military conversations with the Austrian general staff and, despite Austrian reservations, seems to have persisted in the belief that if war did break out as a result of a Prussian move to annex the South German states then the Austrians would be drawn in on the French side by the prospect of avenging Sadowa.

It was certainly a goal of Bismarck's policy to promote closer union with the states south of the Main, and in 1866 success had seemed only a matter of time. However, in the following years opposition to union with the north was growing stronger rather than weaker in the southern states. Catholics, who were in the majority there, had no relish for being absorbed into the mostly Protestant, highly militarized north, or being drawn into a war declared by Prussia in which they would have no say. State patriotism was strong, and there was widespread resentment at Bismarck's attempts at assimilation, all of which seemed to have stalled by the spring of 1870. At times Bismarck thought that union with the south might take another generation to achieve. If the liberal nationalists in the North German Reichstag succeeded in forcing the issue prematurely, they might precipitate a war with France while alienating the south. If on the other hand France provoked a war on some other issue then the treaties of alliance with the south would come into effect and nationalist feeling there would be rallied, helping to ease the path to political union.

If Bismarck, a close observer of French politics, needed any reminder of how excitable the Paris press could be, in February 1869 French rage over the failure of their designs to purchase the Belgian railways led to accusations that his machinations were behind their discomfiture. Napoleon wrote privately to his army commander,

> Since Prussia's successes, France has felt herself diminished; she would like to find the occasion to re-establish her influence in the best possible conditions ... I have no desire at all to drag my country into a war where public opinion, right and justice were not on my side; but, if circumstances unprovoked by me became favourable, I would not shrink from the responsibility that I would incur before posterity.[5]

Speculating at this time on how North Germany might support Russia in the event of a general European war, Bismarck confided to the Russian ambassador that 'nothing would be easier than to compel the French government to mobilize to avoid the consequences and the effect on public opinion in France of measures he had in mind to take in Germany'. France would thus be forced to take the role of aggressor. Bismarck stressed that he would take such a step only reluctantly, and that it would be preferable that the German question were further advanced than it currently was. He mentioned German relations with Spain among several issues that could offer the opportunity for 'diversions' which might bring about German entry into such a war 'without giving it the appearance of an aggressive cabinet war'.[6]

A year later Bismarck took up in earnest the possibility of placing a member of the Prussian royal family on the throne of Spain. The initiative came from the generals who had ruled Spain since the overthrow of the Bourbons in 1868. They approached the South German branch of the Prussian royal dynasty, the Hohenzollern-Sigmaringens, in the utmost secrecy, only after various other candidates for the vacant throne had declined. Prince Leopold of Sigmaringen was a Prussian army officer, but also a Catholic married to a Portuguese princess. The family was initially unenthusiastic. Prince Karl Anton, Leopold's father, had written in December 1868, 'The Spanish candidacy pops up so far only in the newspapers; ... and if this idea were brought to us, I would never advise the acceptance of this dubious position, glittering with tinsel. Besides, because of our relation to Prussia, France could never permit the establishment of a Hohenzollern on the other side of the Pyrenees.'[7] The family declined initial approaches, and during 1869 Bismarck showed little interest in the matter. Only in February 1870, upon a further representation from the Spanish government, did he pursue the opportunity. He urged various advantages of Leopold's candidacy, including dynastic prestige. He was aware of French attempts to ally with Austria and Italy. To secure an ally in France's rear would help offset this anti-Prussian combination, and in the event of conflict would force France to detach a significant body of troops to watch the Pyrenees.

King Wilhelm was unconvinced by Bismarck's arguments when they were aired at a meeting in March, and wanted to let the matter drop. Neither Leopold nor his brother was eager to be a candidate, and by spring the project seemed dead. Bismarck nevertheless kept in contact with the Spanish government and eventually succeeded in reviving the candidacy. By June Leopold had been persuaded to accept, and Wilhelm reluctantly gave his permission. The affair would have become public during July when the Spanish parliament voted on it, but word leaked out at the beginning of that month.

On 3 July, the fourth anniversary of Sadowa, what King Wilhelm called the 'Spanish bomb' burst in Paris with publication of the news of Leopold's candidacy.[8] France was bound to oppose such a move, but the French reaction was particularly violent because this was seen as a deliberate provocation, a direct challenge to France's standing in Europe, and the last straw in a series of humiliations. Not only had France not been consulted about a dynastic change affecting her interests, but the Prussian Foreign Ministry compounded the 'insult' by refusing to discuss the matter. Although Bismarck was for decades to maintain the fiction that he had no prior knowledge of the Hohenzollern candidature and that it was a family matter, the French government was not fooled. It set out to obtain not only Leopold's withdrawal but a formal admission of Prussian complicity.

Had Bismarck deliberately set out to provoke a crisis to further the unification of Germany? The diary of one of his emissaries contains a hint that he was seeking 'complications' with France, but Bismarck's calculations can only be inferred.[9] In any event, when the crisis broke it almost ended in his humiliation and resignation. The French launched a far-reaching diplomatic offensive, making overt threats of war and enlisting other sovereigns and governments to exert pressure on Wilhelm to have the candidacy withdrawn. Prince Karl Anton, head of the Hohenzollern-Sigmaringens, was given to understand that French influence in Spain could soon make Leopold's tenure precarious, and that measures might be taken to undermine the rule of his brother Karl in Romania. These veiled French threats, pressure from Wilhelm and the imminent prospect of a war over the issue persuaded Karl Anton to announce Leopold's withdrawal on 12 July. The French seemed briefly to have won a resounding diplomatic victory; one which, in the words of the pacific *Constitutionnel*, had cost 'not a single tear, not a single drop of blood'.[10]

Neither Gramont, the French Foreign Minister, nor Bismarck had any intention of leaving matters there. Gramont was an advocate of containing Prussia, and sought nothing less than her humiliation, even to the point of proposing to her ambassador that Wilhelm should write Napoleon a personal letter of apology. The first minister, Émile Ollivier, though a liberal who had argued for French acceptance of German unity, felt that this time the Prussian affront was too much to bear. The reports of foreign diplomats and correspondents in Paris all attest that public excitement, whipped up by the right-wing press, was intense. The ability of ministers and the press to communicate rapidly via the electric telegraph heightened tensions and did nothing to encourage measured reflection. The political right, contemptuous of the government's weak handling of the German challenge, was eager for war, in which it saw an opportunity to recover the domestic influence it had lost in recent years. Following the 1869 elections that had gone badly for the government, Napoleon had made concessions to the liberals, introducing many features of a parliamentary system to the Legislature. The Bonapartist Right saw in a foreign war the means to overthrow the liberals and return to the authoritarian regime of the early years of the Second Empire. Their patron was the Empress, whom the Austrian ambassador thought looked ten years younger at the prospect of a political triumph or a war. A successful war would strengthen the dynasty and ensure the smooth succession of her son, the Prince Imperial. If Ollivier experienced some belated hesitations over pursuing a bellicose policy, he was all too aware that any concessions or signs of weakness would provoke the overthrow of his ministry by the Right in the Chamber.

Gramont, in any case, was answerable only to the emperor. On 12 July he persuaded Napoleon that France should demand a personal guarantee from the king of Prussia that the candidature would never be renewed. Recent history showed that renunciations not made by the candidate himself could easily be disowned. In 1863 the Duke of Augustenburg had laid claim to Schleswig-Holstein despite his father's apparently categorical disclaimer; and in 1866 Leopold's own brother Prince Karl had slipped into Romania to become its ruler while supposedly on a family visit. The French demand for a guarantee was presented by Ambassador Benedetti to King Wilhelm during his morning walk in the park at the spa resort of Ems on 13 July.

Bismarck, meanwhile, had been on his estate at Varzin in Pomerania. There was an explosion at the breakfast table when he read in the papers of Gramont's bellicose declaration to the Chamber on 6 July, where to enthusiastic roars the duke had said that if the candidacy were upheld, 'we should know how to discharge our duty without faltering or weakness'.[11] Bismarck found the language 'insolent and bumptious beyond all expectation'[12] and launched a press campaign to stoke German indignation at French arrogance. Maintaining that the affair was not one that involved the Prussian government, he did not leave for Berlin until 12 July, but upon arrival was disconsolate to learn that direct French access to the king had brought about the withdrawal. Bismarck would not have yielded an inch to French threats, and he briefly contemplated resigning, only to be reproached by War Minister Roon and Moltke, the Chief of General Staff. According to the oft-repeated anecdote in Bismarck's memoirs, their dinner together took place on the evening of 13 July, but he may well have confused events with those of the previous evening, as recounted to a British military attaché by the Interior Minister, Count Eulenburg:

> Bismarck appears to have had no inclination for war. Count Eulenburg dined with him, General von Roon making the third. Moltke, who had also been absent from Berlin, came in while they were at dinner, and it was on his urging and assurance that there never was a better opportunity, that the army could be mobilized in thirteen days, and that he had no doubts of the result, that it was agreed to take up the French challenge. It was settled to at once communicate this decision to the King, who it was known would avoid war if he could. Bismarck jumped at Eulenburg's

offer to go to Ems, and he accordingly started that night, reached Ems the next day and obtained from the king permission to return Benedetti an unfavourable answer to the renewed request for an audience ...[13]

Even before receiving news from Ems on the 13th, Bismarck was intent on forcing the issue with France. In a conversation with the British ambassador he presented Germany as the injured party:

> After what has now occurred we must require some assurance, some guarantee, that we may not be subject to sudden attack; like a stroke of lightning in perfect darkness which suddenly reveals to sight a band of robbers, we must know that, this Spanish difficulty once removed, there are no other lurking designs which may burst upon us like a thunderstorm ...[14]

Later that evening, with the support of Moltke and Roon, he telegraphed to the king that a summons should be issued to France demanding that she explain her presumptuous conduct. The king's return to Berlin would be the prelude to the convening of the Reichstag and the issue of an ultimatum to France to explain her bellicose words and preparations. A few minutes later came the telegram from Ems reporting the further French demand for guarantees. Gramont's hot-headed insistence on a Prussian retreat played into Bismarck's hands. With German national feeling strongly supporting it, the Prussian government could not be seen to give way to French threats. Bismarck shortened and dramatized the king's account to make it appear that Wilhelm had answered insolent French demands with a brusque rupture of relations, ending with the flourish, 'His Majesty thereupon declined to receive the French ambassador again, and sent the aide-de-camp on duty to tell him that His Majesty had nothing further to communicate to the ambassador.'

The tone was deliberately inflammatory, as was Bismarck's rapid publication of it and distribution to foreign governments. It had a tremendous effect in Berlin, where crowds gathered in front of the royal palace chanting 'To the Rhine!' in what *The Times* described as 'the explosion of a long pent up anger'.[15]

In Paris there were similar scenes even before the contents of the telegram became known through the evening papers on 14 July. Both sides now believed that the other was intent on war. An enraged Gramont declared that Bismarck's telegram was 'a slap in the face' and that 'after what has happened, a Minister of Foreign Affairs who would not make up his mind for war would be unworthy of his post'.[16] After a long session of the Council of Ministers, presided over by Napoleon, the reserves were called up. Next day, 15 July, the Chamber voted war credits by 245 to 10, encouraged by Gramont's misleading hints that France had allies. In the excitement of the moment Ollivier declared that the government went to war 'with a light heart'. When news of the vote reached Germany, the king, who was travelling back from Ems, was persuaded by Bismarck and Moltke to order general mobilization before being accompanied back to Berlin by cheering crowds.

The French headlong rush to war – for so it seemed to neutral governments – stirred patriotic indignation throughout Germany. The South German states promptly and enthusiastically honoured their defensive alliances and joined the North German Confederation in what was seen as the defence of Germany against French aggression. Thus a Franco-Prussian War (formally declared by France on 17 July and notified to Berlin on the 19th) became within days a Franco-German War. Instead of preventing German unity, France had effectively consummated it at a stroke.

In retrospect the will to German unity took on an aura of inevitability, and German nationalist historians would celebrate Prussia's 'historic mission' to accomplish it. Although Bismarck's daring diplomacy shaped the pattern of events, Prussia's phenomenal economic growth in the two decades prior to 1870 made the adjustment of her relationships with neighbouring powers highly likely. The expansion of her railways since the 1830s, improvements in navigation for steamships along her waterways, the breaking down of internal customs barriers and restrictive trade practices and the development of her banking system had all contributed to rapid industrial growth. In coal, iron and steel production she had become France's equal or superior. In 1820 Prussia had only one third the population of France. Half a century later the North German Confederation and her South German allies together counted 40 million people, marginally more than France. Any French government would have had to choose how to react to these developments, which could not be wished away by nostalgia for the days of French dominance. Napoleon III's error lay perhaps in alternating between two policies, of acceptance and traditional power politics, rather than following one consistently. His inept pursuit of 'compensations' was incompatible with respect for German nationality, and inflamed hostile opinion in a country with a growing will and capacity to defend itself.

The short diplomatic crisis of 1870 is sometimes depicted as a comic opera affair which drew two nations into war for frivolous dynastic reasons. The protagonists certainly behaved more like duellists than statesmen. Yet during that fevered fortnight contemporaries saw great issues at stake. Nor were Frenchmen necessarily mistaken in the belief that Bismarck's Spanish ploy was a deliberate challenge to their European position – a challenge that many believed must be met sooner rather than later, bearing in mind the fate of Denmark and Austria. The French imperial regime could not, for the sake of its own public support, endure another setback. On the German side Moltke and many others believed that German national unity could never be fully achieved or secured without a decisive showdown with France, the old enemy. On both sides the hawks who dominated the final decision-making argued that this was the best opportunity to achieve military victory, and in opting for war both sides were confident of success. The quarrel would now be settled by force of arms.

Chapter 3

The Army of Napoleon III

Confidence in an early French victory ran high. At the height of the crisis *La Liberté*, mouthpiece of Émile de Girardin, pioneer of the cheap press in France, crowed that 'If Prussia refuses to fight we shall boot her back across the Rhine with our rifle butts in her back and force her to yield the left bank.'[1]

A more temperate newspaper complained that 'they talk about crossing the Rhine as if it were as easy as strolling across the Seine bridges'. Yet the high command initially shared in the general mood. On several occasions during the critical days of 14 and 15 July Marshal Edmond Le Bœuf, who as War Minister was the highest authority in the French army below the emperor, assured the Imperial Council and the Chamber that the army was absolutely ready. His confidence, his insistence that France must seize her opportunity by striking first and his urging of mobilization underpinned the French decision for war. Adolphe Thiers, one of the few Deputies with the courage to argue against declaring war, testified that:

> At that fatal epoch, one phrase pervaded every conversation and was on every lip: 'We are ready! We are ready!' ... There are moments in our country when everybody says a thing, repeats it, ends up believing it and, with every fool joining in, the pressure of the crowd overpowers all resistance ... [This phrase] was first heard from Marshal Niel, and daily from Marshal Le Bœuf, and was no more true under the one than the other.[2]

The army of the Second Empire certainly made an imposing sight, as the crowds who watched it on parade at its annual reviews at Châlons Camp every summer could testify. A march-past of over 30,000 men in front of the emperor, the Tsar of Russia and King Wilhelm of Prussia in Paris at the time of the Universal Exhibition in the summer of 1867 prompted the recollection that

> At that time the French army had a rather 'showy' appearance. The tight frogged jackets of the grenadiers and light infantry of the Guard, the shakos with horse-hair tufts and short tunics of the line infantry with their yellow puttees gave the impression of theatrical costumes rather than battledress. However, in the mass these refinements were lost, and you

saw only the thousand colours of an infinite variety of uniforms which led
you to believe that far more men were present than was actually the case.[3]

In 1870 the combatant arms of the French army consisted of one hundred regiments
of line infantry, dressed following the 1867 regulations in blue coats, red trousers,
white gaiters and red-topped kepis, together with twenty battalions of light infantry
(*chasseurs-à-pied*) dressed in dark blue, fifty regiments of cavalry (10 of cuirassiers in
their steel breastplates and helmets, 12 of dragoons, 8 each of lancers and hussars
and 12 of light cavalry (*chasseurs-à-cheval*)), twenty regiments of artillery and three
of engineers. The Imperial Guard, revived by Napoleon III in 1854, was an elite
force which drew the best soldiers from the line regiments and enjoyed higher pay.
It formed in effect a self-contained army corps with regiments of all arms – eight of
infantry plus one battalion of light infantry, six of cavalry and two of artillery. More
exotically clad still were the troops of the Army of Africa based in Algeria. Its
infantry comprised three regiments of Zouaves in their short jackets, baggy trousers
and tasselled fezzes; three regiments of Algerian sharpshooters (*tirailleurs*) known as
Turcos – native troops with white officers; the Foreign Legion and the Zéphyrs –
the latter delinquent types being punished for offences against military discipline.
The cavalry of the Army of Africa was composed of four regiments of the famous
(or to Mexicans infamous) African Light Cavalry (*chasseurs d'Afrique*) in their sky-
blue jackets and tall caps; and three regiments of Spahis – native cavalry wearing
Arab hooded cloaks.

The army was eager for war, which after all was its *raison d'être*. Officers looked
forward to a campaign which would provide opportunities for decorations through
feats of valour, and in which casualties would open the way to promotions that in
peacetime depended largely on having the right connections. The victories of the
last two decades reinforced confidence that they were the best army in the world
and 'had nothing to envy in a foreign army, nothing to borrow from it, and nothing
to learn from it'.[4]

Nevertheless, when pitted against an opponent more formidable than the Russians
or Austrians, the French army proved to be dangerously inferior in strength,
organization, war-planning, training and artillery. Budgetary constraints had kept
troop numbers well below establishment since the Italian war. In 1870, 434,000 men
were nominally serving with the army, but when the results of the plebiscite on
constitutional reform were published in May they showed that only 300,000 men
were actually on duty. Of these, France maintained 64,000 in Algeria and 5,000
at Rome.[5] Awareness of French weakness was an element in the German decision
for war.[6]

Yet the size of her peacetime regular army was not the fundamental source of
French weakness measured against the 304,000 strong standing army of the North
German Confederation, or 382,000 if the South German states are included.[7] The
crucial difference between the opponents was that on the outbreak of war Germany
could call upon a huge pool of fully trained reserves whereas France could not.
In 1862 Prussia had adopted a system of universal military obligation whereby

men aged 20 were conscripted into the army for a relatively short three-year term of service, but thereafter remained in the reserve for another four years and were subject to another five years' service in the *Landwehr*, a territorial force whose role was to relieve the regular army by manning fortresses, guarding communications and maintaining internal order. After 1866 the Prussian system was extended to the North German Confederation and in modified form to her South German allies. Following a carefully prepared mobilization plan, by the first week of August 1870 the Germans had massed three armies on their western frontier with a combined strength of 384,000 men, excluding non-combatant troops.[8] Facing them, by 1 August the French had assembled only 262,000 men, including officers and non-combatants, despite Le Bœuf's promise to the emperor on 6 July that he could put 350,000 men on the frontier within a fortnight of the order to mobilize.[9]

This disparity was due not only to defects in French plans for mobilization and transportation, but to her rejection of the sacrifices required by universal military service. Napoleon III intended the army reforms he initiated in 1866 after Sadowa to give France as large an army as Prussia, but parliamentary opposition emasculated the plan. The Left feared that if the emperor were given a larger army war would become more rather than less likely, as had been the case under his uncle. They mistrusted the army as the compliant instrument of the 1851 coup d'état, feared its increased use for the suppression of liberty at home, and pointed accusingly at Napoleon's record of military adventures in Mexico, Italy and China. They preferred a citizen militia that could be used solely for defensive purposes. 'These gentlemen,' wrote Mérimée, who was close to the imperial family, 'would willingly leave France defenceless against foreigners so that power might fall into the hands of the rabble-rousers of the Paris suburbs.'[10] The issue between the Left and the government, and the enduring dilemma for France, was epitomized during the debate on the new army law, sponsored by the then War Minister, Marshal Niel, in January 1868. Leading republican Jules Favre shouted at the minister, 'Do you want to turn France into a barracks?' Niel turned and responded in a low voice that would send a chill echo down the following decades of French history: 'And you, take care that you don't turn it into a cemetery.'[11]

But opposition to the new law was not confined to the pacifist and anti-militarist Left. Many conservative army officers were contemptuous of the idea of a hugely inflated army composed of short-service conscripts, which in their view would lack the proper military spirit of an experienced regular force, and would be unreliable for maintaining order at home. Thiers, who as a historian of the First Empire considered himself an expert on military matters, ridiculed the idea that Prussia could put over a million men into the field. Deputies loyal to the government were swayed by the intense unpopularity of conscription in the country, and its likely impact on their chances of re-election.

Under the existing system Frenchmen had many chances of avoiding military service when they reached the age of 20. Conscription of the annual contingent – generally set at 100,000 but often much lower in practice for budgetary reasons – was decided by drawing lots. Men who drew a 'good number' did not have to serve.

Even those who drew a 'bad number' could buy themselves out of service, and could even take out insurance for the purpose. A law of 1855 had allowed military service to be commuted for payment of a fixed fee to the government. The money raised was used to pay re-enlistment bounties to serving soldiers whose terms were due to expire.

The effects of this system were that the wealthy could buy themselves or their sons out of the army, leaving its ranks to be filled by the poorest classes. Roughly a quarter of infantry conscripts were illiterate. Nor did the number of men induced to re-enlist ever equal the number who had bought themselves out. The re-enlistment of NCOs under the bounty system encouraged long service, but at the price of pushing up the average age of sergeants and corporals who too often were well past their best and had acquired the bad habits of old soldiers. Lacking the potential for promotion to the officer corps themselves, they blocked the promotion prospects of younger and more able men.

The French army was in some respects the most open to merit in Europe, for by law one-third of junior officer vacancies had to be filled by promoting NCOs from the same unit rather than directly from the officer training schools. That in practice nearly two-thirds of officers had been promoted from the ranks bore witness to the army's failure to attract enough suitable candidates into the officer schools. Compared to Germany, where all officers had to pass through a military academy, standards of education among French officers outside the technical arms remained generally low: 'to get on one had above all to have a good physique, good conduct and a correct bearing'. Slavish obedience to regulations was valued more highly than theoretical study, which was rather frowned upon.[12] Poor pay, slow promotion and restrictions on marriage made life in overcrowded barracks an unattractive prospect to ambitious young men, particularly at a time when commercial prosperity offered more lucrative opportunities elsewhere.[13] Military service was widely seen as a stroke of bad luck, to be avoided if all possible. Nothing so alarmed the Deputies debating the new conscription law than the prospect that 'there will be no more good numbers'.[14]

Thus the new army law was only passed in February 1868 after long and divisive debates, and fell far short of its goal. The period of service was increased from seven years to nine, though the last four would henceforth be in the reserve. Although the system of cash commutation introduced in 1855 was ended, draftees were allowed to hire substitutes and the Legislature insisted on retaining its right to fix the size of the annual contingent. Niel's idea of forming a vast trained reserve of all men who had hitherto escaped military service, whether by drawing a 'good number' or by exemption or early discharge, was rendered virtually useless by the restrictions on its training imposed by the Legislature. This new force, the Garde Mobile, was limited to a fortnight's annual training with no periods of more than 24 hours away from home. Nor could it be mobilized in wartime without the passage of a special law. After attempts to muster it provoked local disorders, Niel's successor Le Bœuf lost interest in the institution, preferring to spend the limited funds available on the regular army. When war came suddenly in 1870 the effects of the Niel law had yet to bear fruit, and France would pay a grievous price for declining to provide herself earlier with a sufficiently large and well-trained reserve.

France preferred to believe that quality would tell over quantity, and her leaders put great faith in her new weapons. In the wake of the Prussian victory over Austria Napoleon had ordered the introduction of the Chassepot model 1866 as the standard infantry weapon. This breech-loading rifle was accurate and robust, with a range of 1,200 metres – more than twice that of the Prussian Dreyse 'needle gun' which had been in service for three decades. The bolt action of the Chassepot allowed the trained soldier to fire up to seven shots per minute. The advantages of fighting the Germans before they could introduce a new rifle of comparable quality were not lost on Le Bœuf.[15] Already the Bavarians were introducing the 1869 model Werder rifle which was superior to the Dreyse.

There was a lively debate within the army as to how infantry tactics should be adapted to the challenges of the modern battlefield, on which troops could fire from the prone position or from behind cover and inflict more casualties at a greater distance than ever before. Far from being blind to the significance of the new fire-arms, many French officers realized that the tactics that had brought them victory in Italy – swarms of skirmishers preceding rapid attacks by formed columns – would be vulnerable to breech-loaders. Many were to err on the side of caution, taking refuge in 'fine positions' with clear fields of fire that would allow them to mow down the attacking enemy. In the novel conditions of 1870 the strategy and tactics of the French infantry, famed for the fury of its bayonet charges, were to appear hesitant and defensive. The Germans, for their part, gave great emphasis to teaching fire discipline and accuracy, and believed with justification that these attributes would go far towards offsetting the technical inferiority of their rifle.[16]

French firepower and overconfidence were further boosted by a newly developed weapon initially funded by Napoleon III personally – the *mitrailleuse*. It had the appearance of a bronze cannon, but its barrel incorporated twenty-five steel tubes firing as many bullets from a pre-loaded magazine at the turn of a handle. Its crews were trained in such great secrecy that on mobilization they were unwittingly posted to other duties. Despite the inexperience of improvised crews and its limited traverse, the *mitrailleuse* had the potential to inflict severe damage on enemy infantry, and French troops were cheered by the sound of the 'coffee-grinders' as they dubbed them. However, it proved to be extremely vulnerable to German artillery.

It was in artillery that the French were most conspicuously outclassed by the Germans, who had more and better guns, used them to greater effect and supplied them with more ammunition than was normally available to French batteries. On 1 August 1870 the French had 780 field guns and 144 *mitrailleuses* present with their optimistically named Army of the Rhine, while the Germans counted 1,206 field guns with their three armies.[17] The French had retained the bronze muzzle-loading rifled cannon that had been developed under the emperor's auspices in the 1850s and had brought them victory in Italy. But the Germans had moved on to breech-loading steel guns with a much longer range. The artillerist Le Bœuf thought the evidence of German gunnery performance at Sadowa inconclusive, and protracted tests on a French breech-loader had not yet been concluded. When, with the wisdom of hindsight, his critics denounced his failure to update the French artillery, he protested that the cost of rearming the infantry with the Chassepot (113 million francs) and of producing the *mitrailleuse* made it extremely unlikely that the Legislature would have granted additional credits to modernize the artillery.[18] In truth, though, he had not foreseen the need.

The Germans had in fact made great advances since Sadowa, which would only become manifest on the battlefield. Their cannon had been fitted with Krupp's superior breech-block, and gunners had practised hard at rapid, aimed fire delivered by running batteries forward to support their infantry. The effect of accurate, concentrated German fire was maximized by the effect of percussion fuses that detonated on impact, whereas the French had opted for a time-fuse system which was intended to simplify the gunners' task but in practice sacrificed flexibility and effectiveness. French artillery practice had also lost sight of the need to achieve an overwhelming concentration of guns early in the battle: an art which the Germans had mastered. If German infantry tactics in the early battles were often inept and costly, they were saved from defeat by the devastating power of their artillery.

German planning and organization were also far better geared to achieving rapid and efficient mobilization than the French, giving them a decisive advantage. The French military attaché in Berlin warned in 1868 that 'the Prussian general staff is the best in Europe; ours cannot be compared to it'.[19] French peacetime military organization was designed to meet internal security needs rather than the demands of mobilization for war. French troops deliberately were not based in their home districts and were periodically rotated to garrisons around the country so that they should not identify themselves too closely with any local community. Their regimental depot, through which supplies and new recruits had to pass, might be at the other end of the country, and those depots in turn depended for their supplies on a highly centralized warehouse system. Generals commanding territorial divisions would command different troops in wartime, and be served by staff officers who might be complete strangers assigned to them by the War Ministry.

In Germany, on the other hand, troops served in the region where they had been raised under the general and staff who would command them in war, and had a well-rehearsed drill for mobilization by rail. German mobilization observed the principle of less haste, more speed. Regiments reported to their local depots where reservists were mustered and everyone was equipped. The fully assembled regiment then embarked on trains that moved at carefully regulated intervals to the concentration area for their unit, with refreshments provided at fixed points en route.

The French by contrast tried to pre-empt their enemies by rushing regiments to the front, leaving their depots to forward batches of reservists and equipment when ready. French troops had not practised railway embarkation, which too often was delayed because officers failed to supervise their men properly, leaving them to be plied with drink by patriotic crowds 'more enthusiastic than well-advised', adding to widespread problems of indiscipline.[20] No central authority at the War Ministry was responsible for planning and co-ordinating railway transportation, as was done in Germany by Moltke's general staff. Le Bœuf had not implemented the report of the railway commission appointed by Niel before his death in 1869. In July 1870 orders came from several different departments at the War Ministry, and despite sterling efforts by the private railway companies in moving men to the eastern frontier French mobilization proved chaotic.

The railways were carrying not only formed regiments to the front, but reservists from all across France who had to report to the chief town of their Département, then be formed into detachments to be forwarded to the regimental depots and thence – if and when the right orders came from Paris – to join their units at the front. This led to some epic journeys as reservists criss-crossed the country. Some living in northern France and assigned to 2nd Zouaves had to travel by rail to Marseille then embark by sea to report to the regimental depot at Oran in Algeria, returning from there to Marseille to join their regiment in Alsace on the eastern frontier, a round trip of 2,000 kilometres. The French attempt to combine mobilization and concentration (which in Germany were distinct stages), the inadequacy of transport planning and the confusion of orders led to reservists arriving at the front from their depots in dribs and drabs. The recall of the reserves on 14 July should have produced 173,507 men, yet by 6 August, when the first major battles were fought, only about half of these had reached their regiments at the front.[21] Many of these reservists were sullen at being recalled to military service and were untrained in the use of the Chassepot, having to be instructed hastily on the eve of battle or even during it.

To the difficulties of assembling the regular army were added those of simultaneously mobilizing the Garde Mobile, for which equipment and officers had to be improvised. This task was a distraction rather than a support to the army command in the first weeks of war, and some units of the Garde Mobile, particularly those from Paris, proved so ungovernable and hostile to the imperial regime that they had to be dispersed.

If bottlenecks in the supply of men were a grave handicap, those of equipment and supplies proved crippling to rapid movement. The army's main base in Lorraine was the fortress city of Metz, where the station became clogged with trains. For lack of sufficient labour, horses, carts and an effective unloading schedule, thousands of tons of material remained stranded in unmarked freight wagons in the marshalling yards, lost to the units for which they were intended. The War Ministry was bombarded with telegrams from desperate generals pleading for the delivery to their units of urgently needed items, from tents to cooking pots, bacon, biscuit or maps. The time needed to untangle these problems was a major impediment to the army's ability to take the offensive.

Napoleon III had envisaged a thrust across the Rhine, through South Germany and on to Berlin, in the hope that he would soon be joined by the Austrians, Italians and Danes. To the manifold problems caused by inadequate preparation he added further confusion by deciding in the days before the outbreak of hostilities to reorganize the order of battle. Instead of two armies on the eastern frontier, commanded by Marshal Bazaine at Metz and Marshal MacMahon at Strasbourg, with a reserve force under Marshal Canrobert at Châlons, he decided to command the entire army personally. Whether he wished to garner the prestige of a victory personally, to influence potential allies or feared to be outshone by his marshals, his intervention necessitated a frantic last-minute redrawing of plans at the War Ministry.

On 28 July Napoleon left his palace of Saint-Cloud for the front by special train, accompanied by the 14-year-old Prince Imperial. Pallid and ill, the emperor could hardly ride a horse without excruciating pain. On reaching Metz he was dismayed at how unready the army was, and was shortly informed that the supply situation meant that a campaign into Germany was not immediately feasible. In the French army there was an expectation that a dynamic strategy would be supplied by Napoleonic inspiration, but from this invalid and prematurely old ruler, by turns hesitant, interfering and fatalistic, came no spark of leadership or even a coherent campaign plan. Despite his habitual wearing of a general's uniform, his close interest in military affairs and personal involvement in matters of armament and uniforms, he was not a professional soldier like King Wilhelm of Prussia. His record as commander-in-chief, whether by proxy in the Crimea and Mexico, or personally in Italy, hardly suggested that his uncle's military genius was hereditary.

The Germans were apprehensive of a sudden French dash into the Rhineland. If they were not preparing such a stroke, why had they rushed to declare war? German intelligence gathering and analysis by the general staff was more professionally organized than on the French side, yet still they could not be sure of Napoleon's intentions. Already German cavalry units were patrolling into France on reconnaissance, cutting telegraph lines as they went, notably in Count Zeppelin's bold raid into Alsace on 24–25 July. French cavalry reconnaissance on the other hand was unenterprising. Napoleon used his infantry like an extended border patrol, spread out to guard the frontiers of Lorraine and Alsace, divided by the massive wooded ridges of the Vosges. For a few days he did little more than shift his lumbering infantry divisions about in response to rumours of German movements.

Marches were slow, partly through poor staff work and partly because the French infantryman was laden with 30 kilograms of equipment, including 90 rounds of ammunition, his pack, water canteen, mess-tin, cooking pot, blanket, tent-pole and half a shelter tent. All this camping gear, which had to be left under guard during battle, was necessary because of the French system of making bivouac every night in a defensible position. This concentration of large units in a giant camp-site made sense in thinly inhabited regions with a warm climate, particularly Algeria. However, it had the disadvantage of limiting the distance that could be marched in a day because of the need to break camp, form the long column in marching order in the morning and to halt early enough in the evening to allow the rearmost unit to reach camp before dark. The Germans differed by following the methods of the first Napoleon, billeting their men in villages strung along their route, where they could take shelter from cold and damp without the need to pitch or strike tents. One

French general, Trochu, was incredulous on hearing that large German units were regularly covering distances that far exceeded French capabilities.[22]

Thus in the first days of August the French army, deficient in numbers, ill-administered, over-extended, ponderous and incapable of mounting its own major offensive, groped towards contact with the enemy. Notwithstanding so many comparative disadvantages, one sharp critic of its pre-war failings believed that it 'still retained enough of its former qualities to conquer; to the extent that, despite the number and skill of its adversaries, it would have been victorious had it only been properly commanded'.[23]

Chapter 4

Defeats at the Frontier

Forty kilometres east of Metz along the main road lies the town of Saint-Avold, from which several routes lead towards the German frontier. Arriving at Saint-Avold on 29 July, the emperor met the commander of 2 Corps, a general he knew well. Charles Frossard had been tutor to the Prince Imperial, and as a military engineer was thoroughly familiar with the uplands of Lorraine. Before the war he had drawn up plans for the French to block a German advance from the north-east by taking up a defensive line along the formidable heights above the Saar valley. His 28,000 troops were now encamped around Forbach, on the road that leads north-east from Saint-Avold to the frontier, beyond which it continues to the German town of Saarbrücken on the left bank of the Saar. Frossard convinced the emperor that it would be useful to take Saarbrücken and, as the army was not yet ready for a major offensive, Napoleon agreed. Such a move would be a sop to impatient French public opinion and to expectations within the ranks of the army itself, and would signal to Austria and Italy, whom Napoleon still hoped to bring into an alliance, that France was in earnest.

Napoleon gave his orders the next day, 30 July, leaving the operational details to his generals. At a council of war they concluded that it would be unsafe to venture beyond the Saar, and drew up elaborate plans for Frossard's advance to be supported by demonstrations by divisions of neighbouring corps: Failly's 5th on his right and Bazaine's 3rd on his left.

Saarbrücken, then a town of 8,000 people, was overlooked by a chain of low hills to its south, one of which was crowned by the drill-ground of the garrison and a pleasure-garden. The French assaulted these hills in mid-morning of a warm 2 August, and soon discovered that they had taken a sledgehammer to crack a nut. The position was held only by a battalion of infantry and three cavalry squadrons, who after a sharp fire-fight followed their orders to withdraw if attacked by a superior force. The whole affair was over by midday, witnessed from a distance by Napoleon and the Prince Imperial, whose exploit in picking up a spent bullet was made much of by the jubilant Paris press. Casualties were about ninety men apiece. From the hills they had captured, the French fired their *mitrailleuses* after the hastily retreating Germans and lobbed shells towards the railway station, which damaged houses in the suburbs, much to the indignation of the German press.

The French made little attempt to occupy the town, and had no thought of exploiting their momentary advantage by funnelling troops across the Saar to engage the heads of the nearest German columns before they could concentrate. Neither did they destroy the telegraph, nor the rail or road bridges across the Saar from which the town took its name. By 5 August, feeling isolated and exposed as reports arrived of the advance of the German First and Second Armies, Frossard asked for and received the emperor's permission to withdraw to a ridge further south, just inside the French frontier. During a night of pouring rain he marched his men to their new positions, where a storm of an altogether different kind was about to break over them.

German cavalry entered Saarbrücken on the morning of 6 August. Probing southwards, it did not take them long to find the new French position on the wooded heights which took their name from the nearby village of Spicheren, but they concluded that this must be a rearguard left to cover a French retreat. A battle this day was no part of Moltke's grand strategy, which envisaged a crossing of the Saar on a wide front on 9 August prior to pinning down the French army while German forces turned its flanks. Nor was the infantry of First Army supposed to be anywhere near Saarbrücken, where the roads had been allocated to Second Army. So eager was the elderly General Steinmetz, commanding First Army, to win the glory of attacking the enemy first that he had wilfully disobeyed Moltke's directives, funnelling his men south of their assigned roads and enraging the commander of Second Army, Prince Friedrich Karl. Thus the nearest infantry unit was 14th Division of First Army, commanded by General von Kameke, who promptly passed through the town and deployed beyond it to drive the French away.

Kameke's decision might have proved suicidally rash had the French counter-attacked promptly and in force, but they remained on the defensive. Even so, the Germans began to suffer heavy losses as they made piecemeal frontal assaults on the central bastion of the French right, a steep red sandstone bluff called the Rotherberg, atop which the French defenders had hastily dug trenches. Under murderous Chassepot fire from the men of Laveaucoupet's division, the surviving Germans were glad to hug the dead ground around the foot of the Rotherberg. Nor could their comrades-in-arms make much headway against the French left, where Vergé's division held a gap in the ridge in front of the industrial village of Stiring, home to the foundry that formed part of the empire of the prominent ironmaster Wendel. For hours the Germans struggled to capture a succession of isolated buildings along the poplar-lined road that ran from Saarbrücken to Stiring, including the customs house and the Golden Bream inn. By early afternoon a full-scale battle was under way, with the French having the advantage of numbers and position.

As the afternoon wore on, that balance began to tilt. However ill-tempered the bickering between the headquarters of First and Second Armies had been that morning about rights of way, the German instinct of solidarity took hold at the sound of gunfire. Every commander within earshot headed for the fighting. Messengers and the telegraph summoned others, who poured into Saarbrücken by road and rail, using the bridges that the French had so considerately left intact. Successive changes of command as more senior German generals reached the scene did not detract from the unfolding of a jumbled but determined offensive, with new units being fed into the line wherever they were most needed. By late afternoon the Germans had at least 35,000 men on the field, and their batteries posted on the drill-ground south of Saarbrücken and the adjacent hills were beating down the French artillery and forcing their infantry under cover as shell after shell burst among them. Even in the village of Spicheren, well behind the French right, German shells perforated the walls of the church and school, killing a few of the wounded who had been evacuated there earlier even as overburdened regimental surgeons worked on them.[1]

Eventually German infantry penetrated the forested ravines right and left of the Rotherberg and secured a foothold despite desperate French counterattacks. The French lacked the strength to hold every part of their 5-kilometre line in sufficient force. Back at his headquarters in Forbach where the telegraph was, Frossard exercised little control. The commander of his reserve division, the aptly named General Bataille, took his men forward on his own initiative to plug gaps in the French line, enabling it to hold for the moment. All Frossard's men were now committed to the fight, but German pressure continued unabated.

Now the French paid for their failure to concentrate their forces. The nearest supporting units, the divisions of Bazaine's 3 Corps, were five or six hours' march away. Bazaine, back at Saint-Avold, was apprehensive that the Germans might cross the Saar on a wide front, threatening his troops at any point, and it was not until 1.25 p.m. that Frossard advised him by telegraph that a battle was in progress. Bazaine was later accused of leaving Frossard to his fate out of jealousy for a rival, but he did order his dispersed division commanders to send support. After a meandering march, one got scarcely halfway to the battlefield by dark; another reached it far too late to be of any help; and a third, after taking up a 'good position' miles from the fighting, was misled by an acoustic quirk of the wooded hills into believing that the cannonade ahead had ceased, and had his men return to their camps. Years of inquiries and accusations about the responsibilities for the events of that sultry August afternoon lay ahead, but the one certainty was that, in glaring contrast to the German commanders, the French generals had failed to hurry support to the threatened point on time: support that would have restored French numerical superiority and enabled a counterattack.

Thus Frossard's men, tired out by their lost night's sleep and six hours of intense fighting, and running low on ammunition, were condemned to fight their battle alone. On the Spicheren ridge the Germans captured the French trenches and hauled some artillery onto the neighbouring hill, forcing the French to give ground. Officer casualties were high on both sides as the fighting swayed back and forth in the smoke-filled woods. Although the Germans could not be dislodged, Laveaucoupet's men held them in check by a bayonet charge at about 7 p.m.

Meanwhile on the left in Stiring-Wendel fighting continued into the dusk among houses, factories, slag-heaps and loaded coal wagons in the railway-yard, as well as in the nearby forest. In a letter home a Breton soldier, Yves-Charles Quentel, described going into battle there:

> When the bugle sounded I was nervous; my poor heart was thumping at the thought of danger. At that moment all the men were under arms, with cartridges issued, awaiting the signal to go. After half an hour of wondering what was happening the command was given to 'fix bayonets' ... Then we advanced to drive out the enemy. We passed through a foundry where the roofs and sheet-iron rang with bullets then, advancing fifty metres, I was ordered behind a pile of masonry ... A short distance from me a *chasseur-à-pied* had been shot in the legs, while another beside him was dead.
>
> A few soldiers were sheltering behind him. A lieutenant under cover ten yards from me ordered us to advance on the Prussians. I ran forward with twenty of my companions. We dashed across the railway tracks, then took cover behind some enormous cast-iron cylinders. We were protected from bullets coming from straight ahead, but not from those coming in from an angle. At my feet was a captain of *chasseurs* with a bullet in his head, lying in a pool of blood. Behind him was a colonel who had taken a bullet in the temple that had passed right through his head. It was enough to make you be sick, but I had no time to think ...[2]

The merciless contest continued in the blazing village after nightfall.

Meanwhile, events beyond his left flank convinced Frossard of the need to retreat that night. Another German division had crossed the Saar downriver and was bearing down on his rear at Forbach, held at bay only by a thin cavalry cordon and 200 reservists who had just arrived by train and were rushed into the firing line. With the fresh divisions of 3 Corps not yet to hand, Frossard concluded that he should withdraw to a better position, and after dark French buglers sounded the retreat. Left in possession of the field, the Germans could claim a hard-fought victory at a cost of 4,871 men to the French 4,078.[3] Next day they also took possession of the immense stores that Frossard had accumulated at Forbach in preparation for an advance into Germany that now would never take place.

Spicheren was but one half of the double blow dealt to France that fatal 6 August, for in Alsace, 60 kilometres away on the far side of the Vosges, MacMahon's 1 Corps had also been defeated.

The German Third Army, commanded by the Prussian Crown Prince Friedrich Wilhelm, had been tasked by Moltke with the invasion of Alsace. It consisted not only of Prussian troops but of the contingents of the South German states. Though Moltke had been impatient for it to advance sooner, it had descended on the French frontier on 4 August. Directly in its path lay the little town of Wissembourg on the River Lauter, where a French infantry division of 6,000 men commanded by General Abel Douay had arrived the previous evening. Douay's immediate superior, General Ducrot, had been contemptuous of warnings from the town's

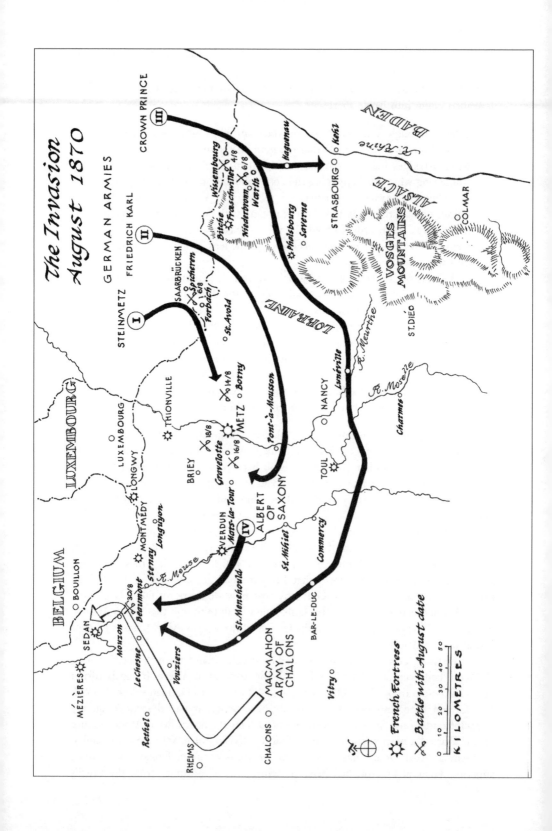

The Invasion
August 1870

GERMAN ARMIES

STEINMETZ FRIEDRICH KARL

CROWN PRINCE

III

II

I

BADEN

R. Rhine

Kehl

Hagueneau

Wissembourg
Frœschwiller 4/8
Niederbronn 6/8
Wœrth
Bitche
Phalsbourg
Saverne
STRASBOURG

ALSACE

VOSGES MOUNTAINS

COLMAR

ST. DIÉ

SAARBRÜCKEN
Spicheren
6/8
Forbach
St. Avold

LORRAINE

R. Meurthe

R. Moselle

Charmes

THIONVILLE

14/8
Borny
METZ
Pont-à-Mousson

NANCY

Lunéville

LUXEMBOURG

LUXEMBOURG

LONGWY

BRIEY

18/8
Gravelotte
16/8
Mars-la-Tour
VERDUN

TOUL

St. Mihiel

Commercy

BAR-LE-DUC

IV

ALBERT OF SAXONY

MONTMÉDY

Longuyon
Stenay
R. Meuse

BELGIUM

BOUILLON

MÉZIÈRES

SEDAN
Mouzon
Beaumont 30/8
Lechesne

Rethel

Vouziers

St. Menehould

Vitry

RHEIMS

CHALONS

MACMAHON
ARMY OF
CHALONS

☼ French Fortress

✕ Battle with August date

KILOMETRES
0 10 20 30 40 50

civilian authorities of a heavy build-up of German forces north of Wissembourg, dismissing the threat as 'pure bluff'.[4] Imperial headquarters wired a warning of an imminent attack early on the 4th, but a reconnaissance sent out by Douay failed to find anything suspicious.

The surprise was complete when Bavarian troops came storming across the meadows bordering the Lauter towards the town walls, and volleys of shells started landing on the French positions. Douay's men fought hard that morning but were forced to retreat as overwhelming numbers of Prussian troops crossed the Lauter to their south and outflanked them. Douay was disembowelled by a shell, one battalion of his men in the town failed to receive the withdrawal order in time and was forced to surrender, while a few hundred men taking refuge in the solid eighteenth-century Château Geissberg on a hill overlooking Wissembourg repelled repeated German assaults until forced to capitulate at around 2 p.m. Their resistance allowed most of the division to get away, less about 2,000 casualties, nearly half of them prisoners. They had inflicted 1,551 casualties on the attacking Germans.[5] There had been no French troops near enough to support Douay. All Ducrot and MacMahon could do was watch smoke rising from Wissembourg from the viewpoint of the Col du Pigeonnier 4 kilometres away. Word spread down other French columns as they toiled along in the heat: 'You had to have been there to understand the effect of this news. So then, things had begun badly.'[6]

The dispersal of 1 Corps at the moment of the German invasion mirrored the overall strategic situation of French forces in Alsace. Although MacMahon quickly pulled his divisions together and took position on the dominating Frœschwiller ridge, guarding a pass through the Vosges and on the flank of any German advance towards Strasbourg, he was far from any support. Like other French units, 7 Corps, with its headquarters at Belfort in the far south of Alsace, had been bedevilled by supply problems following mobilization and was still incomplete. The emperor had insisted that one of its divisions remain in Lyon to keep order in that republican trouble spot, while another of its brigades was on its way back from Rome. The commander of 7 Corps, Félix Douay (Abel's brother), had been led to believe – by decoy German troop movements on the far bank of the Rhine – that the main threat to Alsace would come from the east, rather than from the north where it actually materialized. On 5 August Napoleon belatedly put MacMahon in command of all forces in Alsace. The marshal had a reputation as one of France's most distinguished soldiers, with a record of bravery in Algeria, the Crimea and Italy. The nearest division of 7 Corps was rushed to him by rail, but arrived that evening without its artillery. MacMahon was also given authority over 5 Corps to his north around Bitche and ordered it to join him; but, like other French commanders, General de Failly of 5 Corps was obsessed with the idea that the real threat was on his front, and only belatedly sent one division to MacMahon. It would arrive too late.

Neither MacMahon nor his opponent, the Crown Prince, intended to fight a battle on 6 August, but once the German vanguard made contact with the French along the banks of the little River Sauer fighting began and took on a momentum of its own, sucking in ever more German units whose commanders refused to accept a repulse. On the French left wing, in the woods and clearings north of Frœschwiller, Ducrot's men beat back the advance of a Bavarian corps. In the centre, in the village of Wœrth and the open pine forest called the Niederwald to its south, the Prussian V Corps was unable to make much headway despite the clear superiority of the German artillery which pounded the French from the hills east of the Sauer. After a morning of furious but inconclusive fighting there was a lull before the decisive phase opened. The Prussian XI Corps crossed the Sauer south of the French position, where the slopes of the Frœschwiller ridge were less steep, and began rolling up the overstretched French line while V Corps renewed its assault, bludgeoning its way into the French centre. MacMahon had accepted battle with 48,000 men, trusting in the strength of his position and the mettle of his troops. These included Zouaves and Turcos of the Army of Africa, who amply confirmed their reputation as the best infantry in the French army, but they were facing over 80,000 Germans. MacMahon, successively throwing in cavalry, artillery and infantry, launched desperate but disjointed counterattacks that failed to stem the German tide for long.

The counterattacks by the French heavy cavalry became legendary in the French memory of the war. The cuirassiers in their steel helmets and breastplates had been little used in the wars of the Second Empire, and had preserved a view of themselves as the elite, battle-winning shock arm. They rejected as heretical any notion that in modern warfare cavalry was best employed in gathering information, harassing the enemy's communications and preventing his cavalry from observing your own infantry. However, at Frœschwiller they were asked not to rout a weakened enemy, their traditional battlefield role, but to hold back oncoming swarms of German infantry armed with breech-loading rifles. Their orders required them to charge not over open plains but down steep slopes cut by hedges, vines and hop-poles supporting wire trellises – ground that was totally unsuitable for cavalry. There were two distinct cavalry actions, one by Michel's brigade towards Morsbronn at the southern end of the battlefield at about 1.15 p.m., the other by Bonnemains' division in the centre, down the slopes towards the outskirts of Wœrth at about 3.30 p.m. Yet in the face of a blizzard of artillery and small arms fire their courage could do no more than interrupt the German advance. When the terminally ill General Duhesme protested, he was told that the sacrifice of his men was necessary to save the army's right, and he could only exclaim 'My poor cuirassiers!' The result bore no resemblance to the kind of warfare these cavalrymen had trained for. An eyewitness described the scene in the road that runs through Morsbronn:

> It was there that a great butchery took place. Those unfortunate horsemen, heaped together, confined in a road between banks, were shot at point-blank range by infantrymen posted in the gardens that overlook the lane. There was no combat, not an enemy within a sabre's length of the cuirassiers: it was a defile swept by missiles. The road was so encumbered with the corpses of horses and men that that evening, after the battle was done, the Prussians were obliged to give up their attempt to march that way with their prisoners.[7]

By mid-afternoon the French had been forced back into a ragged line covering the village of Frœschwiller, targeted by every German gun within range. 'The Prussians were gaining ground; their artillery was raking our position; Frœschwiller was on fire,' wrote Major David of 45th Regiment, recording his vain attempts to stem a torrent of fugitives: 'The battle was lost, so much was evident, and already a mass of troops had deserted the battlefield . . . The order to retreat was given.'[8] By 5 p.m. the French had disappeared towards Niederbronn and the mountain gap along a forest road littered with the dead and dying, leaving every building around crammed with wounded who were tended by a handful of doctors. For the next three days the surgeons performed operations from sunrise to sunset. One of them remembered that 'Some of the wounded dragged themselves up to us in order to advance their turn. One of them cried out "People queue here. It's just like at the theatre!" And laughter took hold of all those desperate fellows. Men will laugh, even in Hell.'[9]

Frœschwiller had been a bigger and bloodier battle than Spicheren. The Germans had bought victory at a cost of 10,642 casualties, while French losses approximated 21,000, including 9,200 taken prisoner and 4,188 men who found their way to Strasbourg, which the Germans soon laid under siege.[10] Meanwhile, peasants from the ruined villages on the battlefield were compelled to toil for days at digging burial pits in weather that had turned dismally cold and wet.

The double defeats of 6 August produced a 'veritable panic', an 'indescribable disorder', when they became known at imperial headquarters next day.[11] About a quarter of the army had been directly involved in the defeats, but the psychological effect on the French high command magnified their impact. Over the course of the next week the ailing emperor changed his mind repeatedly about what strategy to adopt. His first thought was that the whole army should fall back and concentrate at Châlons Camp, though that meant giving up much of eastern France without further contest. Other options were only fleetingly considered; for instance either falling back to the south-west so as to stay on the flank of the German advance, or concentrating southwards against the Crown Prince's Third Army as it emerged into Lorraine through the Vosges passes in pursuit of MacMahon. The fact that for two or three days after their victories the Germans largely lost contact with the French army and were in the dark regarding its movements would have favoured such a move. But Napoleon thought only of barring the direct road to Paris. Briefly, on 10 August, it was decided to make a stand on a branch of the River Nied, 15 kilometres east of Metz, with the four corps immediately available, Ladmirault's 4th, Bazaine's 3rd, Frossard's 2nd and the Imperial Guard. However, the position was quickly deemed to be insecure, and next day the army fell back to Metz 'by that sort of passive attraction that fortresses exercise over irresolute commanders'.[12]

The indecision of the high command communicated itself to the troops, who could not understand why they were marching away from the frontier and the enemy. Marches were badly organized, with men having to stand in ranks fully laden for hours on end while waiting their turn to join a column. The appearance of German cavalrymen too often caused French generals to assume mistakenly that enemy infantry must be close behind, and prompted unnecessary night marches in a week of awful weather. On reaching camp, wrote a lieutenant in 4 Corps, 'the men, soaked to the skin, unable to put up their miserable little tents on ground that had become nothing but a sea of mud nor light fires to cook dinner, unable even to eat their ration bread that had turned to pulp in their haversacks, their faces drawn and their clothes filthy, seemed ready to drop from exhaustion'.[13] Things were worse for the men in the defeated 1 and 2 Corps, many of whom had lost all their equipment in the aftermath of battle. Increasingly soldiers resorted to begging and pillage. The cavalry meanwhile provided very little information and seemed to expect to be protected by the infantry rather than vice-versa. The high command kept it in the lee of the marching columns instead of between them and the enemy.

By taking command Napoleon had hoped to garner the laurels of victory, but now he bore the obloquy of defeats that came as an enormous shock to French opinion. The empress recalled the Legislature, which met on 9 August amid large demonstrations by supporters of the republican opposition, who demanded greater parliamentary power and the recall of the incompetent emperor to Paris. Inside the Chamber Ollivier, the butt of public contempt, was swept from power by a vote of no confidence. The motion was proposed by the Bonapartist Right, the very men who had clamoured loudest for war and who exploited their opportunity to eject the despised liberal ministry. Eugénie replaced Ollivier with the Count de Palikao, an old cavalry general who had led the French expedition to China in 1860. The new ministry took a series of measures to raise more men and money to fight the war, and to prepare Paris for a state of siege: steps that would have seemed unthinkable three weeks earlier. The cabinet did not want Napoleon to return to Paris, which would be an admission of defeat, but saw the necessity of appeasing popular feeling by appointing a new commander-in-chief and chief of staff, for Le Bœuf was blamed as much as Ollivier for the war's disastrous beginning.

In the army too, Napoleon's lack of strategic grasp caused him and Frossard to be blamed for defeat. In Paris and among the troops Marshal Achille Bazaine was the popular favourite because he had risen through the ranks and was known to have been out of favour at court after his command of the army in Mexico. Since 5 August Bazaine had nominally had authority over Frossard and Ladmirault as well as his own corps, but had seemed diffident about exercising it because Napoleon and Le Bœuf had continued to issue direct orders to them regardless of the new arrangement. At the urging of the empress, on 12 August Napoleon reluctantly acquiesced, appointing Bazaine commander-in-chief, while a devastated Le Bœuf stepped down as chief of staff. 'We are both sacked,' Napoleon told him.[14] On that day German cavalry entered Nancy, the chief city of Lorraine, meeting no resistance.

Defeat had sapped the emperor's authority and prestige, ushered in a new cabinet and commander-in-chief, and also deepened France's diplomatic isolation.

France already knew that she had nothing to hope for from Britain or Russia, both of whom blamed Napoleon as the instigator of the war and feared the prospect of a French victory. Bismarck had fanned British indignation by supplying *The*

Times with the draft treaty of 1866 in Benedetti's handwriting which envisaged the French acquisition of Belgium. The text, published on 25 July, confirmed Britain's worst fears of French ambitions and her determination to stay neutral. She contented herself with obtaining additional guarantees of Belgian neutrality from both belligerents. Russia, seeing Prussia as her ally, was committed to mobilize against Austria if she showed any sign of joining France. Denmark, with whom France had failed to conclude a meaningful military alliance, was kept neutral by a combination of German threats and Russian diplomatic pressure.

Yet, despite his disappointment at their initial declarations of neutrality, Napoleon still harboured hopes of an alliance with Austria-Hungary and Italy. Both temporized, waiting to see how the campaign would unfold. Austria excused her delay on the grounds that public opinion among both the German-speaking and Hungarian subjects of her Empire was unprepared for war, and that Russia's stance made caution necessary. Besides, like Italy, mobilization would take her several weeks: the autumn would be a better time, when Russia's climate would hinder her intervention. The Austrians and Italians jointly proposed an agreement that both would adopt a stance of armed neutrality prior to effective co-operation with France in mid-September. The document was presented to Napoleon at Metz at the beginning of August, but was unacceptable to him: he must have immediate intervention. Moreover, the price the Italians were asking for their support was a free hand in Rome, given that the French garrison was now withdrawing. Napoleon could not afford to alienate conservative Catholic opinion at home by abandoning the Papal City to the mercy of its Italian secular enemies. 'France', Gramont had pronounced, 'cannot defend her honour on the Rhine while sacrificing it on the Tiber.'[15]

Thus hopes for an agreement were stalled when the French defeats of 6 August supervened. King Victor Emmanuel of Italy, who had been more in favour of intervention than his government, was at the theatre when he got the news. Shocked, he returned to his palace and slumped in a chair. 'Oh! Poor Emperor!' he exclaimed, but added, 'F ... though, I've had a narrow escape!' The changed situation was summed up in Gramont's words to Napoleon, 'Sire, does anyone make an alliance with a loser?'[16] Henceforth both Italy and Austria associated themselves with Britain in a 'League of Neutrals', though that amounted to little more than an agreement not to depart from neutrality without prior mutual consultation. France was left without allies to bring her victory, or victory to bring her allies. Both outcomes were a measure of Napoleon III's shortcomings and miscalculations as a statesman and commander-in-chief.

Chapter 5

The Anvil of Metz

Metz, on the east bank of the Moselle, offered the army a temporary refuge. Although work on constructing its outlying forts remained incomplete, they were a sufficient deterrent against any German frontal assault. The Germans advanced warily towards the Moselle, perplexed by the lack of French resistance and wondering whether a counterstroke was being prepared. It was not. Alarming and often exaggerated reports of huge German reinforcements continuing to pour across the French frontier deepened the oppressive consciousness of numerical inferiority at French headquarters. That inferiority was only partially redressed when, after days of marching back and forth in response to changing orders from the emperor, Canrobert's 6 Corps reached Metz by the 13th, though minus its cavalry, reserve artillery and most of one of its infantry divisions. In addition General de Failly had earlier been ordered to bring 5 Corps up to Metz from the south but, imagining that he was in danger from a flank attack, he disobeyed orders and marched westwards instead, eventually reaching the railway and joining MacMahon's battered 1 Corps at Châlons Camp. Most of Failly's men had not seen action, yet their long and exhausting retreat had demoralized them.

Might the French, by concentrating earlier at Metz and using the fortress as a pivot, have struck a telling blow at one of the oncoming German columns, making the invader more cautious and giving themselves further time to regroup? By bringing superior numbers against a fraction of the German army they might possibly have stabilized the situation, though in any encounter superior German artillery would be a force to be reckoned with. In reality the French army was too cumbrous to be capable of the rapid manoeuvre and co-ordination that the situation demanded. Poor staff work was not improved when Bazaine took command. He had no confidence in General Jarras, the chief-of-staff assigned to him by Napoleon, and barely consulted him on operational planning. The talents of younger officers working for Jarras were largely wasted on routine bureaucratic chores. In any case, the mentality of the high command after the initial defeats was predominantly defensive, focused on finding some delusory place of safety. They saw only the dangers threatening to engulf them, not the opportunities for striking the enemy.

By 13 August the scouts of the German First Army were probing with impunity to within a few hundred metres of the masses of French troops crowded into the area east of Metz. Even more ominously, Second Army was approaching the banks of the Moselle well to the south of the city. Although the bridges across the Moselle above and below Metz had been mined, neither Bazaine nor anyone else gave orders to blow them up to delay a German crossing. The French high command decided that day to leave only one division (Laveaucoupet's) to garrison the fortress of Metz, while the rest of the army continued the retreat westward down the long straight road that leads to Verdun and Châlons. Urged by Eugénie and the cabinet not to return to turbulent Paris, Napoleon remained with the army, warning Bazaine that there was 'not a moment to lose' in carrying out the retreat.[1]

The retreat did not begin until the 14th, and led to an immense traffic jam as long columns of men, wagons and guns struggled to make their way through the narrow streets of Metz and across the bridges. The pontoons, begun on the 9th but disrupted by heavy rains that had raised the river level, were not finished until that morning and funnelled too many men into a confined area. Bazaine had not specified times for the columns to move, nor allocated different roads to each corps, with the result that units crossed each other and stalled for hours. This chaos was still being untangled when at 4 p.m. troops trying to pass through the choked city heard the boom of cannon fire to the east.

In a pattern that was becoming familiar, battle had been joined through the impetuosity of a junior German general eager to win his laurels. Although Moltke had no plans for First Army to advance that day, reports of the French withdrawing through Metz unhindered were too much for General von der Goltz, commander of 26th Brigade of VII Corps. The French troops on the table-land east of Metz belonged to 3 Corps, commanded since Bazaine's elevation by General Decaen. They were awaiting orders to march down to the crossing points when they were attacked by German troops advancing up the steep vine-covered slopes of the Vallières ravine. The French might have been content to hold them off until nightfall while they completed their withdrawal, or have organized a counterattack to punish Goltz's rashness. Instead they accepted a defensive battle, throwing in more and more men to hold their line.

General Ladmirault, commanding 4 Corps, heard the gunfire as his men were crossing the Moselle. On his own initiative he turned around two of his divisions and sent them back to support the one he had left as rearguard. A lieutenant remembered the 'unforgettable spectacle' of his men, dusty and streaming with sweat, double-quicking up the winding roads that lead from the Moselle up to the plateau, eager to get at the enemy at last, while gunners lashing their horses galloped by in a whirlwind of dust.[2]

On the German side substantial portions of I and VII Corps were committed in support of Goltz. Thus the battle, later called Borny by the French or Colombey-Nouilly by the Germans, extended to the high ground on either side of the main highway running east from Metz, until the French had approximately 50,000 men present while the Germans engaged perhaps 30,000.[3]

The improvised contest was a baptism of fire for many. Joseph Marin described its 'incredible intensity', and thought it impossible that he could be spared: 'On all sides I saw my poor comrades falling dead or wounded. Shells burst in our ranks, and grape-shot whistled past our ears like swarms of bees.' However, like other raw French troops, he was heartened by witnessing the impact of the *mitrailleuse* on charging Germans. Alphonse Chantron testified that, 'You have to have seen this weapon at work to comprehend the terrible effect of the destruction it wreaks: its sinister rattle still echoes in my ears; I shall never forget that noise, both terrifying and intoxicating at the same time.' He depicted the gunner 'bent over his weapon, his hands and face blackened, his eyes bloodshot, his cap pulled sideways over his ear ... his teeth clenched, his lips contracted in an anxious yet diabolic smile' as he turned the handle, and his squeal of pleasure on hitting his target.[4] By the time the moon rose over the corpse-strewn fields and woods 4,906 Germans and 3,614 Frenchmen had become casualties.[5] General Decaen had been mortally wounded, and Bazaine had his epaulette torn away by a shell fragment that contused his shoulder: his sixth wound in thirty-nine years of military service.

Tactically the battle was a draw. Although the French had failed to capitalize on their superiority in numbers, their morale was boosted by having successfully beaten off the attack. That night they resumed their retreat across the Moselle as ordered, some of them first taking the opportunity to equip themselves with boots taken from dead Germans. Finding the enemy gone next morning, the Germans too proclaimed victory.

After the war German military writers rationalized the strategic significance of the indecisive Battle of Borny, claiming that it slowed down the French retreat from Metz, so enabling German forces to catch up with them west of the Moselle two days later.[6] But the French delays were predominantly the result of hesitant leadership and poor planning. Any further delay imposed by the battle also affected the Germans, for continuing concerns about a possible French offensive on the east bank induced Moltke temporarily to suspend the crossing of some units of Second Army to the west bank until the situation became clearer.

All through the day of 15 August the French army, over 150,000 men strong, lumbered up the main road westward out of Metz, winding its way up the heights that mark the edge of the great rolling plateau that stretches away towards the Meuse. Such poor use was made of the other available roads, so overburdened was the army with a huge wagon train and so inexperienced was Bazaine in directing the movements of so large a force that progress was painfully slow. By nightfall the leading infantry units had progressed only as far as the little village of Rezonville, having taken thirty-six hours to travel scarcely 15 kilometres from Metz. Ahead of them General Forton's cavalry had encountered some German squadrons and exchanged artillery fire, but made little effort to pursue them when they disappeared. Napoleon was still with the army, embarrassing Bazaine by continuing to communicate his 'wishes' and even issuing orders direct to unit commanders. When they met at Longeville Bazaine claimed that Napoleon, after congratulating him on 'breaking the spell' by the victory at Borny, urged the greatest prudence upon him. Still nurturing the mirage of bringing Austria and Italy into the war, Napoleon enjoined him 'above all to avoid any more defeats'. That night the emperor slept in the village of Gravelotte, and at dawn on the 16th, to Bazaine's great relief, rode off in his carriage accompanied by the Prince Imperial. His parting words to the marshal were to make for Verdun 'as soon as you can'.[7]

The German Second Army spent the 15th crossing the Moselle on a 30-kilometre front south of Metz, finding the bridges intact and meeting no French resistance. From nearer the city, once the sun had burned off the river fog, clouds of dust could be seen to the west, signalling the French retreat. That evening Moltke ordered Second Army to mount a 'vigorous offensive' next day towards the road from Metz to Verdun being used by the French.[8] But the commander of Second Army, Prince Friedrich Karl, detailed only III and X Corps, with the cavalry divisions attached to them, for this mission. No more than Moltke did he know exactly where the French were, for such cavalry reports as had reached headquarters painted a very incomplete picture. Judging that the French must by now be approaching the Meuse, the prince ordered the bulk of his army to march not north but west, in the hope of overtaking them. But next morning, instead of encountering the tail of the French army on the Verdun road, III Corps on his right was to collide with it head on.

Tuesday, 16 August dawned radiant, with the promise of heat. Rather than setting his army in motion without delay, Bazaine postponed the march to Verdun until the afternoon while he waited for 4 Corps to come up. Yet this concentration did not indicate that he was preparing for battle. The army remained in camp, with tents pitched. No attempt was made to occupy rising ground to the south that commanded the road, and the high command was complacent about reports of enemy activity in that direction. A lieutenant with precise information from the outpost line was accused by General Bataille of being 'one of those people who see Prussians everywhere'.[9]

The westernmost troops of the army were Forton's cavalry division, encamped a little beyond Vionville. 'The men were cooking a meal, cleaning their weapons ... whole squadrons were leading their horses to water in the stream' when at 9.15 a.m. a barrage of shells burst among them, 'causing a frightful panic. Men, horses, wagons flooded to the rear in indescribable disorder.'[10] The attacking force was a brigade of German cavalry that had deployed its guns in an arc to bombard the French. Had they been bolder the Germans might have charged home, completing the rout of Forton's men and giving the French no time to recover. As Forton's cavalry fled to the rear the nearest French infantry, Frossard's 2 Corps, had time to form ranks and advanced to drive the attackers away. Hardly had they done so than they found themselves exchanging fire with the leading German infantry units – the Brandenburgers of III Corps, whose commander, Konstantin von Alvensleben, had been urging his men forward to the assault in the wake of the cavalry.

A furious battle ensued, focused first on the village of Vionville, which the Germans captured at about 11.30 a.m., then on the hamlet of Flavigny. On both sides unity of command was quickly lost, the action being shaped by the momentary inspiration of officers and the bravery of individuals. 'Vain would be the attempt to reproduce a true picture of this wild struggle in all its details,' confessed even the authors of the German official history.[11] Alvensleben, a general of superior intelligence and ability, at last discovered that he was confronting not the rearguard of the retreating French army, but the mass of it, with units from four French corps now in the firing line opposing him. He kept attacking nevertheless, trusting in the German aggressive spirit and superior gunnery to disguise his inferior numbers and the immense risk he was running. His boldness paid dividends, albeit at a heavy cost in German lives.

The sun had just passed its zenith when Frossard's two divisions, decimated by artillery fire, were driven back in 'wild flight',[12] their disengagement covered by one of those sacrificial charges that had become the stock-in-trade of French cavalry. Following an abortive charge by 3rd Lancers, three waves of the Cuirassiers of the Guard thundered forward, only to be toppled from their black horses by volleys delivered at close range. A German counter-charge almost captured Bazaine, who was swept along in the mêlée and separated from his entourage until rescued by French horsemen. This was the first of several occasions when the Germans threw in their cavalry to retain the initiative and disguise their desperate situation. By early afternoon their ammunition was running low and help had yet to arrive. 'For the moment the artillery is our only support,' confessed General von Stülpnagel, one of Alvensleben's division commanders: 'If the artillery retires we won't be able to hold the infantry, and the battle is lost.'[13]

Yet Alvensleben had one last trick up his sleeve, and played it at a critical juncture. To relieve pressure on his infantry and spoil any French counterattack, he ordered General von Bredow's cavalry brigade to charge the guns of Canrobert's 6 Corps situated near the Roman road north of Rezonville. Realizing that his mission was sacrificial, Bredow used the cover of shallow depressions to move his two regiments north of the Verdun road at about 2 p.m. before wheeling east, forming line and charging his objective at full tilt. Aided by the cover of smoke and dust his cuirassiers and lancers got in among the French guns, wreaking mayhem among their crews and infantry supports before galloping south amid a hail of fire. On their retreat the survivors were set upon by French cavalry, including Forton's men, who ruthlessly avenged their humiliation of that morning with the points of their sabres.[14] 'Von Bredow's Death Ride' cost nearly half the 800 troopers who set out, but it caused several French batteries to withdraw, made the French high command even more defensive-minded, and created a German military legend similar to that of the Charge of the Light Brigade in Britain.

Help arrived at last for German infantry embattled in the Tronville Woods as X Corps came into line on Alvensleben's left, having marched 27 miles from the Moselle in torrid heat. French reinforcements too were reaching this western sector of the battlefield as Ladmirault's 4 Corps belatedly came into action. Wedell's 38th Brigade of X Corps advanced through Mars-la-Tour against the French right without reconnaissance, only to find itself at the bottom of a ravine, the crest of which was lined with French troops. With supports rushing up to lay down flanking fire, Ladmirault's men raked their exhausted enemies to such murderous effect that they all but annihilated them in a few terrible minutes. As his unit advanced into the ravine with bayonets fixed, 20-year-old Private Jules Louis recounted how he stumbled upon a German officer reloading his pistol behind a large willow tree:

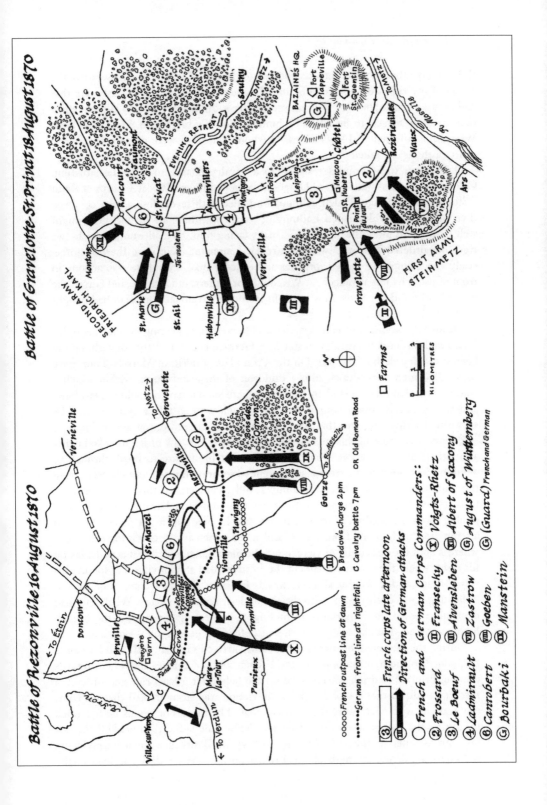

Battle of Rezonville 16 August 1870

Battle of Gravelotte - St. Privat 18 August 1870

KILOMETRES

□ Farms

ooooo French outpost line at dawn
.... German front line at nightfall

☐ French corps late afternoon
◼ Direction of German attacks

French and German Corps Commanders:
③ ◯ French and German
② ◯ Frossard   Ⅹ Voigts-Rhetz
③ ◯ Le Boeuf   Ⅻ Fransecky
④ ◯ Ladmirault   Ⅲ Alvensleben
⑥ ◯ Canrobert   Ⅶ Zastrow
Ⓖ ◯ Bourbaki   Ⅷ Goeben
                      Ⅸ Manstein
                      Ⓖ Albert of Saxony
                      Ⓖ August of Württemberg
                      Ⓖ (Guard) French and German

B Bredow's Charge 2pm
C Cavalry battle 7pm
OR Old Roman Road

'I thrust my sabre-bayonet into his body up to the hilt. Without the cross-guard, the barrel of my rifle would have gone in. My enemy fell, giving me a last stare that had nothing gentle about it. War is a sad business, but it was better to kill the fellow than to allow myself to be killed by him.'[15] Wedell's brigade of 4,641 men from Westphalia suffered 2,614 casualties, of whom some 370 were made prisoner and nearly a thousand killed.[16]

Once again the Germans resorted to a cavalry charge to save the situation. Colonel von Auerswald's Guard Dragoons launched themselves at 4 Corps at about 5.30 p.m. to disengage Wedell. Although repelled with severe losses, they achieved their objective and dissuaded Ladmirault from continuing an advance that might well have swept away the anxious Germans facing him. 'We all wondered why we were not ordered forward,' wrote a French lieutenant. 'We were there in force, ready and willing; we sensed, privates and officers alike, that there was nobody in front of us. Why not advance? ... We could not understand it at all, and cursed the generals who did not know how to profit from the advantages our élan had bought for them.'[17]

Meanwhile, seeing German batteries and horsemen appearing beyond his right, Ladmirault ordered his cavalry to attack. A German counter-charge brought on the biggest cavalry clash of the war. On the Yron plateau north of Mars-la-Tour more than 5,000 men were drawn into a cauldron of dust and noise, within which a confused combat raged. Hand-to-hand fighting of such intensity could not last long, and after a quarter of an hour it was the French who withdrew northward. The Germans let them go, and the battle in the west sputtered out at about 7 p.m.

Bazaine's conduct of this pivotal battle of the war, or lack of it, provoked many accusations after the event. Some suggested that his failure to break through to Verdun was evidence of a treasonable intent to separate himself and his army from the crumbling Empire. Others, less implausibly, conjectured that he was relieved to be rid of Napoleon and was in no hurry to rejoin him. Bazaine had expressed doubts about the wisdom of retreat. In any case he misread the battle as a German attempt to cut him off from Metz, and acted defensively to reinforce his left, whereas both the possibility of victory and the most dangerous threat actually lay on his right, where the Germans had cut the Verdun road at Vionville. Yet forcing his way through to the west at all costs was as far from Bazaine's conceptions as co-ordinating his five army corps with the aim of destroying the enemy. Where German doctrine stressed the importance of finding and defeating the enemy, the French high command thought solely in terms of defending geographical positions.

During the afternoon elements of the newly arrived German VIII and IX Corps had joined in the fighting opposite the French left and centre, and when towards evening Prince Friedrich Karl arrived on the field after a hard ride and ordered a further assault in that sector Bazaine's conviction was strengthened that his communications with Metz were the German goal. The masses of troops he had piled up during the day between Gravelotte and Rezonville sufficed to beat off the last German assaults in the twilight, the artillery of Bourbaki's Guard convincing the Germans of the strength of the French position. After dark the field finally fell silent following twelve hours of an immensely bloody contest. French casualties were 13,761, German 15,799.[18] French accounts typically describe the ravages of German shells 'which burst in the air and showered our men with a veritable hail of iron fragments which tore everything in their path and inflicted atrocious wounds'.[19] Although statistics based on twenty-six regiments suggest that 17 per cent of French wounds during the battle were due to artillery, other units suffered far more severely from German gunnery: in the morning fighting three-quarters of the 411 wounds treated in the 67th Line were caused by shell-fire.[20]

Yet if the Battle of Rezonville or Mars-la-Tour – or Vionville as the Germans called it – testified to the lethal efficiency of modern weapons, in other ways it was reminiscent of the battles of an earlier generation: cavalry in steel breastplates and helmets crossing sabres or wielding lances, red-trousered French infantry in mass formation advancing in neat double lines. Lack of visibility was as much a difficulty as in Napoleonic times, for if the era of the breech-loading rifle and cannon had arrived, that of the smokeless cartridge had not. A participant described 'a mass of white smoke of persistent opacity which extended along the whole fighting front', while the opposing artillery batteries created 'two nearly parallel lines of thick greyish smoke ... lit up at every instant by powerful red flashes'.[21] This literal fog of war made control by commanders as difficult as ever, and there was no ridge or hill from which Bazaine could survey the whole of this vast, sprawling battlefield to understand what was happening. The masses of men involved made the battle-field larger than the average for Napoleonic times, for fighting extended across 12 kilometres of the Verdun road, yet Bazaine had only the means of control familiar in that era, namely verbal commands and messages sent by courier. As he complained during the morning, 'I can't be everywhere at once.'[22]

These difficulties notwithstanding, Bazaine and his corps commanders proved themselves unequal to the demands of the hour, and no match for their deter-mined and professionally competent adversaries. That Bazaine tried to encourage his men was well and good, but he busied himself with tasks like siting batteries and feeding battalions into what he envisaged as a defensive battle against superior odds. The inadequacy of his staff was a reflection of his own preferences, just as the inadequacy of his orders testified to his own limitations and failure to grasp the wider strategic picture. If his intention was to push onwards to Verdun, then he needed to retake Vionville and reclaim the main road which the Germans had cut and obstinately clung to. He had the forces to achieve victory. During the morning Alvensleben was attacking with around 30,000 men when Bazaine had double that number to hand. Even at the end of the day the Germans had engaged only 77,000 men and 246 guns against 137,000 French troops present with 364 guns and 66 *mitrailleuses*: yet a quarter of the French infantry took no active part in the battle.[23] For all that has been written of their superior preparation and general-ship, the Germans had erred in exposing two corps to possible destruction by a closely concentrated French army. Tragically for France, Bazaine failed to grasp the opportunity presented to him.

Late that night, by the light of a candle in a small room at the inn in Gravelotte vacated by the emperor that morning, Bazaine came to a fateful decision. Impressed by the supposed strength of the German forces facing him, influenced by exaggerated reports of a lack of food and ammunition and probably also by the number of demoralized stragglers around the village, he did not for a moment entertain the possibility of an offensive next day. Although a northern road to Verdun via Briey and Étain remained open, he also discounted the option of continuing the retreat. Instead he determined to pull his army back to a defensive position closer to Metz. 'If anyone has a better idea, speak up,' he said to the officers around him. There was a deferential silence before he concluded, 'We must save the army, and to do that we must return to Metz.'[24]

Next morning, 17 August, the army pivoted back through almost ninety degrees to take up a strong defensive position extending a dozen kilometres along high ground running perpendicular to the Verdun road. This short displacement to the east was marked by the usual confusion and disorder. Troops who felt that they had won a defensive victory the previous day were incredulous at being ordered to withdraw. Some units in 4 Corps were so disoriented that when they reached their new position they posted pickets towards the east, facing Metz, with their backs to the enemy. The alleged shortage of rations jarred strangely with the sight of huge quantities of food and equipment being burned near Gravelotte because it could not be removed in time.[25]

Bazaine was confident that his new position would enable him to beat off any attack while protecting Metz.[26] South of the Verdun road Frossard's 2 Corps, with its left on the heights overlooking the Moselle, held the Rozérieulles plateau and the Point du Jour farmstead, and adapted gravel quarries as rifle pits. To the north 3 Corps, commanded by Le Bœuf, was on high ground where solid farmhouses bearing the names Saint-Hubert, Moscou, Leipzig and La Folie were rapidly converted into strong points. Continuing the line northwards Ladmirault's 4 Corps held ground around Amanvillers, the strength of which had long been recognized by military engineers. Only Canrobert's 6 Corps on the French right was initially in a rather exposed position, but that afternoon Canrobert was given permission to pull his troops back into alignment with Ladmirault, anchoring them on the village of Saint-Privat, where they had excellent fields of fire down long open slopes. The Guard was held in reserve behind the French left, near Fort Plappeville where Bazaine had his headquarters.

Meanwhile the Germans too needed to replenish their ammunition after the previous day's battle and were in no position to resume the offensive. On the morning of the 17th they expected to be attacked. Apart from skirmishing as the French withdrew from around Gravelotte, they lost contact with the main French force – an indication that Bazaine could have accomplished a retreat to the north. Moltke's priority for that day was to concentrate his forces. The bulk of Steinmetz's First Army was transferred west of the Moselle, while the remaining corps of Second Army were recalled from their westward race towards the Meuse. By night-fall seven corps and three cavalry divisions were concentrated for the impending offensive. Never again would Bazaine be offered the opportunity to strike at an isolated fraction of the enemy.

Yet when the German Second Army advanced northward from the Verdun road on the baking hot morning of 18 August the high command remained unsure exactly where the French were. After experiencing some traffic problems of their own the Germans groped forward in battle formation, ready to manoeuvre to right or left depending on where contact with the enemy was made. In fact they were marching at right angles to the French position, observed but untroubled by them. Only in mid-morning did Moltke become certain that, rather than retreating northward, the bulk of French forces lay to the east. But where was their right flank? Initially but erroneously it was supposed to be around Amanvillers. Riding forward to reconnoitre French camps there, General von Manstein, commanding IX Corps, observed that they betrayed an air of 'heedless unconcern' and seized his advantage. At 11.45 a.m. his artillery unlimbered and opened fire.[27]

Opposite him Ladmirault's men, who had passed the morning in inspections, cleaning their weapons and cooking, were taken unawares by the bombardment, but quickly fell in to their combat positions. Before long the adventurous German gun crews were being decimated by a storm of rifle and *mitrailleuse* fire, and what French artillery lacked in accuracy it made up for in volume of fire. When Manstein's infantry hurried up in support they proved unable to break into what was actually the French centre rather than their right flank, and were fortunate that the French seemed content simply to hold their ground. The battle in this sector raged with varying intensity all afternoon without decisive advantage to either side.

The sound of Manstein's cannonade prompted First Army to his south to open its own bombardment of the French left. For the moment Moltke wanted it to do no more, for his concept was for First Army to mount only a holding action while Second Army found and turned the French right. However, his note to Steinmetz to that effect made little impact. The skirmish lines of both armies were drawn into a fire-fight as German infantry tried to drive away French sharpshooters targeting their gun crews, and the action rapidly escalated. On this southern portion of the battlefield the Mance ravine served as a dry moat protecting the French positions. It was crossed only by the narrow causeway bearing the poplar-lined road from Verdun past the high-walled Saint-Hubert Farm as it wound over the hill towards Metz. Le Bœuf's and Frossard's men had improved the natural strength of the position by digging trenches. It was 3 p.m. before the Germans were able to force the 750-man French garrison out of Saint-Hubert after a hard fight, but their attempts to push further uphill only lengthened their casualty list.

The 74-year-old Steinmetz, a veteran of the Napoleonic wars and a hero of the war of 1866 with Austria, was a head-down fighter who from the outset of the campaign had been impatient both of Moltke's cerebral, mathematical way of making war and of his own relegation to a secondary role. His artillery was turning the French strong points, notably the Moscou and Point du Jour Farms, into giant braziers, their interiors littered with dismembered limbs and charred corpses. Most significantly, the French artillery, greatly outmatched on this sector, was slackening its fire. Steinmetz believed that French resistance was reaching its breaking point, and ordered an assault. It was a terrible misjudgement, which was to bring First Army to the brink of disaster.

As afternoon turned to evening Steinmetz stubbornly ordered repeated frontal attacks. Obediently his infantry went forward through the Mance ravine, only to be shot down when they emerged onto the bare slopes beyond by French troops firing from their trenches around Moscou and the Point du Jour. Four artillery batteries which managed to cross the causeway could barely maintain themselves on the far side, so heavy were their losses. Steinmetz even ordered a cavalry division across, supposedly to charge the retreating French. Its leading regiment, 4th Lancers, lost fifty men and a hundred horses within minutes, until the division commander wisely turned his men around to avoid their useless sacrifice. The causeway was by now littered with dead and dying and the debris of battle, while the Mance ravine was a vision of Hell where, under a pall of dust and black smoke, huddled the wounded and unwounded of dozens of different battalions.[28]

Convinced that victory required one final effort, towards 7 p.m. Steinmetz threw in the last reserves of his VII and VIII Corps – but far from being on the point of collapse French riflemen and gunners had replenished their ammunition and were ready and waiting in their concealed positions. German infantry went forward into the murderous hail, but bravery could not carry them far. As some troops broke and raced back for the precarious shelter of the Mance ravine they triggered a panic there. Thousands of men together with bolting horses poured back through the main street of the blazing village of Gravelotte, where an excited King Wilhelm and his staff belaboured them with the flats of their swords, and on to Rezonville where at last they were safe from enemy bullets.

Still Steinmetz was not finished. General von Fransecky arrived with his as yet unblooded II Corps after an all-day march from Pont-à-Mousson, and was placed under Steinmetz's orders by the king. Fransecky cheered on his Pomeranians as they advanced across the Mance valley at sunset with 'drums beating and bugles sounding'.[29] Reaching the far side, the leading brigades charged, but none got within a hundred yards of the French lines, now marked only by rifle volleys flashing like lightning in the twilight. This attack too melted away in the missile storm, and a stream of stragglers headed rearward. As night fell the confusion was compounded when German troops near Saint-Hubert mistook the occupants for Frenchmen and exchanged fire with them. Telling friend from foe having become almost impossible, officers sought to put an end to the chaos by breaking off the action, which petered out after 10 p.m.

Moltke had been quite unable to restrain Steinmetz or the king. The consequent repulse of First Army was so severe that a major French counterattack might have turned it into a rout. During the worst of the panic German commanders had taken thought for their vulnerable communications with the Moselle, and for a while were under the impression of defeat. The positions defended by Le Bœuf and Frossard had justified Bazaine's faith in their impregnability. Not until late that night did Moltke learn that his strategy had succeeded after all, though not before Second Army too had suffered appalling losses.

During the afternoon the Guard Corps, under Prince August of Württemberg, had moved into position on Manstein's left, facing the village of Saint-Privat which the Germans now knew to be the bastion of the French right. Further still to the north XII (Royal Saxon) Corps was making a circuitous march to get behind the extreme French right flank, which was lodged in the village of Roncourt.

In order to bring the French positions under effective artillery fire, the Germans had first to take the village of Sainte-Marie-aux-Chênes, which lies on the road from Briey to Metz towards the bottom of the mile-long slope that rises eastwards towards Saint-Privat. Around Sainte-Marie a single regiment acted as an outpost to the main French line. The village was pulverized by German cannon prior to a converging attack launched at 3 p.m. by the left-hand units of the Guard and the right-hand Saxon units. Most of the heavily outnumbered French quickly withdrew up the slopes to Roncourt while they still could, leaving behind at least 200 prisoners who did not manage to escape the shattered village in time.

The capture of Sainte-Marie at about 3.30 p.m. was but the overture to the assault on Saint-Privat, lying just beyond the crest-line of the gentle ridge which the Germans would have to take. For two hours the infantry of Canrobert's 6 Corps were pummelled by German shells which threw up blinding showers of dry earth and stones that could cause injury even when metal shell fragments failed to tear flesh and bone. Partly for want of entrenching tools, Canrobert's men had failed to dig themselves in as extensively as Le Bœuf's and Frossard's further south, and had only the inadequate cover of low dry-stone walls and hedges. Only Saint-Privat itself offered some protection, and its solidly built houses were packed with riflemen on every floor and even on the roofs. Such cannon as Canrobert possessed suffered attrition under sustained German fire, while those remaining were running low on ammunition. Several batteries were withdrawn to replenish their caissons.

The noticeable slackening of French fire towards 5 p.m. convinced Prince August that the moment had arrived to launch his infantry assault. Possibly goaded by a message from his army commander, Prince Friedrich Karl, he became irritable when the commander of his 1st Division, General von Pape, urged a delay to allow further artillery preparation. Prince August was aware that the bulk of the Saxon forces, having a long way to march, had yet to reach their positions, but he was equally aware that Manstein's IX Corps on his right needed support in its stubborn struggle with Ladmirault's men. He became impatient to strike the battle-winning blow with his highly disciplined troops, the pride of the German army. He drew them up in a formation that made no concession whatever to the age of the breech-loading rifle. His Guardsmen lined up shoulder to shoulder in battalion columns as if on parade. First to advance, at about 5.15 p.m., was 2nd Guards Division, south of the road from Sainte-Marie to Saint-Privat. North of the road, 1st Division started forward half an hour later. Both suffered similar fates once they came within Chassepot range. Officers were toppled from their mounts and men were felled in droves as the French fired at will into the dense dark blue ranks, sending up clouds of white rifle smoke. A flock of sheep that wandered into the line of fire was killed to the last animal. Many German battalions quickly lost all their officers and continued forward under the command of ensigns or NCOs until some got to about 500 metres from their objective. Against such a storm of fire they could make no further headway.

The survivors of this hecatomb flung themselves down to take what meagre cover they could, whether in the slightest undulation in the ground or in the shallow drainage ditches that lined the road. From there they could at least bring the French under fire from their needle-guns. The slaughter might have been greater still had Canrobert's men possessed any *mitrailleuses*. As it was, nearly half the 18,000 Guardsmen who advanced had been cut down within an hour. No starker illustration occurred during the war of the cost of employing the close-formation infantry tactics of the eighteenth century in the face of the weapons of 1870.[30]

The discipline and training of the Guard in the face of this bloody repulse helped contain any repeat of the mass panic that had taken hold on Steinmetz's front. The remaining troops clung to their positions, while their artillery deterred local French counterattacks. More Saxon batteries were joining in with those of the Guard, so that 144 guns were targeting Saint-Privat. At last, too, the Saxon infantry came into action and drove the French out of Roncourt. They had found and turned the weakly held extremity of the French line. For, though Marshal Canrobert's personal bravery was much in evidence throughout that long August afternoon, his tactical dispositions were faulty. He had heaped battalions into Saint-Privat, where they made a dense target for enemy shells, at the expense of more vulnerable parts of his line. Saint-Privat could now be attacked from three sides.

The final assault, involving both the Saxons and the Guard, came at about 7.30 p.m. Canrobert's men, tired, hungry, thirsty and shaken after hours of bombardment, were reduced to searching the pockets and cartridge pouches of dead and wounded comrades for ammunition, for fresh supplies had failed to reach them in sufficient quantity. Their numbers dwindling under enemy shell-fire, they were overborne by the final German onrush. Saint-Privat became the scene of murderous combat with clubbed rifles and bayonets as the French made a last stand in its streets and burning buildings, notably around the church and cemetery. Amid the savage fighting the wounded suffered the consequences of the unwise decision to establish hospitals in the village. Disaster occurred when a staircase in the chateau collapsed under the weight of a terrified horde of wounded, including amputees, rushing to escape shells bursting in their makeshift wards and bullets passing through windows and ricocheting. In the church the blazing roof collapsed on the helpless wounded screaming below.[31] Finally, as dusk fell, the carnage ceased and the Germans established control, taking 2,000 prisoners. One of the French troops streaming away to the south-east recalled:

> Only upon reaching the road, all puffed out, did we look back. Night was spreading over the battlefield; Saint-Privat and [the nearby hamlet of] Jérusalem were on fire; great masses of Germans were pouring in from

north, south and west . . . In front of us, above the flames and through the smoke, the huge red sun was sinking beneath the horizon. I can still see that sinister end to a great day of battle.[32]

The defeat of Canrobert's 6 Corps left Ladmirault's right exposed, and it too began to give way under assault. The exhausted and defeated troops of the French right retreated in disorder down the forest roads towards the western outskirts of Metz, where they were rallied next morning.

Marshal Bazaine had given no direction to the battle, the sound of which reached his headquarters at Plappeville only faintly and intermittently due to the prevailing wind.[33] As on the 16th, he was concerned only with the security of his left and of his communications with Metz. From Mont Saint-Quentin the distant view of German movements on his southern flank reinforced that fixation. He ordered part of his reserve, the Imperial Guard, to take position behind his left in case it was needed. Otherwise, he diverted himself for a long while with some heavy cannon. With regard to his right he remained utterly complacent, convinced that it was secure and that the Germans were only probing it. In response to repeated messages from Ladmirault and Canrobert he gave orders for two batteries and some ammunition to be sent to the right, but without betraying any concern. Already he was planning for the army to fall back closer to Metz. Out of his depth as an army commander, he appeared to have no conception of the magnitude of the threat facing his army. While the fate of the battle, and indeed of France, hung in the balance, he failed to fulfil the commander-in-chief's role of purposefully engaging his reserves: the Imperial Guard, the reserve artillery and two cavalry divisions.

Towards 6.30 p.m. the commander of the Imperial Guard, General Bourbaki, did lead a brigade forward in response to an appeal from Ladmirault for his intervention. Yet Bourbaki, ignorant of the general situation, hesitated to commit his men, particularly over what he deemed to be unfavourable ground. When he saw many of Ladmirault's men melting away to the rear, he upbraided the staff officer from 4 Corps who had been urging him forward, saying, 'You promised me a victory, but you have led me here to witness a rout. You have caused me to abandon my magnificent positions. You had no right.' Thereupon he turned his column about, away from the enemy.[34] Although Bourbaki subsequently sent some men and guns to Canrobert, they arrived too late to do more than protect the retreat of the right against German pursuit until darkness fell. Disbanded infantrymen heading for Metz greeted them with shouts of 'Filthy Praetorians!'[35] How the fortunes of that momentous 18 August might have turned had the Imperial Guard been at hand to counterattack in late afternoon, either on Canrobert's front or against Steinmetz's shattered battalions, would remain only a subject for rueful speculation in the post-war years of defeat.

Gravelotte–Saint-Privat had been an immense battle involving some 300,000 men, creating suffering on a scale that marked witnesses for the rest of their lives. Reflecting on the inadequacies of French systems for retrieving the wounded and providing first aid in comparison to the German system, a French regimental surgeon wondered, 'How many victims might have survived had they been picked up and bandaged in time? How many might have lived had they not been crushed by horses hooves and the wheels of caissons, which left flesh in bloody shreds, heads flattened, chests crushed, limbs torn, entrails spilling out and trailing, in the most horrible spectacle that the imagination can conceive?'[36] Virtually every building for miles around was crammed with wounded. The Germans, attacking with their faces towards Berlin, had floundered in their attempts to find the French positions, then employed clumsy tactics that maximized their losses, which totalled 20,163 (the Guard Corps accounting for 8,230 of these).[37] The French, with their faces towards Paris, had conducted a successful defence all along the line until evening, despite being outnumbered and outgunned. Their losses were 13,218.[38]

Ultimately Bazaine's passivity and failure to use his reserves allowed the Germans to recover from their blunders and to find and turn his right flank. Defeated on his right, Bazaine ordered his left too to withdraw early next day to positions around Metz. By 20 August the Germans had invested the city. Like malleable iron, the French army had been beaten back on the anvil of Metz by the three hammer blows of 14, 16 and 18 August. Bazaine's communications with the rest of France, to which he had attached such little weight, were cut, and as a result of his lack of strategic grasp the fate of his army was sealed.

Chapter 6

Sedan and the Fall of the Empire

Moltke, as ever, reacted rapidly to the changed strategic situation. On the day following the battle of 18 August King Wilhelm signed orders for a new division of German forces. The bulk of First and Second Armies, consisting of seven army corps under Prince Friedrich Karl, would remain to blockade Bazaine in Metz. (Besides meeting changed operational requirements, this reorganization enabled Steinmetz to be removed. He was appointed Governor of Posen.) Three corps, including the Guard, plus two cavalry divisions, were formed into a separate force, the Army of the Meuse under Crown Prince Albert of Saxony, who had so success-fully directed the flanking movement at Roncourt. This new force would continue to advance westwards, towards Châlons, where the remainder of the French army was concentrating. The Army of the Meuse would co-operate with Third Army under Crown Prince Friedrich Wilhelm of Prussia, which had continued its advance through Lorraine after its victory at Frœschwiller. The superiority of the German military system of trained reserves thus allowed Moltke to detail 150,000 men[1] to contain Bazaine while combined mobile striking forces totalling 224,000 men with 813 guns[2] would seek to bring the French forces still at large to a decisive battle.

Marshal MacMahon, forming his new army at Châlons Camp with troops trans-ported there by rail, had only half that number of men. The hastily amalgamated Army of Châlons included his 1 Corps, now under General Ducrot. These survivors of the campaign in Alsace presented a stark contrast with the reservists who had been sent to make up the losses of Frœschwiller: 'MacMahon's defeats and famous retreat inevitably showed in the slovenly, dust-covered and varied uniforms of the officers. Their beards were unkempt, their faces emaciated and sunburnt.'[3] Failly's 5 Corps was equally demoralized by the prolonged and disorderly retreat from the frontier in abysmal weather, without yet having fought. Félix Douay's 7 Corps had been transported from Belfort. While piled into railway wagons its men 'enjoyed an unhealthy and alcohol-fuelled idleness and learned contempt for their officers and for discipline from the tub-thumpers of every regiment'.[4] The newly formed 12 Corps under General Lebrun combined an excellent division of Marines and a regular division which until recently had formed an observation corps on the Spanish frontier with a third composed almost entirely of raw troops. Not only were the reservists and recruits who had been called up to swell the ranks of the new force inadequately trained, but one regular officer noted a lack of enthusiasm. Surprised by their sudden recall because of a dynastic quarrel that meant little to them, the city dwellers had no love for the Empire, while the rural recruits resented being called away at harvest time. Insubordination and indiscipline were rife, but officers seemed disinclined to impose exemplary punishments.[5] A junior officer doubted that such a force 'could hold together in open country in the face of such a determined enemy with such formidable artillery fire'.[6]

MacMahon was under strong pressure from the imperial government in Paris to advance directly to Bazaine's rescue. If Napoleon III himself had become a liability, the Empress Eugénie and her ministers still hoped to save the dynasty. The republican opposition in the Chamber was becoming ever bolder, demanding that the people of Paris be armed and parliamentary control of the war effort: both measures that would in effect signal the end of the regime. For the moment War Minister Palikao was feeding public opinion with portentous hints that French forces were on the verge of a great victory. An embittered survivor of Frœschwiller, arriving on the evening of 18 August, found the capital prey to the wildest rumours:

> The idlers of Paris, deceived by official bulletins and the reticences of
> Palikao, by the journalists and their own proverbial stupidity, insisted that
> the success of France was assured, and their bragging was equalled only
> by their naïve credulity ... I thought of the feast day of lunatics that used
> to be celebrated in the Middle Ages.[7]

In an age of revived interest in the military history of antiquity, there was speculation that the defeat of Attila and the Huns, believed to have taken place near Châlons in 451, was about to be repeated. Palikao was adamant that the rescue of Bazaine was a political and military necessity and was 'our only chance of salvation'.[8]

MacMahon did not share Palikao's confidence. When on 20 August the approach of German cavalry to within 50 kilometres of the indefensible Châlons Camp was reported to him, he feared that a raid by those 'bold buggers' might cause panic among his men if he lingered.[9] Abandoning and burning large quantities of supplies at Châlons, next day he marched his army north-westward to Rheims, from where it could cover the approaches to Paris. His strategic assessment was that 'It is impossible to go to rescue Bazaine. Bazaine has no munitions or supplies and will be forced to capitulate, and we shall arrive too late.'[10] He thought it more important to conserve his army as the nucleus of a larger force which France could organize given time. On 22 August he was in the process of giving orders for a withdrawal towards Paris when a message smuggled through the lines from Bazaine caused him to change his mind entirely.

Dated 19 August, Bazaine's message indicated that he intended to break out northward to reach Montmédy. From there, if he found the direct route westward to Châlons barred, he would try to reach it by continuing down the Meuse valley towards Sedan.[11] The phrasing betrayed all the vagueness and irresolution that Bazaine's chief of staff, General Jarras, shrewdly diagnosed in his saturnine master, and in the event Bazaine made no determined attempt to break out.[12] Yet MacMahon felt honour-bound to march to his aid: not, however, by lunging straight for Metz, as Palikao was urging, for that would take him into the jaws of the advancing German armies. Instead, MacMahon would skirt to their north, hoping to avoid any contact with the enemy before making junction with Bazaine around Montmédy. Next day the Army of Châlons began its march to the east.

All the shortcomings of the French army exposed by the campaign so far combined to rob it of the speed and secrecy upon which the success of the plan depended. Poor staff work, the rapid breakdown of supply arrangements, the inability of the infantry to march fast or of the cavalry to provide an effective screen against enemy observation all helped to seal the army's doom, and progress was slowed even further by heavy rains. On only the second day MacMahon had to divert northward to the railway at Rethel to feed his men, losing a day's march. The shortage of food encouraged widespread marauding and indiscipline during the advance through Champagne and into the Argonne Forest. After five days his army had covered only some 60 kilometres from Rheims, scarcely two-thirds of the distance to Montmédy.

By this time the Germans had picked up his trail and were in pursuit. Analysis of the Paris press, which seldom showed restraint in publishing military information, convinced Moltke that the French were indeed marching eastward to the north of the axis of the German advance on Paris. The Army of the Meuse was ordered to wheel northward to intercept them, and Third Army on its left conformed to the movement. Already Moltke saw the possibility of trapping the whole of MacMahon's army as it attempted to join Bazaine.

With German cavalry already nipping at his flanks and keeping his movements under observation, MacMahon realized that a junction with Bazaine was no longer feasible, particularly as Bazaine's army was still in Metz. (Although MacMahon did not know it, Bazaine had cancelled a projected sortie on the 26th.) MacMahon determined to save his army, and from his headquarters at Le Chesne-Populeux on 27 August wired Palikao that he was going to head northward to Mézières, whence he could put his men on trains back to Paris. The army had set off in this new direction on the morning of the 28th when Palikao countermanded the retreat. Backed by the empress regent, he insisted that 'If you abandon Bazaine, there will be revolution in Paris ... the anxiety with which we follow your movements is extreme.' Albeit with misgivings, MacMahon obeyed unprotestingly. He had already resumed the march on Montmédy when an even more imperative order arrived from Palikao: 'In the name of the Cabinet and the Privy Council, I demand that you go to help Bazaine.'[13]

Napoleon III, now emperor in name only, remained with the army, where he and his baggage train were nothing but an encumbrance. Although he did not realize it, he escaped assassination by a disaffected soldier on the morning of the 28th. A lieutenant of *franc-tireurs* later recounted how he had knocked away the rifle of one of his men who had drawn a bead on the emperor from behind a hedge. The soldier coolly explained that 'I was going to shoot down that c—, who is the cause of all our troubles.'[14] An ambulance-man who caught glimpses of Napoleon on subsequent days thought him 'pale, dull-eyed', and suspected that his moustache was dyed and his face made up. Cries of '*Vive l'Empereur!*' from a few peasants were drowned out by 'vigorous and coarse swearing from the troops'.[15] As ever, Napoleon's ability to recognize mistakes seemed utterly divorced from the will to avert them. He wrote later that he had wanted to lead France's last army back to Paris, but 'political considerations forced me to make the most imprudent and strategically unsound advance'.[16]

MacMahon continued eastwards to Montmédy, only to learn that the Germans already held the bridge over the River Meuse at Stenay. He diverted northward, intending to cross further downstream. His two southernmost corps, 5 and 7, were already being harassed by German cavalry which forced them to deploy and lose precious time. The capture of a staff officer bearing orders from MacMahon to Failly not only put Moltke in possession of French plans but condemned 5 Corps to continue down the road to Stenay while the rest of the army turned away from it. Only after a brush with Saxon infantry at Nouart on the 29th did Failly learn of the mistake and send his men slogging northward on a night march down narrow, boggy, woodland roads.

The morning of 30 August found Failly's exhausted men encamped around the village of Beaumont, close to the west bank of the Meuse. They spent the morning cleaning their weapons and equipment and cooking in preparation for resuming their northward march. Many of the troops were camped on low ground, security arrangements were minimal and, despite warnings from local people, Failly was complacent about the possibility of an early German pursuit. In fact the forest stretching south of the French camps concealed the vanguard of the Army of the Meuse. Once again in this war German officers could stare through their binoculars at unsuspecting French troops, who 'presented rather the appearance of an encampment of gipsies than one of soldiers'.[17]

German artillery opened fire on this tempting target towards half past noon. The local priest wrote: 'I cannot begin to describe to you the effect produced by the first cannon shot: the brief silence, the immense uproar that followed, the disorder, the frightful confusion of shouts, the horses, caissons and wagons of all sorts careering along, crossing each other, colliding, becoming jammed together in the main square of Beaumont as they attempted to force a way through ...'[18] Nevertheless, when German infantry charged they were met by fierce fire from French units which had rallied after the first shock. Though soon driven out of the village, the French managed to maintain some resistance as they fell back northward to the river crossing at Mouzon, where units of Lebrun's 12 Corps re-crossed the Meuse to provide a rearguard to cover Failly's retreat across the river. In a pursuit that extended over 8 kilometres and as many hours, the Germans suffered 3,564 casualties,[19] but they had inflicted more than double that number on the French, including 2,000 unwounded prisoners. The majority of French casualties, 4,700, were from Failly's 5 Corps, but a misdirected brigade from 7 Corps had also been routed when it strayed across the path of the German advance.

The inexcusable surprise and avoidable defeat at Beaumont left the Army of Châlons mauled and disorganized. Abandoning for the moment any hope of reaching Montmédy and Bazaine, MacMahon herded his troops northward up the east bank of the Meuse towards the nearest fortress. 'That dismal night march, during which everybody felt a presentiment of disaster, soon turned into a confused shambles,' remembered an officer.[20] During 31 August MacMahon's disheartened forces took positions on the hills above the textile weaving town of Sedan.

MacMahon still imagined that he had options once he had resupplied his army – either to renew the attempt to reach Montmédy or to continue north-westward to Mézières. Whilst he was contemplating these possibilities, oblivious to the strength of the forces he was facing, the Germans forestalled him. Moltke had not managed to destroy the French while they were still on the west bank of the Meuse, but he grasped that MacMahon had placed himself in a 'mousetrap' by entering the narrow strip of French territory between the Meuse and the Belgian frontier a dozen kilometres away.[21] On 31 August the Army of the Meuse, having crossed the river, pursued the French along the east bank. Meanwhile Third Army advanced to secure the crossings west of Sedan to cut off any French withdrawal. Thus MacMahon would be caught by a pincer movement on the east bank, while sufficient German forces would remain on the west bank to prevent any French breakout in that direction. By afternoon German artillery on the west bank had begun shelling Lebrun's men posted across the river around the village of Bazeilles, south-east of Sedan. Bavarian infantry dashed across the intact railway bridge, throwing barrels of gunpowder placed by French engineers into the river before they could be detonated. Although the Bavarians were pushed out of the village by French marines after a sharp fight, they retained their bridgehead.

Similarly, at Donchery, west of Sedan, French engineers were prevented from blowing up the bridge when the train carrying their equipment pulled away under shellfire before they could unload it. The vanguard of Third Army seized the undefended bridge and began laying pontoons, enabling their columns to cross the river during the night.

The speed and scope of the German operation, covered first by darkness and then by dense river fog, took MacMahon completely unawares. Two Prussian corps, V and XI, of Crown Prince Friedrich Wilhelm's Third Army, crossed the Meuse at Donchery in the early hours of 1 September. Moltke had been unsure whether the French were already making good their escape to Mézières, where a fresh corps commanded by General Vinoy awaited them, but when Prussian troops reached the main road to Mézières at about 8 a.m. they were relieved to find it deserted. They turned right, following the loop in the Meuse, meeting little resistance until they rounded it and bore down on the French positions on the hills covering Sedan. Even before they opened fire they had cut off any possibility of a French escape westward.

Meanwhile the assault on French positions east of Sedan had begun before dawn, with General von der Tann's I Bavarian Corps stealing across the railway bridge and nearby pontoons and storming into Bazeilles, held by the Marine Division.

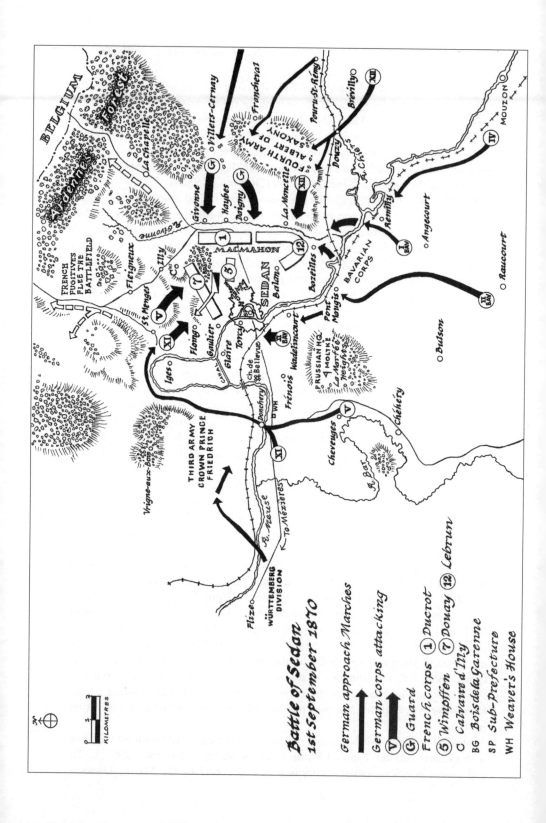

Battle of Sedan
1st September 1870

Germans approach Marches

German corps attacking

Ⓥ Guard
🄶 Guard
French corps ① Ducrot
⑤ Wimpffen ⑦ Douay d'Illy
C Calvaire d'Illy
BG Boisde la Garenne
SP Sub-Prefecture
WH Weaver's House

Intense house-to-house fighting raged for seven hours as both sides fed in more troops 'like coals onto a fire'.[22] Rumours that German wounded had had their throats cut by local women incensed the Bavarians, who gave no quarter to civilians who joined in the defence of their village or who were unlucky enough to get in the way.[23] Forty-two inhabitants of Bazeilles were killed during or soon after the fighting, a few by summary execution. While some houses were set alight by shells or to smoke out enemy riflemen, many were deliberately torched as a punitive measure after the fighting had ceased.[24] By nightfall Bazeilles was a furnace and the savagery of the struggle there stirred opinion throughout France and in the neutral countries, where the horrors of war seemed especially shocking after two generations of peace.

Having believed that the Meuse afforded his army security, MacMahon was awoken to be told of the German attack at Bazeilles. Riding out with his staff to assess the situation, he had reached the hills north of the village when he was caught in the increasingly heavy bombardment of the French positions and wounded by a shell fragment at about 6 a.m. – perhaps fortunately for his later reputation. When he revived he nominated Ducrot to succeed him, but amid the hazards of the battlefield it was over an hour before Ducrot learned the news. Ignorant of MacMahon's intentions, he could see that the attack was extending progressively northward up the steep-sided valley of the Givonne opposite his own position. Diagnosing correctly that the Germans would try to turn his northern flank, he began giving orders for a phased withdrawal north-westward to high ground beyond the village of Illy, which he considered a more defensible position. Lebrun objected that his men were more than holding their own in Bazeilles. Why not exploit their advantage? Besides, Lebrun feared 'that a retreat would discourage the men and soon turn into a rout'. Ducrot responded: 'While the enemy is playing with us on your front, he is manoeuvring to envelop us.'[25]

Ducrot was attempting to implement his plan when he received a note from General de Wimpffen, who had reached the army on the evening of the rout of Beaumont to replace the discredited and unpopular Failly in command of 5 Corps. En route from Algeria to the front Wimpffen had conferred with Palikao, and shared his seething indignation at what they saw as MacMahon's hesitant and dilatory handling of the campaign. Wimpffen now informed Ducrot that he had an order from Palikao appointing Wimpffen to command the army in the event of any mischance to MacMahon. When the two men conferred Wimpffen grew impatient of Ducrot's explanations, declaring 'What we need is not a retreat but a victory.'[26] Later, around 10 a.m., Wimpffen declared to the emperor his intention to throw the Prussians into the Meuse.[27]

The dispute between the two generals over the best strategy to adopt erupted in a heated verbal exchange on the evening of the battle and continued as a pamphlet war for more than a decade until both were dead. In their subsequent eagerness to present themselves as the potential saviour of the army and the other as responsible for its loss, neither conceded that it actually made little difference whether the army attempted to move north-west as Ducrot advocated or south-east as Wimpffen wanted. It was too late for Wimpffen's offensive spirit to save the situation, and the most to be said for Ducrot's plan was that if the army did not disintegrate under attack while attempting it, it might have allowed more men to escape into Belgium. Soon after midday the German Third Army advancing from the west had established contact with the Army of the Meuse advancing from the east, and the French were soon surrounded.

Not only had MacMahon failed to delay the German pincer movement by defending the river crossings, but he had placed his army in a very confined position, its eastern face defended by 12 and 1 Corps and the western face held by Douay's 7 Corps. These wings formed two sides of a triangle, with Sedan and the Meuse at its base. Even at the time of the Crimean War fifteen years earlier such a position, with the French holding high ground, might have enabled a prolonged defence, but the power of modern German artillery made it a death-trap. Once the Germans had closed a ring around the French they were able to bring over six hundred guns to bear from all points of the compass, many from ground overlooking the French positions, creating a devastating cross-fire.

From a hill on the west bank King Wilhelm, Roon, Bismarck and a host of German and foreign dignitaries were surveying the spectacle 'laid out for them as if they were looking at a diorama in a peep-show' under a brilliant September sun, while their staffs 'were dispersed in groups, smoking or munching sandwiches, or looking through their glasses'. Joining them, *The Times* correspondent William Howard Russell described the sky 'flecked with wreaths of bursting shells' as 'from every knoll, and from the edges of detached clumps of trees, spurted continual jets of smoke from literally dozens of batteries ... directing a concentrated fire upon the French, who, we could see, were suffering horribly ... The roar of the musketry was deafening in volume ... The air quivered to the roaring of artillery' while dark masses of German troops could be seen completing the encirclement.[28]

There was no hiding place for the French under this unprecedented volume of fire, and only Douay's men had some semblance of field entrenchments. Local counterattacks by Ducrot's men in the Givonne valley were beaten back, and by noon the weight of German shellfire was making the apex of the French position at the Calvaire d'Illy untenable. Thousands of French fugitives were already fleeing through the Ardennes, either to Mézières or over the frontier into Belgium. In desperation, towards 2 p.m. Ducrot ordered General Margueritte's cavalry division to charge westward down the slopes towards Floing to try to break out. The German fire was so intense that Margueritte was shot down before he could even give the order to charge, but as his *chasseurs d'Afrique* in their sky-blue uniforms moved from a walk to a trot to a gallop they looked as if they might run over the ragged line of Prussian infantry facing them. Yet when they got within 200 yards came 'the whiff and roll of a volley'. 'The result was almost incredible,' wrote Russell:

> The leading squadron was dissolved into a heap of white and grey horses
> ... The survivors, dropping fast, passed around each flank of the infantry,
> and as the second and third squadrons came in a confused mass over

the plain, filled with the carcasses of horses and men, they swerved from rushing upon their fate, and wheeling past the infantry rode off right and left, as water divides upon a rock . . .[29]

A further charge led by the Marquis de Gallifet was also beaten back with crippling losses, and as the cavalry retreated through the ranks of Douay's infantry it caused great disruption. Watching the French cavalry charges from the west bank, King Wilhelm could not help but admire their courage. Bismarck too conceded that it was a brilliant feat, but 'a heroic folly' against unbroken infantry.[30]

Chastened by the experience of Gravelotte, the Germans to a marked extent (except at Bazeilles) let their artillery reduce French resistance before launching their infantry assaults. By mid-afternoon the pulverized French had fallen back, many taking refuge in the dense Bois de la Garenne, where, however, they found no respite from the relentless shelling. Many French batteries had been destroyed by accurate German gunnery, or had retired for want of ammunition. Tens of thousands of disorganized French troops were streaming back towards the illusory safety of Sedan, which had become crammed with fugitives as the concentric advance of the Prussian, Saxon and Bavarian troops squeezed them into an ever-tighter perimeter around the town. Officers who tried to re-establish order amidst this chaos soon found the attempt hopeless. As Ducrot had predicted the previous evening, Sedan itself was a shell trap (or a chamber-pot, as he graphically put it)[31] where German shells wrought carnage in the densely crowded streets, sending roof tiles and masonry crashing down on the troops milling below, and starting fires. The town's antiquated fortifications offered little protection. Amid scenes of panic, troops who had given way were quick to blame their plight on the 'treason' of their leaders.

At the Sub-Prefecture Napoleon III saw that the situation was hopeless and that the time had come to surrender. During the morning he had ridden aimlessly around the battlefield, a 'useless spectator ... whom death itself seemed to disregard',[32] before returning to town. Although his staff thought that he was seeking death, it might be truer to say that he abandoned his fate to the falling shells. He did not venture right to the front line, nor answer Wimpffen's exhortation to put himself at the head of his troops. Although towards 3 p.m. he ordered the white flag to be raised, he could not persuade Ducrot to open negotiations. Ducrot insisted that, as Wimpffen had assumed command, the responsibility must fall to him. Eventually Lebrun was prevailed upon to go and find Wimpffen and ask him to come to see the emperor. Wimpffen angrily refused, and had the white flag (actually a serviette) borne by Lebrun's orderly thrown to the ground. Gathering whatever remnants of troops he could, and persuading Lebrun to join him, Wimpffen launched a final forlorn attack south-eastward towards Balan, where bitter fighting had continued after the French withdrawal from Bazeilles. Briefly it made headway, until fresh German troops and cannon brought it to a halt amid the rubble of the ruined village. To the north, advancing German infantry was extinguishing the last resistance in the splintered Bois de la Garenne, taking thousands of prisoners.

At last the German high command made out a white flag through the black smoke billowing from Sedan. Gradually word spread to the artillery to cease fire. Already Bavarian troops had reached the city walls and were attempting to open negotiations for surrender. An officer of Moltke's staff was admitted to see Napoleon, whose presence the Germans had not suspected. Napoleon had written a letter which was presented by his aide, General Reille, to Wilhelm on the La Marfée heights above Frénois, from which the king had watched the German victory unfold:

> Having been unable to die amidst my troops, it only remains for me to place my sword in Your Majesty's hands.
>
> I am Your Majesty's dear brother,
>
> Napoleon.[33]

The emperor having refused to accept his resignation, Wimpffen rode that night to Moltke's headquarters in Donchery to settle the formal terms of surrender. His attempts to extract concessions were rebuffed. The French could either surrender or face renewed bombardment next morning – which, as the implacable Moltke pointed out, would mean a slaughter of French troops penned within the walls of Sedan. The following dawn, 2 September, Napoleon rode out towards Donchery in a carriage to seek a personal interview with Wilhelm in the hope of obtaining better terms for his army, but it was Bismarck who met him. Their interview took place in a 'poor and unclean' weaver's cottage near the road, with both men seated on rush chairs. Bismarck hoped that the emperor would surrender on behalf of France, ending the war, but Napoleon maintained that as a prisoner he could make no agreement that would bind the government in Paris.[34] Only when Wimpffen had signed the capitulation was Napoleon allowed a brief meeting with King Wilhelm at the Château de Bellevue: 'We were both much moved at seeing each other again under such circumstances,' wrote Wilhelm. 'What my feelings were – I had seen Napoleon only three years before at the summit of his power – is more than I can describe.'[35] Next day Napoleon, anxious to avoid further contact with his own troops, was escorted by German cavalry over the Belgian border, and on into captivity in the chateau of Wilhelmshöhe in Germany.

Six weeks earlier France had been considered by many the foremost military power in Europe. The epic scale of her defeat, and of the German victory, astounded Europe. Engaging 150,000 men at Sedan, the Germans had captured an entire army, reckoning their prisoners at 21,000 during the battle and a further 83,000 (including wounded) at the capitulation. In the fighting they had lost 8,932 men,[36] while inflicting perhaps 12,000 casualties on the French. For a fortnight the disarmed French were penned into the desolate Iges peninsula formed by the loop in the Meuse below Sedan, where they camped in the rain and mud, tormented by hunger, fever and gangs of marauders from their own ranks, until they could be transported to prisoner-of-war camps in Germany.

In only a month of combat, from Saarbrücken on 2 August to the capitulation on 2 September, 74,000 Germans had been put out of action, nearly 17,000 of them killed in battle, the rest wounded or missing. The number of Frenchmen killed or wounded in that period was in the order of 60,000, but the number captured or missing, including the bag at Sedan, was over 130,000. Of the French army concentrated on the eastern frontier a month previously, those men not mouldering in shallow graves or languishing wounded in hospital were either captives or were surrounded by German forces in Metz or in smaller fortresses, with little hope of escape.

The Second Empire could not survive such a catastrophic military defeat. During August republican discontent had been simmering in the big cities, and when news of Sedan reached Paris, Lyon and Marseille the imperial regime was toppled by popular uprisings. On Sunday, 4 September a revolutionary crowd in the capital invaded the Legislature in the Palais Bourbon. Léon Gambetta proclaimed the deposition of the Bonapartes, and he and other republican leaders formed a Government of National Defence. The empress fled to England. The débâcle of Sedan had given birth to the Third Republic, but simultaneously to the greatest challenge it would have to face over the next three-quarters of a century – a united and heavily armed Germany. Although Bismarck faced weeks of difficult negotiations with the South German states before the formal proclamation of the German Empire in the Hall of Mirrors at the Palace of Versailles on 18 January 1871, at the popular level German unity was consummated at Sedan, a victory achieved by the troops of every German state. The subjection of France was the foundation stone of the new German Reich, and was seen by Bismarck and Moltke as the pre-condition of its continued existence.

Chapter 7

Siege and Surrender

The Germans hoped that Sedan would bring an early end to French resistance. Conversely, advanced democratic circles in Paris nursed a fleeting illusion that, having toppled the empire that had declared war, 'our German brothers' would be content to go home.[1] Both hopes were dashed. The new Foreign Minister, Jules Favre, who declared that France would yield 'not an inch of our territory, nor a stone of our fortresses',[2] met Bismarck at Ferrières on 19–20 September to see whether the Germans would settle for payment of a war indemnity. Bismarck refused, demanding that France surrender Alsace and the German-speaking portion of Lorraine as the price of peace. Such a vindication of their historic 'right' was the minimum Germans would accept in compensation for their sacrifice. Moltke insisted on the new frontier as a safeguard against future French aggression. Bismarck saw the value of a conquest achieved by joint enterprise for binding together the nascent German Empire. His demands helped unite Frenchmen of all shades of political opinion in a national struggle against the invader. Weaned on legends of the Revolutionary Wars of the 1790s which had instilled a faith in the invincibility of the Republic, the new government declared that it would fight to the bitter end.

Yet, with very little of her regular army left, France could offer no effective obstacle to the advance of the German armies from Sedan to Paris, which was invested on 19 September. An attempt that day by the Paris garrison to check the oncoming Germans at Châtillon quickly ended in fiasco and rout. South of the River Loire, in the heartland of France, attempts to raise new armies to relieve Paris got off to a disappointing start with defeats at Artenay on 10 October and outside Orléans the next day, following which the Germans occupied that major city. In the east, after besieging and bombarding Strasbourg for seven weeks, they captured it on 28 September and pressed on through the Vosges, defeating French forces that tried to bar their advance and capturing Dijon, the capital of Burgundy, on 31 October.

Escaping from besieged Paris by balloon on 7 October, Gambetta put all his formidable energy into galvanizing the war effort in the provinces. From the temporary capital of Tours he oversaw the raising of new armies. Since the outbreak of war France had been calling more and more categories of men into military service, and a huge national effort was made to arm, equip and train them. To provide officers for the new forces the Government of National Defence had to rely on a mixture of retired imperial officers, escapees from Sedan or Metz, naval officers and its own appointees, regardless of seniority or regulations governing promotion. An impressively large army was assembled behind the Loire under General d'Aurelle de Paladines, and on 9 November it achieved a significant victory by defeating General von der Tann's much smaller force at Coulmiers and recapturing Orléans.

Yet this great fillip to French morale could hardly offset the blow of the capitulation of Metz on 27 October. Having allowed himself to be blockaded in the city following the Battle of Gravelotte-Saint-Privat on 18 August, Bazaine's attempts to break out proved at best half-hearted and ineffectual. Believing that the war must soon end, Bazaine, who remained loyal to the Bonapartes, entered into negotiations with the Germans in the hope of keeping his army intact and restoring the imperial dynasty. As weeks of dismal weather passed, his army had to eat its horses, rendering it by October unfit to mount an offensive or escape through the strongly entrenched German lines. On 29 October 173,000 French troops, who had constituted the best part of the imperial army, marched out of Metz on their way into captivity in Germany. Bazaine, hailed as a hero by the opposition in August, was now reviled and would become the national scapegoat for the failures of the war. Gambetta issued a proclamation denouncing him for treason. In Paris the news sparked insurrection by the Left on 31 October, which the Government of National Defence survived only by a mixture of luck and the disunity of its opponents, which allowed loyal forces to rescue the ministers held hostage in the Hôtel de Ville.

The fall of Metz was a crucial success for the Germans because it released the army of Prince Friedrich Karl to take on the hastily levied French provincial armies and to try to force the war to a decision. Marching rapidly, his Second Army arrived in the Loire theatre a fortnight after Coulmiers. The climactic struggle of the war began towards the end of November. On 28 November the right wing of the French Army of the Loire assaulted the left of Second Army at Beaune-la-Rolande but was repulsed. After an initial success at Villepion on 1 December the French left wing too was beaten next day at Loigny and Poupry. On 3–4 December the Germans went over to the offensive, driving the French out of Orléans and capturing another 20,000 prisoners. Meanwhile at Paris the garrison had made a determined attempt at a sortie to join hands with the provincial armies. Led by Ducrot, who had escaped captivity after Sedan, it tried to punch its way through German lines south-east of Paris by crossing the River Marne and assaulting the heights beyond Champigny. But, because of a failure to lay pontoons, the offensive had to be postponed for a day, until 30 November, and the Germans were on the alert. Strongly entrenched on the heights, they beat the French back. The French flanking movement that was supposed to dislodge them miscarried. On 2 December the Germans launched a surprise counteroffensive, and although they were held off Ducrot withdrew across the Marne the next day.

In the face of these major defeats in the same week, Gambetta became increasingly isolated in his faith that the Germans could yet be driven out of France, and French morale began to wane. Still the French provincial armies made final forlorn efforts in appalling weather conditions. The rain, mud and frosts of autumn were succeeded by the snow and ice of an exceptionally severe winter that tried the stamina and cohesion of the new armies to the limit. In northern France the German First Army had defeated the French at Amiens on 27 November and invaded Normandy, capturing its capital Rouen on 5 December. They shortly found their railway communications under threat from the small but well-officered French Army of the North under General Faidherbe, but responded quickly to his bold advance. At the Battle of La Hallue on 23 December Faidherbe was driven away from Amiens. Despite winning a victory at Bapaume on 3 January 1871, his army was brought to bay and finally routed at Saint-Quentin on 19 January.

Meanwhile General Chanzy, leading what had been the left wing of the Army of the Loire, stood and fought the pursuing Germans at Beaugency on the Loire on 7–10 December, inflicting heavy losses on them before retreating by stages on Le Mans, where, however, Friedrich Karl eventually followed and defeated him on 11–12 January. The right wing of the former Army of the Loire became the Army of the East under General Bourbaki. It attempted a sudden thrust to the east to relieve Belfort, one of the few French fortresses still holding out, but its transportation by rail was botched, it was beset by supply problems and, despite a victory at Villersexel on 9 January, Bourbaki proved a hesitant commander. The Germans were given time to react, and Bourbaki found his road to Belfort barred at the River Lisaine. In three days of desultory fighting in arctic conditions he failed to break through. Retreating to Besançon, he found himself in danger of encirclement by a German army that had made a rapid march to intercept him. Bourbaki attempted suicide, while his army of 90,000 men avoided another Sedan only by the desperate expedient of marching into Switzerland, where it was disarmed and interned on 1 February.

Life in besieged and frozen Paris had become grim indeed as stocks of food and fuel diminished, and from 5 January the Germans had subjected the capital and its forts to bombardment by heavy artillery by day and night. On 7 January Edmond de Goncourt noted: 'The sufferings of Paris during the siege? A joke for two months. In the third month, hardship drove out humour. Today, the laughter is stilled and we are heading rapidly for famine ...'[3] On 19 January the Paris garrison made a final attempt to break out to the west, but after a day of fighting around Saint-Cloud and Buzenval was unable to pierce successive German defence lines. Following the failure of the Buzenval sortie the Military Governor, General Trochu, was compelled to resign and a small insurrection by the revolutionary Left outside the Hôtel de Ville was put down on 22 January with fatalities. For the first time during the conflict French troops had fired upon fellow citizens in the capital. With no further hope of relief from outside and food supplies approaching exhaustion, Favre signed an armistice with Bismarck on 28 January. The Paris garrison was disarmed, except for one division to keep order. The ring of forts that had protected the capital from assault was occupied by the Germans and the city paid a war indemnity of 200 million francs.

The faith of French republicans in the efficacy of citizen armies had not been vindicated by their performance in the field. France had paid a heavy price for the failure of her military reforms to keep pace with German military expansion in the 1860s. Some 482,000 men had fought in the French provincial armies. At the armistice tens of thousands more were in training camps or waiting to be mustered into national service. But the rare and inconclusive victories of Coulmiers, Villepion, Bapaume and Villersexel could not reverse the tide of war, and the failure of the provincial armies to break the German stranglehold on Paris set a limit to resistance. Although French republicans and military theorists of other nations were to make much of the guerrilla resistance to the Germans in the countryside, the 'republican' phase of the war was actually decided by conventional campaigns fought by armies organized by the opposing nation-states. Before the war Bourbaki had warned regular army colleagues against the dangers of underestimating German short-service troops, whom it was all too easy to dismiss as an 'army of lawyers and opticians'.[4] The discipline and training of German forces, combined with superior artillery and generalship, prevailed even against superior numbers of raw French conscripts. Moltke gave intelligent and well co-ordinated direction to German strategy, while French efforts were ill co-ordinated. As one great French historian of the war pithily concluded, 'In the first phase of the war France had neither numbers nor organization, though the Empire could and should have provided both. In its second phase she had the numbers, but did not and could not have the necessary organization.'[5]

The north-eastern quarter of France had endured the ravages caused by the passage of armies and the heavy demands of the German occupiers. French guerrilla activity incensed the Germans and provoked harsh reprisals, but it was poorly co-ordinated. Furthermore, the conduct of these undisciplined *francs-tireurs* towards the inhabitants and their property was all too often 'worthy of bashi-bazouks, and not of fellow countrymen'. Some peasants willingly sold produce to the Germans, but often they had little choice. Their plight in the midst of the fighting was sympathetically depicted by a French captain:

> I often heard the peasants of the invaded regions reproached in the most severe terms for having given the enemy a better welcome than they gave our troops: of having hidden their foodstuffs when our men arrived and of having got them out eagerly when the Germans appeared in our place ... but this was very much the exception.

Given that resistance by non-combatants risked death or destruction of their property,

> Should one judge them so very harshly? And should we expect that, after having given their sons to the army to defend the soil of the country ... they should expose themselves and their kin – women, old men, children – to having no roof for shelter and to dying of hunger? Then it would be well to admit that their best course is to act as they acted in 1870, as their forebears acted in 1814 and 1815, and as all civilized people have acted in like circumstances.[6]

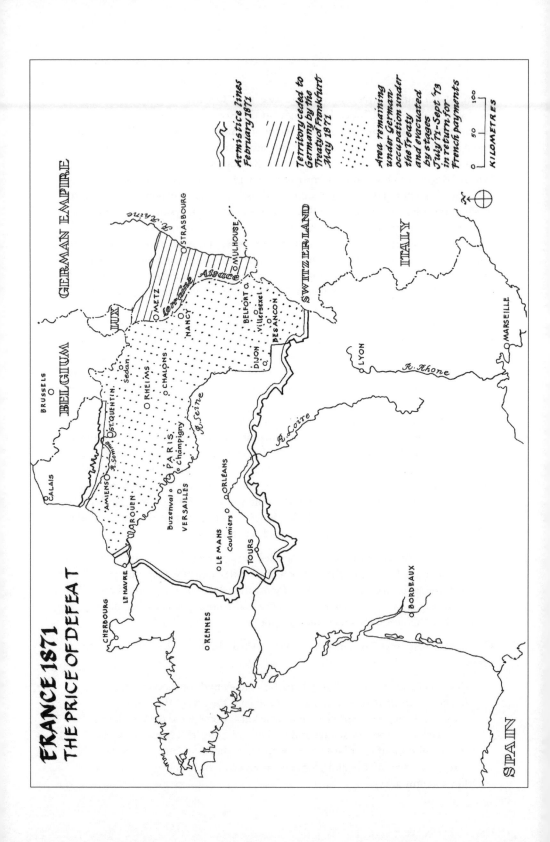

FRANCE 1871
THE PRICE OF DEFEAT

GERMAN EMPIRE

BELGIUM

BRUSSELS

LUX.

CALAIS

CHERBOURG

LE HAVRE

ST QUENTIN

R. Somme

AMIENS

ROUEN

Sedan

RHEIMS

CHALONS

PARIS

Champigny

Buzenval

VERSAILLES

R. Seine

METZ

Lorraine

STRASBOURG

Alsace

MULHOUSE

NANCY

BELFORT

Villersexel

BESANÇON

DIJON

SWITZERLAND

R. Rhine

RENNES

LE MANS

Coulmiers

ORLÉANS

TOURS

R. Loire

LYON

R. Rhone

ITALY

MARSEILLE

BORDEAUX

SPAIN

Armistice lines
February 1871

Territory ceded to
Germany by the
Treaty of Frankfurt
May 1871

Area remaining
under German
occupation under
the Treaty
and evacuated
by stages
July '71 – Sept '73
in return for
French payments

0   50   100
KILOMETRES

By the end of January 1871, with all the French armies defeated and the Germans seemingly invincible, enthusiasm for continuing the war was largely confined to Alsace and Lorraine, whose future was at stake, and the radicals of Paris and the big cities. When national elections were held in February they were in effect a referendum on whether to resume a war that was manifestly lost, and the vote was overwhelmingly for peace. The humiliating peace terms imposed by Bismarck at Versailles demanded the cession of Alsace and the German-speaking region of eastern Lorraine plus Metz, and a war indemnity of 5 billion francs. German troops would remain in occupation of north-eastern France at French expense initially up to the line of the River Seine until the indemnity was paid off by instalments. On 1 March the Germans entered Paris and staged a victory march through the Arc de Triomphe, though ratification of the peace terms that day by the French National Assembly by 546 votes to 107 curtailed the German occupation of the capital. The final peace treaty was signed at Frankfurt on 10 May. To Frenchmen the peace seemed draconian, and few were inclined to reflect that Napoleon I had inflicted harsher terms on Prussia after her defeat at Jena in 1806; or that had France won in 1870 she would have taken at least the Rhineland and would have divided Germany into client states.

For France the cost of the lost war was measured not only in a toll of 139,000 servicemen dead and 143,000 wounded, plus at least 60,000 civilian deaths, in the 384,000 troops in German prisoner-of-war camps, in the amputation of her eastern provinces and in the high financial cost, but also in the bloody civil war in Paris that flowed from defeat.

During the siege of the capital the government had yielded to popular demand by arming the National Guard, a strongly republican citizen militia that had become increasingly radicalized by five months of hardship, the failures of the political and military leadership and the political atmosphere of the Paris clubs. Whilst most regular troops were disarmed under the terms of the armistice, the National Guard was allowed to keep its weapons, making it the dominant force in the capital. Revolutionary fever ran high, fuelled by patriotic disgust at the capitulation, unemployment, resentment at the actions and attitude of a largely conservative, rural majority in the National Assembly – especially its withdrawal of the pay of the National Guard – and fears of a monarchist coup. On 18 March the army's attempt to seize cannon claimed by the National Guard sparked a popular uprising, during which a furious mob slaughtered two generals captured at Montmartre. For two months Paris was under the control of its own insurgent government of the far Left, the Commune.

Based at Versailles, the Government of France under Adolphe Thiers built up a new army under Marshal MacMahon (now recovered from his wound) which laid a second siege to the capital, while German forces looked on from the forts east of the city. In the last week of May the army re-entered the city, where a rump of perhaps 20,000 National Guardsmen defended their home districts in the east after torching many of the landmark buildings of central Paris. With some generals determined to make an example of the 'Reds', and all tolerance extinguished by the deliberate arson of the city, no quarter was given to the Communards in the street fighting by which the army re-established control. Summary executions continued for days, until possibly 17,000 revolutionaries had been shot dead in hot blood or in cold.

Victor Hugo lamented 1870–71 as 'The Terrible Year'. Bitter memories of invasion, defeat and civil war were to haunt a generation of Frenchmen and gave rise to much partisan recrimination. An officer of royalist sympathies wrote that he could never afterwards bear to hear the *Marseillaise*, 'prelude and accompaniment to all our defeats'.[7] The war had reversed the power relationship between defeated France and her German conqueror for decades to come. Reflecting dolefully on the shame borne by his generation for the defeat, one exile from Alsace could find consolation only in the hope 'that our children will be more fortunate than us'.[8]

Part II

1914:
The Ghosts of August

The generations born since the war [of 1870–71] still bear the weight of that war, and in everything we do, in everything we undertake, we sense our defeat hovering over us.

André Tardieu, May 1913

Chapter 8

In the Shadow of the Reich

For two-and-a-half years following the Treaty of Frankfurt the relationship between Germany and France was that of occupier and occupied. German forces under General von Manteuffel, with his headquarters first at Compiègne, then Nancy, remained in possession of the north-eastern portion of France bounded by the Seine and the Somme. The French authorities found Manteuffel more polite and reasonable to deal with than Bismarck; but, despite the general good discipline of German troops, occupation inevitably generated friction with the civilian population. Anti-German feelings ran high both inside the occupied region and on its fringes, and there were occasional incidents involving the death or wounding of German soldiers that triggered reprisals.

The Thiers government made the liberation of French territory its priority, both as a point of national pride and to minimize the cost of supporting an occupation force of 120,000 men and the interest payable on the war indemnity. France paid the first half-billion francs in July 1871, following which the Germans evacuated Normandy. The launch of a government loan at rates of interest attractive both to foreign bankers and patriotic French savers was a great success. It enabled another billion to be paid off in September, securing the German evacuation of a further four Departments, including the eastern forts of Paris. In return for tariff concessions and early payment of another half billion, the Germans marched out of another six Departments that autumn and the occupation force was reduced to 50,000 men. Another over-subscribed loan launched in 1872 allowed the French to pay off the outstanding three billion francs far sooner than expected. Under a revised schedule negotiated in March 1873, France agreed to complete the outstanding instalments by September. After dismantling the fortresses of Belfort, Toul and Mézières the German Army of Occupation headed homeward at the beginning of August 1873, retaining only Verdun as a gage against the final payment. Once that was received, Manteuffel and the last German soldiers evacuated French territory entirely on 16 September.[1]

Bismarck had agreed to the accelerated payment of the war indemnity with misgivings at the unexpected speed of the French financial recovery. The presence of German troops on French soil had provided him with a convenient means of intimidating the French and cowing them into compliance with their obligations.

French governments became accustomed to his frequent threats to renew hostilities or to extend the occupation over comparatively minor incidents. Bismarck dubbed such episodes 'giving the French a cold shower'. The French, alarmed at his continual picking of what they called 'German quarrels', had little choice but to be conciliatory and avoid provocations.[2]

Such incidents reflected Bismarck's natural penchant for bullying, but they were also carefully contrived for political effect, as much at home as abroad. For instance, he ratcheted up tension in 1873 over a pastoral letter of the Bishop of Nancy urging prayers for the reunion of Alsace and Lorraine with France, and subsequent support by French bishops for the opposition of their German counterparts to Bismarck's campaign against the power of the Catholic Church – the *Kulturkampf*. Professing to see in this evidence of an ultramontane plot against Germany and the peace of Europe, Bismarck demanded not only formal explanations and apologies but that the French bring prosecutions against the offending clergy. Eventually the French defused the situation by closing down an ultra-Catholic newspaper that had printed an anti-German article. It was a reminder of how useful it was to Bismarck to associate his domestic enemies with the French threat, which he was not averse to exaggerating in order to impose his will on the Reichstag.

By early 1875 there was evidence that the French were rearming more rapidly than expected. Bismarck received reports that they were building up currency reserves and importing horses. A new army law created a fourth battalion in every French regiment. If this would not produce the dramatic expansion of manpower some claimed, it would provide the officer cadres necessary for such an expansion upon mobilization. There was apprehension in Germany that the war of revenge many considered inevitable was in the offing. Among the German general staff there was a strong body of opinion in favour of a preventive war before Germany lost her military advantage. Bismarck later protested that he had no serious intention of launching a pre-emptive attack, but he did follow the familiar route of mounting a campaign of intimidation against the French. In March he prohibited the export of horses to France. In April *Die Post* in Berlin pointedly asked 'Is War in Sight?', which, if not directly inspired by Bismarck, was of a piece with escalating diplomatic menaces and press excitement. In May one of Bismarck's subordinates made overt threats of a preventive war to the French ambassador in Berlin.

The French Foreign Minister, the Duc Decazes, made foreign governments aware of the threats, and insisted that if attacked France would withdraw her forces behind the Loire and offer no resistance. The London *Times* expressed consternation at German behaviour. Rather than sharing Bismarck's view that the French were still the troublemakers of the continent, Britain and Russia were becoming apprehensive at the apparent bellicosity of the new dominant power of central Europe. By joining the 'Three Emperors' League' with Russia and Austria in 1873, Bismarck was assured that those powers recognized Germany's gains by the Treaty of Frankfurt, but the League by no means ensured French isolation. The Russian Foreign Minister, Gorchakov, now visited Berlin and added his warning to the representations of British diplomats, who had no wish to see France crushed by

Germany and the balance of power upset. Bismarck was furious at the Russian intervention, and bore a long grudge against Gorchakov. It was on hearing this news that the Hungarian Foreign Minister Andrassy performed three hand-stands on his table, exclaiming 'Bismarck will never forgive it!'[3] Bismarck thought of resigning over the humiliation, but Emperor Wilhelm, who had strongly opposed a new war, nevertheless refused to part with his Iron Chancellor.

For a decade following the 1875 crisis Franco-German relations entered a period of relative détente. With republican victory in the 1877 French elections the question of the country's regime seemed to have been settled. A monarchist restoration, which had seemed probable after the conservative victory of 1871, had been thwarted by the obduracy of the Legitimist pretender to the French throne, the Comte de Chambord ('Henri V'), who refused to make any concessions to the changes wrought in France by the Revolution of 1789. As Thiers quipped, Chambord's adhesion to the royalist white flag made him the Washington of the French Republic, because he ensured its foundation.[4] Bismarck was glad to see the Legitimists and their clerical supporters discomfited, for he suspected that they would favour a French war in Italy to restore the temporal power of the Pope. As a republic, France would remain an unattractive ally for the monarchies of Europe. Moreover, the defeat of President MacMahon in the constitutional struggle of 1877, during which he tried to impose a conservative cabinet which lacked majority support in the Chamber, permanently weakened the French executive. Henceforth France would be governed by ministries reliant on precarious parliamentary majorities. However deep popular anti-German feeling might run in France, her conservative, bourgeois, republican leadership had no appetite for a war of revenge against her formidable neighbour. Even Gambetta, who in 1871 had seemed to incarnate the spirit of revenge, had privately renounced the idea, and in 1880 publicly expressed only a hope that one day 'immanent justice' would somehow enable France to recover her lost provinces.[5] When he came to power in 1881 his short-lived ministry was preoccupied with domestic and colonial issues, and he died at the end of 1882.

By 1878, the year in which the last of the three commissions charged with winding up the administrative business of the Treaty of Frankfurt completed its work, France had recovered materially from the war. The Universal Exhibition in Paris that year was a great success, though Germany thought it discreet to participate only through a small display of artworks. In that year too France returned to the European conference table at the Congress of Berlin, which attempted to settle the troubles of the Near East, and found Bismarck positively amicable. Indeed, he was eager for France to divert her energies into colonialism, and German encouragement and covert diplomatic support facilitated French expansion in Tunisia, Morocco, Madagascar and China. Moves towards a Franco-German rapprochement seemed close to realization during the second ministry of Jules Ferry (1883–5), and there were even a few advocates of an alliance in both countries. Bismarck told the French ambassador, 'I hope to reach a point when you will forgive Sedan as you have forgiven Waterloo. Renounce the Rhine, and I will help you to secure everywhere else the satisfactions you desire.'[6] Whilst welcoming improved relations, the French government was nevertheless wary that Bismarck's overtures were aimed at embroiling them with Great Britain.

Any French government attempting reconciliation with Germany did so at its peril while the scars of the war remained raw. Whilst Gambetta and Ferry saw colonial expansion as a means of reaffirming French prowess, a vociferous nationalist lobby criticized it for distracting France's attention from 'the blue line of the Vosges'.[7] Paul Déroulède, whose patriotic doggerel *Chants du soldat* (1872) enjoyed wide popularity, became the leading figure of the League of Patriots, founded in 1882 to agitate for the recovery of Alsace-Lorraine. The poet denounced Ferry's colonialism with the rebuke, 'I have lost two children and you offer me twenty domestics.'[8] The Radical Georges Clemenceau accused Ferry of being Bismarck's creature and, following the minor defeat of a French force in China in 1885, forced him to resign amid extraordinary scenes inside and outside the Chamber.[9] The phenomenal popularity enjoyed by Clemenceau's protégé, General Georges Boulanger, in the years 1886–9 derived in large measure from hopes that here at last was a man who could restore French prestige and stand up to Bismarck. The handsome general, a former commander of French troops in Tunisia, a reforming War Minister from 1886 and a gifted if unscrupulous self-publicist, was celebrated in French café-concerts as 'General Revenge'.

Bismarck saw Boulanger's popularity as a potential threat, but more as an opportunity that he could exploit to the hilt. In the winter of 1886/7 he was at loggerheads with the Reichstag over the bill for funding the army for the next seven years and increasing its size to restore Germany's margin of superiority over France. Unable at first to get the bill through, he dissolved the Reichstag and fought the election campaign on the danger of a French war of revenge led by Boulanger. Because it did not suit his purposes, Bismarck pressured the German ambassador to France to withdraw a report to Emperor Wilhelm which observed that actually the French were unprepared for war and greatly feared it. Bismarck's alarmist press campaign, accompanied by the mobilization of 72,000 reservists in Alsace-Lorraine, carried the day, and a new Reichstag approved the Army Bill in March 1887.

The passions fanned by Boulanger and Bismarck for domestic political purposes were the background to the most serious Franco–German confrontation since 1870. In April 1887 a French border police official named Schnaebelé was lured across the German border in order to be arrested on charges of espionage. French popular opinion mistakenly attributed the peaceful resolution of the resulting crisis to German fears of Boulanger. In reality President Jules Grévy, an erstwhile republican opponent of Gambetta and a firm believer in keeping the peace, restrained his prime minister from issuing an ultimatum and Boulanger from initiating a military demonstration that might provoke the Germans. Though Schnaebelé was in fact part of a spy ring organized by Boulanger, the French forwarded correspondence to Berlin demonstrating that he had been inveigled across the border and therefore illegally arrested.[10] Bismarck, who had no further need of a crisis, intervened to have him released. Boulanger had become an embarrassment and a threat to peace.

Braving taunts of being a 'German Ministry'[11] a new cabinet ousted him from the War Office in May. Protest riots in Paris that July could not prevent him being posted to a provincial command. Although another brief excitement blew up in the autumn when a German border guard shot dead a French gamekeeper accompanying some huntsmen who had wandered too near the border near Vexaincourt, it was rapidly smothered by a German apology and payment of compensation.

Mutual restraint had preserved peace, but two decades after the war Franco-German relations remained mired in fear and suspicion. Bismarck told the Reichstag in 1888 that 'God has placed us beside the most bellicose and restless of nations, the French . . .' It was fortunate, he added, that 'We Germans fear God but nothing else in this world . . .'[12] Given the state of feeling in both countries, he refused when the French invited German participation in the 1889 Paris Exhibition. When Bismarck finally fell from power in 1890 France rejoiced, and the new Kaiser, Wilhelm II, seemed eager to improve relations until a conciliatory gesture on his part backfired. When his mother, the former empress, visited Paris and Versailles in 1891, protests orchestrated by Déroulède outraged the German press and the Kaiser.

Yet, however volubly French nationalists might lament the lost provinces, the question of their eventual liberation languished in the realm of patriotic sentiment rather than practical politics. German suspicions notwithstanding, a war of revenge never formed the programme of any French government after 1871. As the vogue for Boulanger demonstrated, the scandal-ridden parliamentary regime of the Third Republic remained vulnerable to attacks using the convenient stick of its allegedly pusillanimous foreign policy; especially since the enemies of the Republic shared few coherent aims in domestic politics. Boulanger's electoral success in 1888–9 drew support from an unlikely combination of monarchists (who saw him as a stalking horse and secretly funded him), leaderless Bonapartists, socialist revolutionaries, and workers feeling the economic pinch who were disillusioned by bourgeois politicians with no interest in social reform. Realizing the danger Boulanger posed to the regime, the government showed ruthless determination in driving him from politics in 1889 and dissolving the League of Patriots. Having exhibited little of that quality himself, Boulanger committed suicide in exile in 1891. After him the nationalists – increasingly identified with the political Right – typically expended more of their bile against fellow Frenchmen than against Germany. Frustrated by their poor showing at the polls, their priority became the overthrow of the hated Republic, with the recovery of Alsace-Lorraine relegated to second place at best.

The passage of time, and the coming of age in the 1890s of a generation either too young to remember 1870 or born after the war, was diluting the strength of feelings on that issue. In the lost provinces themselves residual loyalty to France persisted among the generation who had lived through the war, and there was keen resentment of repressive German measures that muzzled the press, suppressed the teaching of French in schools and outlawed its use except in private. When in 1874 the provinces were allowed to send fifteen representatives to the Reichstag, seven refused to take their seats in Berlin in protest. The size of the protest vote in the annexed territory in 1887 was so displeasing to Bismarck that in the wake of the Franco-German crisis that year a new series of punitive measures was introduced restricting contacts with France. Yet in their daily lives and business dealings Alsace-Lorrainers had by degrees to accommodate themselves to being part of the Reich, and the programme of enforced Germanization and economic integration with Germany was taking effect. A generation grew up having learned only German in schools, and young men served as conscripts in the German army. The Roman Catholic clergy, who had been amongst those most loyal to France, were repelled by the aggressively anti-clerical policies pursued by French republican ministries in the three decades from 1880. Alsatians increasingly took refuge in nurturing the distinctive qualities of their own culture and language as a means of asserting an independent identity, and focused on advancing their own interests. In 1898 twelve out of fifteen representatives elected to the Reichstag professed loyalty to the Reich, and over the next four years many of the restrictions on civil liberties imposed in the Bismarck era were lifted. In 1900 German law replaced the *Code Napoléon* in the provinces.[13]

In France the 1870s and 1880s had seen an outpouring of books, poems, songs, pictures and school texts, mostly of maudlin quality, celebrating wartime feats of bravery and stirring emotions over the loss of the provinces. Popular illustrations showed Alsace and Lorraine as young women dressed in traditional folk costume or in mourning. The loyalty of the provinces and their burning desire to be reunited with France were never doubted. By 1890 this literary and artistic vein was nearing exhaustion, and some among the new generation were reacting to the values of their parents by embracing internationalism, pacifism and anti-militarism. Bored by a surfeit of patriotic literature, the writer Rémy de Gourmont dared aver in 1891 that he would not give the little finger on his right hand for the reconquest of Alsace-Lorraine because he needed it for writing, nor that of his left hand which he needed to flick the ash off his cigarette.[14] Although his article was considered so scandalous that it cost him his government job, many Frenchmen were becoming resigned to annexation. Some nursed a pious hope that the provinces might be allowed self-determination or neutral status, or even that Lorraine might one day be purchased by France or exchanged for a French colony. Others were frankly indifferent.

Yet if France would not make war to regain the provinces, neither would she renounce them.[15] They remained a barrier to conciliation with Germany, despite the exchange of such courtesies as the attendance of the French navy at the opening of the Kiel Canal in 1895 and the successful German presence at the 1900 Paris Exhibition. Even a shared resentment of British imperial expansion, particularly fierce in France, failed to produce a Franco-German entente. A series of diplomatic feelers between 1896 and 1901 aimed at co-operation in applying pressure on Britain foundered on mutual mistrust. The Germans were suspicious of the instability of French governments and the chauvinism of the Paris press. The French were aware that any open moves towards an alliance would be unpalatable to public opinion, and shied away from German suggestions of a mutual guarantee of their European frontiers. Such an agreement would have been tantamount to French acceptance that the loss of Alsace-Lorraine was permanent – a step she would not take.

If the impasse on her eastern frontier seemed likely to endure for the foreseeable future, in other respects France had recovered her diplomatic freedom of action. The series of defensive alliances woven by Bismarck to ensure German security and keep France isolated had begun to decay even before the ageing Chancellor lost power. Germany's Dual Alliance with Austria-Hungary (1879) had become a Triple Alliance in 1882 with the adherence of Italy, France's rival in North Africa and at odds with her over tariffs. In 1881 Bismarck drew Russia into an arrangement whereby she, like Austria, would remain neutral in a Franco-German war, and he was able to extend treaty arrangements with her in 1884 and 1887 (the 'Reinsurance Treaty'). Increasingly, however, opposing Austrian and Russian interests in the Balkans militated against Germany being able to avoid a choice between them. In response to Russian designs on Bulgaria, Bismarck closed the Berlin bond market to Russia only months after signing the Reinsurance Treaty in 1887. Meanwhile, high tariffs to protect German farmers were seriously harming Russian grain exports and revenue. After Bismarck's departure the Reinsurance Treaty was not renewed. Russia, in urgent need of large loans to finance her industrialization, turned instead to French financiers, who were most willing to oblige, and by degrees economic and political ties between France and Russia were strengthened.

Although it took time to overcome Russian reservations, mutual apprehension of Germany resulted in a secret military agreement, drawn up in 1892 and finally ratified in 1894. By its terms, if either party was attacked by Germany the other would come to its aid, France with 1,300,000 men, Russia with 800,000. Any mobilization by the forces of the Triple Alliance would trigger mobilization by France and Russia. An attack on France by Italy supported by Germany, or on Russia by Austria supported by Germany, would oblige both France and Russia to attack Germany.[16] News of the diplomatic alliance triggered extravagant celebration in France that the long isolation imposed upon her by Bismarck had been broken. 'What joy after this night of twenty years!' exulted a Lyon newspaper: 'At last, the horrible nightmare has vanished; at last, we are no longer the beaten and almost disdained nation which the insolent victor attempted to place in quarantine.'[17]

French financial strength also helped her compose her differences with Italy towards the end of the century, culminating in an agreement in 1902 that Italy would remain neutral in the event of German aggression against France. Moreover, after a decade of rivalry that had brought them to the brink of war at Fashoda in 1898 over conflicting claims to the Upper Nile, France and Britain settled their colonial disputes in 1904. In the division of respective rights and spheres of influence that constituted the *Entente cordiale*, France, in return for renouncing her claims on Egypt, gained a free hand in Morocco. She proceeded to expand her interests there, having cleared her way by agreements with Spain and Italy, but without consulting Germany.

The days when Bismarck had been eager to encourage French colonial ventures were past. Whereas he had been concerned only to maintain Germany's security in Europe, his successors pursued global aims – *Weltpolitik* – urged on by the zealous nationalists of the Pan-German League and similar pressure groups. Germany had modest business interests in Morocco, and was a signatory to the Madrid Convention of 1880 that guaranteed the country's independence, which French activity had flouted. Germany therefore had legitimate grounds for concern and diplomatic protest. It was the manner of her intervention that roused consternation. The Kaiser unexpectedly landed at Tangier in March 1905 and made a speech approved by Chancellor Bülow asserting Germany's rights and positioning her as the Sultan's protector. Alarmed at so brusque a challenge, the French government sought to be conciliatory. Prime Minister Maurice Rouvier, who had sacrificed Boulanger to appease Germany in 1887, under German pressure now sacrificed his Foreign Minister, Théophile Delcassé, the architect of the *Entente cordiale* and advocate of a firm line against Germany. Germany insisted on an international conference, which took place at Algeçiras in Spain in 1906.

The German motive, beyond asserting her prestige, was evidently to weaken the *Entente* by demonstrating to France that she could not rely on her allies and was dependent on German goodwill. Bülow calculated that Britain would not stand by France. Nor would Russia, humiliated in her war against Japan (1904–5) and weakened internally by revolution, be of any help to France in pursuit of her colonial ambitions. Yet it was Germany that was left humiliated and virtually isolated at Algeçiras. Although France made some concessions, she remained dominant in Morocco, and received the support of other powers. Britain, in particular, alarmed by German threats and by her intention to build a fleet that could challenge Britain's, backed France strongly. The inept German challenge had aroused popular feelings and actually pushed the *Entente* partners towards closer co-operation. Though Britain resisted any formal defensive alliance, military talks between the French and British staffs began in the wake of the crisis. Urged to do so by the French, the British and Russians reached an accommodation regarding their imperial disputes in 1907. Sabre-rattling diplomacy by Germany risked making her fears of encirclement a self-fulfilling prophecy.

Emboldened by international support, France continued her forward policy in Morocco, to the mounting irritation of the Pan-Germanists. A further incident blew up in 1908 when the French seized German and other deserters from the French Foreign Legion who had been attempting to escape with the assistance of the German consul in Casablanca. With British and Russian encouragement, France withstood Bülow's hectoring demands for the men's release and his threats to break off relations. Arbitration at The Hague found in France's favour on the principal points at issue.

The colonialists who dominated the French Foreign Office – the counterparts of the Pan-Germanists – extended the French hold over Morocco further. German resentments simmered at French disregard of the letter and spirit of both the Algeçiras agreement and an economic pact signed between the two countries in 1909. Matters came to a head when in the spring of 1911 France sent a military expedition to Fez to protect Europeans in the capital, which was besieged by rebels. Suspecting that this was merely a pretext for a French takeover of the whole country, Germany chose to make her point, in the expression used by her Foreign

Minister, by thumping her fist on the table.[18] In July she sparked another international crisis by sending a gunboat to Agadir. Passions were aroused not only in Germany and France but especially in Britain, where it was feared that Germany intended to seize the Moroccan port as an Atlantic naval base. With Anglo-German relations inflamed by naval rivalry, Lloyd George, echoing German language at the time of the Tangier incident, declared that Britain would not allow herself 'to be treated, where her interests were vitally affected, as if she were of no account in the Cabinet of Nations'.[19] The war scare lasted for several weeks.

Yet Germany's aim had once more been to force France to an agreement through threats – her now habitual style of diplomacy that Lloyd George characterized as 'blundering and blustering'.[20] Eventually she moderated her demands after taking alarm at the withdrawal of French funds from the Berlin money market in September. After hard bargaining France and Germany settled their rivalry over Morocco in November. In return for recognizing a French protectorate, Germany received stronger guarantees of her economic interests there and 'compensation' in the form of two undeveloped strips of the French Congo. The settlement left nationalists on both sides angry, disappointed and accusing their governments of caving in.

Thus, forty years on from the Treaty of Frankfurt, despite periods of détente, Franco-German relations continued to be rocked by occasional war scares that both expressed and perpetuated a deep antagonism. Resentful as France was of Germany's too ready resort to menaces, she had always made concessions, acutely aware in every crisis that the military odds weighed against her. In the period following the Agadir crisis the size and state of the French army again came to the forefront of French politics as military competition between the two countries added to the political tensions in a Europe divided into armed camps.

Chapter 9

The Army of the Republic

When France and Germany fought in 1870–71 their populations were roughly equal, with France narrowly trailing Germany's 40 million people. In the decades following the failure of her appeal to arms and her loss of two provinces France found herself in a situation of widening inferiority to Germany, not only in population but in many key areas of economic production such as iron, coal and steel. At the time of the Napoleonic Wars France had been easily the most populous nation in Europe. By 1910 a rapidly industrialized and booming Germany had surged to 65 million people while the French population remained stable at 39 million, well behind Austria-Hungary and Great Britain.[1] This growing disparity weighed on French minds, provoking much soul-searching about the supposed moral causes of her decline in relation to other powers. For four decades French military thinking was dominated by the problem of defending the country against the possibility of another German invasion.

France cherished her army all the more enthusiastically following the crushing defeat of 1871. Indeed, the army became the focus of a patriotic cult as the country's shield against the foreign enemy, the guardian of internal order and the symbol of battered national pride. Wounded patriotism conveniently attributed defeat to overwhelming German numbers, an incompetent emperor and the alleged treachery of Bazaine, who was court-martialled and imprisoned in 1873. The blackened buildings of central Paris had scarcely ceased smouldering from the fires of the Commune when Thiers sought to rally the morale of the army and the country by reviewing a grand march-past at Longchamp on 29 June 1871. Even republicans who had been vocal anti-militarists under the Second Empire had changed their views as a result of the bitter experience of defeat. Jules Ferry, one of the more determined members of the Government of National Defence, wrote after the war,

> Do you recall the vague longings for general disarmament, the manifest detachment from any military spirit, and the tendency to favour a kind of universal National Guard that characterized the democracy of that

day? These ideas had their adherents; some amongst us professed them, inclined towards them, or let themselves be convinced. But today is there even one man, I ask you, who has not been converted by events? This country has witnessed the War of 1870; it turns its back for ever on these perilous and disappointing utopias.[2]

Thus in the aftermath of war, although Frenchmen could not at first agree whether their country should be a monarchy or a republic, there was a consensus that the army must be made fit for national defence. All could agree, as the sponsor of the 1872 conscription bill pronounced when introducing it to the National Assembly, that 'great disasters produce great lessons'.[3] Nevertheless, there was much debate about what exactly those lessons were, and how they should best be applied. In the Assembly Trochu was prominent amongst those officers who believed that France must adopt shorter service on the Prussian model in order that she too could draw on a larger army with a greatly expanded pool of trained reserves. For in the military sphere, as in so many other fields of French scientific and educational endeavour, the concomitant of fear of the invader was an earnest desire to study and imitate German methods, which were seen as more modern and efficient.

To the relief and satisfaction of anxious German diplomatic observers, President Thiers blocked adoption of the Prussian model. With overweening confidence in his own expertise on every subject, Thiers considered that his histories of the Revolution and the First Empire made him a supreme authority on all things military. In the face of the evidence of the recent campaign, he insisted that short-service conscription gave no advantage and that long-service soldiers were far preferable. Appealing to conservative opinion, he argued that foreign institutions were not transferable to French social and political conditions, nor suited to the French temperament. To MacMahon's objections in a committee of senior generals convened by the president that regional recruitment had given the Germans a crucial advantage in the speed of their mobilization, Thiers countered that in France it would undermine national unity and the discipline of troops who might be called upon to keep order in their own communities. With the events of the Commune still fresh, Thiers warned that universal conscription would 'inflame every head and put a rifle on the shoulder of every socialist. I want a professional army, firm, disciplined, capable of making us respected at home and abroad, very limited in number but superior in quality. This system is more defensive than offensive, and no one has any reason to object to it.'[4] He would have preferred a seven- or eight-year term of service, and threatened to resign if the Assembly voted for anything less than five years. As the majority still considered him the indispensable man to lead the country, he got his way. Nevertheless, despite his scepticism, the preamble to the 1872 Conscription Act passed by the Assembly established the fundamental principle that 'Every Frenchman has a personal obligation to perform military service.'[5]

The 1872 Act gave France an army of about 440,000 men. In practice, conscription remained selective because France could not afford to maintain every eligible man who turned 21 in active service for five years. The two-tier lottery system of the pre-war army was retained, so that a varying portion of men every year underwent only six months' training, whilst few of those retained for full service actually served even four years before being discharged. The 1872 Act also permitted various exemptions, notably for young men training to be teachers or priests. Those meeting certain educational requirements could enlist for one year's officer training on payment of a fixed fee. Intended to safeguard educational standards, in reality such exemptions favoured the sons of the wealthy over those of workers and peasants, as substitution had before 1868.

Subsequent debate about conscription centred not on the principle of national service, which was generally if unenthusiastically accepted, but on making its burden genuinely universal and equal. If in the 1870s conservative partisans of 'moral order' saw the army as a school for discipline and sought to impose observance of Catholic practices throughout the army with a large contingent of chaplains, so in the 1880s anti-clerical republicans seeking to break the political influence of the Church and its grip on education took up the symbolic demand that priests should be forced to shoulder a knapsack. The comparatively small number of men involved did nothing to reduce the time and passion expended on such issues on the hustings and in parliamentary debate. After years of intermittent debate, the 1872 law was modified in 1889 by the formal reduction of the period of active service to three years. The purchase of one-year officer training enlistments and exemptions for priests and teachers were abolished, but the two-tier lottery system was retained and the Senate insisted on keeping educational exemptions, thereby boosting the popularity of university courses which excused students from two years in barracks. Not until 1905 were all exemptions abolished at the same time that the period of service was equalized at two years for all conscripts, Germany having taken that step in 1893. Many French officers were unhappy with such short service, which they believed allowed insufficient time to inculcate proper discipline and military spirit, and would make them more dependent upon reservists to meet any German attack. It was for precisely these ideological reasons that the reduction was championed by the Left which, in the aftermath of the Dreyfus affair, was determined to override the high command and to democratize and republicanize the army thoroughly.

In order to maintain France's overall military capability, reductions in the length of active service for conscripts were counterbalanced (nominally at least) by extending the time they remained liable to service afterwards in the Reserve and the Territorial Army, which required short periods of training every year. The Territorial Army was created in 1872 to replace the Garde Mobile and National Guard, which had been found wanting in wartime. Its role was to guard rear areas and communications while the active army sought to parry an invasion. Successive changes to the periods of military service required of Frenchman can be conveniently summarized in tabular form:

Military Service Obligation in France, 1872–1914[6]

Conscription Act	1872	1889	1905	1913
Active Army	5 years	3 years	2 years	3 years
Reserve	4 years	7 years*	11 years	11 years
Territorial Army	5 years	6 years	6 years	7 years
Territorial Reserve	6 years	9 years**	6 years	7 years
Annual classes available for mobilization	20	25	25	28

*10 years from 1892   **6 years from 1892

The 1870s saw another major military reorganization aimed at producing an army better geared to the demands of modern warfare. MacMahon's willingness to succeed Thiers as president in 1873 was partly explained by his concern to see through necessary changes to the army which the opinionated elder statesman had frustrated. To avoid a repeat of the slow and chaotic mobilization of 1870, France was divided into eighteen military regions (nineteen including Algeria), each constituting the base of an army corps under the command of a general who would lead it in wartime. On the German model, each corps would consist of only two divisions, rather than the three or four of 1870. Troops on active service in each region would continue to be recruited nationally, so meeting concerns about their coming to identify too closely with the local population. But, for rapidity of mobilization, the reservists for that corps would be drawn from that region, as in Germany.

A range of other reforms sought to improve the quality of the army. Training for officers and NCOs was markedly improved by the establishment of new schools, and officers were encouraged to read officially sponsored professional journals. In the post-war years good officer candidates were attracted by the status and respect afforded to the uniform. The inevitable war with Germany would bring opportunities for winning distinction and promotion; so much so that few were tempted by service in colonial adventures, because they hoped that the real action would take place on the eastern frontier. The Germans having rearmed their infantry with the Mauser rifle, in 1874 the French adopted the Gras rifle, which used metal-cased cartridges instead of the paper that had proved so vulnerable to the weather in 1870. From 1877 the artillery rearmed with steel breech-loaders which fired shells with percussion fuses. Meanwhile, at immense cost, the Assembly voted funds for constructing a series of fortifications along the new eastern frontier. Initially directed by General Séré de Rivières, the forts were intended not only to delay the invader but to channel enemy offensives away from strong points like Toul and Verdun, Belfort and Épinal, into corridors where he could be counterattacked. After ten years of effort, 166 forts and 43 secondary works had been constructed and armed by 1884.

By 1890 public pride and confidence in the reformed army remained high, and the signing of the alliance with Russia fed hopes that when the day of revenge did come France would prove equal to the challenge. Yet most well-informed military commentators remained pessimistic about French prospects in the event of a renewed German onslaught. As we have seen, successive French governments shied away from any new trial of strength. By conscripting a higher proportion of her young men, France had managed until the mid-1880s to maintain parity with Germany, or even a margin of superiority, in the size of her peacetime army. Thereafter Germany maintained a widening lead over France: from 16,000 men in 1887, to 99,000 in 1900, and 165,000 by 1912.[7] Serious flaws remained in French organization. For example, the number of trained artillery officers fell far below requirements; for lack of adequate inducements the infantry failed to persuade sufficient good quality NCOs to re-enlist; and in training and preparation the Territorial Army long remained more impressive on paper than in reality. The Germans, determined to maintain their edge over France, managed always to be a step ahead in numbers, organization and armaments, and in the quantity and professional quality of her officers and NCOs.

The command structures of the two armies also seemed to give the Germans an advantage. Although the French staff was reorganized in the 1870s and recruited the best officers who passed through a new war academy, experts considered it too focused on bureaucratic routine and no match for the German general staff. The French chief of staff was subordinate to the war minister, a post which, in the volatile politics of the Third Republic, changed hands forty-two times between 1871 and 1914. For many years the nominated head of the field army in case of war was simply a senior corps commander, endowed with little peacetime authority over the chief of staff or over the army he would lead into battle.

This weakness of the high command derived in some measure from the insecurities of a recently established parliamentary democracy, for it was only in 1879, with the departure of MacMahon, that the Republic was governed by a republican majority. It was only then that the *Marseillaise* became officially the national anthem, and the following year that 14 July, Bastille Day, was celebrated as the national festival. French politicians remained sensitive to the threat of a military coup against the Republic like the one staged by Louis-Napoleon in 1851 with the support of the army. They wanted no military figure with a stature comparable to Moltke's in Germany. Such fears surfaced during the constitutional crisis of 1877, when Ducrot was indeed urging MacMahon to stage a coup, and again with the rise of Boulanger a decade later. MacMahon, with a greater sense of political reality than his hot-headed subordinate, stuck to a strict sense of legality and constitutional duty, while Boulanger felt sufficient loyalty to the Republic to refuse the urgings of extremists like Déroulède to stage a coup. In any case, Boulanger had no following in the army, which actually had a strong tradition of obedience to the legal regime. War Ministers occasionally made examples by suspending or dismissing serving officers of whatever stripe who ventured too boldly into the political arena with unauthorized and partisan statements. The army accepted the role of 'the great mute' with the removal of the right of serving soldiers to vote in 1872 or to stand for election as a Deputy in 1875. Yet tension and mistrust persisted between republican politicians and a military hierarchy whose sympathies were predominantly 'reactionary', that is monarchist or Bonapartist in the 1870s and conservative and nationalist thereafter.

Notoriously, that tension came to a head in the Dreyfus affair which convulsed and divided France in 1898–1900. The passions released by what came to be known simply as 'The Affair' fed on fears of Germany and of spies, and were envenomed by a virulent and widespread anti-Semitism. Hatred of Jews was fanned by the journalist Edouard Drumont, who found ready tinder in traditional Catholic prejudices, anti-capitalism inflamed by the prominent role played by certain Jews in the Panama scandal of 1893 which hurt many small investors, and the perennial temptation to blame a feared minority for every disagreeable or frightening change to familiar ways of life. In extreme nationalist circles it became an article of faith that the parliamentary republic was nothing but a Jewish and Masonic conspiracy against the 'true' France. In 1894 the Army general staff discovered that military secrets were being sold to the German embassy by a French officer. An investigation all too readily concluded that the culprit must be Captain Alfred Dreyfus, an Alsatian of rather aloof personality who happened to be the only Jew on the general staff. A military tribunal convicted him on flawed handwriting evidence and sentenced him to hard labour on Devil's Island. The twists and turns of the affair need not be rehearsed here – how it resurfaced in the public arena, how in the face of mounting doubts about Dreyfus's guilt the military establishment conspired to pervert justice in its determination to justify its original verdict, even to the point of fabricating incriminating evidence and acquitting the real culprit, Esterhazy, and how after years of campaigning by the family and mounting public uproar Dreyfus was pardoned and finally vindicated and reinstated.

The fault line that divided the Dreyfusards who believed in the captain's innocence and the anti-Dreyfusards who insisted on his guilt pitted many of France's leading intellectuals, artists, liberals, radicals and socialists against conservatives, nationalists and anti-Semitic enemies of the Republic. Although most army officers were anti-Dreyfusards to whom the honour of the army and the integrity of military justice were the issue, the army made no move to overthrow the Republic. At the funeral of President Faure on 23 February 1899, at the height of the excitement, the ultra-nationalist Paul Déroulède leading a few hundred followers urged the anti-Dreyfusard General Roget to lead his brigade to the Élysée Palace to stage a coup. Roget indignantly refused, accusing Déroulède of wanting to reduce France to the level of Spain.[8] Déroulède was arrested and later tried and banished.

The Affair brought to power a government of republican defence intent on taking a tough line against the anti-Dreyfusards. Following decisive electoral victory in 1902, a Left wing coalition of radicals and socialists determined on vigorous measures to further the ideals of the Revolution and to inculcate democratic, republican and secular principles. This meant reform of what they saw as the remaining bastions of aristocracy and privilege, the Church and the Army. Religious schools were closed, all but a few religious orders were dissolved, relations with the Vatican were broken off, and finally Church and State were separated in 1905. The requirement to make inventories of church property caused some disturbances, particularly in the west, which the army was called upon to suppress. The task was distasteful and provoked a number of resignations and refusals to obey orders. As one Catholic officer put it, 'I joined the army to serve my country and to defend it against foreigners, sacrificing my life to it if necessary, but not to make war on God.'[9]

Within the army itself, many of the most vehement anti-Dreyfusard officers were removed or transferred, and loyalty to republican principles became the touchstone for promotion. This was a reversal of the position before 1879, when the minority of republican officers, particularly those who had achieved spectacular advancement in Gambetta's armies of the National Defence, had felt themselves unduly discriminated against and viewed with suspicion by a staunchly conservative hierarchy. A so-called 'affair of the card-indexes' caused a scandal in 1904 when it was revealed that the War Minister, General André, had been deciding promotions on the basis of information about officers' political opinions and religious practices supplied by the Grand Orient lodge of Freemasons. Practising Catholics and conservatives had been discriminated against, and such was the uproar in the Chamber that André was assaulted by a nationalist Deputy and forced to resign.

Nevertheless, André had made perhaps more effort than any War Minister since Boulanger to improve conditions for the common soldier. National service had all too often consisted of harsh discipline applied by remote and haughty officers in overcrowded and sometimes insanitary barracks. Such conditions had been pilloried since the 1880s in a stream of anti-militarist novels written by sensitive, literary young men repelled by the rougher side of military life.[10] The republican vision was that the army should become the school of the nation, and that officers should be responsible for the civic education and welfare of their men. Some of the more doctrinaire anti-militarist Deputies seemed to regard the army as having no value except as a teaching institution, though conservative critics retorted that an army's primary purpose was to defend the country, and that strict discipline was necessary to prepare men for the trial of battle. Fearing that the army was losing its effectiveness, a corps commander lamented in 1907 that, 'We owe the country the truth: the army is falling apart.'[11]

Undoubtedly, in the first decade of the twentieth century the army's politically driven loss of status was reflected in a steep drop in the number of officer candidates. Pay was poor, promotion slow, the uniform no longer carried the prestige it had, and the prospect of a war of revenge seemed to have receded into the indefinite future. Instead the army found itself used to quell an increasing number of violent strikes, particularly under the Clemenceau government. The disturbances of 1907–8 alone saw nearly 700 protesting workers shot down by troops, a score of them killed. There was widespread unrest among the vine-growers of southern France in 1908, and when 17th Infantry Regiment stationed at Agde mutinied rather than follow orders to suppress crowds of protesters at Béziers, 500 men were punished by postings to Tunisia. Such incidents fuelled a spate of pamphlets inspired by anarchism and revolutionary socialism portraying the army as merely the tool of employers for the suppression of their workers, and the instrument by which the bourgeois state oppressed its citizens and reduced them to obedience. Whilst moderate socialists dissociated themselves from the more violent anti-militarist and anti-patriotic rhetoric, they feared that standing professional armies constituted a dangerous threat to both international peace and the interests of the working class.

A sea change in the national mood followed the Agadir crisis in July 1911, to an extent sometimes characterized as a 'national revival'. That month a new Chief of General Staff, Joseph Joffre, was appointed. When asked point-blank by Prime Minister Caillaux whether France had at least a 70 per cent chance of victory if the crisis led to war with Germany, Joffre replied negatively.[12] The revival of the German threat concentrated minds on defence, and helped restore trust between the government and the high command. Joffre himself could hardly be suspected of being a reactionary aristocrat. He had good republican credentials, being of modest social origins (his father was a cooper in a small town in the Pyrenees), a former Freemason, and an engineer by training. He had the initiative and independence characteristic of senior commanders who had spent most of their careers in the colonies, and was given far more authority over the army than his predecessors. He was allowed to select on merit officers known to have been anti-Dreyfusards, notably General de Castelnau, 'the Friar in Jackboots', as his chief of staff. While Joffre set to work to galvanize the army, the government showed its support for improving morale by a number of measures, such as the Millerand law of 1912 which introduced stiffer penalties for inciting soldiers to disobey orders or desert, and general improvements in pay and conditions. After a decade of being officially discouraged, military bands and parades were back in fashion. 'Every Saturday evening in summer in every garrison town,' recalled Charles de Gaulle, 'tattoos by torchlight inspired popular enthusiasm for martial music.'[13]

Joffre helped impart a new confidence to the army, manifested through an emphasis on the offensive at both the tactical and strategic levels. French analysis of the failings of 1870 seemed to point irrefutably to the dangers of relying on a defensive strategy. Remaining on the defensive had allowed the enemy the initiative, and led ultimately to envelopment and capitulation. The writings of military analysts of the period abounded in warnings that passivity led to disaster, as well as with paeans to the offensive spirit of the French soldier, whose temperament and traditions were held to be best suited to the bayonet charge. As Lieutenant Colonel Rousset, an instructor at Saint-Cyr and distinguished historian of the Franco-Prussian War, expressed it in 1896, 'Happily in France we have reverted to the wholesome ideas on which our former power and glory were founded; and we now know that in order to defend ourselves we must above all know how to attack.'[14]

With the passage of years, as the generation of veterans who had fought in 1870 passed, the experience of what it was like to face concentrated artillery and rifle fire faded, and the conviction grew that discipline, élan and the sheer will to win were all-sufficient to carry men through the killing zone created by modern weapons. French officers studied the posthumously published writings of Colonel Ardant du

Picq (mortally wounded by a shell outside Metz on 15 August 1870), emphasizing psychological preparation for the attack, Foch advocated the offensive at the École de Guerre, and the influential lectures of Lieutenant Colonel de Grandmaison in 1911 exalted moral over material factors and the imperative of taking the battle to the enemy. Japanese victory over Russia in 1904–5 seemed to demonstrate that modern weapons by no means precluded successful offensives.

As a general proposition it was undeniable that an offensive spirit and high morale are essential to success, and that wars cannot be won by defensive tactics alone. German doctrine hardly differed in that respect, but German tactics and training had adapted better to the problems of attacking successfully.[15] Events would prove that the prevailing French cult of the all-out offensive dangerously underestimated the need to support heroic determination with the right weaponry and an adept combination of infantry and artillery tactics. Whereas the 1875 infantry regulations, born out of combat experience, prescribed open-order combat tactics and advances by short rushes under protective fire in order to overcome the power of defensive fire, the 1913 regulations laid great stress on the offensive spirit, and included the precept severely condemned by later critics: 'The artillery no longer prepares attacks, it supports them.'[16]

There were a few dissenters: for instance, Colonel Philippe Pétain, a former infantry instructor, who impressed upon his men that 'fire kills' and that superior firepower, accurately directed, could prevail over any amount of raw courage. Watching a flamboyant bayonet charge staged during the 1913 autumn manoeuvres, the caustic Pétain spoiled the mood of self-congratulation by commenting that the display embodied 'all the mistakes that a modern army must no longer make'.[17] Observing the same manoeuvres, General Palat noted that 'our infantry were seen to make premature assaults, to advance without taking account of the effects of fire, without profiting from cover or sheltered approaches, without making contact with neighbouring troops or with their supports'.[18] Yet these warnings ran counter to the fashionable faith in the bayonet, and Pétain was nearing retirement.

In strategy, too, Joffre went beyond the defensive plans that had been elaborated over the years by his predecessors, from Plan I originated in 1875 to Plan XVI in 1909. For three years he toiled over Plan XVII, which aimed to concentrate French forces closer to the frontier. It envisaged not merely withstanding a German invasion but, as soon as hostilities had commenced, taking the battle to them and forcing them to react. However, the government made it clear to Joffre in 1912 that his idea of advancing into southern Belgium to meet a German advance there was off limits, because it would alienate the British and might jeopardize bringing them into a war on France's side.[19] Any offensive must therefore be directed towards the heavily fortified Franco–German border. Nevertheless, to attack seemed the surest route to a quick decision, and France's alliance with Russia provided another powerful reason for adopting an offensive strategy. At a conference between the French and Russian general staffs in 1912, Joffre argued that 'it is in the interest of the Germans to advance successively and separately, first against France and then against Russia. The plan of the allies, in contrast, must be to launch a simultaneous attack on both fronts with the maximum combined effort.'[20] In other words, if France and Russia fought defensively they would be beaten by the Germans one at a time: only if they attacked in combination did they have any hope of victory against a stronger opponent.

To implement an offensive strategy in co-operation with the Russians the French generals would need more men than the 1905 conscription law provided. Yet the most compelling reason for increasing the size of the army was provided by the Germans, who, fearing the combined strength of the Entente powers, and having offensive plans of their own, rapidly expanded their army in 1912–13. To trust that a standing army of 532,000 available for service in Metropolitan France could adequately defend the country against German forces that would reach 876,000 in 1914 was, in the French government's judgement, too great a risk to run.

Unusually, the National Assembly had chosen a strong president in 1913. Raymond Poincaré, a dour lawyer from Lorraine, did all he could to support legislation reintroducing conscription for three years in response to the German measures. The debate was impassioned, and for a while threatened to reopen some of the wounds of the Dreyfus Affair. Some regiments staged unruly protests at the prospect of their two years' service being arbitrarily extended. Socialists and some Radicals saw the move as a reactionary ploy aimed at militarizing the country, and argued that the army already had enough men to defend the frontier if only the high command would make proper use of the reservists it had available. The formidable intellect and booming voice of the bearded Socialist leader Jean Jaurès advocated an alternative scheme which he had expounded in his 1910 book, *L'Armée nouvelle* (The New Army). Drawing on republican arguments current during the debate over the Niel law before 1870, Jaurès argued that national defence should be entrusted to a short-service patriotic citizen militia, with little place for a professional army except for a reduced officer corps to provide training and leadership. Such a force, he argued, could never be used for aggressive warfare beyond the borders of France. Yet even his eloquence could not convince the Assembly that such a force would be a match for the German army, or that this was any time to jeopardize national security by radical experiments. His proposals were voted down by 496 to 77.[21]

The high command did not necessarily believe the claims of the sensationalist press that the three-year law was imperative because the Germans were planning to take advantage of their superior numbers to launch a sudden attack on French defences without waiting for a declaration of war or general mobilization. Such stories were useful all the same for persuading moderate opinion that the law was necessary. Although the general increase to three years' service was in some respects a crude instrument for swelling the army's ranks, it had the virtue in the eyes of the Left and Centre of the Assembly of retaining the principle of absolute equality established by the 1905 law. The three years' law, passed in the summer of 1913, extended the total period of military obligation to twenty-eight years, and brought forward the age for commencement of service from 21 to 20. Thus France was able to incorporate two annual classes of eligible men, those of 1912 and 1913, in October and November of 1913, closing the manpower gap with Germany.

The sacrifice required to keep up in the arms race was great in terms of both manpower and money. The strident patriotism of the Right in demanding an enlarged army was matched only by its stubborn resistance to proposals for an income tax to pay for it. Money had to be found to build new barracks to house the influx of recruits, amongst whom epidemics spread in overcrowded conditions, and training so many men proved a challenge. Many viewed the law as only a temporary expedient, especially once the wave of patriotism that had supported its passage subsided. The victory of the Left in the elections in the spring of 1914 made it possible that the widely unpopular Act might be repealed within months: an eventuality Poincaré used all his constitutional powers to prevent.

In the summer of 1914 the French army under Joffre was in far better shape to meet the German challenge than it had been before Agadir. It was significantly larger and had recovered confidence in its own élan to achieve victory. In more senses than one it was prepared to re-fight the war of 1870. Its uniforms had been little modified since the days of the Second Empire. Despite three attempts since 1900 to introduce a camouflage uniform comparable to the British khaki or German field-grey (introduced from 1897 and 1907 respectively), the nationalist press had insisted that French troops retain their scarlet breeches[22] – even though, ironically, since 1882 the red dye had been supplied by German factories.[23] Officers still wore their red kepis and carried swords. Zouaves still wore their baggy breeches, cuirassiers their steel breastplates and crested helmets.

Yet this traditional garb disguised the extent to which technological changes over the previous generation would make the battlefield a far more deadly place. It was not merely that over the last dozen years the army had begun to harness inventions like wireless telegraphy, the bicycle, the aeroplane and the lorry. A quiet revolution was laying up murderous consequences for the young men born in the 1890s who every year were sent off from their towns and villages to do their military service, their passage to manhood marked by ceremony and celebration, for the destructive power of weaponry had been transformed.

The invention of virtually smokeless powder in 1884 did more than make it hard to detect firing positions on the battlefield. It greatly extended the velocity and range of missiles, allowing rifles to use smaller ammunition and the infantryman to carry more of it. The Lebel rifle, the first model of which appeared in 1886, fired an 8mm bullet, was accurate up to 1,000 metres and effective up to 3,000, far exceeding the Chassepot. Although its reloading mechanism was inferior to the 1898 model German Mauser, which could fire 25 shots per minute to its 14, the Lebel was robust and had a greater range than the Mauser thanks to the adoption of the modern ogival-shaped bullet in 1898. The same ammunition could be used in the new generation of *mitrailleuses*, machine guns with little in common with the crank-fired weapon of 1870 but the name. Yet such weapons remained in disfavour following disappointed expectations in 1870. The emphasis on the offensive and rejection of a war of position meant that little faith was placed in them. According to General Sarrail, they were acquired only 'to please public opinion'.[24] The

Saint-Etienne, adopted in 1907, was superseded by the more reliable Hotchkiss from 1914. No light mortar had been adopted to accompany the troops.

The power of artillery had increased even more dramatically than that of infantry weapons, thanks to the invention of the high explosive melinite in 1885 and advances in metallurgy. The disadvantage of developments in gunnery for the French was that they rendered many of the Séré de Rivières forts obsolete, and there was money to protect only a portion of them with thick concrete and earth emplacements and steel gun turrets. Also, as exposed by Senator Charles Humbert early in July 1914, the French heavy artillery was inferior to the Germans' and needed modernizing. On the other hand, the French had taken full advantage of the new technology to develop a superb field gun. They felt justifiable confidence in their 75mm gun, secretly developed in the years prior to its adoption in 1897. Light and accurate, with a range of over 7,000 metres, its hydraulic recoil system removed the need to re-lay the gun after each shot, and it had a much faster rate of fire and a heavier shell than the German 77. In tests it could fire more than 20 rounds per minute and, even if this rate was difficult to attain in the field, a four-gun battery could decimate infantry attacking in open country. The fact that the flat trajectory of the 75 made it less effective against men in trenches or behind cover, and that the French were sadly deficient in mobile heavy artillery, hardly seemed to matter in what was expected to be a fast-moving campaign that would be decided by a climactic battle within a matter of weeks.

Chapter 10

The Chain Reaction

The build-up in armed forces in the period following Agadir was accompanied by numerous manifestations of Franco-German rivalry and antagonism. Pan-Germanist calls for Germany to exploit her superior power at the expense of her neighbours were exemplified by such publications as General Friedrich von Bernhardi's widely translated and reprinted *Germany and the Next War* (1912), advocating the total destruction of France. Bernhardi was not alone amongst bellicose German nationalists in calling for a final settling of accounts with the French, who were portrayed as a degenerate race in terminal decline. Although trade between France and Germany was flourishing, the commercial atmosphere was tainted by a series of tit-for-tat customs measures following a sustained German drive from 1911 to sever remaining French commercial and cultural ties with Alsace-Lorraine. In response, campaigns in the French press roused hostility against German-controlled businesses in France and encouraged the boycott of goods made in Germany. French and German banks competed for influence in Turkey, Russia and the Balkans, where French loans funded Serbian armaments.

French nationalism found expression in the literary works and journalism of such prominent authors as Maurice Barrès, who in 1914 succeeded Déroulède as chairman of the League of Patriots, and Charles Maurras and Léon Daudet, who were associated with the right-wing *Action française*. Their writings emphasized French historical identity and the sacredness of French soil, keeping alive the memory of the lost provinces: patriotic sentiments that found expression in the growing cult of commemoration of the dead of 1870. Among a younger generation of French writers, Charles Péguy, a pacifist and internationalist until aroused by the first Moroccan crisis, came to see triumph over Germany as the route to national salvation, and in 1912 dreamed of 'entering Weimar at the head of a good platoon of infantry'.[1] The novels of his admirer Ernest Psichari meanwhile exalted the profession of arms and war as a purifying force. Amongst the elite of French youth a new spirit of muscular patriotism and self-sacrifice had taken hold. In 1912 General Lyautey declared that 'what I like about today's young men is that they have no fear of war; neither of the word, nor of the thing itself'.[2]

At the popular level, antagonism towards Germany was expressed in a series of incidents in April 1913, coinciding with the debates over the Three Year Law. A

German Zeppelin flew over the French frontier and landed at Lunéville. Suspected of being on a spying mission, the craft had to be protected by French police from a howling, stone-throwing mob. Shortly afterwards a party of German travellers were beaten up in Nancy, where the local authorities did little to protect them. Further incidents were highlighted in the press.[3] In November that year feelings in both countries were inflamed by the Zabern (Saverne) incident in Alsace, when a German junior officer, von Forstner, insulted Alsatian recruits and the French flag, leading to violent incidents with local people resentful of the authoritarian arrogance of the German military. A steady trickle of young men from Alsace-Lorraine made their way into France to avoid having to serve in the German army in the event of a conflict. That same month Kaiser Wilhelm II told the visiting King Albert I of the Belgians that the irreconcilable attitude of the French made war 'inevitable and imminent'. On the same occasion his Chief of General Staff, Helmuth von Moltke (nephew and namesake of the conqueror of 1870), spoke with confidence of German victory and was certain that nothing would withstand 'Teutonic fury' once it was unleashed. 'It would be of great advantage to the small states to be with us,' Moltke told Albert, 'for the consequences of the war will be harsh for those who side against us.'[4]

In February 1914 the French ambassador in Berlin, Jules Cambon, who had worked tirelessly for détente, complained of the militarist and nationalist party in his own country, 'which excites the aggressive tone of a great number of news-papers'. He feared that another incident between the two countries could blow up 'a powder-barrel' at 'the slightest imprudence'.[5] The Belgian Minister in Paris thought it beyond doubt three months later that 'the French nation has become more chauvinistic and more self-confident'.[6]

Yet in both countries the chauvinists were a strident minority. In France, nationalist sentiments were marked among the clerks and students of Paris and other large towns, but less so among the mass of peasants and workers.[7] Cambon thought it undeniable that 'the majority of Germans and Frenchmen want to live in peace'. On 20 January 1914 a thaw in relations was indicated by Poincaré's accept-ance of an invitation to dine at the German embassy in Paris, the first President of France to do so. Behind the scenes, diplomats worked towards colonial agreements between the two countries. The spring elections of 1914 indicated that French opinion was moving to the Left, not the Right. Nationalist arguments were strongly challenged by socialists, who hoped to thwart any war by a concerted general strike, as well as by various religious and other groups promoting international peace.

The serene summer of 1914, like the summer of 1870, seemed to augur an easier period in international relations. The threat to peace posed by the Balkan wars seemed to have been settled by agreement among the Great Powers the previous year. On Sunday, 28 June President Poincaré was attending the races at Longchamp amid a 'carefree and happy' crowd when he was handed a telegram announcing that the heir to the Austrian throne, the Archduke Franz Ferdinand, and his wife had been assassinated by a Bosnian-Serb nationalist at Sarajevo.[8] Nearly a month passed before Europe awoke to the realization that these killings had lit the fuse that would ignite a world war. There seemed no reason for Poincaré to cancel his long-scheduled state visit to Russia. He set sail from Dunkirk on 16 July, accompanied by René Viviani, who held the offices of both Prime Minister and Foreign Minister. Meanwhile Paris was rapt with excitement – not about some diplomatic complication in the far-off Balkans, but over the sensational trial of Madame Henriette Caillaux, who on 16 March had shot dead the editor of *Le Figaro*, Gaston Calmette, in his office, emptying a revolver into him. Her husband, former Premier Joseph Caillaux, had been the object of a particularly dirty press campaign by his political enemies, which Calmette had been about to escalate by publishing Henriette's love letters to Caillaux at a time when he was still married to his first wife. The trial preoccupied the capital from 20 July to Madame Caillaux's acquittal on the 28th. The trial had threatened to embarrass the government by revealing that it was intercepting the telegrams of foreign governments to their ambassadors in France. Thanks to an indiscretion by Caillaux, the Germans had already discovered this in 1911 and had changed their codes, leaving the French unable to read their messages.[9]

One government can incontrovertibly be said to have been deliberately seeking war in the weeks following Sarajevo – that of Austria-Hungary. The assassins had been armed by elements within the Serb military. The decision-makers in Vienna intended to seize their opportunity to crush Serbia once and for all by military action, to prevent her becoming the nucleus of a South Slav state that would precipitate the unravelling of the multi-racial Habsburg Empire. Believing that Austria-Hungary's status as a great power was at stake, they looked to their German ally to back them and to deter Russia from intervening to protect Serbia. Germany's rulers in their turn believed that if they did not stand by their ally Germany's future as a great power was in peril. In taking that stance they set the pattern for every other great power during the crisis. Some in Berlin, possibly including the Kaiser, believed that Russia would back down, but in any event they accepted the risk, come what may. On 5 July they assured Vienna of their support: the so-called 'blank cheque'. Urged to prompt action by Berlin, Austria's rulers had no interest in an international conference – the kind of compromise brokered in London that would have left Serbia intact and in possession of her gains from the Balkan wars of 1912–13. The Tsar's last-minute proposal of arbitration at The Hague was dismissed by Austria and Germany for the same reason.

Austria-Hungary's ultimatum to Serbia, designed to be unacceptable, was not delivered until 23 July. The delay was partly because Austria's military preparedness lagged far behind her bellicose designs, partly to allow her reservists time to get the harvest in, but also to hinder a co-ordinated Entente response by waiting until President Poincaré had left Russia. For Serbia to have accepted all of Austria's conditions would have been tantamount to surrendering her sovereignty. Immediately upon receiving her qualified reply the Austrian ambassador broke off relations and left. Both sides having begun mobilization against each other, Austria declared war on Serbia on 28 July and the next day bombarded her capital, Belgrade. Any German calculation that Russia would be deterred from intervening by fear of revolution proved unfounded. Having backed down to German threats during the

1908–9 Bosnian crisis, and having begun to rebuild her military strength, Russia's rulers believed that to refuse Serbia's plea for help and abandon her to her fate would be to abdicate as a great power and protector of the Slavs. After some hesitation by the Tsar, on 30 July Russia moved from partial mobilization against Austria to full mobilization. A German threat to stop only sharpened the issue of whether Russia should once more submit to intimidation and forfeit her influence in the Balkans.

If Germany's civilian leaders had initially calculated on a confrontation that might split the Entente, military considerations now exerted a pressure that would unite Germany's potential enemies. Driven on by ultimatums from Berlin, a Balkan war became a general European war within a week. Germany's military plans were based on the assumption that she would have to fight a war on two fronts. Russia having begun her slow mobilization, 'military necessity' dictated immediate German mobilization in order to defeat France in the few weeks available before Russia was ready. But this put Germany in the position of having to declare an unprovoked war on France. Moreover, to attack France where her defences were weak, along her border with Belgium, Germany must incur the odium of violating the neutrality of two unoffending countries, Belgium and Luxembourg, thereby making highly probable the entry of Britain into the war against her. A last-minute attempt by the mercurial Kaiser to order an attack on Russia first, involving the reversal of years of planning, reduced his Chief of General Staff to despair. Moltke pleaded that it was impossible to reverse the direction of the planned offensive at short notice, and any attempt to do so would produce not an army ready to strike 'but a messy heap of disorderly, armed men without supplies'.[10] Such a move would also expose Germany to an attack from the French, who in any case would hardly stand aside and could mobilize much more rapidly than the Russians.

A certain fatalism among Germany's civilian and military leaders, a 'now or never' attitude, played its baleful part in the fraught final days of the crisis. Moltke and Falkenhayn, the War Minister, had long been advocates of a preventive war. Believing war 'inevitable', they were convinced that it was in Germany's interest to begin it sooner rather than later. In three years' time Russia would have completed her rearmament and built the strategic railways to her western frontier that the French had been pressing her to construct for some years and providing the loans for. She would then be able to mobilize as fast as the French, making Germany's position hopeless. Chancellor Bethmann Hollweg had confided at the beginning of the crisis that Russia 'grows and grows and weighs upon us like a nightmare'.[11] As time went on the Entente would become stronger while Germany's ally Austria-Hungary, beset by racial unrest, would grow weaker. On 1 August Germany ordered general mobilization and declared war on Russia amidst widespread scenes of enthusiasm.

Already, on 29 July, Germany had attempted to buy British neutrality by offering not to annex any French territory except her colonies – an offer Asquith thought 'shameless' and which enraged Foreign Secretary Sir Edward Grey. On that day Poincaré and Viviani were greeted by immense crowds on their return to Paris as

tension mounted. Both France and Germany were already taking military pre-
cautions. On the 30th Joffre was authorized to deploy troops to cover the frontier as
unobtrusively as possible, but to keep them strictly 10 kilometres behind the frontier
line itself, both to avoid giving any provocation to Germany and to demonstrate
France's peaceful intentions to the British. That day too a telegram was despatched
urging the Russians not to give Germany any pretext for mobilization, but Russia
had already made her decision.

After the war Poincaré's political enemies, eagerly followed by some German
writers, laboured rather unconvincingly to portray him as a warmonger who had
manoeuvred Germany into war. Certainly his chosen ambassador to Russia, Maurice
Paléologue, exceeded his instructions by encouraging the Russians to count on
French support. Yet Paléologue's influence on the Russian decision to mobilize was
less decisive than portrayed, and the charge that he deliberately withheld news of
the Russian general mobilization from his own government has been discredited.[12]
Poincaré's visit to Russia had been intended to affirm the alliance, which he believed
was the best way to deter Germany. It is known that the Tsar expressed concern
at any weakening of the Three Year Law in France, and that on 21 July Poincaré
observed to the Austrian ambassador that strong measures against Serbia could give
rise to complications because Serbia was allied to Russia and Russia was allied to
France. But by the time the crisis broke Poincaré was at sea, and five days after his
visit the Russian military attaché in Paris was still uncertain whether France would
mobilize in Russia's support if Germany attacked her.[13] There is insufficient
evidence of any pre-concerted Franco-Russian response to the crisis that broke
immediately after Poincaré's departure from Russia, beyond a mutual determination
to keep to the terms of their alliance.

Nevertheless, that alliance was the bedrock upon which France's security rested
in the face of a menacing Germany. France had a strong financial interest and
compelling strategic stake in Russia's survival. If she stood aside and let Russia be
defeated by the German armies, she would be left at Germany's mercy: whether
that meant the military conquest of France or her reduction to a vassal state. The
great majority of Frenchmen of all political persuasions were determined to resist
that humiliation, which would almost certainly be worse than that she had suffered
in 1871. In contrast to previous crises, this time France had confidence that her
military strength and her Russian ally gave her an alternative to submitting to
perennial German threats. Poincaré therefore had no intention of deserting Russia,
but also no intention of being labelled the aggressor. He confronted the crisis with
calm authority, seeking to rally opinion at home and in Britain. The French government knew enough of German military plans to realize that France would be attacked
first. For political reasons they determined to wait for that attack to develop.

Domestic unity was threatened on 31 July by the murder in Paris of one of
France's most prominent figures. Within the past week there had been significant
anti-war demonstrations by socialists in several cities, and only two days previously
Jean Jaurès had been at a conference of the Second International Working Men's
Association in Brussels discussing whether war might be prevented by strikes in

France and Germany. As he was dining that sultry evening in the Restaurant du Croissant in the rue Montmartre, near the offices of his newspaper, *L'Humanité*, he was fatally shot through the open window. The assassin was a deranged nationalist, Raoul Villain, who had been influenced by the strident insistence of the right-wing press that Jaurès's plans and his contacts with German socialists made him a traitor. Political opponents from Poincaré, a moderate republican, to Maurice Barrès on the nationalist Right joined in condemning the crime and offering condolences to the family. Rather than creating a dangerous political rift, Jaurès's death brought Frenchmen together at a moment of extreme danger. Just as German workers saw defending the Fatherland against the Slav hordes as a duty that overrode international socialist solidarity, so French socialists were aware that support for an anti-patriotic stance was dwindling in the face of the German menace. On 1 August the headlines of the once virulently anti-militarist *La Guerre sociale* proclaimed, 'National defence above all! They have assassinated Jaurès! We shall not assassinate France!'

That morning the German ambassador called to ask the French government for a response to the question he had posed the previous day: would France stay neutral in a war between Germany and Russia? Having consulted with Poincaré, Viviani replied only that France would act according to her interests. Had France been willing to stay neutral the German ambassador had instructions to demand the surrender of the key fortresses of Toul and Verdun as gages of French 'sincerity' – a provocative demand that France was bound to refuse. Joffre was impatient for the order to mobilize. Like Moltke in Berlin, he saw his own nation losing precious hours while its neighbour proceeded with obvious preparations for an impending attack. He warned the government that every day's delay would put France behind the Germans and cost her territory, and threatened to resign. The cabinet ordered the notices for general mobilization to be posted up across France that afternoon, the first day of mobilization to be Sunday, 2 August. On that Sunday reports that the Germans were invading Luxembourg and that their patrols were operating well within French territory left no doubt that their offensive had begun. Corporal Peugeot, formerly a primary school teacher from Montbéliard, was the first French soldier to be killed. President Poincaré declared a state of emergency, giving the military wide powers over civilian life, including censorship. The 10-kilometre withdrawal order was lifted, but Joffre ordered that no French troops were to cross the frontier. In Paris, where frequent newspaper extra editions ratcheted up the tension, there were instances of Austrian and German businesses being attacked and looted while the police looked on.

In drafting a message to be read to the National Assembly, Poincaré at first included the phrase '*Vive l'Alsace Lorraine!*' but was dissuaded by cabinet colleagues who thought it would make a bad impression at home and abroad.[14] France was, and must be seen to be, on the defensive in a war that was being forced upon her. The pressure of time weighed most upon her enemy, who could wait no longer. Unable to find any better pretext for hostilities than alleged French violations of Belgian neutrality and a false report that a French aeroplane had dropped a bomb near Nuremburg, Germany declared war on France at 6.30 p.m. on Monday, 3 August.[15]

There remained only the question of what Great Britain would do. French military planning did not depend heavily on a British presence. 'Army W' as the French designated it in honour of General Henry Wilson, the Francophile Director of Military Operations who had represented Britain in Anglo-French staff talks, was assigned only a supporting role on the flank of the French deployment. Nevertheless, the French attached great moral importance to British participation. When Wilson asked Foch in 1910, 'What would you say was the smallest British military force that would be of any practical assistance to you?', Foch replied, 'One single private soldier, and we would take good care that he was killed.'[16]

On 31 July Poincaré had addressed a plea for support to King George V, but the British cabinet, preoccupied with Irish troubles, remained divided and undecided, with some members extremely reluctant for Britain to become embroiled in a European war. The French ambassador in London, Paul Cambon (brother of Jules and in 1870–71 secretary to Jules Ferry, Mayor of Paris during the siege) came at one point close to despair at the persistent British refusal to give any formal commitment to support France. After a discouraging conversation on 1 August, during which Sir Edward Grey had to tell him that the cabinet, ignorant of the Anglo-French staff talks that had resumed in 1911, had decided not to send the British Expeditionary Force to France, Cambon supposedly groaned, 'They are going to leave us in the lurch! They are going to let us down!'[17] That day in Paris the British ambassador began to prepare his embassy for a mob attack, while the embassy porter feared that if Britain failed to join in, 'these Frenchmen will have our heads off, and I don't blame them neither, we'll have deserved it'.[18]

In London Cambon pointed out that in 1912 France and Britain had signed a naval agreement, following which France had concentrated her fleet in the Mediterranean on the assumption that the British fleet would secure the Channel. Grey deployed this argument in the cabinet meeting of 2 August. Although Britain had no binding obligation to France, the cabinet agreed that Grey should warn Germany that Britain would not tolerate a naval attack on the French coast. Germany responded that she would refrain from entering the Channel so long as England remained neutral.

On 3 August the Belgian question forced itself to the fore, providing Grey with a welcome unifying issue that rallied both those for whom Britain's strategic interests took precedence and those whose Liberal consciences were outraged by the violation of a small nation whose neutrality had been guaranteed by the Great Powers in 1839. Germany had demanded free passage for her troops, a request refused by the Belgian government. Could Britain allow a small state in which she had a strong strategic interest and which had appealed to her for protection to be crushed by the Central Powers, with all that might portend for her own future prosperity and security? Grey that day gained the support of a majority in the Commons for making respect for Belgian neutrality a condition of British neutrality. British interest in supporting France, let alone the danger to her imperial interests in Asia of not supporting Russia, could never have aroused the same public emotion or unanimity.

Although no formal alliance with France existed, the consequence for Britain of allowing her to be defeated would be that her own naval rival Germany would become supreme on the continent: and how long thereafter could Britain maintain her power, her empire and even her independence? That evening Sir Edward Grey looked out from his office over St James's Park and uttered his elegiac words about the lamps going out all over Europe. No reply to Britain's ultimatum requiring German troops to evacuate Belgium having been received, on 4 August she entered the war against Germany on the side of France and Russia.

Thus France was again facing invasion, but this time with two strong allies. In following a policy of restraint, Poincaré had been mindful of Gramont's errors and impetuosity in 1870 and had reaped both moral and material rewards. Because Austria and Germany were the aggressors, the terms of the Triple Alliance did not require Italy to mobilize and she declared her neutrality.

Not only had the German attack in the west created a united allied front against her, it had ensured French national unity as nothing else could. In explaining the need for mobilization, the French government had proclaimed: 'In this hour, there are no more parties. There is eternal France, peaceful and resolute France. There is the country of right and justice, totally united in calm, vigilance and dignity.'[19]

These words struck a deep chord. On the Left, Jaurès himself a fortnight earlier had written that 'there is no contradiction between making the maximum effort to secure peace, and, if war breaks out in spite of us, making the maximum effort, even in the most terrible anguish, to assure the independence and integrity of the nation'.[20] Following his murder, the ex-Communard Edouard Vaillant, now aged 74, declared on 2 August: 'In the face of aggression, socialists will do their duty: for the country, for the Republic, for the International.'[21] The funeral of Jaurès on the morning of 4 August was an impressive demonstration of political unity. That afternoon the National Assembly was brought to its feet by Viviani's reading of Poincaré's presidential message, which began, 'Messieurs, France has just become the victim of a brutal and premeditated aggression, which is a flagrant insult to the right of peoples . . .'.[22] He called for unity in the face of the enemy, and Poincaré's phrase '*union sacrée*' was to become a watchword.

In case of war, the government had prepared a list of about 2,500 individuals whose 'attitudes and actions might tend to disturb public order and hinder the smooth operation of mobilization'. The suspects named in this *Carnet B* were mostly anarchists and anti-militarists. In the event, the Interior Minister decided not to order the arrests.[23] France, so recently and bitterly divided by the Dreyfus Affair, by the subsequent struggles between Church and State and between employers and workers, was seeing one of its finest hours. Charles Péguy wrote on 3 August, 'Anyone who didn't see Paris yesterday and today hasn't seen anything.'[24] Of course Left and Right would continue to hold very different views of the meaning of the war. For the Left it was a struggle against German militarism and for the establishment of international peace and a universal republic, whilst for the Right the war represented a national revival, revenge for 1870 and a return to the values of patriotism and duty that they had found lacking in recent years. But all could agree that, whatever ideas France represented to them, defence of its soil against the invader was paramount.

The news of mobilization stirred a gamut of emotions as it was spread across France by the ringing of church bells, followed by formal notification by gendarmes and local mayors. In rural areas the news came as a shock, and the call-up of the men just at harvest time was a heavy blow. On hearing the bells, one old Breton woman was heard to mutter, 'They are tolling the funeral knell of our young lads.'[25] Nevertheless, whether observers recorded enthusiasm, calm, or anxiety and apprehension in different communities, the prevailing mood was overwhelmingly one of patriotic resolution to defend the country. The military authorities had calculated that as many as 13 per cent of men might not report for duty.[26] The actual figure was less than 1.5 per cent: a smattering of conscientious objectors, anti-militarists, disaffected clergy, and men who for whatever reason chose to remain abroad or to flee there. But many of the approximately 1,600 men arrested for failing to report turned out to be criminals, illiterates, vagabonds or drunks, blithely oblivious to the sacrifice the state demanded of them.[27] Their number was more than offset by volunteers, who included men who had failed to report for duty in previous years.

The moment of the troops' departure and of their leave-taking of loved ones was often solemn and poignant. Certainly there were scenes of enthusiasm and cheering as regiments set off for the station, with bands playing the *Marseillaise* or the *Chant du départ*, of crowds casting flowers as the men marched by with their rifles at the slope, the tramp of their hobnail boots sounding on the *pavé*.[28] But such pictures were less typical outside Paris and the big cities. Even at the Gare de l'Est, Paris's eastern rail terminus that was the gateway to the frontier for so many departing regiments, André Maginot recalled a vast but silent crowd which seemed

> oppressed by the expectation of the great drama impending. There were no noisy demonstrations, no idle bluster: just handshakes, passionate embraces, lingering hugs and gazes exchanged between those about to be separated at any moment. Some women wept, the faces of the old people were a picture of distress, yet all sought to steel themselves against their emotions so as not to sap the courage of their departing menfolk.[29]

Some participants described experiences of confusion that recalled the chaos of 1870: of men disembarking from delayed trains or ensconcing themselves in cafés, of scrabbling for equipment that was not where it was supposed to be. Press reports of the fatal accidents that invariably accompany large-scale troop manoeuvres were censored – like the decapitation of some hapless soldiers of 61st Infantry Regiment who were riding atop wagons when their train entered a tunnel.[30] Yet the overall picture is of how well French planners had learned the lessons of 1870, of how smoothly years of military preparation and training enabled France to transform itself within days into a nation in arms. A British liaison officer, Edward Spears, was impressed that every man had mobilization orders telling him exactly when and where to report: 'There was no confusion and no fuss.'[31] This time, based on the German model, mobilization and concentration were implemented in an orderly sequence over sixteen days. The scale of the operation remains impressive.

Charles de Freycinet, Gambetta's right-hand man during the war of 1870–71, had from 1878 as Minister of Public Works overseen a programme to expand the French railway network by more than a third, primarily for military purposes. (Freycinet, one of the more competent and longest serving of War Ministers of the Third Republic, was still active in 1914 as Chairman of the Senate Army Commission.)[32] The French military authorities now requisitioned fourteen lines, running over 5,000 trains packed with singing, wine-drinking troops to the eastern frontier at well-regulated intervals in the three weeks up to 18 August.[33] The operation was supported by 90,000 motor vehicles, 9,500 of them requisitioned from civilians, together with hundreds of thousands of horses. Marc Bloch noted that the sudden departure of so many men and vehicles made the streets of Paris seem unusually silent and solemn.[34]

France in 1914 made a far greater military effort per head of population than any other power except Serbia. From a total population not much greater than in 1870, she fielded a much larger army. When war broke out she had 882,000 men on active service (classes of 1911 to 1913). Mobilization added 2,220,000 reservists (classes of 1900 to 1910). For rear area service she could in addition call on 1,540,000 men of the Territorial Army (classes of 1886 to 1899), giving her a potential total military manpower of 4,640,000 men. In practice, however, many of the older Territorials were either not put in uniform or were detailed to help bring in the harvest. The total number of men actually available for service in Metropolitan France was 3,580,000, about 700,000 of whom initially remained in their depots, ready to replace losses at the front. The total present for duty in the frontier zone was 1,700,000, of whom some 400,000 were non-combatants. Thus 1,300,000 fighting men were available for the opening campaign, 700,000 of whom had been on active service when war broke out (including 60,000 troops safely shipped from North Africa despite a brief shelling of their embarkation ports by German cruisers).[35]

The balance of forces in the west was more even than either side had anticipated or hoped. The boldness of the German gamble lay in their decision to leave only three of their twenty-five active army corps to guard East Prussia against the Russian advance while throwing the remaining twenty-two corps against France and Belgium. The total German strength in the west was about 1,700,000 men. Against them France could field twenty-one corps, but the addition of two British corps (i.e. four strong infantry divisions) helped even the balance for the Entente. The French and Germans each had ten cavalry divisions, the British one. Neither side had attached great importance to the possibility of Belgian resistance. Belgium's six large divisions were of variable quality and lightly armed, yet their weight in the military balance was to prove far from negligible. The Belgian field army totalled 117,000 men, the British Expeditionary Force about 100,000.[36]

Legend notwithstanding, there was no decisive difference in the number of machine guns available, each side possessing two per battalion. In the skies the French could deploy twenty-four squadrons of six aircraft each against thirty German squadrons, but three British squadrons helped close the gap. In any case, aircraft were initially for reconnaissance rather than combat. In field artillery the Germans did have an edge, with 4,812 guns deployed in the west against 4,092 French and 328 British. Though three-quarters of the German guns were 77s, which compared poorly to the French 75s, the remainder were 105mm howitzers capable of dropping shells on concealed targets, which the French had nothing to match. The German superiority in mobile heavy artillery would become apparent all too soon.[37]

How would the German offensive develop? Rather than wait to see, Joffre planned to seize the initiative and spoil their plans. Colonel de Grandmaison had argued that 'What the enemy plans to do matters little,' and the 1913 instructions for the employment of large units enshrined the doctrine that attack is the best form of defence.[38] Making his headquarters at Vitry-le-François from 5 August, Joffre ordered his covering troops to probe forward while mobilization and concentration were completed, when he would launch major offensives of his own.

Chapter 11

Slaughter on the Frontiers

At five o'clock in the morning on Friday, 7 August 1914 troops of the French 7 Corps under General Bonneau entered Alsace, triumphantly uprooting the German frontier-posts as they advanced. Watched by curious but smiling peasants, they headed up the main road leading eastward from the French bastion of Belfort. French forces that day took the town of Thann, and after a skirmish with outnumbered German defenders stormed into the village of Altkirch. By the evening of 8 August they had entered the industrial centre of Mulhouse, where they were enthusiastically received. A proclamation to Alsatians signed by Joffre announced that 'After forty-four painful years of waiting, French soldiers once again tread the soil of your noble region. They are the first labourers at the great work of revenge! ...'[1] Now that the day of liberation had arrived, the years since 1871 appeared in retrospect to have been only a foredoomed truce between France and Germany. Already the French government had made the recovery of Alsace-Lorraine a war aim.[2] Like the success of Saarbrücken in August 1870, news of Altkirch and the occupation of Mulhouse caused rejoicing in France.[3]

Bonneau's men were the southernmost unit in the French deployment of five armies, each of several corps, which extended 300 kilometres along the Franco-German border, from Belfort near Switzerland to beyond Mézières on the River Meuse, facing southern Belgium. The army commanders on both sides were mostly men born in the 1840s or 1850s who had served as young officers in the war of 1870–71. Joffre had seen service (though not action) with an artillery battery during the Siege of Paris. General Dubail, commanding First Army, had first distinguished himself at Spicheren and Borny. General de Castelnau, commanding Second Army, had served in Chanzy's Army of the Loire. General de Langle de Cary, at the head of Fourth Army, had been an orderly to General Trochu during the Siege of Paris and had been wounded in the chest at Buzenval, while General Lanrezac, commanding Fifth Army, had seen action around Orléans and in Bourbaki's Army of the East. Now the French army had the opportunity to redeem its earlier defeat and recover its reputation.

Unlike its German counterpart, Plan XVII did not prescribe a particular line of operations: Joffre confided detailed instructions to his army commanders on 8 August, stating his intention to seek battle with all his forces united.[4] Bonneau's foray into southern (Upper) Alsace, besides its psychological impact, was meant to destroy the Rhine bridges and to support the right flank of Dubail's First Army as it advanced further north.

Yet despite the comparative ease of his initial advance, Bonneau was hesitant and pessimistic, and his campaign quickly stalled. Not everyone in Mulhouse was glad to see the French, and telephone lines carried news of events to the headquarters of the German Seventh Army at Strasbourg. By the evening of 9 August the Germans had launched their counterstroke. To avoid encirclement, the French evacuated Mulhouse the next day and retreated back across the frontier, fighting several rear-guard actions.

Although the portly, white-moustached Joffre had the appearance of a benevolent station-master,[5] his staff knew well enough that his apparent placidity masked a fierce temper. He knew how to make his authority felt, and did not tolerate failure. If he did not go as far as the excitable War Minister, Adolphe Messimy, who reportedly claimed, 'Give me the guillotine and I'll give you victory',[6] Joffre made it plain that no general suspected of weakness or incompetence could expect to keep his job. Bonneau and some of his subordinates were sacked, the first of dozens of senior generals who, fairly or otherwise, would receive short shrift from him over the coming weeks. A new French verb would gain currency, *limoger*, meaning to send generals to report at Limoges, far behind the front. (The British equivalent, to stellenbosch, had been coined during the Boer War.) In the face of this first setback Joffre also demonstrated a penchant for creating new armies for particular tasks, which he was to employ several times in the coming weeks. Reinforcing 7 Corps with additional divisions, he designated the new force of 150,000 men the Army of Alsace and put it under the command of General Pau, a veteran who had lost a hand in 1870.

Pau swiftly recovered the ground abandoned by Bonneau, fighting his way back into Mulhouse on 19 August. Yet he proved unable to exploit his success or to provide the support urgently demanded by Dubail. The Germans had fallen back to more defensible positions, and within days Upper Alsace had become a strategic backwater for both sides as heavy fighting developed further north. Pau was shortly ordered to withdraw, and his army was dissolved because its divisions were urgently needed elsewhere. By the end of August French troops in Alsace retained only a toe-hold around Thann and the wooded passes of the Vosges, captured by trained Alpine troops in a series of savage actions simultaneous with the abortive advances on Mulhouse.

Meanwhile, by mid-August the main French concentration was largely complete. From their railheads the troops marched to their assigned positions, suffering from the stifling heat in their thick woollen uniforms and heavy packs, their feet bloody and blistered in their stiff hobnail boots. On 13 August Joffre received the news he had been waiting for: that the Russian army was preparing to cross Germany's eastern frontier. Next day, 14 August, the French offensive into Lorraine began too. It involved two armies, Dubail's First, concentrated around Épinal and Saint-Dié, and de Castelnau's Second, concentrated around Nancy. Because the Germans had

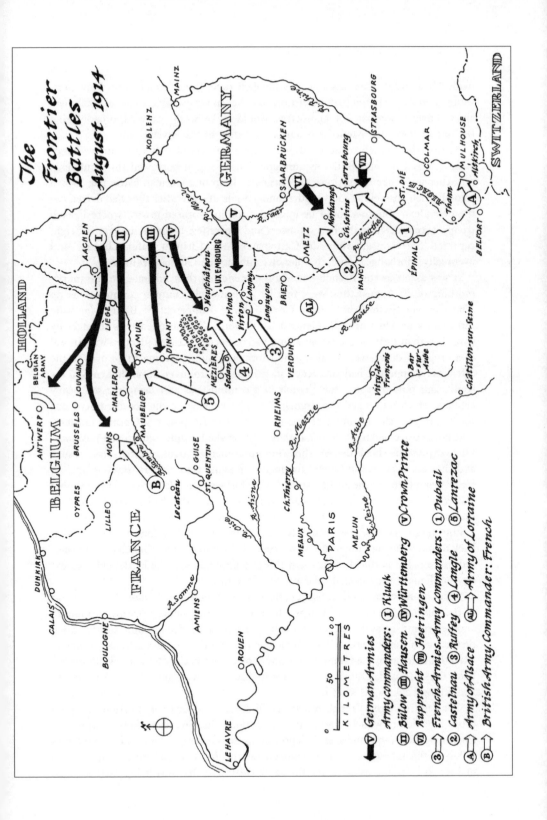

The Frontier Battles August 1914

HOLLAND

GERMANY

MAINZ

KOBLENZ

AACHEN

ANTWERP
BELGIAN
ARMY
BRUSSELS LOUVAIN
LIÈGE
NAMUR
CHARLEROI
DINANT
MEZIÈRES
Sedan
MONS
MAUBEUGE
B

BELGIUM

OYPRES

LILLEO

FRANCE

Le Cateau
GUISE
ST. QUENTIN

DUNKIRK

CALAIS

BOULOGNE

AMIENS

LE HAVRE

ROUEN

R. Somme

R. Oise

R. Aisne

Ch. Thiery

MEAUX

PARIS

MELUN

R. Marne

R. Seine

RHEIMS

Vitry-le-
François

Bar
sur
Aube

R. Aube

Châtillon-sur-Seine

LUXEMBOURG

Neufchâteau
Arlon
Virton Longwy
Longuyon
BRIEYO
AL
VERDUN

R. Meuse

METZ
NANCY
ÉPINAL

OSAARBRÜCKEN
Morhange
Ch. Salms
Sarrebourg
ST. DIÉ

ALSACE
Thann
COLMAR
MULHOUSE
Altkirch
BELFORT

STRASBOURG

R. Saar
R. Meurthe
R. Moselle
R. Rhine

SWITZERLAND

I II III IV V VI VII
1 2 3 4 5 A B

KILOMETRES
50   100

⬇ German Armies
Army commanders: ① Kluck ③ Hausen ⑥ Württemberg
② Bülow ④ Rupprecht ⑦ Heeringen
⇧ French Armies. Army commanders: ① Dubail
② Castelnau ③ Ruffey ④ Langle ⑤ Lanrezac
Ⓐ Army of Alsace ⒶⓁ Army of Lorraine
⇨ British Army. Commander: French

made Metz and its environs a heavily fortified zone, Joffre launched his blow to its south, across the central plateau of Lorraine. Seven army corps, some 300,000 men, arrayed over more than 100 kilometres, would strike north-eastward, broadly from the line of the River Meurthe towards the valley of the River Saar.

At first the French made headway, despite pockets of stiff German resistance and the onset of rain. Bulletins announced feats which borrowed the symbolism of earlier wars, like the capture at Niargoutte farm of a German battle-flag, which some French chasseurs found hidden under a pile of straw after they had driven out the defenders.[7] Success could be measured too in captured towns, where French troops were greeted with cheers, flowers and cigarettes. Dubail's men on the right captured Sarrebourg, while de Castelnau's took Château Salins, Dieuze and eventually Morhange, some 20 kilometres inside the German frontier.

It was as far as the French got. As they renewed their advance on the murky morning of 20 August they were met by a formidable German counteroffensive. The German Sixth Army under Crown Prince Rupprecht of Bavaria (actually directed by his chief of staff, General Krafft von Dellmensingen) was stronger by two corps than Joffre had estimated, and had been conducting a planned withdrawal to a prepared defensive line along the Morhange Ridge. Itching to go over to the offensive, Rupprecht had succeeded in gaining control over Seventh Army to his south, and now overbore the French in a combined assault using massed heavy artillery which outranged the French 75s. The violence of the bombardment was the first large-scale encounter of French troops with the power of German artillery. The horizon seemed to be on fire as thousands of shells inundated French positions. Huge explosions shook the air, throwing up immense clouds of pitch-black smoke and showers of stones and metal fragments, gouging giant craters, sending ancient trees 'flying through the air like straws in a whirlwind' and leaving acrid fumes that clawed at the throat.[8] This onslaught was combined with a hail of small-arms and machine-gun fire from swarms of oncoming spiked-helmeted grey-clad infantry. Within hours most of the French Second Army was in headlong retreat, passing back through burning towns it had so recently 'liberated'. The French dead in their red trousers lay so thickly that when Prince Rupprecht saw the battlefield the next day he thought they looked 'like a field of poppies'.[9]

Accusations were made subsequently in the French press about the behaviour of the southern troops of 15 Corps who had given way under pressure, leading to another round of sackings. Only Foch's 20 Corps yielded ground slowly. Soon de Castelnau's men were back on the French side of the frontier, rallying in time to defend the ridges of the Grand Couronné protecting the city of Nancy. With his left flank thus exposed, Dubail too was compelled to retreat, abandoning Sarrebourg and falling back to his start line.

The failure of the French offensives in Alsace and German Lorraine exposed those inhabitants who had welcomed and aided the French to harsh reprisals – shootings, house-burnings and deportations to Germany. Once German forces followed the retreating French armies over the frontier, the towns and villages of French Lorraine came in for the same treatment that was being meted out to

Belgian civilians. No doubt some citizens did join in the defence of their villages, but German reaction to real or suspected acts of civilian resistance was both brutal and disproportionate, and became a mainstay of Entente propaganda.

So imbued were German soldiers with stories of the war of 1870–71 that during their advance they attributed any shot fired at them from an unseen source to 'treacherous' civilian *francs-tireurs*, though in the majority of cases such fire seems to have come either from French rearguards or to have resulted from German 'friendly fire'. Paranoid about the ubiquitous presence of snipers, nervous German troops entering hostile territory and braced for combat were in no mood to make nice distinctions as to who was guilty. As in 1870, rumours were rife in their ranks that civilians had mutilated German wounded, whether by eye-gouging, throat-slitting, castration or beheading. Reprisals were encouraged and condoned by officers at all levels, who held that such measures would cow resistance and deter insurrection, and were justified by the 'laws of war' – or the German version of them, at least, which was at odds with the Hague Convention of 1907 to which Germany was a signatory. Thus after fighting their way into the village of Nomény on 20 August Bavarian troops torched it and massacred fifty-five civilians, including women, children and old people, creating panic in nearby Nancy. Similar incidents occurred at Badonviller on 12 August, where ten civilians died, at Gerbéviller on 24 August where there were sixty victims, and at Lunéville on 25 August where nineteen were killed. Village mayors and priests were commonly taken hostage and, if they were unlucky, were shot on the orders of a junior German officer who wielded the power of life or death over them, as happened at Vexaincourt, Luvigny and Allarmont. German troops pillaged and burned as they went, and at Saint-Dié and elsewhere used civilians as human shields during street-fighting. In all, about 900 French civilians were killed by German soldiers in the opening weeks of the campaign.[10]

The apparently deliberate German practice of spreading terror wherever they went filled the roads from Belgium and Alsace-Lorraine with civilian refugees – mostly women, children and old men wearing their Sunday best. Seeking safety, they tramped forlornly westward in their thousands, having piled such possessions as they had been able to save onto carts drawn by oxen.[11] Their strange accents occasionally caused them to fall victim to French fears that German spies were concealed among them. In the fevered atmosphere of August 1914, when advertisements for beef stock cubes produced by a supposedly German company had to be removed because rumour insisted that they contained concealed codes to guide German saboteurs to strategic points, suspected spies were apt to be dealt with summarily. A young officer noted that 'The most fantastic rumours are going around; everyone is seeing spies unbolting railway track or trying to blow up bridges,' whilst a British officer warned that 'the French are brusque in their methods with spies'.[12]

The flood of refugees from Belgium was one indicator of the strength of the German advance there which was already forcing Joffre to modify his dispositions. He had expected that some German troops would pass through southern Belgium.

A flurry of German railway-building in the northern Rhineland, and particularly around the city of Aachen, in recent years had not gone unnoticed by French intelligence; who, however, had convinced themselves that German troops would not pass north of the line formed by the Rivers Sambre and Meuse.[13] Having miscalculated the number of troops Germany could bring to bear in the west in the first weeks of the war, Joffre gravely underestimated the size and direction of the coming blow. Not only had the Germans kept a bare minimum of troops to face the Russians in the east, but they had put reservists into the front line to reinforce the hammerhead of three armies that was swinging through Belgium aiming to envelop the French left flank. In reality, those armies would comprise three-quarters of a million troops.

In France, reliance on reservists was seen by the high command and the Right as both militarily and politically suspect, and less had been invested in their training than in Germany. As Joffre later confessed, because the French would not have used what they considered inferior troops in this way, it did not occur to him that the Germans might do so.[14] Joffre and his staff were complacent about and irritated by repeated warnings from General Lanrezac, commanding Fifth Army, about the potential German threat to his left flank. After all, Sordet's cavalry corps had ridden deep into southern Belgium from 6 August and returned ten days later without encountering any significant body of German troops, for the good reason that none was there. Sordet's men – elegantly uniformed hussars, lancers and chasseurs, helmeted dragoons and cuirassiers whose steel breastplates were concealed by covers – had been cheered as they rode through Belgium, but they had failed to bring any material aid to the beleaguered Belgian army and achieved little save to wear out their mounts. Their reports seemed to confirm Joffre's preconceptions and to justify his reassuring Lanrezac on 14 August that 'the Germans have nothing ready' beyond the Meuse.[15]

In these days when every history student has heard of the 'Schlieffen plan', we should remember that Joffre was not gifted with the powers of hindsight enjoyed by his post-war critics. The general German westward advance through Belgium did not begin until 18 August, after the forts of Liège had been pounded into surrender by the heaviest guns available. Brussels fell on the 20th – the date, Joffre claimed, 'when for the first time we had precise information about what was going on north of the Meuse'.[16] His response was to attack. If there was a larger than expected German presence in Belgium, thought his chief of staff, 'so much the better: that will allow us to cave in their centre'.[17] Joffre therefore proceeded immediately with the next phase of his planned offensive, sending Third and Fourth Armies across the Belgian frontier into the Ardennes forest, where he believed the Germans must be weak. Eight army corps, roughly a third of a million men, would advance on a 60-kilometre front, broadly between Bouillon and Longwy.

The densely wooded hills of the Ardennes, traversed by few roads but intersected by many streams that turned the ground marshy in places, made an uninviting battleground. Beyond the occasional pasture fenced with barbed wire, only the cultivated areas around the settlements in the river valleys afforded opportunities

Emperor Napoleon III (1808–73).

Marshal Edmond Le Bœuf (1809–88), Minister of War.

Helmuth von Moltke the Elder (1800–91).

German troops storm the Chateau of Geissberg during the Battle of Wissembourg, 4 August 1870. From an 1884 painting by Carl Röchling (1855–1920).

Defence of Stiring station near Forbach, 6 August 1870. From an 1877 painting by Alphonse de Neuville (1835–85).

French troops in retreat, August 1870. Sketch by Alphonse de Neuville.

A convoy of French wounded, August 1870. Sketch by Alphonse de Neuville.

On the Firing Line: A Memory of 16 August 1870. Engraving after an 1886 painting by Pierre-Georges Jeanniot (1848–1934).

Marshal Achille Bazaine (1811–88). Photograph taken during the Mexican campaign.

Storming of the Cemetery of Saint-Privat, evening of 18 August 1870. After an 1881 painting by Alphonse de Neuville.

The French retreat towards Metz, 18 August 1870. Engraving after a painting by Richard Knötel (1857–1914).

The White Flag at Sedan, 1 September 1870.

Proclamation of the German Empire in the Hall of Mirrors at
Versailles, 18 January 1871. From an 1885 painting by Anton von
Werner (1843–1915). Bismarck is in the white uniform at centre.

Kaiser Wilhelm II (1859–1941) and, at right,
Helmuth von Moltke the Younger (1848–1916) on
manoeuvres before the First World War.

A French regiment departs for the front, Paris, August 1914.

General Joseph Joffre (1852–1931) at centre with Generals Paul Pau (1848–1932) at right and Edouard de Castelnau (1851–1944) at left. Note Pau's artificial left hand, the result of a wound in 1870.

A German infantry column marching through a burning Belgian village, August 1914.

Joffre's counteroffensive depended on moving units rapidly by train. Men of the 6th Territorial Infantry Regiment prepare to embark at Dunkirk, August 1914.

General Joseph Gallieni (1849–1916), Military Governor of Paris. Photograph dated 2 September 1914.

French artillery in action during the Battle of the Marne, September 1914. This photograph was taken near Varreddes, north-east of Meaux.

The aftermath of the Marne. Dead horses and men near Etrépilly (Marne).

Philippe Pétain (1856–1951) being presented with his marshal's baton by Premier Georges Clemenceau at a victory ceremony in Metz, 8 December 1918. President Raymond Poincaré has his back to the camera at right, while at left Marshal Foch, Field Marshal Haig and General Pershing look on.

German tanks waiting to be deployed in an assault, May–June 1940.

General Heinz Guderian (1888–1954) directs the advance of his XIX Panzer Corps from his armoured command vehicle.

German columns advancing after their victories on the Meuse. In this photograph of 17 May 1940 smoke rises from the burning village of Tétaigne, south-east of Sedan in the valley of the River Chiers.

Chaos on the roads: civilians and defeated French troops caught in the exodus of May–June 1940.

From left to right in this photograph of 10 June 1940 – the day the government evacuated Paris – are General Maxime Weygand (1867–1965), Paul Baudouin (1894–1964), Premier Paul Reynaud (1878–1966) and, in civilian dress looming prophetically over his shoulder, Marshal Pétain.

German infantry advancing, having broken through the Weygand Line. Photograph taken on or about 14 June 1940.

Burning buildings in Rouen after its capture, 10 or 11 June 1940.

The tears of the vanquished. A Frenchman weeps as German soldiers march into Paris, 14 June 1940.

for manoeuvre. But Joffre did not intend his armies to fight there, only to pass through. French columns entered the forest virtually blind on the mist-shrouded morning of 22 August, assured that they could expect no contact with the enemy that day. Once again French intelligence and reconnaissance were inadequate, and the French deployment invited catastrophe. They entered the Ardennes not in a connected line but in a stepped or echelon formation, with the left flank corps leading. As they did so they collided with the German Fourth and Fifth Armies.

German scouts kept their infantry commanders better informed, and in the series of disconnected encounters that ensued German troops repeatedly demonstrated the superiority of their training and small unit tactics. If they had no more machine guns than the French, their machine-gun companies showed greater proficiency in deploying and concealing their weapons. If the French 75 was a fine gun, co-operation between infantry and artillery left much to be desired. When the sun burned off the mist many French batteries were caught out in the open by German gunners, who made short work of them. German riflemen in their grey uniforms were less conspicuous than their enemies, whose only concession to camouflage was a blue-grey cover for their red-topped kepis. The glint of mess-tins strapped on top of the French infantrymen's packs, even more than their red trousers, helped German marksmen draw a bead. French officers, identifiable by their shorter coats, paid a heavy toll. A staff officer of Third Army trying to glean information met an old friend emerging from the fight: 'He told me how his brigade had met disaster ... of his commander killed at his side, of whole ranks of men mown down by machine guns; of the horror of fighting in the fog; of a frightful nightmare ... And this officer, whose courage I had no reason to doubt as he was known to me, put his hands over his eyes as if to see no more of this terrifying spectacle.'[18] Even in areas of this vast battle-zone where the Germans did not enjoy numerical superiority, they took the fight aggressively to the enemy, infiltrating between French units and making use of cover. One German division succeeded in putting the French 17 Corps to flight.[19]

On the French side command and control often broke down in the excitement of combat, and the hesitations of some commanders in terrain affording such poor visibility left the flanks of neighbouring units exposed. Some French units, notably 3rd Division of the Colonial Corps, found their retreat cut off by German infantry working their way through the woods to their rear and by German artillery laying down a curtain of shrapnel. These marines, hardened professional soldiers and the successors of the men who in 1870 had made their last stand at Bazeilles near Sedan (only 40 kilometres away), sold their lives dearly but were surrounded and cut to pieces by units which included German reservists. The division lost 10,500 out of 17,000 men, and several other regiments suffered over 30 per cent losses.

Over on the right flank of Third Army, 23-year-old Desiré Renault described how:

> The battle began at dawn. I fought all day, and was very lightly wounded the first time by a bullet that passed through my pack, which I had placed in front of me, hit my hand, went through my greatcoat and grazed my

chest. I found the bullet, which I showed to a comrade, Marcel Loiseau, then put it in my purse. I continued the fight, when my comrade Loiseau was hit in the leg. I also saw my lieutenant fall, shot through by a bullet. The battle continued; a great many of my comrades lay dead or dying around me. About three o'clock in the afternoon, while I was firing at the enemy who was occupying a trench two hundred metres away, I was hit by a bullet in my left side. I felt terrible pain, as if someone were breaking my bones. The bullet travelled right down the length of me, passing through my pelvis and lodging above my knee. I immediately experienced great suffering and a burning fever.

Renault crawled into a hole and spent a frightful night tortured by thirst, listening to the groans of the wounded and the bombardment of Longwy by German guns while a machine gun swept the ground around him. The next day the sun brought out swarms of flies drawn by so much blood. Not until the evening was he found by Red Cross workers who rescued him under German fire. Narrowly surviving the bombardment and burning down of the hospital he was taken to, Renault was to spend four years in captivity.[20]

Amongst the thousands killed on 22 August was the writer Ernest Psichari, celebrant of the military virtues, who was shot through the head while directing a battery. The Germans were the clear victors, with significantly fewer casualties than the French. Nevertheless, their losses too had been severe. After the battle they took savage vengeance on the inhabitants of the towns and villages whose little-remembered names evoke the combats of that bloody Saturday – Neufchâteau, Rossignol, Bellefontaine, Tintigny, Bertrix, Virton, Ethe.[21] The French Third and Fourth Armies, decisively repulsed but not routed, withdrew across the French frontier.

Meanwhile to the north Lanrezac's quarter-million strong Fifth Army had also been ordered to launch an offensive, and had moved up to the line of the River Sambre in southern Belgium to meet the developing German threat. The Germans struck first, bringing on a general engagement on 21–23 August known to the French as the Battle of Charleroi. Lanrezac failed to communicate in time to his corps commanders that he intended to fall back to a defensive line on hills south of the Sambre. Left to their own devices, they chose to defend the built-up industrial area extending eastward from Charleroi along the south bank of the Sambre. General von Bülow's German Second Army had descended on the Sambre in force, and quickly found an unguarded railway bridge across the river. German units, including the Prussian Guard, passed across to the south bank and gradually gained ground against uncoordinated French resistance. As villages changed hands in attack and counterattack, fighting amongst factories, slag-heaps and narrow cobbled streets proved costly for both sides, and the shelling made it seem as if it were 'raining coal-scuttles'.[22] Among the French infantry, 25th Regiment from Cherbourg suffered 1,200 casualties, the 36th from Caen 1,000, 1st and 3rd Tirailleurs 950 and 900 respectively, the 49th from Bordeaux 700, the 74th from Rouen 800 and the 129th from Le Havre 650.[23] As they fought they could hear the roar of German siege guns pulverizing the Belgian fortress of Namur, which stands at the confluence of the Sambre with the River Meuse.

The fortress of Namur was evacuated on 23 August. On that day too the German Third Army, composed of Saxon forces under General von Hausen, crossed the Meuse around Dinant and prepared to fall upon Fifth Army's right flank. General Franchet d'Espérey of 1 Corps, who was emerging as one of the most effective French commanders, ordered a counterattack. One of his brigades under General Charles Mangin, whose credo was that 'To make war is to attack,'[24] succeeded in checking the Germans temporarily at Onhaye. Nevertheless, for Fifth Army to try to maintain its position the next day risked it being rolled up and crushed by superior numbers. Lanrezac's thoughts were of Sedan, 'that appalling disaster which rendered our defeat irreparable'. To avoid a repetition, on the evening of 23 August he acted to save his army by withdrawing.[25]

To his north that day part of the British Expeditionary Force had fought its first battle, fending off attacks by General von Kluck's First Army at Mons. Lanrezac, a sarcastic Creole who had not troubled to hide his disdain for the British and their commander, Field Marshal Sir John French, at their first meeting at Rethel on 17 August, left it to the initiative of the British liaison officer, Lieutenant Spears, to carry word of his withdrawal to his ally. Sir John was deeply affronted, and henceforth nursed a conviction that he had been left in the lurch in the face of the enemy. A cycle of Anglo–French suspicions and recriminations had taken hold which would have damaging consequences for the conduct of the campaign, with each blaming the other for failing to protect their endangered flank. Informed by Joffre's headquarters of the strength of the German forces facing him, and realizing his danger, on the night of 23 August Sir John ordered the BEF to begin its long and gruelling retreat.

Joffre recognized the necessity of approving Lanrezac's withdrawal. On 25 August he ordered his left wing armies to fall back, pivoting on Verdun. The French offensives of the third week of August had been a costly failure. What came to be remembered as 'The Battle of the Frontiers' had consisted of distinct offensives in varying terrains: the expeditions in Upper Alsace, the thrust into central Lorraine culminating in the double battle of Morhange-Sarrebourg (called the Battle of the Saar by the Germans), the disastrous foray into the Belgian Ardennes and the combats along the south bank of the Sambre. Total French casualties in the three days from 20 August have been calculated at 130,000, plus 15,000 unwounded men taken prisoner. The number of dead or mortally wounded on 21–23 August came to 40,000, of whom 27,000 were killed on 22 August alone, making it the bloodiest day in French military history.[26] After years of preparation, and for all its self-confidence, the French army had been bested by the Germans in the first encounters.

For those who survived, their baptism of fire remained an indelible memory. The ordinary French soldier's experience in the opening battles was captured by Corporal Jean Galtier-Boissière, a Parisian of 31st Infantry Regiment, who glanced at his comrades while 'shrapnel balls rained down, ricocheting from mess tins, a punctured canteen pissed out its wine, and a shell hummed through the air for ages like an annoying mosquito'. His men 'were panting, trembling with nerves, their mouths contracted in a hideous rictus, their teeth chattering. Their faces, distorted by fear, resembled the grotesque gargoyles of Notre-Dame.' A corporal stuttered, 'If this is what it's going to be like, I'd rather die straight away.' When the order came to fix bayonets and charge they did so with spirit, but after taking heavy casualties were quickly pinned down: 'The air was riven by screeching, howling, whistling, buzzing and ululating noises: it was an infernal din.' As he hugged the ground listening to the *tac-tac-tac-tac* of German machine guns, thinking of loved ones he feared he would never see again, Galtier-Boissière's world was reduced to that of the tiny insects crawling in the grass in front of him, with whom he felt a sudden affinity: 'A stray shell might suddenly blow me to smithereens, without my being able to protect myself any better than a carelessly squashed gnat. Expecting death at any second, I had a bitter sense of my own insignificance as a humble pawn on the chess-board of war.' Eventually his unit broke to the rear under a withering cross-fire, many men desperately seeking shelter in a roadside ditch. Galtier-Boissière saw a heavy shell land 'with the crash of a thunderbolt' among his comrades a few metres away. 'When the smoke cleared, nothing was left but a mangled heap of men from which came a kind of horrible death-rattle. From this pile of flesh and smouldering cloth a bloody upper body suddenly shouldered its way out. The face was nothing but a bright red disc, with no more nose or eyes. I saw only a hole, a gaping hole that was shrieking.' Unnerved by this bloody vision, Galtier-Boissière's men ran in panic, like hunted animals fleeing death, ignoring even the cries for help from the hideously mutilated wounded, who crawled on their stomachs 'like crushed slugs'. That evening the regiment was in mourning as survivors spoke of their losses in hushed tones.[27]

Nothing was known at the time of the scale of the defeats, for Joffre insisted on strict military censorship, particularly with regard to prying politicians, several of whom were already lobbying for his removal on grounds of incompetence. Nor was the cost of failure to be measured solely in terms of so many lives so quickly lost. In withdrawing from the frontier region the French armies abandoned coalfields that had accounted for 40 per cent of national production, plus the precious iron ore deposits of the Briey region, so important to her war industries.[28] French mine-owners and their spokesmen in the National Assembly were amongst Joffre's most vocal critics in the post-war enquiries into what had gone so terribly wrong in August 1914.

In the aftermath of the defeats, Joffre blamed his subordinate commanders, more of whom were removed. He insisted (erroneously) that he had sent his armies into battle with numbers on their side. If they had failed, the fault lay in the execution. To the War Minister he confessed disappointment at his troops' 'lack of aptitude for the offensive'.[29] It is tempting to dismiss this judgement as the insensate obstinacy of a general and his staff out of touch with murderous battlefield realities and ready to blame the consequences of their own intelligence failures and mis-judgements on the badly trained men who risked and too often lost their lives trying to carry out their orders without the support of heavy artillery. Belatedly Joffre issued new tactical instructions that in important respects reversed the pre-war offensive doctrines for which he bore ultimate responsibility. They amounted to a commentary on what had gone wrong:

> ... attacks must be prepared with artillery, holding back the infantry and sending it forward only at a distance from which it is certain that it can reach its objective ... Throwing infantry units into the attack straight-away in dense masses exposes them immediately to enemy fire which decimates them, stops their attack dead and leaves them at the mercy of a counterattack.[30]

His army commanders issued similar instructions which, coming in mid-campaign, were an extraordinary admission of the deficiencies of French pre-war tactical training.[31]

Yet Joffre's strictures were not wholly unjustified. In combat some unit commanders had indeed proved unfit for their jobs, and too many junior officers had shown themselves ignorant of their tactical manuals. An observer of manoeuvres at Saint-Dié on 22 July 1914 reported that the officers 'have no idea, no suspicion, of the power of fire. The bayonet and the charge are the answer to everything.'[32] Many showed reckless bravery, disdaining to delay attacks for fear of being thought cowards, or allowing themselves to be killed standing upright rather than taking cover. Lieutenant Charles de Gaulle of 33rd Infantry Regiment, who was hit in the leg near Dinant on 15 August, later reflected that all the heroic gestures and bravery in the world could not prevail against modern fire.[33]

One modern historian has dismissed the French offensive strategy as 'mad'.[34] The initial French operations were certainly blinkered in conception and tactically inept, but an offensive strategy was not irrational, given that France wanted to recover Alsace-Lorraine and that she was fighting the war in alliance with Russia, with whom she needed to concert her action. It was understandable, too, that France should try to avoid fighting the war on her own soil. Joffre's critics sometimes failed to notice that the Germans won their early successes through the relentless momentum of their offensive, at both the strategic and the tactical levels. They met French advances with attacks of their own. It was doubtless true that prevailing notions of patriotism, duty and sacrifice, and of war as a test of honour and manhood, predisposed all the commanders of 1914 to accept the necessity of heavy losses. Yet neither side had reason to believe that the defensive offered a 'safe' strategic option capable of achieving victory.

In the event, the strength of the French offensive in Lorraine induced the Germans to send six-and-a-half Ersatz divisions (depot troops) to that front rather than to their right wing. The retreat of the French First and Second Armies also paid a quite unintended strategic dividend, in that it tempted the pursuing Germans to batter themselves against the prepared defences around Nancy in the hope of breaking the right wing of the French army while its left was rolled up by the great turning movement from the north. To Moltke in his headquarters at

Koblenz it seemed possible that the so far invincible German armies now marching across the French frontier could achieve a double envelopment. They seemed well on the way to winning the victory in six weeks that was their goal.

In his instructions of 25 August Joffre envisaged a counterstroke, but the swiftness of the German advance threatened to deny him the time he needed to prepare one. Kluck's First Army pursued the British so closely that on 26 August Smith-Dorrien's II Corps felt compelled to stand and fight at Le Cateau, losing 8,000 men before resuming its retreat that evening. The Germans were prevented from turning the British left flank by the resistance of Sordet's cavalry and 84th Division of French Territorials under the command of General d'Amade.

In contrast to Moltke, who stayed at his headquarters with the Kaiser, Joffre was in the habit of visiting his army commanders in a car driven at speed by an ex-motor-racing champion. While the fighting at Le Cateau was in progress, Joffre was holding a dispiriting meeting in Saint-Quentin with Lanrezac and Sir John French. Sir John had veered from his initial stolid optimism to despondency. He felt that he was bearing the full brunt of the German onslaught, and had almost been led into a trap by over-optimistic intelligence reports from Joffre's headquarters. He was intent on giving his force several days' rest. His depressing assessment was echoed by subsequent reports from French liaison officers at British headquarters, which painted an exaggerated picture of defeat and loss of cohesion.

Joffre's hope of rallying his left on the line Amiens-Verdun was already beginning to unravel. He judged that the immediate need was to relieve the British. On the 27th he ordered Lanrezac to halt his retreat and attack westward. Lanrezac, a former teacher of strategy at the Army War College, was as ever full of criticisms and objections, pointing out that if he changed front Bülow's oncoming Second Army would strike him in the flank. An exasperated Joffre visited his subordinate on the 28th and, following an angry outburst, insisted that his orders be obeyed.

Lanrezac sought support for his attack from the British right. Sir Douglas Haig, commanding I Corps, was eager to co-operate, but Sir John overruled him, ordering him to rest his men for the day. Yet I Corps had seen only minor action so far, the fighting at Mons and Le Cateau having fallen almost entirely on Smith-Dorrien's II Corps. When he was informed of French's order it was a furious Lanrezac's turn to feel betrayed and exposed as he prepared to do battle south of the Oise.

Fifth Army's offensive towards Saint-Quentin opened in thick fog on the morning of 29 August but soon lost momentum, not least because, as Lanrezac had predicted, the Germans began attacking him from the north. By late afternoon they had regained the upper hand on the French left, and were holding their ground south of the Oise on the French right despite determined resistance. At sunset the French played a last trump on their right, sending in a fresh corps well supported by concentrated artillery. General Franchet d'Espérey, mounted on a chestnut charger, cheered the troops of his 1 Corps into battle with flags flying and bands playing. His fierce determination revived the spirits of neighbouring units which also surged forward and drove the Germans back, enabling the French to claim a victory in what they called the Battle of Guise and the Germans the Battle of Saint-Quentin.

The action at least bought the French and British time to continue their retreat. Although Bülow too claimed 'complete victory', he paused after this unexpectedly severe encounter and called for First Army to close up on his right. Kluck, believing that the British had been swept aside, responded on 31 August by angling his march to the south-east, aiming to find and turn the French left flank. It was the beginning of a manoeuvre that, over the following days, would expose the Germans to an attack from the direction of Paris.

The French public, meanwhile, had been led by newspaper bombast to believe that their troops were everywhere advancing beyond the frontier, driving the *Alboches* (broadly the French equivalent of 'square-heads', soon shortened to *Boches*) before them at bayonet point. Bayonets had indeed been much on display during the initial French advance, but bafflingly few opportunities had arisen to use the long, thin, triangular-bladed *Rosalie* against an enemy usually seen only at a distance if at all. Now it was French illusions, rather than Prussian posteriors, that were rudely punctured. On 29 August the papers published a lapidary official bulletin announcing: 'The situation on our front, from the Somme to the Vosges, remains what it was yesterday. German forces appear to have slowed their rate of advance.'[35] This oblique admission that the Germans were invading France and had already reached the Somme conjured the spectre of an earlier defeat. 'It's just like in 1870' was heard on many lips, particularly among older people.[36] Paris itself was under threat, and the railway stations saw an exodus to the west and south of tens of thousands of panicked citizens who could afford to go. The recently retired General Joseph Gallieni, veteran of Sedan and of campaigns in the Sudan, Tonkin and Madagascar, where he had ruled as virtual viceroy, was recalled and appointed military governor of the capital on 26 August. Defying the civilian lobby which believed that Paris should be declared an open city, with characteristic authoritarian vigour Gallieni pressed forward work on the defences of the capital to prepare it for imminent attack. Since the last siege an outer ring of forts had been built in the 1880s and a fortified zone 20 kilometres deep extended around the city, giving a defence perimeter of 125 kilometres. Food was stockpiled, more guns and ammunition were brought forward, concrete was poured, trenches were dug and barbed wire strung, trees were felled and buildings demolished to clear lines of fire.

Meanwhile the field armies continued their retreat. Passing a column of Lanrezac's men on 1 September, Lieutenant Spears thought they looked like ghosts: 'Heads down, red trousers and blue coats indistinguishable from dust ... they shuffled down the endless roads, their eyes filled with dust that dimmed the scalding landscape.' As they stumbled blindly along, the roadsides became littered with dead or dying horses that had dropped from exhaustion. 'As the heat increased and the air vibrated white under a sky of brass, many men, utterly worn out, overcome by fatigue or sunstroke, dropped and lay where they had fallen ...'[37] The rear of the columns was protected by artillery which, following Joffre's recent instructions, held the pursuing Germans at bay by smothering them with shellfire. Some batteries of 75s consumed up to 2,000 rounds per day, inflicting significant casualties.

Despite the apparent similarities to 1870, the French army counted several advantages denied it in the earlier campaign. It could draw on its large pool of trained reserves in their depots who soon filled the gaps left by the opening battles. Although several accounts speak of days of hunger, the supply system operated better than in August 1870: indeed, supply became easier as French troops drew nearer Paris. Despite their bloody first encounters and their grumbling as they marched, French troops generally maintained their discipline, cohesion and confidence. 'Our faith in the ultimate success of our arms was not seriously dented,' wrote one junior officer, though he admitted that 'it took all the energy of the officers to sustain their courage and keep them in the ranks'.[38] Deserters and soldiers caught pillaging were unceremoniously executed by military police.[39] The writer Charles Péguy, who as a lieutenant in 276th Infantry Regiment led by example, challenged one of his men who spoke of treason, retorting angrily that 'We are very far from being sold or defeated. You will see in due course that we have capable leaders.'[40]

Above all, France in 1914 had a high command that did not lose its nerve following the first defeats. Joffre, a former Director of Rear Area Services, had a sound grasp of logistical questions and a highly competent staff. Even while his troops were retreating he was transferring units from his right to his threatened left. Earlier he had assembled an Army of Lorraine under General Maunoury to mask Metz. Finally convinced that a German offensive would not after all come from that direction, Joffre made Maunoury commander of a new Sixth Army and began transporting its component units north-westward by rail to support the British left and prepare to strike the German right flank. Although the German advance drove Maunoury's scratch force away from its originally designated concentration area around Amiens, by good luck the south-easterly inflection that Kluck gave to the march of his First Army after Guise-Saint-Quentin allowed Maunoury to reassemble his force north-east of Paris undetected and undisturbed. Meanwhile, to fill the gap that had opened between Fourth and Fifth Armies, Joffre pulled units from where he could spare them to create a Ninth Army under Foch. Joffre's adaptability and clear sense of strategic purpose in this second phase of the campaign were vital to the French recovery following the failure of Plan XVII.

As the German armies advanced, their confidence remained high. Yet in the west so far they had failed to surround or inflict a decisive defeat upon any major part of the Entente armies. In Lorraine the German counteroffensive had been launched too soon to catch the French First and Second Armies in an envelopment battle. They had merely been forced back, and by 25 August had so far recovered as to be capable of a counterattack in the Charmes Gap south of Nancy, where the Germans suffered heavy casualties. The French Third and Fourth Armies, though mauled in the Ardennes, mounted a stubborn defence of the line of the Meuse before falling back. In the north, as we have seen, both Lanrezac and the BEF had retreated too quickly to be ensnared. Nowhere could the Germans show tens of thousands of unwounded French prisoners or hundreds of captured guns that might have signified an enemy teetering on the brink of disintegration.

The pace of the German advance was exhausting their troops. The infuriating obstinacy of Belgian resistance was denying them the full use of the Belgian railway network that they had counted upon. Radio transmissions were proving unreliable, and the destruction of telephone wires both by Belgian sabotage and by over-enthusiastic sabre-wielding by German cavalry was hindering communication with General Headquarters – now relocated to Luxembourg. Crucially, too, while French units were being reinforced the Germans were being weakened by detachments. One army corps was diverted to mask Antwerp, where the Belgian Army was holding out, another to besiege the French fortress of Maubeuge, whilst a brigade was left to garrison Brussels. To counter the menace posed by the Russian invasion of East Prussia, Moltke, still confident that victory in the west was in sight, despatched two more corps from his right wing to the eastern front.

As it happened, by the time those two army corps arrived the crisis in the east had passed. Although defeated by the Russian First Army at Gumbinnen on 20 August, outnumbered German forces manoeuvred boldly south of the Masurian Lakes to surround and utterly defeat the Russian Second Army at Tannenberg on 26–31 August. The fate of Samsonov and his men in the mosquito-infested forests of East Prussia invited comparison with the annihilation of the Roman legions of Varus in the Teutoburg forest in AD 9 at the hands of Hermann (Arminius), to whom German nationalists had dedicated a giant monument in 1875 in the wake of unification. The new command team who had presided over this victory were Hindenburg – a dug-out veteran of 1870 who would in his turn be commemorated by a huge statue – and his formidable chief of staff Ludendorff, whose transfer from the western front on 21 August was perhaps not the least of the German decisions to which France would owe her salvation. For the moment the French public knew nothing of the disaster suffered by the ally in whom they had invested so many hopes. Nor were they aware of Joffre's anxiety that the British might be about to abandon the campaign altogether.

Sir John French was becoming daily more convinced that he needed to take the BEF out of the battle line to rest and refit, and was retreating so fast as to leave a dangerous gap in the allied line. Although British losses so far had been modest by the standards of continental warfare, they had made a deep impact on Sir John, whose career had been made in colonial campaigns. In his own view he had done his best to co-operate with the French, despite the language barrier and their generals being not quite gentlemen, but it was they who had let him down. On 30 August he wrote to Lord Kitchener, who had become War Minister on the outbreak of war:

> My confidence in the ability of the leaders of the French army to carry this campaign to a successful conclusion is fast waning, and this is my real reason for the decision I have taken to move the British forces so far back ... I have been pressed very hard to remain, even in my shattered condition, in the fighting line, but have absolutely refused to do so, and I hope you will approve of the course I have taken.[41]

It was true that Kitchener's original instructions to Sir John had stressed that his command was entirely independent of the French, and that he should take care to ensure 'a minimum of losses and wastage'.[42] Neither man wanted to be responsible for Britain's small army being squandered in some ill-considered French offensive. Kitchener was no admirer of the French army, having seen it after its rout at Le Mans in January 1871. As recently as 1911 he had declared that it was 'rotten, and ours was not much better', and held that the Germans would scatter it like partridges.[43] But he took a large view of allied strategy and had taken alarm at the pessimistic tone of Sir John's recent messages. Joffre, anxious that the British might desert on the eve of the crucial battle for France, had requested diplomatic pressure at the highest level. Realizing what was at stake, Kitchener, with cabinet backing, took a destroyer to France and in a plain-speaking interview in Paris on 1 September sought to impress upon a resentful Sir John that he should conform to Joffre's plans and that there must be no more talk of British withdrawal. For his part, Joffre had determined to dismiss Lanrezac who, however brilliant intellectually, was too given to outspoken criticisms of Joffre and to cavilling at his orders. At a difficult interview on 3 September Joffre told him that he was 'hesitant' and 'indecisive',[44] and replaced him with Franchet d'Espérey, a fighting general with the will to win. The change was also intended as a conciliatory gesture to the British, who welcomed it.

At that date the left and centre of the French armies were still falling back southwards, presenting a concave line to the Germans, who began crossing the River Marne in pursuit. The left horn of the French deployment, Maunoury's Sixth Army, was positioned east of Paris while the right, Third Army now under Maurice Sarrail, was anchored on Verdun. Joffre had allowed for the possibility of falling back even further, if necessary as far as the line of the Rivers Seine and Aube, before launching his counterstroke. He was mindful that his left was growing daily stronger, while the Germans were pushing further into the net that had been spread for them. With his headquarters now in a school at Bar-sur-Aube, Joffre listened to intelligence reports and the arguments of his staff, studied the situation map and deliberated over the optimum time to begin the battle on which the fate of France would depend.

In Paris, Gallieni was convinced that the moment to strike had come. On the previous day, 2 September, the anniversary of the capitulation of Sedan, the government had departed for Bordeaux to avoid being trapped in a besieged capital as in 1870. Already Kluck's army was only 40 kilometres from the city, with German cavalry patrols venturing within 30 kilometres. Every evening German *Taube* aircraft dropped small bombs on the city, which killed a few people, together with leaflets calling on Parisians to surrender. On the 3rd Gallieni issued a proclamation to the Army and People of Paris which, eschewing inflated rhetoric, caught the gravity of the moment:

> The Members of the Government of the Republic have left Paris in order
> to give new impetus to the national defence.

I have been charged with defending Paris against the invader. I shall fulfil that mission to the last extremity.[45]

On his orders the bridges over the Seine, the Eiffel Tower (which housed a radio transmitter) and other public buildings were prepared for demolition in the event of a German breakthrough. Yet during the day British and French aerial reconnaissance confirmed that the long German columns, leaving a trail of burning villages behind them, were continuing their south-easterly course, leaving Paris on their right. Kluck was presenting his flank to an enemy whose presence in force he did not suspect. Gallieni's headquarters were a hive of activity. The next day, the 4th, he ordered Maunoury to prepare to attack and sought permission from Joffre, formerly his subordinate and protégé in Madagascar, to launch it.

Joffre was aware of Kluck's change of direction from a map found on a wounded German officer. Yet he had to consider not just the situation in front of the capital, but that of all his armies. If they were not yet ready to turn and fight, an isolated blow struck by Maunoury would have little effect. With the calm that both awed and reassured those around him, Joffre sent enquiries to his army commanders, then sat waiting in the shade of a weeping ash tree in the sun-baked schoolyard of his headquarters for their responses.

That evening word came from Foch that his Ninth Army could be ready on the 6th. To his left, Franchet d'Espérey on his first day as commander of Fifth Army admitted that his troops were 'not in brilliant condition', and would continue their retreat for another day. Nevertheless, he undertook to fight on the 6th and proposed objectives for the four armies of the left wing – the Ninth, Fifth, BEF and Sixth.[46] To Joffre, reflecting that he would have received no such positive response from Lanrezac, d'Espérey's plan was the key to the forthcoming operation. That night, with d'Espérey's memorandum to hand, Joffre's staff drew up General Orders No. 6 for a counteroffensive on the 7th, though, after a telephone call from Gallieni, Joffre changed it to the morning of the 6th. Maunoury's Sixth Army would take position on the 5th, advancing towards the River Ourcq, a tributary of the Marne.[47]

Franchet d'Espérey had warned Joffre that unless Maunoury protected their flank, 'the British will not advance'. D'Espérey had discussed his plan with Henry Wilson, stressing that 'It is essential that you fill the gap between the Fifth and Sixth French Armies.'[48] Wilson, as ever, was keen to fall in with French plans, but when he got back to British headquarters at Melun he discovered that Chief of Staff Sir Archibald Murray had ordered a continuation of the retreat towards the Seine, notwithstanding a personal plea from Gallieni in good English to co-operate with the French offensive.[49] When Sir John returned that night to find several conflicting proposals awaiting him, he allowed the cautious Murray's orders to stand while he studied the situation. From the French point of view, this would put the British too far back to play their assigned role. 'It is simply heart-breaking,' wrote Wilson.[50] Alerted by his liaison officers, Joffre dashed to Melun by car on 5 September. He could neither command Sir John nor sack him. Instead he made a direct personal appeal, telling French that he intended to fight a battle to save France, 'in whose name I come to you to urge British co-operation with all the power that is in me. I cannot believe that the British army will refuse to do its part in this supreme crisis – history would judge its absence severely ... *Monsieur le Maréchal*, the honour of England is at stake!'[51] Sir John may have been more receptive than French liaison officers had indicated. According to Wilson, he had already, at 7 a.m., 'agreed to retrace his steps and join in the offensive'. In any event the British commander, flushed and emotional, struggled to reply to Joffre in French before exclaiming, 'Damn it, I can't explain. Tell him that all that men can do our fellows will do,'[52] which Wilson translated as: 'The Field Marshal says "Yes".'

With this welcome reassurance, Joffre drove to his new headquarters at Châtillon-sur-Seine and prepared two communications. One was a letter to the new War Minister, Millerand, explaining that 'the strategic situation is excellent and we cannot count on better conditions for our offensive'. He warned of 'the gravest consequences' for the country in the event of a reverse, but declared his determination 'to engage all our forces without stint and without reservation to achieve victory'.[53] The other was a proclamation to his men, to be issued next morning, announcing that 'the time for looking backward has passed; every effort must be devoted to attacking and driving back the enemy. Troops that can no longer advance must hold ground won at any cost, and be killed where they stand rather than retreat. In the present circumstances, no weakness can be tolerated.'[54]

Chapter 12

The Price of Miracles

Before Joffre reached British headquarters on 5 September the immense battle that would decide the fate of France had begun – sooner than he wished. It raged for five days along some 300 kilometres of front from the Paris region to Lorraine, drawing in 2 million exhausted, hungry and thirsty armed men who fought each other across rolling fields of cereal or sugar beet, in ruined villages or in woodland or marsh, paying a terrible toll in casualties to artillery, machine-gun and rifle fire. By day the guns thundered from the capital to the frontier; by night the battlefield was lit for miles around by burning farms and hayricks. The great confrontation had been foreseen for a generation, but for neither side did it begin or end as planned; and tactically neither succeeded in pressing home a decisive advantage. Yet the balance might have tipped either way on any of the successive days of what Joffre in its aftermath chose to call the Battle of the Marne.

The French had finally turned to face their pursuers, but they did not succeed in surprising the Germans and rolling up their right flank as intended. As the leading columns of Maunoury's 150,000-strong Sixth Army, composed largely of reservists and North African troops, advanced eastwards from Paris towards the valley of the Ourcq they were spotted before midday on the 5th by German cavalry near Monthyon, north of the town of Meaux on the Marne.

The main body of General von Kluck's First Army was by now well south of the Marne. Kluck had been bent on pursuing the French Fifth Army when his role was changed by Moltke, who now saw more chance of defeating the French by aiming blows at the right and centre of their front than by persisting in the attempt to envelop their left. Kluck had little taste for the role of flank guard to which Moltke was relegating him, and did not take the possibility of a French counteroffensive very seriously. Even so, he had not committed the error of leaving his right flank and rear facing Paris totally denuded. In Maunoury's path was the IV Reserve Corps commanded by General Hans von Gronau, who as a young man had been present at Gravelotte. With scarcely 23,000 men, Gronau took the bold decision to conceal his weakness by attacking. Thus it was the Germans who commenced the battle and the French who were forced to react. Charging forward into German fire with inadequate artillery support, a crack Moroccan brigade was decimated, setting a pattern in this sector for the failure over the coming days of successive French frontal assaults on fortified villages and farms. Gronau held his own until evening before withdrawing to a ridge running northward along the west bank of the Ourcq. Another of Kluck's corps was already under orders to support him and made a forced overnight march to stabilize the German position.

Among the French casualties on that broiling afternoon of 5 September was Lieutenant Charles Péguy, who had written a month earlier, 'If I do not return, remember me but don't mourn me. Thirty years of life are not worth what we are going to achieve in the next few weeks.'[1] Ignoring the shouts of his men to lie down as he stood directing their fire through his lorgnette as they advanced up the long, open slopes towards Monthyon, the poet was felled by a shot through the forehead. As his men charged forward one glanced back and saw him 'stretched out on the hot, dusty earth among the broad green beet leaves, one fleck of black and red among so many others . . .'[2]

The battle west of the Ourcq continued for another four days, with both sides hurrying up reinforcements. As French troops arrived in Paris by rail from Alsace and Lorraine, Gallieni forwarded them to Maunoury by road or rail, heedless of pleas by some commanders for a day's rest. Although most troops were moved by lorry, one minor episode that seized the public imagination was the transportation to the front of two infantry regiments (the 103rd and 104th, totalling about 4,000 men) in hundreds of requisitioned taxi cabs. Under the direction of Lieutenant Alexandre Lefas, an able politician in uniform, the cabs in their red, yellow and black livery were mustered on the Place des Invalides on the evening of the 6th. From there they travelled north-east to pick up five armed and equipped soldiers apiece from their barracks, motoring on in convoy to deposit the men on Sixth Army's left flank near Nanteuil-le-Haudouin, where on the 8th the troops were fed into the fighting.[3]

The furious contest between Maunoury and Kluck along the Ourcq was but one sector in a struggle in which another five French armies were heavily engaged. The eastern horn of the French offensive was supposed simultaneously to strike the left flank of Crown Prince Wilhelm's German Fifth Army as it advanced southward.[4] Instead, when General Sarrail's Third Army, aligned south-westward from the fortified bulwark of Verdun, went forward on 6 September it encountered the advancing Germans head on. Like Maunoury in the west, Sarrail was soon on the defensive: on his left a German assault broke so deeply into French positions that a divisional commander, General Roques, was shot dead point-blank in fighting at his own headquarters, and the situation was salvaged only with difficulty.[5] Sarrail became focused on preventing the Germans from cutting him off from Verdun. Yet, as an anxious Joffre repeatedly reminded him, the greater danger lay on his left, where the Germans might enter the Revigny Gap. After all, Verdun was well protected by a ring of forts and a strong garrison. The weak point lay at the junction between Sarrail and Langle de Cary's Fourth Army, which was beating off attack after German attack.

Although the fighting on Third Army's front was desperate, Sergeant Galtier-Boissière could at least savour the advantages of the defensive as his unit held a trench at the edge of a wood near Revigny on 8 September. The first German assault

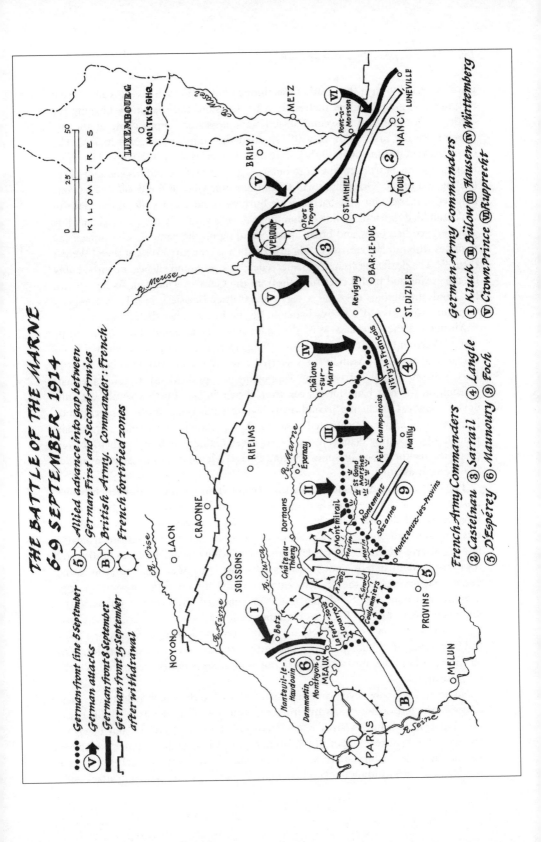

THE BATTLE OF THE MARNE
6-9 SEPTEMBER 1914

⇨ 5 Allied advance into gap between
      German First and Second Armies
⇨ B British Army. Commander: French
   ⊛ French fortified zones

⤑ German front line 5 September
⬆ German attacks
▬ German front 8 September
⌐ German front 15 September
      after withdrawal
••••
Ⓥ

German Army commanders
Ⓘ Kluck Ⓘ Bülow Ⓘ Hausen Ⓘ Württemberg
Ⓥ Crown Prince Ⓥ Rupprecht

French Army Commanders
② Castelnau ③ Sarrail ④ Langle
⑤ D'Espérey ⑥ Maunoury ⑨ Foch

LUXEMBOURG
MOLTKE'S GHQ.
METZ
BRIEY
PONT-À-MOUSSON
ST. MIHIEL
NANCY
LUNÉVILLE
TOUL
VERDUN
Fort Troyon
BAR-LE-DUC
Revigny
ST. DIZIER
Vitry-le-François
Mailly
Châlons-sur-Marne
Sézanne
Fère Champenoise
St. Gond Marshes
Mondement
Montmirail
Montceaux-les-Provins
RHEIMS
Épernay
CRAONNE
LAON
SOISSONS
NOYON
Château-Thierry
Dormans
Coulommiers
La Ferté-sous-Jouarre
MEAUX
Monthyon
Dammartin
Betz
Nanteuil-le-Haudouin
PROVINS
MELUN
PARIS

R. Meuse
R. Moselle
R. Meuse
R. Marne
R. Marne
R. Aisne
R. Oise
R. Ourcq
R. Petit Morin
R. Grand Morin
R. Seine

0 25 50
KILOMETRES

wave that tried to rush the position was thinned out by French fire: 'Finally it went to ground about a hundred metres from us, invisible and seemingly hugging the earth ... But suddenly a second assault wave appeared, approaching at the run to reinforce the first. "Fire at will!" shouted the company sergeant-major.' The Germans kept coming on until they were only 40 metres away. Deafened, his nerves fraught and his heart pumping fit to burst, Galtier-Boissière and his comrades kept loading and firing: 'Once night had fallen the whole edge of the wood was just one long jet of flame. Our rifle barrels were burning. Under our volleys, the German ranks tumbled down like a line of dominoes ... and suddenly the whole enemy line gave way, eddied back, and broke apart. Standing on the parapet, we dropped the fugitives with our last cartridges, shouting with a savage joy, "We got them! We got them!" ' The deafening frenzy was succeeded by a profound silence, disturbed only by the groans and pitiful cries for help from the German wounded. As he sat with his hands trembling, smoking a cigarette, Galtier-Boissière heard his company sergeant-major say, 'It's always better to be the hunter than the rabbit.'[6]

Meanwhile the Germans were also launching attacks along the Meuse south-east of Verdun, threatening to open a dangerous breach in the French line on Sarrail's right. This possibility was averted only by the obstinate defence of little Fort Troyon, whose garrison and supporting troops held off a whole German division on the east bank for a week from 8 September. Further south-east still, outside Nancy, Castelnau's Second Army had its hands full in trying to repel Prince Rupprecht of Bavaria's repeated assaults. Joffre dissuaded Castelnau from any thought of evacuating Nancy, just as he reproved Gallieni on 8 September for even preparing for the possibility of evacuating Paris if Maunoury's line gave way under the German assaults.

The heavy engagements fought by the Second, Third and Fourth French armies during the first fortnight of September are sometimes hardly thought of as an integral part of the Marne battle. Yet the capacity of those armies to keep fighting was crucial to redeeming Joffre's risk in stripping units from his right to achieve a numerical preponderance on his left. Ironically, Moltke's deference to headstrong royal army commanders – each adamant that his army was about to achieve the decisive victory against the French centre or right – inverted the pre-war strategy devised by Count von Schlieffen that had governed the opening phase of the campaign. Instead of the French expending their strength on vain assaults against fortified positions in Lorraine held by a minimum of German divisions, the roles had been reversed. Although taking a pounding, the thinly stretched French armies on the right held the line, and German hopes of an impending breakthrough were never realized.

No army was more severely tested than Foch's Ninth, which held the French centre to the left of Fourth Army, from which it was separated by a 20-kilometre gap. For two days Foch's army maintained itself by counterattacks, but its right, posted in the featureless plains of Champagne, nearly crumpled under a surprise assault launched before dawn on 8 September. The typhus-stricken General von Hausen, commanding the German Third Army, ordered his men to attack with bayonets fixed and rifle-bolts removed, and without any preliminary bombardment that might alert the sleeping French. His Saxons, supported by the Guard on their right, advanced by moonlight, smashed three French divisions in their path, and advanced up to 8 kilometres before their own exhaustion, as much as continuing French resistance, brought them to a halt.

Foch's centre was partially protected by the mist-prone solitudes of the Saint Gond Marshes, passable by only a few narrow causeways. French forays to the north side resulted in heavy casualties, but induced the Germans not to weaken that sector. By 8 September German offensives had won them a footing on the dry ground south of the marshes. From there the next morning two Hanoverian battalions charged forward to seize a key point on the heights above, the château of Mondement, whose turret light served as a beacon for tardy travellers through the treacherous marshes. If the Germans could hold that position and consolidate their grip on the ridge upon which it stood they would hold the heights overlooking the Seine valley and have the French army at their mercy.

The battle for the Mondement château later took on legendary qualities, for in a sense it represented the crisis of the first campaign of the war in a way that fitted popular preconceptions of what a traditional battle should look like. Fearing it would be an artillery trap, the French had not occupied the village or château in great strength and were taken unawares. The Germans burst in through the open château gates and established themselves on all floors of the buildings, which they defended all day. Wave after wave of French battalions counterattacked from the south in formations that were too dense, their white-gloved officers brandishing their swords as they went forward, only to be cut down by machine guns and rifles trained on the breaches artillery had made in the garden walls. French guns kept up a barrage on the forward slopes of the ridge, preventing significant German reinforcements from reaching Captain Purgold and his beleaguered men, but failed to suppress fire from the spiked-helmeted defenders of the château itself. Only when two French guns were run up within close range by volunteers and began demolishing the building were the Germans compelled to evacuate in the evening, leaving the French to storm the château in which only the ashen-faced wounded remained. It was a dramatic contest, fought under a louring sky, but in reality the Germans had not possessed the strength to exploit their initial success. Foch's men kept their hold on the high ground.[7]

Ninth Army had withstood all assaults, though only with the help of a corps readily lent by Franchet d'Espérey to support Foch's left. Foch's repeated orders to attack sometimes bore little relation to the situations his commanders faced, and could not always be carried out,[8] but his exhortation to his men on 9 September that 'success will go to the side that holds out longest'[9] had seldom been more apt. If the Germans had not been driven back on his front, neither had they broken through. His troops' ability to withstand four days of punishment had kept German troops tied down while the French achieved success elsewhere. When Foch attempted a counteroffensive on 10 September he found only enemy rearguards. When his staff proposed to toast victory with champagne he declined, saying, 'No, there are too many dead!' He had yet to learn that his own son and one of his sons-in-law were among them.[10]

It was along the front that extended between Foch's left and Maunoury's right that the Germans were vulnerable, and where their lack of reserves proved their undoing. Leading the assault in this sector was Franchet d'Espérey's Fifth Army. Its commander had lost none of his offensive spirit, but his tactical instructions on the eve of the battle breathed a determination that the lessons of the frontier battles must be learned. Attacks must be prepared methodically with artillery, and bunching up of infantry must be avoided.[11] One of his division commanders in particular needed no prompting in applying the new methods. On the brink of retirement at the outbreak of war, by the end of August Philippe Pétain was wearing a brigadier's stars: the very stars worn by General de Sonis, a hero of the 1870 war, with whose daughter Pétain happened to have his headquarters when he heard of his promotion.[12] Like most senior commanders on the Marne, Pétain was learning the value of aerial reconnaissance for identifying targets. On 6 September he held back his Sixth Infantry Division all day while the Germans in the village of Montceaux ahead were pounded with artillery, before personally leading his hesitant Norman troops up the ridge. He summed up his doctrine as 'The artillery conquers, the infantry occupies.'[13]

On that first day of his offensive Franchet d'Espérey was content that his men had achieved a modest but measurable advance against stiff opposition. Their morale, like that of the British troops on their left, was boosted by the realization that for the first time in a fortnight they were no longer retreating but advancing. Over the following two days, despite pockets of fierce fighting, it became evident on Fifth Army's front that the Germans were withdrawing, and that the French advance had become a pursuit. French infantrymen could see with their own eyes signs of German exhaustion and the blackened bodies of Germans killed by French 75s, whose dry, sharp detonations were as reassuring to them as they were unsettling to the enemy. The aura of German invincibility had been punctured. On the 7th the French crossed over the Grand Morin, a tributary of the Marne. Next day they pushed on over the Petit Morin and after a long contest captured the village of Marchais-en-Brie on the ridge beyond, forcing the Germans to pull back even further.

The commander of the German Second Army, General von Bülow, was drawing back his heavily outnumbered right flank which had been left exposed by the gap that had opened up between his army and Kluck's: a gap into which allied forces were advancing in strength. That gap was widened when Kluck ordered his two remaining corps, which had been on Bülow's right, to march back north-west to join the battle against Maunoury. To cover a 40-kilometre void in their line, the Germans had only a 10,000-strong cordon of cavalry and light infantry – backed, however, by well-handled artillery.

The situation had been aggravated by the independence of the German army commanders, who too often behaved like rivals intent on fighting their own battles. Only the Saxon Hausen responded wholeheartedly to requests from his comrades-in-arms for troops, and was rather despised by his haughty Prussian counterparts in consequence. Between Kluck and Bülow there simmered resentments which kept their communications to a perfunctory minimum. Nor did they trouble to keep Moltke fully informed or to seek his orders. Moltke in any case was far away in Luxembourg, and there was no intermediate theatre commander to set priorities and ensure co-ordination. To make matters worse, German communications remained poor and overloaded. Because of difficulties with their radios the Germans, like the Russians before Tannenberg, sent some unencrypted messages that were intercepted by their opponent – in this case by French receivers on the Eiffel Tower. At the moment of crisis there were holes in the German command and communication systems, as well as in their battle line.

Seeing opportunity beckoning, Joffre was impatient for the British to bring succour to the hard-pressed Maunoury by pushing into the gap between the two right wing German armies. Franchet d'Espérey became livid with exasperation at their slow progress – an attitude that has continued to colour French accounts of the battle. With no less choler one of his corps commanders, General Maud'huy, tongue-lashed French cavalry for its lack of enterprise, ordering one commander in no uncertain terms to get out of his infantry's way. Although one French cavalry division (Bridoux's) raided in Kluck's rear on 8 September, incidentally forcing that formidable warrior to take cover and his staff to use their side-arms, other units were of limited use because poor horsemanship had left their mounts with sore backs.

Starting from its rearward position the British Expeditionary Force, now reinforced by an under-strength 3rd Corps, certainly moved with deliberation, being wary of ever again having its flanks exposed as at Mons and Le Cateau and of walking into a German trap. The skill and determination of the German rearguards it faced, occupying good positions, should not be underestimated. Even so, General Haig's intelligence chief admitted privately that on 7 September 'our own troops, though the men were very keen, moved absurdly slowly'.[14] The BEF covered only 40 kilometres in three days, passing through ransacked villages littered with thousands of empty wine and champagne bottles and unmistakable signs of a hasty German departure. Overcoming successive obstacles, by the evening of the 8th it had crossed the two Morins and reached the south bank of the Marne, fighting its way across on the 9th between La Ferté-sous-Jouarre and Château-Thierry, which was taken by French troops. A wedge had been driven between the German First and Second Armies.

National pride has to an extent warped the history of the Battle of the Marne. Some early British popular accounts came close to suggesting that the BEF turned back the German invasion of France almost single-handedly, while German and French accounts for differing reasons sometimes belittled the significance of the British intervention. The German commanders had been contemptuous of British capabilities, but the enemy presence on the Marne forced them to confront a potentially disastrous strategic situation. On the morning of 9 September Bülow's Second Army began its retreat behind the Marne. Kluck, meanwhile, had taken a calculated risk in pulling each of his corps in turn back towards the north-west, believing that by striking rapidly he could defeat Maunoury before the British intervened. That morning he used his last reinforcements to drive in Maunoury's northern flank, pushing it close to collapse. Even as he did so, however, he was pulling back his left in response to the British advance, diminishing the value of the success on his right. The attack was halted in the early afternoon when an emissary from Moltke arrived and a retreat was ordered.

Argument has not yet ceased over the role played by Lieutenant Colonel Richard Hentsch, a trusted staff officer who had been sent with verbal instructions from Moltke and who reached First Army after having visited the other commanders. Even before the end of the war, when it was becoming apparent just how critical a turning point the withdrawal from the Marne had been, Hentsch was made a scapegoat for a retreat represented by many German commentators as needless. He was accused of exceeding his authority and of taking a defeatist view. Even before the stab-in-the-back legends to explain away the army's defeat in 1918, there was insistence that there had been no defeat in September 1914, only a bad command decision.

It was true that, in the tactical sense, the German army had not been beaten, and at several points along the front it had had the best of its encounters with the French. The disbelief and anger of German troops at being ordered to withdraw are well attested.[15] A few days earlier they had felt elation at being on the verge of entering Paris. Some had even had a distant glimpse of the Eiffel Tower. Now, instead of a triumphal end to their marches and sufferings, they were heading for the rear even though they felt themselves undefeated. No doubt the chaotic scenes Hentsch had witnessed on his drive through its rear areas had given him an unduly pessimistic view of First Army's condition.

Nevertheless, much of the indictment of Hentsch smacks of shooting the messenger, and subsequent claims that the German army was on the verge of a decisive tactical success owe much to wishful thinking. The fact remains that in four days of fighting the Germans had failed, however narrowly, to break the French army, and their attacks had frequently been heavily punished by the French 75s. As Second Lieutenant Maurice Genevoix put it, 'their enormous shells had not battered down the fragile wall; and when the spiked-helmeted hordes surged in behind the avalanche of steel that preceded them, their obstinate offensive spirit and their repeated hammer-blows delivered with desperate fury over five days proved unable to open the breach that they sought'.[16] Even German success against Maunoury's left would have run up against a French second line and eventually the defences of Paris. However grudgingly, Kluck and his chief of staff accepted that Bülow's retreat and the advance of the British made First Army's withdrawal a military necessity. That the army found itself in a strategically compromised situation and that at the critical moment it did not have fresh divisions available to plug the gap in its line were facts not of Hentsch's making.

Thus the German army withdrew northward not because it had been decisively defeated, but to avoid that possibility. To ever admit that the French army had got the better of them remained too much for most Germans. Official announcements of events were as sparing and oblique as those on the French side in August. Before the war the German high command had regarded their French counterparts as amateurs, a view encouraged by the outcome of the frontier battles. Yet since then Joffre had out-generalled Moltke, amassing his strength where his enemy was weakest. For all that the battle had not conformed to his conception and that he had been favoured by German mistakes and failures to find or exploit his weak points, Joffre had achieved an undeniable and historic victory, halting the Germans and turning them back. His imperturbable, methodical and confident approach contrasted markedly to that of the increasingly depressed and pessimistic Moltke, who had failed to give strong direction to his forces or to achieve the quick victory in the west that was the holy grail of German military planning in 1914. The psychological impact on senior German commanders of being so unexpectedly counterattacked in force by an enemy they had considered beaten should not be underestimated. As even the aggressive Kluck admitted to a Swedish journalist at the end of the war, '... That men who had retreated for ten days, that men lying prostrated on the ground half dead from exhaustion could pick up their rifles again and attack at the sound of the bugle, that was something we had never reckoned with; that was a possibility never considered in our military academies.'[17]

Notwithstanding that there was credit enough to go around on the French side, squabbles subsequently broke out as to who deserved the lion's share, particularly between the supporters of Gallieni and Joffre. Such disputes distracted attention from evidence that during the battle itself the French army commanders – mostly Joffre's appointees – had by and large co-operated well, more like the German generals of 1870 than those of 1914. As to the controversies, the most apt comment may have been Joffre's wry sally in 1923 that, 'I don't know who won the Battle of the Marne but, had it been lost, I know very well who would have lost it.'[18] As Foch said of Joffre, 'If we had not had him in 1914, I don't know what would have become of us.'[19]

On 11 September Joffre claimed victory. General Maunoury had already issued an order thanking his troops warmly for what they had achieved, 'for to you I owe the realization of the objective towards which all my energies and efforts have been bent for the last forty-four years – the reversal of the verdict of 1870'.[20] Wary of making inflated claims, and perhaps also of the authoritarian Joffre's intentions towards it, the government was more cautious in its announcements. The public reaction was predominantly one of relief that the Germans had been turned back – a chance to breathe again now that the immediate threat to the capital had passed. It was only months later that the religious and right-wing press began to descant upon 'The Miracle of the Marne' that had saved France.[21]

In the aftermath of the battle Joffre was keen to press his advantage, but the opportunity slipped. The Germans in September, like the French in August, withdrew in reasonably good order, battered and bloodied but unbroken. Instead of the victorious drive towards the Rhine that some French and British generals hoped for, the allied 'pursuit' was more of a cautious following at a distance by worn-out troops in weather that had turned wet and cold. By 12 September Kluck was safely over the River Aisne without molestation. Within days, German troops released by the capitulation of Maubeuge on 8 September and others sent from Seventh Army in Alsace closed the gap in the German line by the narrowest of margins. Moltke had been compelled to mirror Joffre's strategy, pulling divisions out of Alsace and Lorraine to feed them north-westward. In consequence, the southern portion of the German line also gave ground, falling back to defensive positions. Moltke was painfully aware that high German hopes at the outset of the campaign had been dashed, and he paid the price. Having disappointed the Kaiser and lost the confidence of many of his officers, he was effectively superseded by Falkenhayn on 14 September, lamenting from his retirement a few months later that, 'It is dreadful to be condemned to inactivity in this war which I prepared and initiated.'[22]

Along several sectors of the front during the Marne fighting both sides had resorted to field entrenchments for protection. The Germans, being better trained and equipped for the task, had quickly made their positions west of the Ourcq almost impregnable to frontal assault. Once established on the formidable ridges north of the Aisne they again put their entrenching skills to excellent use, as the allies discovered to their cost when attempts to assault those positions from 13 September ended in bloody repulse in 'a regular monsoon downpour'.[23] It was not immediately apparent that the phase of mobile warfare was at an end, as over the next six weeks both sides tried but failed to turn each other's flank in the so-called 'Race to the Sea'. After the culminating slaughter on the banks of the Yser in Belgium in late October and early November, the western front was set solid, as if the hot molten lava flow of the German invasion of August and September had cooled to a carapace of cold grey rock encrusting and smothering Belgium and north-eastern France, impervious to any hammer blow or weight of explosive to dislodge it. So prodigious had been the consumption of ammunition on the Marne that stocks on both sides were running very low indeed.

The cost in men, too, of the first phase of the war had been heavy on both sides, and the medical services had been stretched to the limit and beyond. Once the stretcher-bearers had gathered the wounded, the dead of the Marne became prey to more than crows and dogs. Scavengers from Paris who managed to slip through the cordon of gendarmes were soon picking over the battlefield for booty. Photographs show harvested fields dotted with bodies lying like heaps of crumpled rags. Whilst many men had been mutilated by shrapnel and shell fragments, others appeared to be quite unwounded, yet their internal organs had been ruptured by the blast of exploding shells.[24] Among the victims of artillery fire, and of still imperfect co-ordination between arms, lay some French troops who had been caught by their own guns. In the September heat the bellies of the dead became bloated, and Galtier-Boissière was one of the many who gagged at the 'atrocious, unbearable, pestilential' stench of decaying carrion. He and his comrades covered their faces with hand-kerchiefs, 'Yet still this frightful smell clutched at our throats and pursued us.'[25]

Before long France was to experience battles even more murderous than the Marne, but only because they were of longer duration. Although France lost more men killed in 1915 and 1918 than she did in the last five months of 1914, the average monthly losses later compiled by the army medical service revealed that August and September 1914 were by far the costliest two months of the war for France.[26] The official figures for killed, wounded and missing were given as 206,515 for August (excluding officers) and 213,445 for September (including officers but also casualties incurred in three weeks of costly operations after the Marne) giving a total of 419,960.[27] Within this total, the number of French troops killed, taking into account those who later died of their wounds and those officially reported as 'missing' but who were actually dead, has been calculated in round figures at 80,000 in August, 8,000 in the first five days of September and 25,000 in the Battle of the Marne itself, or about 120,000 from the commencement of hostilities up to the Battle of the Aisne[28] – approximately one man in eleven of the combat troops who two months earlier had been peaceably going about their business in fields, shops, factories, offices or barracks. German battle casualties in the first ten days of September were reported as 27,417 dead or missing and 47,431 wounded.[29] British casualties for 6–10 September totalled 1,701.[30]

In all armies the losses among officers and NCOs had been damaging, though the French were soon able to fill the gaps in their ranks from depot troops. Many commentators were to agree that if there had been a 'miracle' at the Marne then it lay in the spirit of resistance of the French soldier. One junior officer attributed high morale during the battle to the sense of discipline and duty instilled in his men during their peacetime training.[31] This in turn rested on a profound patriotism imbibed in the schoolroom and the community. In these early weeks of the war, disillusion had yet to take hold. There were also more immediate influences whose relative importance varied from unit to unit and man to man: not only the threat of draconian discipline against deserters enforced by the high command, but also outrage at reported German atrocities, which was felt particularly keenly among troops whose homes lay in the invaded regions. French troops understood that they were fighting to save their country and their capital, and felt a growing confidence that the tables were at last being turned on the Germans. 'Even in the darkest hours of the retreat,' wrote Galtier-Boissière, '... I always retained in the bottom of my heart, not the hope, but the certainty of victory.'[32] If Joffre's order of the day on the eve of battle reached the German high command rather more quickly than it did many French units in the field, it nevertheless struck a chord. Maurice Genevoix, having lost forty-nine of his seventy men in five days of brutal combat, did not read Joffre's stirring injunction to drive back the enemy until after the battle, on 12 September. Nevertheless, he thought that Joffre's words exactly matched the hour: 'I felt that sentiment, and so did my men and all of us to whom nothing had been said. *To be killed rather than retreat.* Nobody had read us those words at ... the time we had turned about to face north. Yet we had carried them within us.'[33]

The Marne had shown that Germany had been unable, after all, to end the war in the west quickly by knocking out France with one blow. Germany was thereby condemned to fight a war on two fronts with a weakened ally, for the Austrians had simultaneously been heavily defeated by the Russians around Lemberg. Conversely, even with allies, France had not possessed the initial strength to defeat Germany, to liberate Alsace-Lorraine, or even to prevent the Germans from occupying a significant portion of French territory, including the major city of Lille. Nine Departments were wholly or partly occupied, leaving 2 million French people subject to German rule. Rheims, though reoccupied by French forces, was at the mercy of German heavy guns which proceeded to pulverize it. While German forces remained on French soil there could be no question for France of a negotiated peace. As Clemenceau's paper reminded its readers daily, 'The Germans are at Noyon', that is, only 90 kilometres from Paris.[34] On 5 September representatives of the Entente powers meeting in London agreed to make no separate peace with the enemy.

On 9 September in Berlin, where victory still seemed imminent, the German Chancellor Bethmann-Hollweg initialled the so-called 'September programme': a list of demands envisaging the annexation in the west of Luxembourg, Liège and Antwerp, and from France Belfort, the western slope of the Vosges, the Briey iron ore field, plus a coastal strip around Dunkirk and Boulogne. To ensure German security and economic dominance Belgium was to become a vassal state and France 'must be so weakened as to make her revival as a great power impossible for all time'.[35]

The failure of the 1914 campaign to produce a victor ushered in a long war – something that neither side had wanted or prepared for. Having already sacrificed so much blood, and believing their national survival to be at stake, neither side would accept less than victory. In their quest for it, both were condemned to a brutal war of attrition on a hitherto unimaginable scale. The contest became a giant mutual siege extending 700 kilometres from the Channel to Switzerland. Its radically changed nature was symbolized by the metamorphosis of the French soldier from picture-book mannequin to mud-daubed trench dweller. Gone were the red trousers, so dear to the nationalist press, along with blue greatcoats and kepis. From 1915 the picturesque uniform of the last century was superseded by horizon-blue great-coats, puttees, gas-masks and the Adrian steel helmet which offered at least a little protection from flying fragments of earth and metal. Men struggled to survive in a squalid Stygian trench-world infested by rats and lice where the danger of death or mutilation inflicted by bullets, shells, mines, bombs, grenades, flamethrowers or gas was omnipresent. To sustain the struggle each nation had to mobilize all its available manpower, but also to gear its economy to arm and equip its armies, keep them supplied and ensure that both they and the civilian population could be fed. Over four years France, keystone of the Entente, produced 24,000 artillery pieces, including heavy guns and mortars, and 331.5 million shells, 90,000 machine guns, 2,375,000 rifles and 6.3 billion cartridges, 52,000 aircraft, over 3,000 tanks and 98,000 military vehicles.[36] Though hampered by the loss of coal and iron from the occupied regions, with the aid of imported raw materials and foreign loans her industries were able to meet most of her war needs while fulfilling large orders from allies such as Belgium, Serbia, Russia, Italy (which joined the Entente in 1915) and later the USA, which was to rely heavily on France for aircraft, guns and tanks.

Yet all this industrial and agricultural effort and staggering expenditure of life at the front produced no decisive breakthrough for four years: not for the French in the Champagne and Artois offensives of 1915, not for the Germans in the ghastly mincing machine of Verdun in 1916 nor for the great Franco-British offensive on the Somme that summer, any more than for the French on the Chemin des Dames or the British at Ypres in 1917. The terrible cost of his failed offensives, and accusations that he had left Verdun unprepared, undermined Joffre. By 1916 his aureole as victor of the Marne had become tarnished, and his ruthless sackings in 1914 had made him many enemies with political connections. He was effectively 'kicked upstairs' by promotion to marshal in December 1916 as the politicians reasserted their control over strategy. Yet his successor, Robert Nivelle, who had distinguished himself as a gunner at the Marne, did no better. After the bloody failure of his Chemin des Dames offensive he was replaced by Pétain, whose leadership and defensive skills had seen the army through the supreme ordeal of Verdun. Pétain was confronted by a series of mutinies – collective refusals by a minority of troops to sacrifice themselves in attacks that too evidently were ill-planned and mismanaged. In reimposing discipline he had some of the mutineers shot, but also addressed the troops' legitimate demands for long overdue improvements in conditions of service, such as better food, more leave and proper periods of rest. Morale remained a cause for concern, and for the remainder of that year the French army confined itself to local offensives methodically prepared by massed artillery. The major offensive that autumn was undertaken by the British army which, to ease the strain on French manpower, had progressively taken over nearly a third of the western front, holding 200 kilometres at the start of 1918 compared with 40 in 1914.

Might the war continue until the last German and Frenchman had slaughtered each other? Talk of a negotiated peace in certain political circles was scotched when President Poincaré appointed his bitter enemy Georges Clemenceau as premier in November 1917 to bring new vigour to the war effort. Despite deadlock on the western front, elsewhere the balance seemed to be tilting in Germany's favour. By December Russia, in the throes of revolution, had dropped out of the war, depriving France of the support of an ally whose co-operation had been fundamental to her strategy. German victory in the east, together with her conquest of Romania in 1916, opened the prospect of greater sources of food to offset the severe shortages being imposed by the British naval blockade. Italy needed the support of French and British divisions after a severe defeat by German and Austrian troops at Caporetto in October. On the other hand, the German submarine offensive in the Atlantic had provoked the USA into declaring war on her in April 1917, giving a great morale boost to France and Britain: but it would be summer 1918 before America's fresh, if inexperienced, divisions could make their weight felt in France.

In March 1918 it was the Germans who broke the deadlock, gambling on using divisions released from the eastern front to strengthen them sufficiently to defeat the battle-drained British and French before the Americans could arrive in force. Ludendorff's succession of fast and furious blows, using short but overwhelming bombardments and infiltration tactics, fell first upon the British, who were pushed back within sight of Amiens before stabilizing their line. On 27 May the Germans struck at the French front and again made alarming inroads, particularly where some commanders paid insufficient heed to Pétain's prescriptions for defence in depth. By summer the Germans were back astride the Marne, pushing to within 60 kilometres of Paris. Since January the capital had experienced occasional air-raids by Gotha bombers, and from March had come under bombardment from a huge gun (nicknamed Big Bertha by Parisians with reference to Krupp's wife) from a distance of 120 kilometres. Between them these bombardments killed or wounded over a thousand citizens, giving front-line troops the satisfaction of knowing that civilians who had been living comfortably in the rear were now also exposed to the daily risk of death or dismemberment. As the Germans again approached the capital there was a fresh exodus of Parisians.[37]

The gravity of the crisis, and the danger that spring that the British and French armies might be forced apart, had persuaded the British to accept the offensive-minded Foch as commander-in-chief, with control of the strategic reserves. Though allied counterattacks at first met limited success, by July, with the Americans joining in, the tide of battle began to turn. As in 1914, the Germans proved unable to break the allies and had overextended their strength, leaving themselves exhausted and vulnerable to a counterstroke. As at the First Battle of the Marne, so in the second: the allies retained the manpower, weaponry and will to fight back. By August the Germans were in retreat as Foch orchestrated a series of offensives that pushed them back towards the frontier, capturing hordes of prisoners in the process. By September Ludendorff was in despair at looming defeat, and Germany's allies began to capitulate. In October she sought an armistice on the basis of President Woodrow Wilson's Fourteen Points. Finally, with revolution breaking out in Germany's fleet and cities, the Kaiser abdicated. With the authorization of the high command, a civilian delegation representing a new socialist-led German government accepted the armistice terms drawn up by the allies.

The armistice was signed at Marshal Foch's headquarters in a railway carriage at Rethondes in the Forest of Compiègne on 11 November 1918. By its terms German forces in the west were required to evacuate within fifteen days those parts of Belgium and France which they still occupied, as well as Luxembourg and Alsace-Lorraine. Within thirty-one days they must withdraw east of the Rhine, leaving the allies to occupy the left bank and three bridgeheads on the right bank at Mainz, Koblenz and Cologne. Germany was to repatriate all prisoners of war and civilian internees. To cripple her ability to resume hostilities, she was required to surrender specified large quantities of weapons, aircraft and vehicles plus all her submarines, while her surface fleet was to be disarmed and interned.[38]

In the French trenches news of the armistice was greeted with an ineffable relief. An army chaplain recorded that in his unit, 'There was not a single cheer, nor any drinking. Men just came together to shake each other's hands. The joy was too profound, too solemn, to be expressed in words or celebration.'[39]

Behind the lines it was a different picture. In Paris, huge crowds celebrated victory while all the bells pealed. 'Paris is joyful, fevered, delirious,' wrote President

Poincaré,[40] while far away in the Pyrenees a crowd gathered in tribute outside Joffre's family home in Rivesaltes. Still in exile in England, the exultant 92-year-old former Empress Eugénie exclaimed, 'Today I understand why God has made me live so long ... Our dead of 1870 have finally been repaid for their sacrifice.'[41] As French troops entered Alsace-Lorraine in the wake of the German evacuation, they were welcomed enthusiastically. Henri Desagneaux recorded in his diary that 'All the towns are decked out in the French colours, and the inhabitants are on their doorsteps.' Where his unit was billeted, 'the whole village is in a festive mood. We are received by the local dignitaries. Each one has got out his coat, his top-hat, and his Sunday-best suit. Everyone, young and old, is wearing a rosette. The children, led by the village priest, are carrying little French flags ...'[42]

Such scenes were repeated on a large scale when President Poincaré, in company with the leading allied generals, paid a triumphal visit to Metz on 8 December. At the station, at the Esplanade (where, in Joffre's presence, the president conferred a marshal's baton on Pétain), at the Hôtel de Ville and again in the cathedral, the cheers were deafening. Next day at Strasbourg the reception was if anything more frenetic still, and once again a group of veterans of 1870 were prominent in the ceremonial, receiving from Poincaré 'a long and respectful salute'. When he spoke of the dignified protest against annexation to Germany by the Deputies of Alsace-Lorraine in 1871 and turned to Clemenceau, who had voted with them in the French Assembly nearly half a century earlier, there was a huge ovation. Overcome by emotion at the French recovery of the 'lost provinces', Poincaré wrote of 'a supremely beautiful day', sighing, 'Now I can die.'[43] Victory was sweet, but amid the euphoria there was scarcely a community or household in France unmindful of the unimaginably terrible price that had been paid for it.

Part III

1940:
The Collapse

Night fell slowly. The leaden sky glowed red. Some of the men wondered whether war had already been declared ... Then in the silence a woman began weeping and wailing ... We could no longer doubt it. The war had begun.

Georges Sadoul, Metz, 3 September 1939

Part III

1940:
The Collapse

Chapter 13

In Search of Security

The scale of the killing in the Great War cast a shadow over a generation, marking the survivors and the families and friends of the dead as they grappled with its consequences for their own lives, for their communities and for France. The cold as marble figures still possess a bleak eloquence that defies commentary. In four years France had mobilized 8,410,000 men, roughly a fifth of her population and a greater proportional effort than any other major power.[1] The total of French servicemen who had died was established after the war as 1,397,800, or approximately one-sixth of those mobilized.[2] By one computation this meant that during the four years of the war on average 890 French servicemen died every day.[3] The French loss of nearly 1.4 million men compared to Germany's over 2 million, Russia's 1.8 million, Austria-Hungary's 1.1 million, the United Kingdom and British Empire's combined 921,000, Italy's 578,000 and the USA's 114,000.[4] In addition, 806,000 French soldiers had been invalided out for serious wounds and 2,800,000 were classified as wounded, even excluding those lightly wounded men who had returned to their units after a few days. Half the wounded had received two wounds.[5] As in every European country, severely disabled and disfigured men were to be a common sight for years to come. Less visible was the immense weight of grief and mourning which strove to find expression in the proliferation of national and local war memorials in the post-war years. Civic war memorials alone numbered over 36,000 in France, where the war left at least 630,000 widows and 719,000 fatherless children, counting only those relatives most immediately affected by soldier deaths.[6] For the bereaved, as for soldiers maimed in body or mind, the Armistice could bring no end to their suffering.

The material damage in the fought-over and occupied zones was also immense. Large areas of France's most productive and agriculturally most fertile regions in the north-east had been utterly laid waste. Over 220,000 houses had been destroyed and over 120,000 seriously damaged, along with 62,000 kilometres of road, 5,600 kilometres of railway and 1,800 kilometres of canal, plus hundreds of bridges, mines, factories, schools, churches and other public buildings.[7] To fight the war, France had spent some 143 billion francs, almost twenty-nine times her budget of 1914,[8] and had incurred a huge national debt through borrowing from her allies.

After such an ordeal, what kind of peace did France want, and was it within her power to attain it? The armistice terms imposed on Germany had reflected the French desire for occupation of the left bank of the Rhine. Some, like Poincaré, argued that the allies should have fought on until they had demonstrably defeated German armies on German soil.[9] Yet, as Foch pointed out, to have continued the campaign into 1919 would have cost tens of thousands of allied lives which they could ill spare, France least of all. There were fears too in British and French governing circles that it would become more difficult to maintain domestic unity and order if they opted to fight on after Germany had shown willingness to accept an armistice. Moreover, had the fighting continued, the USA would within months have built up the largest army in Europe, empowering her to dictate terms to enemies and 'associates' alike. As it was, Foch maintained, the armistice had given France all she could have hoped to gain by fighting on.[10]

Her sacrifice had been desolating, but France was victorious: her army was the strongest in Europe, while Germany was mired in civil turmoil. Yet France was still a nation of not quite 40 million, while Germany's population stood at around 65 million. Even the recovery of Alsace-Lorraine's 1.7 million inhabitants[11] could do little to offset the long-term consequences of France's declining birth rate, which had been aggravated by the war and the influenza epidemic that followed in its wake. In reality France had been able to win only with the support of allies. Germany's industries and fields remained undamaged by war, whereas it would take France a decade to repair the destruction hers had suffered. French statesmen knew from their own experience that defeated nations can rise again and recover by arms what has been lost by arms. The problems facing French politicians and generals were therefore twofold: the immediate challenge of repairing material losses and how to pay for them; and the larger, longer-term question of how France could protect herself from the recurrence of such a calamity given that her powerful neighbour must sooner or later revive. In practice these two questions became intertwined. In an atmosphere suffused with hatred for an enemy who had inflicted so much suffering, the peace conference convened in Paris in January 1919. It was chaired by the brusque, authoritarian 77-year-old prime minister, Clemenceau, whose caustic disposition was not improved by a bullet wound in the back inflicted by an anarchist who attempted to assassinate him on 19 February.

Majority opinion in France held that Germany must be permanently weakened through limitations on her armaments, loss of territory and huge payments in cash and kind. In formulating a peace treaty reflecting these aims, Clemenceau's problem was his need to gain the agreement of France's allies to her demands. Because France 'made war with allies,' he explained, 'we could not avoid making an allied peace'.[12] While Britain and the USA shared some of France's concerns, each had differing interests and priorities. Neither country had Germany as a land neighbour, and neither shared the acute apprehensions of the French about the potential danger to their frontier.

The British, for whom Germany had been a naval and imperial competitor, could take satisfaction from the elimination of Germany's fleet and the division among the victor nations of her colonial empire. There was broad agreement among the allies on measures to curtail her offensive capacity: strict limits on ship building, the prohibition of submarines, heavy artillery, tanks, aircraft, poison gas and the importation of arms and ammunition, and the abolition of her General Staff. Differences arose over the size and nature of the army Germany was to be allowed. Foch was content for her to retain an army of 140,000 short-term conscripts. The British prime minister, David Lloyd George, preferred to abolish conscription because in time it would furnish a large pool of trained men. Instead he urged that Germany should be limited to a long-service (twelve years) army of volunteers. Clemenceau accepted the British principle, but it was agreed to limit the German army to 100,000. Foch was ill content. Would not a small professional army provide Germany with the highly trained cadres that would enable its rapid expansion at a later date? He recalled Marshal Bugeaud's warning that 'an army of donkeys led by lions was more to be feared than an army of lions led by donkeys'.[13]

When it came to territorial claims the French generals of 1919, like their German counterparts in 1871, sought to deny their enemy his forward concentration areas from which any future invasion could be launched. This meant denying the Germans the Rhineland, and ensuring the demilitarization of a 50-kilometre zone beyond the river. For Foch, France's true defence line lay on the Rhine. Some of his generals dallied with German regional separatist groups. Right-wing pressure groups in France urged that the opportunity should be seized to undo Bismarck's handiwork by making the Rhine the western limit of German sovereignty. The Rhineland would become one or more buffer states under French protection, while France herself would extend her border eastward by reverting to her frontier of 1814. This would yield her not only Landau adjoining Northern Alsace, but the coalfields of the Saar, so necessary to the revival of her heavy industry.

When Clemenceau advanced these claims at the peace conference he met strong resistance from the British and Americans. They had shown some scepticism even about the return of Alsace-Lorraine without plebiscites, and dismissed claims that Rhinelanders still nurtured residual French sympathies. Wilson threatened to leave the conference after a heated exchange with Clemenceau over the issue, and Lloyd George warned of the dangers of creating an Alsace-Lorraine in reverse by annexing German territory. Neither wanted to see France revert to her Revolutionary and Napoleonic borders and suspected her of aiming to establish hegemony in Europe. They were prepared to accept only the restoration of the frontier of 1815–70. Nevertheless they agreed to the French government taking over the German state-owned coalmines of the Saar in compensation for the Germans' deliberate destruction of French mines. The Saar region would remain under allied occupation for fifteen years under the auspices of Wilson's proposed League of Nations. A plebiscite would then decide its future. The Rhineland would also remain under allied occupation for a temporary period only, but to assuage French anxieties Wilson and Lloyd George offered to guarantee France against unprovoked aggression. Clemenceau accepted, realizing that he was unlikely to get more and that allied co-operation and assistance were essential to French security. Besides, the clauses governing the

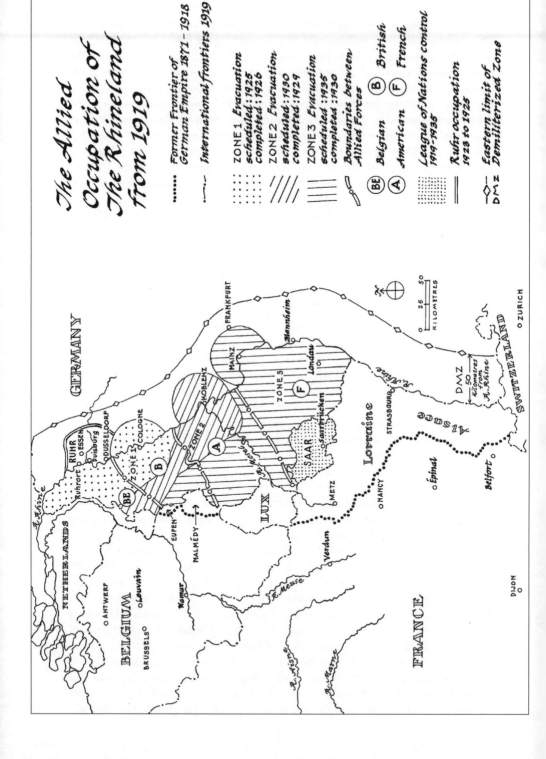

The Allied
Occupation of
The Rhineland
from 1919

Former Frontier of
German Empire 1871 – 1918

International frontiers 1919

ZONE 1 Evacuation
scheduled : 1925
completed : 1926

ZONE 2 Evacuation
scheduled : 1930
completed : 1929

ZONE 3 Evacuation
scheduled : 1935
completed : 1930

Boundaries between
Allied Forces

(BE) Belgian   (B) British
(A) American   (F) French

League of Nations control

Ruhr occupation
1923 to 1925

Eastern limit of
DMZ Demilitarized Zone

phased evacuation of the Rhineland at three five-year intervals gave France the right to remain if Germany failed to fulfil her treaty obligations. Clemenceau expected Germany to default, so calculated that this opened a way for France to exert pressure indefinitely.

The peace conference also agreed that Germany should be weakened by losing some of her borderlands. In the west, Eupen and Malmédy went to Belgium in partial compensation for her losses. In the north, a plebiscite was to be held which resulted in the return of northern Schleswig to neutral Denmark, so finally fulfilling a stipulation which at French insistence Bismarck had included in his peace treaty with Austria in 1866 but had never honoured. In the east about 2 million Germans found themselves living in a revived Polish state which incorporated parts of the old Prussia. To make Poland viable it was given access to the Baltic by the award of a corridor of territory running down to the largely German port of Danzig, which was designated a free city. Although Germany lost no territory to her south, she would be bordered by the new state of Czechoslovakia, which included 3 million German former subjects of the defunct Austrian Empire living in the Sudetenland. The successor states to the shattered empires remained weak, quarrelsome and internally divided, and several contained a significant German population. They looked to France for patronage and protection, particularly given the turbulent and often desperate condition of post-war Central and Eastern Europe following the disintegration of Austria-Hungary. France in turn saw the successor states as instruments both for containing Germany and as a *cordon sanitaire* against the spread of communism from Russia, and hoped that they might at least partially fill the void left by the collapse of the old Russian Empire as her military partner. Over the coming years France would conclude defensive alliances with Poland (1921), Czechoslovakia (1924), Romania (1926) and Yugoslavia (1927).

In seeking to truncate and isolate Germany, Clemenceau was applying Bismarck's techniques towards France in reverse, and he did not neglect the third means employed by the Iron Chancellor to weaken his opponent: the imposition of severe financial penalties. Like Bismarck, he had no faith that moderate terms would diminish the danger to his country. Initial French claims included a requirement for Germany to repay the indemnity France had paid under the Treaty of Frankfurt, with interest. They and the British at first talked of making Germany responsible for the entire war expenses of the allies. President Wilson was opposed to war indemnities in principle, and would not countenance inflated claims. Nevertheless, the French and British insisted Germany must bear the full cost of all the damage it had caused during the war, including the cost of war pensions. As a legal basis for reparations, the peace treaties included what the allies considered a simple statement of fact, the so-called 'war-guilt clause' (Article 231), whereby Germany accepted responsibility for having caused 'all the loss and damage to which the allied and associated governments and their nationals have been subjected as a consequence of the war imposed upon them by the aggression of Germany and her allies'. What the amount of reparations should be set at, how it should be divided between the allies, and how much Germany could realistically be asked to pay were discussed at length and inconclusively by commissions of experts. Although Lloyd George, like Clemenceau, had to meet the expectations of an electorate that was in no mood for moderation or conciliation, upon reflection the British delegation became anxious lest Germany be destroyed as a trading partner or turned into a fertile seedbed for the spread of Bolshevism. As Lloyd George put it, 'We cannot both cripple her and expect her to pay.'[14] All that could be agreed in Paris was that Germany should pay 20 billion gold marks pending a full assessment of her liability by a panel that would report in 1921. This open-ended arrangement suited the French, for it provided a means not only of keeping Germany weak, but of transferring a significant share of her financial and mineral resources to France to help her rebuild, pay down her debts and reduce the disparity in strength between the two nations.

In Russia and Romania Germany had shown what kind of terms she imposed when she was the victor. Now it was her turn to pass under the yoke. In May 1919 the German delegation was summoned to Paris to be presented with the allies' peace terms. They could only protest. The common German view was that they had accepted the armistice on the basis of Wilson's Fourteen Points, and considered themselves cheated by being compelled to submit to a dictated peace. Wilson's high-flown principles now seemed to them only a cover for the despoliation of Germany. The principle of national self-determination was, it seemed to them, to be applied to everyone except Germans. (At Clemenceau's behest, the allies specifically forbade the 6½ million Germans of the rump state of Austria to join Germany, despite their wish to do so.) The 'war-guilt clause' provoked fierce and abiding resentment, and Germany was being asked to sign a blank cheque for reparations. Yet the armistice terms had deprived her of the means of resuming the war, and the allied blockade remained in place. Faced with the threat of allied invasion and occupation, the German government agreed to sign.

Germany was regarded in allied countries as a pariah state, and Germans as a nation of criminals. On 16 June their delegation was stoned by French nationalists. The signing ceremony took place on 28 June, the fifth anniversary of the assassination of Franz Ferdinand and his wife. To emphasize the reversal of 1871, the ceremony was held in the Hall of Mirrors in the Palace of Versailles, where Bismarck had proclaimed the German Empire nearly half a century before. Thenceforth in Germany the new republic bore the stigma of having submitted to national humiliation. No German government would ever accept the Versailles settlement as fair and reasonable, any more than the French had ever accepted the peace treaties of 1815 or 1871 as final.

An impressive victory parade was staged in Paris a fortnight later, on 14 July 1919, for the Bastille Day celebrations. A thousand war-wounded passed through the Arc de Triomphe, preceding Marshals Joffre and Foch riding at the head of allied and French troops. In a sense the day marked the apogee of French power in the twentieth century and the Versailles settlement bore a strong French imprint. Yet the allied solidarity that underpinned victory was already fraying. Britain and France were reverting to colonial rivalry, squabbling over the carcass of the late Ottoman Empire, and were beginning to view each other as potential enemies. The

British were having second thoughts that the treaty was too severe and risked provoking Germany into seeking to overthrow it at the first opportunity, particularly along her eastern frontier. Clemenceau was contemptuous. If the British wanted to appease the Germans, said he in effect, let them hand back some of their own gains. 'The Tiger' was equally scathing about those at home who attacked him for not being harsh enough and for having conceded too much to the allies. For if his disputes with other members of the 'Big Three' had been occasionally stormy, his confrontations behind the scenes with hard-liners like Poincaré and Foch had been scarcely less explosive. Urging the National Assembly to approve the treaty, Clemenceau argued that its detailed provisions mattered less than the will to enforce it. 'It will be worth what you make it worth,' he warned.[15] The treaty was approved by a comfortable majority in October, with only the socialist minority voting against and some disgruntled nationalists abstaining.

In January 1920 Clemenceau left the scene, retiring to private life after a parliamentary manoeuvre by his opponents denied him the presidency. In March his handiwork seemed to have been vitiated when the United States Senate failed to ratify the treaty. This meant that Wilson's grand project of a League of Nations to keep the international peace would have to function without the participation of the USA. The League would in any case have no army of its own. When France had championed such a force her allies would not hear of it. Worse still for France, America's desire to disengage from European commitments meant that Wilson's promise of a formal guarantee of France's eastern frontier had evaporated. The British guarantee, which had been contingent upon it, also failed to materialize, leaving France bitter at having been let down by '*les Anglo-Saxons*'. Privately Foch complained of the folly of having accepted an 'English peace' which left France insufficiently protected, and that the chance to dismember Germany had been traded for a worthless promise: 'The prey we held has been abandoned for a shadow.'[16]

Successive French governments intended to enforce the treaty nevertheless, with or without allied support. They were backed by the strongly conservative and patriotic majority of the *Bloc national*, the so-called 'Horizon-blue Chamber' elected in November 1919 – the French equivalent of Britain's khaki election. Rather than impose heavier taxes at home or incur even larger debts, French governments were adamant that Germany would pay for reconstruction and war pensions. 'Germany will pay' was the watchword.[17] However, even with a strong will to exact payment, obtaining the sums envisioned from Germany proved frustratingly difficult. The Germans, pleading inability to pay, used delaying tactics. At the Spa conference in July 1920 the allies agreed that France should receive 52 per cent of all reparations, but Germany would not agree to a figure, and had her scheduled deliveries of coal and coke scaled down with the support of Britain, which had no wish to see her coal squeezed out of the French market. Nor were any 'war criminals' ever handed over to the allies as stipulated in the treaty, and inspections to enforce disarmament raised doubts about German compliance. Allied frustration at German evasions led to harsher measures. In March 1921 a Franco-British force occupied Düsseldorf, Ruhrort and Duisburg. In April the allies unilaterally fixed the amount Germany must pay at 132 billion gold marks, payable in annual instalments. Premier Briand threatened that if Germany attempted to wriggle out of paying she would feel 'a firm hand fall upon her collar',[18] and in May the allies issued an ultimatum to Germany that she must accept that figure and fulfil her obligations or face the occupation of her industrial heartland of the Ruhr.

When Germany accepted, Britain declared herself satisfied; but the French suspected, not without some justification, that the German move was purely tactical. By December Germany was asking for a moratorium on payments because of her chronic financial difficulties. Yet there was evidence that German heavy industry was on its way to recovering pre-war production levels, while that of France languished. Far from being crippled by the loss of Lorraine iron ore, as the French had expected, Germany had found alternative sources of supply in Sweden and Spain. German industrialists, who heavily influenced policy, were building up gold reserves in foreign banks. By the end of 1922, after the latest in a series of German requests for a moratorium on reparations, this time for four or five years, French patience was exhausted.

The wartime president, Raymond Poincaré, who had been critical of recent ministries for their failure to make Germany pay her due, had been recalled to the premiership. Unconvinced by last-minute German offers, he ordered French troops to occupy the Ruhr on 11 January 1923, securing a large vote of confidence from the Chamber. His only opponents were the socialists and the new Communist Party, which had split off from them in 1920 and was affiliated to the Third International in Moscow. France had one willing ally, Belgium, which had abandoned the neutrality that had failed to protect her in 1914. Otherwise she was isolated. The British and Americans disapproved and did not participate. Increasingly they saw France as the aggressor and the main obstacle to the stabilization of Europe.

Franco-Belgian forces met a hostile reception in the Ruhr. German civilians resented foreign occupation as much as Belgian and French citizens had in 1914. Berlin organized a campaign of passive resistance with payments for strikers. France retaliated by expelling 37,000 German officials and strikers.[19] There were bloody incidents: thirteen died in a clash at the Krupp works in Essen on 31 March. Resistance was not always passive. Nationalist Freikorps volunteers sabotaged trains carrying coal and coke to France, among them a veteran of Verdun named Schlageter. His execution by the French made him a martyr in Germany. In all, 141 German civilians died during the occupation. A virulent propaganda campaign portrayed the Germans as innocent victims of brutal French militarism and imperialism, just as lurid German cartoons had made much of alleged rapes by French North African troops in the Rhineland. German nationalism was inflamed to fever pitch against France. The Franco-Belgian forces were undeterred, sticking to their purpose of protecting their own engineers and workers who extracted the coal and transported it to France without German co-operation. French customs barriers divided occupied from non-occupied Germany. French generals indicated that they might stay for years, and provided encouragement and arms to regional separatist movements.

In this 'Battle of the Ruhr' it was the Germans who backed down. Their hyper-inflated currency, the mark, had finally been reduced to worthlessness by the crisis. Hopes of British mediation proved vain, and the country seemed in danger of breaking up as social unrest and revolutionary outbreaks by the extremes of Left and Right multiplied. In September a new government in Berlin under Gustav Stresemann ordered the end of passive resistance and co-operation with the allied authorities. Poincaré had carried his point, but at high cost. The value of the raw materials France had extracted from the Ruhr fell below expectations. As in Germany, though not to the same degree, the weight of government debt was weakening the currency, and by late 1923 the franc was falling alarmingly. Revived French plans for making a buffer state of the Rhineland were shelved as Poincaré yielded to the need for British and American loans. A committee of experts under the American General Dawes was convened to find a solution to the reparations issue. Amid disillusion at the meagre results of Poincaré's hard-line policy, inflation, government cuts and rising taxation, in the May 1924 elections the *Bloc national* was defeated by a left-of-centre coalition, the *Cartel des gauches*, which from ideology and necessity was more inclined to conciliation. Poincaré left office, denounced by the Left and by liberals abroad as a 'warmonger', a view encouraged by the dissemination of German-subsidized literature arguing tendentiously that the Franco-Russian alliance bore responsibility for the outbreak of war in 1914. After the Ruhr, France lost her appetite for armed intervention in Germany.

The Dawes committee produced a plan that was accepted by all parties in 1924. In return for American loans to help put her economy back on its feet, Germany agreed to a firm schedule of reparations payments. For her part, France would evacuate her troops from the Ruhr within a year and dismantle the administrative regime she had established in the Rhineland. The agreement laid the basis for a few years of improved relations under leaders who sought to steer their countries away from confrontations neither could afford and towards compromise – Stresemann in Germany and in France Aristide Briand who, despite frequent changes of government, held the Foreign Ministry from 1925 to 1932. As prosperity revived in the mid-1920s, Franco-German relations appeared to be returning to normality. In the autumn of 1925 the Locarno agreements saw Germany recognize the eastern frontiers of France and Belgium, which Britain and Italy guaranteed against aggression. In 1926 Germany took a permanent seat on the council of the League of Nations in Geneva, having equal status with the victors of 1919. In 1926–7 the French and Germans settled their commercial disputes by treaty and signed an agreement allocating production quotas for coal and steel. In 1928 France and Germany were among the nations which signed the Kellogg–Briand pact outlawing war as a means of settling international disputes and committing themselves to seeking arbitration. Shortly afterwards Poincaré who, despite the left-wing press campaign against him, had been recalled as premier in 1926 to stabilize the falling franc, met with Stresemann and agreed that the reparations issue which had so embittered Franco-German relations must be finally resolved. In 1929 another conference agreed the resulting plan produced by American financier Owen

D. Young, which effectively reduced Germany's reparations liability and spread the payments over fifty-nine years to 1988. Under the plan, France withdrew her occupation troops from Germany in 1930, five years ahead of the date fixed by the Treaty of Versailles. Meanwhile, in 1929 Briand presented a proposal to the League of Nations for a European Federation, with every member guaranteeing the others' frontiers.

These developments went hand in hand with a growing spirit of optimism and enthusiasm for conciliation, often called the spirit of Locarno. Pacifism had become an article of faith for a large portion of the French Left as a tide of revulsion at the barbarity and waste of war ran strongly. Exchange visits between French and German students and other professional and religious groups were encouraged, and there were high hopes that humanity was moving towards a better future without war. In 1926 Stresemann and Briand received the Nobel peace prize.

Yet Stresemann and Briand were not pacifists or doctrinaire idealists, nor did they place naïve trust in the intentions of the other. Both were pragmatists who recognized that they had to pursue their strategies within the limitations imposed by the reduced strength of their respective countries. Behind a genuine desire for compromise and glowing public announcements of harmonious agreement lay a history of hard bargaining, disappointments and serpentine attempts to out-manoeuvre the other. Both worked in the knowledge that their attempts to build bridges with the ex-enemy would draw suspicion and fierce criticism from the nationalist Right.

Stresemann had been conspicuously successful in negotiating the early evacuation of French troops from German soil, and through a policy of co-operation had ensured a continuing flow of American and British money into Germany. Any concessions he had made on reparations could, after all, be renegotiated at a more favourable time. If he had recognized France's eastern frontier, he had by the same token reaffirmed German sovereignty west of the Rhine. Moreover, while stabilizing Germany's position in the west he had eluded all French attempts to get Germany to recognize her frontiers with Poland and Czechoslovakia as permanent. If he had accepted Germany's loss of Alsace-Lorraine, it was already evident that French attempts to re-assimilate the 'lost provinces' were proving far more troublesome than had been imagined amid the euphoria of 1918. The French government's doctrinaire imposition there of the anti-clerical regime applied to the rest of France before the war revived the Alsatian autonomist movement, which Germany covertly subsidized. Covertly, too, Germany was experimenting with new weapons in violation of Versailles, and allied armaments inspections ended in 1927. By negotiation Germany was dismantling both the sanctions imposed on her in 1919 and the means by which the ex-allies might bring pressure to bear on her. The continuing strength of nationalist feeling in Germany was revealed by the widespread celebrations that accompanied the departure of the last French troops in June 1930.

On the French side, Briand could point to the less tangible benefits of his policy. Rather than persisting in attempts to ruin and destabilize Germany, was it not more advantageous to France's long-term security to encourage and work with the

Weimar Republic, since a stable democracy was more likely to be pacific than a Germany led by its opponents? France was collecting regular reparations payments without the costs of occupation. Locarno had committed Germany to accepting at least part of the Versailles treaty voluntarily rather than by *diktat*, including the frontier of Alsace-Lorraine and the demilitarization of the Rhineland, and France had a British guarantee of her frontier, albeit in limited terms.

Yet France had failed in successive attempts to strengthen the powers of the League of Nations as a means of reducing her isolation. Britain had positioned herself as a mediator between Germany and France rather than as an ally. The anodyne pacifist declaration of the Kellogg–Briand pact was a poor substitute for the American guarantee of her frontier that France had sought. Alerted by the Americans to the negotiations, Stresemann thwarted French intentions by suggesting a broadening of the agreement into a general multi-lateral declaration. German co-operation with the west also strengthened her argument (echoed within France by socialists and communists) that France too should disarm, and that her failure to do so was inconsistent with a genuine desire for conciliation. Beneath the rhetoric, a quiet contest of wills was being waged between the French desire to maintain and strengthen the frontiers set by the Versailles settlement and the German desire to revise them as soon as she could. The Germans assisted in burying Briand's proposal for a European Federation because it would have committed them to accept existing frontiers.

From the time of the Wall Street crash in October 1929 (three weeks after Stresemann's premature death), Franco-German relations deteriorated once more. With the flight of American capital from Germany and the growth of mass unemployment there, Germans increasingly saw reparations payments to a vindictive France as the root of all their hardships. Wracked by economic crisis, Germany ceased all payments under the Young Plan in June 1931. The German government, supported by Britain, requested France to abandon reparations. At the Lausanne conference in 1932 France agreed that Germany should make one final payment of 3 billion gold marks, but even that was never to be paid. By one estimate Germany had paid about 22 billion of the 132 billion gold marks imposed in 1921.[20] Less than 9 billion of that went to France, which had after all to meet the cost of her own war pensions and about 70 per cent of the costs of reconstruction. It remained a source of deep resentment in France that British and American leniency with regard to Germany's reparations had appeared to go hand in hand with their insistence that France repay them its war loans in full.

Another aspect of Versailles seemed to be unravelling. In March 1931 there was alarm in Paris when Berlin, pleading economic necessity, announced a plan to form a customs union with Austria, and during the summer announced commercial agreements with Romania and Hungary. The leaders of the faltering Weimar Republic were being stridently denounced by Hitler and his National Socialist Party as 'November criminals' and traitors who by accepting the Young Plan had condemned Germans to generations of slavery. Eager to outbid nationalist attacks by claiming some foreign policy success, they sought to extend German influence into the lands of the former Austro-Hungarian Empire. Concerned that these moves were a prelude to German political domination, France persuaded Britain to join with her in using financial leverage against Austria to block the German move. It was the last instance of a successful French initiative to try to control the expansion of her restless and internally troubled larger neighbour.

The disarmament conference at Geneva in 1932 brought confrontation between Germany and France. Wilson's idealism had inspired the Versailles treaty to commit all members of the League of Nations to 'the reduction of national armaments to the lowest point consistent with national safety'. Now Germany challenged France either to reduce her armaments or to agree to German parity. On the horns of a dilemma, France countered by proposing a joint collective security force under the League of Nations. The Germans withdrew from the conference in protest, and were lured back only by support for their position from the British and Americans.

The French feared that German rearmament had already begun, and that in a new arms race Germany's industrial strength must make her the winner. French military planners had already accepted that the revival of German power was inevitable, that France's post-war moment of superiority was passing and with it her ability in isolation to coerce Germany by reoccupying the Rhineland. Studies conducted during the 1920s recommended the construction of strong fortified zones to protect her eastern frontier against a possible sudden attack by a resurgent Germany.

The planning of a new line of fortresses owed much to the memory of 1914, when France had been handicapped by the early loss of key industrial areas and much territory besides, at a heavy cost in casualties. By fortifying her newly recovered frontier most strongly around Metz and Longwy she sought to keep it inviolate. Further fortified zones along the northern frontier of Alsace and the mountainous frontier of Italy would enable France to make the most economic use of her manpower and buy her time to mobilize her reserves. The experience of attempting to recapture their own forts from the Germans at Verdun had convinced the French that fortresses could still impose a significant delay on an enemy. The latest advances in design and technology developed from wartime experience would make France's defences more formidable than the outdated Belgian and French structures that the Germans had reduced within weeks in 1914. Priority was given to building fortifications on suitably defensible hilly ground along the new frontier with Germany. Preliminary work began in 1929, with funding voted early in 1930. The bill was pushed through by War Minister André Maginot – the same who had described the solemn crowds at the Gare de l'Est in August 1914. A wounded war hero, Maginot died of typhoid in 1932, and in 1935 the new fortifications were officially named in his honour – the Maginot Line.

France's embrace of concrete and steel gun-turrets and bunkers was aimed partly at deterring Germany, partly to demonstrate to other powers that her own intentions were not aggressive. Yet the Maginot Line was not conceived as an all-sufficient shield from German attack, rather as the keystone of a strategy that would allow French forces to manoeuvre in the flat open plains of the north where the ground was less suitable for building a dense and hugely costly chain of fortresses. If the Germans again came through Belgium it would make sense for the French to advance to meet them there and to fight them beyond her own borders. The area between Montmédy and the Channel was only lightly provided with fortifications. Sometimes portrayed with hindsight as a monumental folly, at the time it was constructed the Maginot Line seemed a logical solution to France's strategic need to defend Alsace and Lorraine with the fewest possible forces against an enemy likely to grow more powerful with every passing year.[21] With the upsurge of aggressive nationalism in Germany fuelled by defeat and the depression, with allies that were uncertain at best, France looked to her own defences for that lasting security which, despite all her sacrifices only a dozen years earlier, still eluded her.

Chapter 14

Facing Hitler

On 30 January 1933 Adolf Hitler became Chancellor of the German Reich and began consolidating his power within Germany. Within months he embarked on a series of brazen challenges to the victors of 1918, each time testing their resolve to stop him dismantling the Versailles settlement step by step. His initiatives would dictate events in Europe for the rest of the decade, yet in every confrontation he proved a master at presenting Germany as an oppressed victim and himself as the restorer of justice. His success in posing as the aggrieved party was important not only in carrying German opinion with him but in persuading those willing to be persuaded in Britain and France that he was acting with justification. In October 1933 he justified Germany's withdrawal from the disarmament conference and the League of Nations as a protest against France's refusal to grant Germany 'equal rights' in the matter of armaments, all the while professing his devotion to peace. 'Only a madman', he declared in a reassuring radio broadcast that evening, could dream of a war between Germany and France.[1] A referendum in Germany the following month overwhelmingly approved his action. In press interviews and well-publicized meetings with French war veterans Hitler professed his horror of war. He had assured the French ambassador in Berlin of his willingness to abide by the Locarno agreements. 'If I have one ambition,' he declared, 'it is that some day a monument will be raised to me as the man who reconciled France and Germany.'[2]

Louis Barthou, who became French Foreign Minister in 1934, was unconvinced. Aged 71, he was perhaps the last French statesman in the Poincaré mould. As prime minister in 1913 he had introduced the three-year conscription law and had lost his son at Thann in 1914. To him vigilance against Germany and restraining her ambitions remained the primary goal of French foreign policy. He was among the few Frenchmen who had read Hitler's *Mein Kampf*, publication of which in French the Führer attempted unsuccessfully to prevent. In it France was variously characterized as 'the most terrible enemy', 'the hereditary enemy', 'the moral enemy' and 'the mortal enemy' of the German people. In Hitler's world-view France supposedly was in thrall to the occult power of international Jewry, while her African immigration threatened to achieve the 'racial pollution' of Europe. Because France 'inexorably strangles us and robs us of our strength', Germany must ally herself with other powers who found French hegemony intolerable and prepare 'for a reckoning' with France. 'Every sacrifice' must be made for the overthrow of the power of 'our grimmest enemy'.[3] When Hitler's emissary Ribbentrop visited Barthou in March 1934 he made light of the book, written under the impression of the Ruhr occupation and published in 1925, as outmoded by events. Then why, queried Barthou, was it being constantly reprinted in Germany?[4]

A fortnight later Germany announced a substantial increase in her military budget, whereupon the French government determined to stand up to continuing pressure from Britain to disarm. In a note of 17 April 1934 it made clear to London that 'The French government refuses to legalize the rearmament of Germany, which has rendered all negotiations pointless. Henceforth France will assure her security by her own means.'[5] In practice, this amounted to little more than continuing work on the Maginot Line. The rest of the French forces were starved of funds by deep budget cuts: for instance, France produced only three tanks that year.[6] That summer's events – Hitler's 'Night of the Long Knives' in June and the murder of the Austrian Chancellor Dollfuss by Nazis in July – convinced Barthou that 'no one could count on Germany's peaceful intentions or honest purposes'[7] – a truth that was to dawn rather more slowly on some of his colleagues. Barthou spent months touring central Europe, Russia and Italy in attempts to foster co-operation with France in containing Germany. His efforts were cut short on 9 October when he was mortally wounded at Marseille as he sat with King Alexander of Yugoslavia at the moment when a Croat terrorist approached their car unchallenged and shot the king dead.

In January 1935, as stipulated by the Treaty of Versailles, the inhabitants of the Saarland voted on their future, 90 per cent opting for reunion with Germany against only a tiny percentage for France. A delighted Hitler had declared that this was the last issue dividing France and Germany.[8] Nevertheless, on 10 March Göring announced the creation of the Luftwaffe. Seeing German rearmament proceeding apace, France took heed of the gaps that would open in the ranks of her army during the 'hollow years' of 1935–9 as a direct consequence of the fall in her birth rate in 1914–18. In the wake of victory she had reduced her period of conscription to eighteen months in 1923, then to one year in 1928. To keep her forces up to strength, on 15 March 1935 conscription was increased to two years' service. Hitler's riposte the very next day was to reintroduce conscription in Germany. On the 25th he announced a naval rebuilding programme, but stressed his 'moderation' with an assurance that the tonnage of his fleet would be only 35 per cent of Britain's. To French dismay, Britain accepted the situation by signing the Anglo-German Naval Agreement in June without consulting France.

French diplomatic initiatives to build bridges with fascist Italy and communist Russia bore little fruit after Barthou's death. Mussolini understood from his conversations with the new French Foreign Minister, Pierre Laval, that in return for an alliance France was prepared to allow him a free hand to conquer Ethiopia. But Mussolini's attack on that African member of the League of Nations stirred outrage in Britain, both on moral grounds and from apprehensions of a potential threat to British interests in Egypt. To retain the British friendship that was essential to France, Laval reluctantly supported British proposals for League of Nations sanctions against Italy: sanctions that failed to halt Italy's campaign of conquest, but were sufficient to enrage Mussolini and to drive him into Hitler's orbit. Meanwhile, Laval's talks with the Russians, who showed signs of wanting a closer military alliance, produced only a rather convoluted mutual assistance pact which, when ratified by the French legislature in February 1936, gave Hitler the pretext for his boldest coup yet.

On Saturday, 7 March German forces rapidly reoccupied the Rhineland as far as the border with France, flouting both the Treaty of Versailles and the Locarno agreements. Hitler justified the move by asserting that the Franco-Soviet pact had already made Locarno a dead letter. He explained to the Reichstag that centuries of useless strife between France and Germany could be ended only on the basis of equality for Germany. Once again he covered an aggressive act with a barrage of proffered peace negotiations, stressing that the forces he had sent into the Rhineland were merely 'symbolic'. He offered to discuss a demilitarized zone on both sides of the Franco-German border – which would have required the French to demolish the Maginot Line.

Some of Hitler's generals had been anxious about the move, scarcely daring to hope that the French would tolerate it. In retrospect the reoccupation appeared as a great lost opportunity to stop Hitler in his tracks. Even at the time Pope Pius XI told the French ambassador that, 'Had you ordered the immediate advance of 200,000 men into the zone the Germans had reoccupied you would have done everyone a very great favour.'[9] Hitler himself later boasted privately of the success of his bluff, asking, 'What would have happened ... if anybody other than myself had been at the head of the Reich! Anyone you care to mention would have lost his nerve. I was obliged to lie, and what saved us was my unshakeable obstinacy and my amazing aplomb.'[10]

Beyond an empty assertion by Premier Albert Sarraut that 'We will not leave Strasbourg exposed to the fire of German guns,'[11] French reaction resulted only in a protest. Subsequent explanations for their lack of a military response emphasized the refusal of the British to join them in resisting the move. In Britain the conviction prevailed that German forces were merely entering their own back yard. After all, they had been enthusiastically welcomed by the German population and a referendum on 29 March showed that Germans endorsed Hitler's actions with near unanimity. Moreover, France had no operational plan for a rapid military response and the advice of the general staff was discouraging. French military planning was based on the expectation of a long defensive war requiring the call-up of successive classes of reserves. While a light mechanized division had recently been created, there was no plan to deploy it offensively. Proponents of the creation of highly trained armoured divisions for the offensive, like Lieutenant Colonel Charles de Gaulle, found little favour. De Gaulle found a champion in the right-wing politician Paul Reynaud, but his advocacy of an elite professional military force was suspect to many republicans. The Left feared that his proposals would subvert the democratic ideal of 'the nation in arms' embodied in a conscript army whose only legitimate mission was national defence. De Gaulle's book *Vers l'armée de métier* (1934 – published in English as *The Army of the Future*) was more widely read and studied in Germany than it ever was in France: Hitler claimed to have read it 'again and again' and to have 'learned a great deal from it'.[12]

In reality, French acceptance of the remilitarization of the Rhineland was not determined solely by military considerations and lack of an ally, important though these were. There was no desire to repeat the Ruhr episode. To oppose Hitler by force meant launching a war against Germany from a standing start. However legally justifiable France's position, she could be portrayed as the aggressor, and would have to invade German territory against the will of the inhabitants. Claims that victory could have been won cheaply and easily need not be taken at face value.[13] Hitler's gamble was actually well calculated and timed – France was unlikely to mobilize while she had a caretaker government pending parliamentary elections in the spring. Although the long economic depression had aggravated corrosive class and ideological divisions within French society, a great majority across the political spectrum viscerally opposed another war, so oppressive was the memory of the last conflict. In France, too, the idea that Versailles had been an unfair settlement had gained credence. The fact that the Communist Party, after years of denouncing French militarism and imperialism, had lately veered around in favour of resistance in conformity with the latest instructions from Moscow, aroused the suspicions of many on the Right whose traditional Germanophobia had become subordinated to fear and hatred of Russian communism. Some warned that Moscow was trying to embroil France in a war with Germany for its own ends. The extreme Right admired the authoritarianism and much-vaunted 'dynamism' of the fascist states, sharing their contempt for an apparently outworn parliamentary democracy with its revolving door cabinets which seemed helpless in the face of the depression. Whilst a minority admired Hitler, more mistrusted him but regarded him as a lesser of evils and a necessary bulwark against communism. Nor were communists the only enemies they shared with Hitler. The residual anti-Germanism of the Right vented itself increasingly against the tens of thousands of German Jews already seeking refuge in France, and there was a revival of anti-Semitism not seen since the days of the Dreyfus Affair. Meanwhile the Socialists, who abhorred Hitler and Nazi ideology, were wedded to pacifism. In all, in the spring of 1936 the French public was no more prepared to risk war over the Rhineland than the military.

France paid a price for her passivity in the face of a direct challenge. She now seemed an unreliable ally to the states of eastern and central Europe. The Germans rapidly began building the Siegfried Line opposite the Maginot Line, both to protect German territory and to erect a strategic barrier against French forces if they attempted to march to the aid of Poland or Czechoslovakia, to whom in due course Hitler's attentions would turn. Even France's defensive strategy was undermined when Belgium, wary of compromising her independence and of provoking Germany, withdrew from her military alliance with France. French plans for a common defence of Belgium's eastern frontier in the event of a German attack would henceforth have to await the outbreak of hostilities and a Belgian invitation to French troops to enter her territory.

The passionately contested French elections of May 1936 saw the Left triumph as Socialists, Radicals and Communists joined together to form a Popular Front to demand social reforms such as paid holidays and the forty-hour week. The stimulus to unite had come not just from the reluctance of a National Assembly dominated by employers to deliver reform, but from the rise within France of right-wing Leagues which, whether or not they avowed it, were to a greater or lesser degree inspired by fascism, with all the trappings of paramilitary uniforms, flags, salutes, mass rallies and authoritarian leaders. The Leagues had fomented violent riots in Paris on 6 February 1934, triggered by revelations that a swindler, Stavisky, had been protected by members of the political establishment. Had the rioters been better organized they might have invaded the National Assembly. In the bloodiest scenes in Paris since 1871 the police opened fire. Seventeen people died in the riots, with nearly 1,500 injured. Violence flared again in a communist counter-demonstration three days later.

The Popular Front was the Left's response to the internal threat to the democratic, parliamentary republic from fascism. Heading it was the Socialist leader Léon Blum who, as a Marxist, Jew and intellectual, was a hate figure to the Right. In 1935 Charles Maurras, in the venomously anti-Semitic *Action française*, had pronounced him to be 'a man to be shot: in the back',[14] and in February 1936 Blum was severely beaten by right-wing thugs, only being saved by the intervention of some nearby building workers. One of the first items of business for the Popular Front was to ban the Leagues, which generally complied peacefully by transforming themselves into political parties. Yet political extremism and violence continued to simmer. The retired Marshal Franchet d'Espérey was amongst establishment figures secretly funding army officers who laid plans to thwart a feared communist coup, whilst a secretive right-wing anti-communist group called the *Cagoulards* committed occasional terrorist outrages.

Foreign affairs were low on the agenda of the Popular Front as it came to power amid a wave of euphoria among workers who occupied their factories for weeks on end in the belief that better lives and social justice were at last within their reach. The conservative, property-owning classes were on the other hand alarmed that they were seeing the beginnings of a communist revolution. As prime minister, Blum was at first preoccupied with brokering a deal with employers and then with trying to persuade strikers to return to work. Yet within weeks he had to confront the dilemmas posed by the outbreak of the Spanish Civil War in July. That brutal conflict exacerbated still further the ideological struggles that had superimposed themselves on the traditional pattern of French politics. Among Socialists, pacifism and opposition to fascism had seemed complementary beliefs, but now presented themselves as alternatives. Blum's first instinct was to provide support to the kindred left-wing republican government in Spain, the *Frente Popular*, against General Franco's nationalist uprising. Other members of his cabinet counselled caution. Might intervention conceivably ignite a similar struggle in France – with the Right, the Catholic Church and elements of the army arrayed against left-wing republican forces? With German and Italian forces openly intervening on Franco's side and the USSR supporting their opponents, might French participation bring on a wider European ideological war: one in which France could find herself encircled by fascist powers? In that scenario Italian and German forces in Spain would be well placed to cut France off from her North African colonies, on which Mussolini was already casting covetous eyes. Blum opted to join with Britain in a cautious policy of non-intervention, which in effect meant turning a blind eye to blatant German and Italian involvement. Unofficially a flow of volunteers and weapons did pass from France across the Pyrenees, but not in sufficient quantities to save Spanish republicans from defeat in early 1939, following which almost half a million refugees crossed into France and had to be housed in improvised camps. A neutral stance at least allowed the rapid establishment of correct relations with the victorious Franco, to whom Marshal Pétain was accredited as French ambassador.

Meanwhile in August 1936 Germany extended her period of conscription to two years, increasing the size of her army to 700,000 men. That November Mussolini referred publicly to the 'Rome-Berlin Axis'. In the face of mounting threats to France's position in Europe, the Popular Front government accepted the necessity of strengthening her defences. A major rearmament programme was begun under the direction of Defence Minister Édouard Daladier.

In March 1938, following a campaign of intimidation and subversion against its government, Hitler ordered German forces into Austria, extinguishing its independence. He had already overcome Mussolini's objections and was confident that there would be no reaction from the west. France was caught between governments when Hitler acted. He shortly organized a plebiscite in Austria which approved union with Germany almost unanimously, enabling him to claim legitimacy on the grounds of self-determination. His vision of a Greater Germany was gaining momentum, accompanied always by the siren call of his raucous, mesmerizing voice, the strident acclamations of the party faithful – and the covert arrest, beating or murder of any who dared oppose his regime.

By the spring of 1938 the Popular Front was moribund, beset as it was by intractable economic difficulties, continued strife between workers and employers, and resistance to its reforms by vested interests. The leader of the Radicals, Daladier – a dumpy, balding former history teacher from the south – became prime minister in April. Within weeks it became apparent that Hitler had set his sights on Czechoslovakia, with whom France had allied herself in 1924. Would France stand by her treaty obligations, forged in the days when Germany was militarily weak? The cabinet concluded that it could offer only diplomatic support. In July Foreign Minister Georges Bonnet, another wounded war veteran and a thoroughgoing appeaser, informed the Czechs that France would not support them militarily. The French government in its turn was aware that it could not expect armed support from Britain, whose Prime Minister Neville Chamberlain feared that a Franco-German conflict might draw Britain into a quarrel in which she had no direct interest and in which the support of her Dominions could not be guaranteed. Neither the British nor the French government wished to begin a war they might well lose.

Exaggerated estimates of German strength deepened their gloomy apprehensions, and the French were glad to play second fiddle to Britain as Chamberlain took the initiative in seeking a settlement with Germany, for the most part keeping the French informed after the event.

Chamberlain's policy was based on the assumption that Hitler's demands had some limit, and that addressing rationally all alleged German grievances arising from the Treaty of Versailles could bring peace and stability to Europe. Both the British and French considered offering to restore some of Germany's colonies surrendered in 1919 as the price of appeasement. When Hitler forced the crisis in September with a military build-up against Czechoslovakia, supposedly to protect the oppressed German minority in the Sudetenland, Britain and France agreed to accept his demands. They applied intense pressure not to Germany but to France's ally, Czechoslovakia, to yield the Sudetenland to Hitler, who responded by ratcheting up his demands, threatening to invade Czechoslovakia if the Sudetenland was not handed over immediately. This, he declared, 'is the last territorial claim which I have to make in Europe'.[15] Reluctantly, Britain and France prepared for war, Britain mobilizing her fleet, France her army. In eastern France station names were removed and windows were prepared for blackout as a precaution against the devastating air raids that were expected to follow immediately upon the outbreak of war. A civilian exodus from Paris began. As Daladier prepared to depart for the conference convened at Munich on Chamberlain's initiative, he was warned by General Vuillemin, the head of the Air Force, who had recently witnessed a Luftwaffe fly-past over Berlin, that if war broke out the French Air Force might be destroyed within a fortnight.[16] Daladier himself had served through the Great War, including at Verdun, and had earlier confessed to 'but one thought: to prevent the return of such atrocities'.[17]

At Munich Hitler stepped back from the brink of war, allowing Chamberlain to claim that the agreement signed on 30 September was 'peace with honour'.[18] Daladier allowed himself no such delusions about the humiliating concessions made by France. When he flew back to Le Bourget airport after Munich he expected to be booed and hissed. When he saw the huge cheering crowd welcoming him he was amazed, muttering, 'They're mad.'[19] Joy and relief that peace had been saved at the last minute were brief but intense in France, and reactions cut across traditional party lines. Broadly, many Socialists and the Far Right approved of Munich, while the Communists and a significant portion of the moderate Right were opposed or sceptical. Thus while the Communist paper *L'Humanité* described Munich as 'a diplomatic Sedan',[20] Socialist leader Blum wrote that 'There is not a woman or man in France who would refuse Mr Neville Chamberlain and Édouard Daladier their just tribute of gratitude. War has been averted.'[21] Blum's bitter opponent, former premier Pierre Flandin, was so ecstatic that he sent congratulatory telegrams to all the principals involved, including Hitler – an act for which the nationalist lawyer Jacques Renouvin publicly slapped his face during that November's remembrance ceremony at the Arc de Triomphe.[22] Although Daladier's stance was overwhelmingly approved by the Chamber, one dissenter, Henri de Kerillis, prophesied, 'Germany is insatiable and pitiless towards the weak, and you have just shown yourselves to be weak. Germany only respects the strong. You may think she will become quiet and peaceful but I tell you she will become demanding and terrible.'[23]

France's apparent weakness at Munich caused her prestige to slump in Europe and across the world. She had, after all, brought peace by sacrificing her ally, a democratic state with a significant army, defences and armaments industry. In the Italian Chamber on 30 November Deputies were emboldened to stage a scene in the presence of the French ambassador clamouring for French territories to which they laid claim, Tunisia, Corsica, Savoy and Djibouti.[24] Daladier responded that 'France will not give an inch of its territories to Italy, even if it means an armed conflict,'[25] and made a point of visiting Corsica, Algeria and Tunisia in January 1939, so signalling a new spirit of firmness towards both Mussolini and British pressure to make concessions to him.

Bonnet, on the other hand, still sought conciliation with the dictators. In December 1938, not long after the anti-Semitic attacks of *Kristallnacht* in Germany, Ribbentrop came to Paris and signed a document with him recognizing the Franco-German frontier. French ministers who were Jewish were not invited to the accompanying reception. In this era of 'pactomania', the agreement served only to further alarm the Russians, who had been excluded from the Munich conference despite their professed readiness to guarantee Czechoslovakia. They suspected the western powers of seeking to direct German aggression eastward, towards them. The British and French governments for their part remained suspicious of a communist regime they believed to be bent on subverting them, and whose bloodily purged army they thought likely to be ineffective. For Daladier, as for Blum before him, strengthening the alliance with Britain had to be the priority if France were to avoid being left to face Germany alone.

Before long Hitler's actions propelled Britain from appeasement of Germany towards a policy of deterrence and eventually resistance. The consequence was a marked shift in her attitude to France. For years British policy had been guided by an extreme reluctance ever again to become entangled in a costly European land war: hence her inclination to restrain the French and conciliate the Germans. Yet with every passing month after Munich evidence accumulated that Hitler's expansionist ambitions could never be sated. Alarmist reports suggested that he might be contemplating a strike eastwards into the Ukraine, or perhaps westwards against Switzerland or the Netherlands, accompanied by a bombing raid on London. In early February the British cabinet authorized staff discussions with the French and Chamberlain told the Commons that 'any threat to the vital interests of France ... must evoke the immediate co-operation of Great Britain'.[26] Since the 1920s many arguments had been advanced that alliances and military commitments had 'caused' the Great War, and Britain had been wary of them. Yet in the presence of a common danger, the necessity of Franco-British co-operation reasserted itself as a matter of survival, as it had in 1914–18. Germany's annexations had increased her population to 76 million[27] – an addition of 11 million – making her nearly twice as populous as France and endowing her with ever more of the resources she needed to wage war. Further expansion might make her unbeatable.

Chamberlain was influenced by another myth about the origins of the last war that enjoyed an undeservedly long life in France as well as Germany, namely that war might somehow have been prevented had the British government stated its intentions clearly at the start of the crisis.[28] That he had no intention of opening himself to similar allegations became evident after Hitler's next blow, which fell neither east nor west but south, against the defenceless remnant of Czechoslovakia, in March 1939. This time there was little pretence that self-determination for a German minority was the issue, any more than some supposed injustice arising from the Treaty of Versailles. The invasion was a naked act of aggression against a Slav state, ignoring the guarantee of Czechoslovakia's borders given at Munich by Britain and France. Neither at first reacted, but at the end of the month in a gesture of deterrence Britain guaranteed the independence of Poland and France followed suit. Meanwhile Hitler seized the German-populated city of Memel from Lithuania, while Mussolini added to the tension and sense of menace by occupying Albania on Good Friday, 7 April. Britain and France responded to the Axis by extending guarantees to Greece and Romania. Urged to do so by the French, in April Britain introduced conscription for the first time in peacetime. In May the French and Polish staffs met in Paris, and agreed that France would launch an offensive fifteen days after any German attack on Danzig or Poland. Bonnet, however, wished to pursue his own policy of disengaging from France's eastern commitments rather than increasing them, and deferred the political agreement with Poland that would have made the military protocol binding. German demands for Danzig escalated from March, and as summer passed signs of an impending attack were unmistakable.

In an editorial of 4 May the pacifist Marcel Déat asked why Frenchmen should die for Danzig, but his protest found few echoes. French opinion had hardened since Munich. The new tool of opinion polls had shown that at that time 57 per cent of people were in favour of the agreement, but also that 70 per cent thought that France and Britain should resist any new demand by Hitler. By July 1939 76 per cent of people thought that France should fight if Hitler attacked Danzig.[29] Both sides were locked in an armaments race and intelligence services scrutinized the other's military preparations assiduously. French rearmament was aided by the revival of the economy. Daladier's tough stance against an attempted general strike in November 1938 and his extension of the working week reassured French investors, who repatriated much of the gold they had invested abroad through mistrust of the Popular Front.[30] Acutely aware of how far they lagged behind Germany in aircraft numbers, the French belatedly strove to increase production. Nationalized in 1936, the French aircraft industry (like much of French industry generally) remained small scale and ill-geared to mass production compared to the German, British and American organizations. In an effort to close the gap with Germany some orders had to be placed in America. In the first eight months of 1939 French factories produced almost as many aircraft as in the previous three years combined.

With war looming, the last hope of deterring Germany appeared to lie in reviving the old military alliance with Russia. Taking the rather reluctant British in tow, Daladier sent a delegation to Moscow, but mutual distrust caused the negotiations to drag. A major difficulty was how the Russians could engage the Germans except by passing across the territory of Poland or Romania. Having beaten Russian armies back from the gates of Warsaw as recently as 1920, the Poles feared that once across their frontiers Russian troops would never leave, and refused to agree. Despite this impasse, the French and British hoped that the conduct of negotiations would in itself deter Hitler, whose military build-up along the Polish border they monitored anxiously. Then on 23 August came the thunderbolt of the Nazi–Soviet Pact, turning upside-down western assumptions that the ideological gulf between Nazis and communists made agreement between them unthinkable. Britain and France had been outbid by the Germans, who secretly offered to divide Poland with the Russians. Stalin, preoccupied with fighting the Japanese in the Far East, embraced the opportunity for peaceful gains in the west.

The Nazi–Soviet Pact was Hitler's signal for the war against Poland he was intent on starting. His previous successes had persuaded him, his generals and the German people of his genius and luck, and he did not intend this time to be cheated of military victory. Chamberlain reiterated Britain's intention of standing by her guarantee to Poland. Daladier wrote Hitler an emotional letter on 26 August pleading with him as one war veteran to another to keep the peace – to no avail.[31] Hitler believed that the French and British would back down as they always had before. 'But, ...', he wrote to Mussolini on 27 August, 'If ... it should come to a major war, the issue in the East will be decided before the two Western Powers can score a success. Then, this winter, at the latest in the spring, I shall attack in the West with forces that will be at least equal to those of France and Britain ...'[32] His attempts to isolate Poland from the west misfired, but nothing induced him to call off the attack. After a week of mounting tension and manufactured border incidents, the German invasion of Poland began before dawn on 1 September. The Poles, who had refused throughout to be bullied, fought to defend their independence.

The French cabinet meeting on the evening of 31 August was marked by tensions between appeasers and resisters. Bonnet wanted to accept an Italian proposal for a four-power conference at San Remo to consider all outstanding grievances deriving from the Treaty of Versailles. A prickly Daladier snubbed him, asking forcefully what purpose further conciliation would serve. It could only end in another Munich and more concessions to Germany: 'Suppose that we go and carve up Poland and dishonour ourselves ... then end up with a war anyway? The lesson of Munich is that Hitler's signature is worthless. We can't mobilize three million men every six months.'[33]

With news of Hitler's attack, general mobilization was ordered on 1 September and the National Assembly was convened on the 2nd, when it voted 69 billion francs in war credits. Yet, much to the impatience of the Poles, it took the British and French nearly three days to declare war formally on Germany. The delay was largely because the French Chief of General Staff, General Maurice Gamelin, wanted time both to evacuate civilians from the eastern frontier and to mobilize the army without the disruptive air raids the Poles were suffering. Bonnet meanwhile was still seeking a way out by pursuing the Italian conference idea. Unlike the British, he was prepared to negotiate even with German troops on Polish soil. Finally, Bonnet's tortuous attempts to wriggle out of French obligations to Poland were brought up short by pressure from London. Facing a revolt in the Commons at his apparent dilatoriness, Chamberlain despatched an ultimatum to Berlin on the morning of 3 September. The French followed the British lead a few hours later. Ambassador Robert Coulondre presented the ultimatum in Berlin at 12.30 p.m. 'Well then!' said Ribbentrop, 'France will be the aggressor.' 'History will judge,' replied the Frenchman. The ultimatum expired at 5 p.m.[34]

Thus France went to war, officially because her ally Poland had been attacked. It was a war that nobody in France had wanted or sought, but which the French government chose to accept rather than submit to the domination of Europe by an aggressive Germany bent on devouring her smaller neighbours at an accelerating rate. Some were to see French determination to resist as misplaced nostalgia for the days when her manpower and wealth permitted her to dominate the continent, coupled with an unwillingness to accept her reduced status. Yet self-defence was the prevailing motive. It needed no great foresight to grasp that sooner or later Hitler would turn his attentions to France, of whose ultimate defeat the Nazi rank and file sang and had long dreamed.[35] It seemed to make sense to accept his challenge before Germany grew any stronger, and to fight in alliance with Great Britain.

The decision for war was accepted without protest, even if there were none of the patriotic demonstrations of 1870 or 1914 – no flags, no flowers, no shouts of 'To Berlin!' This time nobody had any illusions about the nature of war. As in London and Berlin, grim resignation was the prevailing mood. Some even felt a sense of release after weeks of 'grotesque suspense'. American observers in Paris noted the impressive calm and order with which mobilization was carried out,[36] and reports from Prefects revealed the same picture in the provinces. One official wrote that the war was accepted as inevitable, 'because no one doubts that the peaceful governments have gone to the utmost limit possible'.[37] An editorialist at *Le Figaro* noted mournfully on 1 September: 'We knew that war had become inevitable with this gangster regime established in the heart of Europe, and yet now it has happened we can scarcely believe in the reality of this catastrophe.'[38]

Although a handful of pacifists were arrested for encouraging desertion, the percentage of men failing to report for duty was very small, as in August 1914. The phrase heard then was again current: 'We've got to put an end to this,' or sometimes more specifically, 'We've got to have things out with these people' [the Germans] or 'We've got to put an end to this Hitler nonsense.'[39] Yet the soldiers of 1939 were embarking on a very different war from the one fought by their fathers.

Chapter 15

A Peculiar Sort of War

'What now?' Hitler asked Ribbentrop when told of the British ultimatum on 3 September. Later that day he expressed his belief that the British and French would limit themselves to a war of economic blockade – 'a potato war', as he put it.[1] The allies had indeed settled on a mainly defensive strategy of blockade, which would have the double advantage of allowing them to mobilize their strength fully and increase war production while sparing lives until they were ready to take the offensive, perhaps in 1941. They believed that a long war would favour them, and were at first optimistic that cutting off Germany's raw materials would soon put her in difficulties and perhaps precipitate Hitler's overthrow.

Allied quiescence had its price: it abandoned the Poles to their harsh fate. General Gamelin had supposed that they could hold out until the spring, but within a month German forces crushed the Polish army and occupied Warsaw. Meanwhile, on 17 September the Russians advanced to claim their share of Polish territory. German and Russian troops met and shook hands at the River Bug. Gamelin had once urged the strategic advantages to France of 'a conflict beginning in central Europe, so that we would act as a secondary force against a Germany already engaged there with her principal forces'.[2] During the summer of 1939 he had insisted that French honour was bound up with its guarantee to Poland and on the importance of arming the Poles. He had also assured Daladier that the French army was ready for war. In the event, French weapons production was stretched to meet France's own needs, with little to spare for her allies. It also became apparent that Gamelin had meant only that the army was ready to defend France's frontiers. On 5 September the Poles were formally promised the offensive that they were pressing for, but what followed fell far short of their expectations.

The most inviting option for an advance into Germany – a rapid strike at the Ruhr through Belgium and Luxembourg – was politically off limits. That left the Franco-German border in Lorraine as the only feasible theatre of operations, but there the French faced the newly constructed Siegfried Line. From 8 September eleven divisions drawn from the French Third, Fourth and Fifth Armies probed cautiously into Germany on either side of Saarbrücken, meeting only light resistance from German rearguards but slowed by their first encounters with a new weapon – anti-personnel mines, which the Germans had sown along roads or rigged as booby-traps in abandoned villages. Newspapers and newsreels presented the advance as a triumphant major offensive, which was the impression Gamelin sought to give the Poles, assuring them on 10 September that 'More than half our active divisions ... are engaged ... The Germans are putting up vigorous resistance ... Prisoners indicate that the Germans are reinforcing their front with new large units ... We know that we are pinning down a considerable portion of their air strength.' He insisted that 'I have exceeded my promise to take the offensive with the bulk of my forces on the fifteenth day after mobilization. It has been impossible for me to do more.'[3]

None of this bore much resemblance to reality as the French crept forward about 15 kilometres into Germany, occupying some fifty villages, before halting when they came within range of the guns of the Siegfried Line. Gamelin quickly concluded that the Poles were finished and ordered his men to withdraw to their original positions, having lost 308 killed and 1,378 wounded.[4] The Germans followed them up in October, re-establishing themselves close to the frontier. They were greatly relieved, for in early September their western front had been held by only thirty-five mediocre divisions, poorly equipped and with not a single tank. France at that time had eighty-five divisions deployed, and would never again enjoy such favourable odds.

Why did Gamelin hold back? He pleaded the inadequate training of many of his reservists and the necessary delay in bringing up heavy artillery,[5] and insisted that it was better to stick to the agreed long-term strategy, noting on 8 September that, 'Whatever fate awaits Poland, it would be an error to blunt our military weapon prematurely.'[6] The only military benefit France had gained from her eastern alliances was the time to complete her mobilization without disruption, which for the moment Gamelin considered sufficient. The memory of the bloody offensives of August 1914, so heavily criticized since 1918, weighed upon him. As a staff officer, Gamelin had at that time been at Joffre's right hand. It was he who had drawn up some of the key orders for the Battle of the Marne, and who had suggested the name of the battle to Joffre. Gamelin, a grandson of General Uhrich who had commanded at besieged Strasbourg in 1870, had a superior intellect. He was polished and cultivated, had a gift for lucid strategic analysis and well-developed political antennae. In him, wrote Colonel de Gaulle, 'intelligence, fineness of perception and self-control attained a very high degree'.[7] Yet critics detected in his philosophical detachment and skill in writing memoranda the hallmarks of a mere desk general, not a leader. His aversion to commitment and responsibility recalled the elder Moltke's warning that 'In every headquarters there are men who know how to demonstrate with great perception all the difficulties attending every proposed enterprise. The very first time something goes wrong they prove conclusively that they had "said so". They are always right. Because they never counsel anything positive (much less carry it out), success cannot refute them.'[8] Undoubtedly there existed at French headquarters a deep reluctance to join battle, and a desire to keep the war at a distance for as long as possible. When the British suggested bombing German targets the

French objected, fearing German retaliation at a time when their own bomber force was weak.

Thus Hitler was spared a war on two fronts, and after digesting Poland was able to start shifting forces to the west. He pressed his generals to prepare for an early offensive against France, but meantime on 6 October announced to the Reichstag his willingness for a peace conference if the West would accept his gains in Europe. In France a small number of Deputies – appeasers, pacifists, Anglophobes, men of the far Right – argued within the confines of the National Assembly that France should consider negotiations because Poland, the country France had gone to war to defend, no longer existed. What else was France fighting for? To serve British purposes? Wasn't it more 'realistic' to reach an accommodation with Germany? Daladier retorted that to negotiate meant in effect to accept German victory and domination of Europe. Like Chamberlain, he firmly rejected Hitler's 'offer', such as it was. Nevertheless, French official propaganda, unlike British, downplayed ideological opposition to fascism. This was partly because the French were less inclined to observe the polite distinction made by the British between Germany and the Nazi party, this being to many Frenchmen simply another German war. The French government was also mindful that Italy had not yet declared herself and did not wish to provoke Mussolini unnecessarily. Some figures on the Right, notably Laval, still hankered after an Italian alliance.

Opposition to the government came not only from a minority on the Right but from the Communist Party, which was preparing another volte-face following the Nazi–Soviet Pact. Moscow now required the party to denounce the 'capitalist' and 'imperialist' war and to agitate for peace. In the France of 1939 there was no *Union sacrée* as there had been in the face of invasion in 1914. Courting the support of the Right, Daladier struck hard against his erstwhile allies of the Popular Front, dissolving the French Communist Party by decree on 26 September. Its leader, Maurice Thorez, serving as a chauffeur at the front, fled into Belgium to escape arrest. The party's newspapers were banned, the civil service was purged and internment camps began to fill with thousands of communists and other suspects. The Nazi–Soviet Pact had revived and intensified all the French anger at Russia's 'betrayal' in 1917, and adherents of Russian communism were denounced as being in league with German Nazism. Between the two, said Daladier, the only difference he saw was that between the plague and the cholera.[9]

French indignation against the USSR reached new heights when the Russians, taking advantage of western preoccupations, invaded Finland on 30 November. Having been reluctant to go to war at all, the French momentarily seemed bent on taking on the Germans and Russians simultaneously. Early Finnish successes in their winter war encouraged hopes that intervention could be effective, and the press took up the Finnish cause. Plans were drawn up both to aid Finland directly and to bomb the Baku oilfields in the Caucasus, so denying oil supplies to both totalitarian states: for Russia had agreed to supply Germany with huge quantities of raw materials, so undermining the allied blockade. A scheme was even concocted for General Weygand, commanding French forces in the Levant, to occupy the

Caucasus oilfields before marching north on Moscow, where he would rendezvous with allied forces marching southward from Finland. That the Western allies did not find themselves at war with Russia owed nothing to sober second thoughts. Daladier seemed intent on launching an anti-Soviet crusade to help the Finns, despite warnings from the British navy that the means did not exist to transport and supply the number of troops required. Such fantasies ceased only when the Finns were forced to accept terms in March 1940.

Daladier had become so identified with the project to aid them that he was forced to resign as premier on 20 March. Once dubbed 'The Bull of Vaucluse', as a war leader he was now judged to have proved 'a bull with snail's horns'. He stayed on as Defence Minister under his successor, the dapper, diminutive and energetic conservative lawyer Paul Reynaud. The focus of allied plans for intervention in Scandinavia shifted to a strike into Norway to disrupt the supply of Swedish iron ore to Germany. Getting wind of the move, Hitler anticipated it by swiftly invading Denmark and Norway in April. The botched allied expedition ended in a fiasco which brought down Chamberlain in Britain. The so-called 'peripheral strategy' against Germany had met an embarrassing check.

That there had been no action on the western front all winter had not been by Hitler's choice. After the rejection of his 'peace offer' in October, he intended 'to destroy France' as the means of bringing England to its knees.[10] He set the date for 'Case Yellow', the attack on the west, for 12 November 1939, and furiously browbeat General von Brauchitsch, the Commander-in-Chief of the Army, when he timidly suggested that it was not ready. Only the onset of the autumn weather forced postponement of the operation – the first of many postponements, largely due to the exceptionally cold winter which imposed delays until the spring. These delays worked to the advantage of the German army in several ways. It was badly worn down and in need of a refit after the Polish campaign, and by the spring of 1940 was a much stronger instrument than it had been in the autumn of 1939. The postponements gave time for the arrival of fresh divisions, for the intensive training of officers and men, and for the supply of new weapons, equipment and ammunition. For example, in October 1939 the Wehrmacht possessed 151 Panzer Mk III tanks and 147 Mk IVs – the best available German tanks. By the following May those numbers had risen to 785 and 290 respectively, and other weapons in comparable proportions.[11] But the greatest dividend from the delays came through the trans-formation of the German operational plan for the campaign.

At Hitler's demand, the general staff obediently set to work drawing up plans, nursing the sullen hope that in the meantime someone else would take responsibility for assassinating the dictator. (Acting quite alone, a Swabian joiner named George Elser did plant a bomb which exploded in the Munich Beer Hall on 8 November, but Hitler, expecting to launch the western offensive, had left for Berlin ten minutes earlier.) The first plan the general staff produced was for an offensive through Luxembourg, Belgium and Holland into northern France, which would meet Hitler's wish to gain as much territory as possible there 'to serve as a base for the successful prosecution of the air and sea war against England and as a wide protective area for the economically vital Ruhr'.[12] Hitler was dissatisfied with their efforts. On 25 October he asked about the possibility 'of making the main attack south of the Meuse – perhaps with a secondary operation against Liège – in order to advance west and then northwest to cut off and destroy the enemy forces in and moving into Belgium'.[13] A fortnight later, on 11 November, he threw in the idea of an armoured strike against Sedan, where the Meuse could be crossed without the obstacle of steep banks. The generals were not impressed. The Führer was forever haranguing them with amateur ideas, of which this was only one. They were similarly dismissive when the chief of staff of Army Group A, General Erich von Manstein, submitted a plan that also involved an armoured thrust at Sedan. They considered it far too adventurous and risky, and were fearful that Hitler would get carried away with it if it came to his attention. The outspoken Manstein was banished to a command in East Prussia.

Manstein had developed his plan while at Koblenz, and had discussed it there with Panzer General Heinz Guderian, Germany's leading advocate of using armour in a concentrated mass. Guderian had taken part in the 1914 Ardennes campaign and knew Sedan well from his service in the First World War. The town lay beyond the end of the Maginot Line at Longuyon, and aerial reconnaissance suggested that French defences in that sector were weak. By stages, Manstein formulated a strategic conception of extraordinary boldness: more imaginative, broader in scope and more thoroughly thought out than anything Hitler had envisaged. Instead of being the main thrust, the attack on the Netherlands and Belgium by Army Group B would serve initially as a giant decoy operation, intended to lure allied forces into Belgium. As they advanced there, the bulk of the German army's armoured and motorized divisions, spearheading a strengthened Army Group A, would take advantage of the cover of the Ardennes Forest to descend on the Meuse at Sedan in a surprise attack and force a crossing. From there they would drive rapidly for the mouth of the Somme on the Channel coast, cutting off the retreat of allied forces advancing in the north and so encircling them. Once across the Meuse, other German columns would peel off southwards to contain any French counterattack and eventually achieve a second encirclement, pinning the southern French army group back against the Maginot Line. Manstein's ambitious plan offered not merely the prospect of winning a battle and gaining territory, but of delivering a knock-out blow against the enemy's army, so avoiding a drawn-out war of attrition. Despite the initial resistance of the general staff, the idea made headway. Hitler picked it up and on 2 February ordered them to modify their plans. When his chief adjutant contrived a meeting between Hitler and Manstein on 17 February, the Führer for once listened attentively, quickly convincing himself that Manstein had merely interpreted his ideas. Manstein's daring concept of a concentrated thrust to break the centre of the French line and drive north-westward was incorporated into the general staff's plan of 24 February.[14]

While the Germans planned and trained for their offensive, the French army lapsed into the routines and mentality of a peacetime garrison. French troops received training too, of course, but much of it was routine instruction in the use of infantry weapons, sometimes amounting to no more than half a day per week. Practice in the use of terrain or in how to counter tank attacks was barely known on the scale rehearsed by the Germans. French commanders were obliging when farmers asked for troops to help out on their farms, and men detailed for such work welcomed the change of scenery and food and an escape from training. Also, in the time-honoured manner of the French army, a disproportionate number of men were absorbed in administrative tasks or as officers' servants. For the rest, much of their time was spent digging trenches, anti-tank ditches or gun emplacements, burying telephone cables or setting rails upright in the ground as anti-tank defences, pouring concrete for blockhouses or stringing barbed wire – though occasionally leaving gaps so that local farmers could continue to graze their livestock. If much of this work was indifferently done, it was at least an occupation. When the snow set in, lasting from early December until late February, work came to a halt and the army postal censorship observed a steep decline in morale from the early weeks of the war. Time hung heavy on the men. 'Nothing new here,' one soldier wrote home on 20 February, 'I'm bored to death. We do absolutely nothing here but wait ... Wait for what? We're beginning to have had more than enough of this imbecile existence. Let's hope it will soon come to an end.'[15]

Monotony begot boredom, and boredom begot grumbling. Whilst the 1935 pattern khaki uniform was comfortable, there was a shortage of footwear needed to withstand the mud of the trenches and of blankets for protection against the cold. Delays to the postal service were another cause for complaint, and so was low pay as prices soared. Inequalities were resented, especially the higher pay of skilled men who had been mobilized but were subsequently detailed to industrial jobs in the rear where their absence had caused an alarming slump in war production. Peasant soldiers felt that the burden of the war was once again falling on them. These discontents were played upon by communist and German propaganda.

Following the suppression of their party, known communists in the army were kept under surveillance and posted to duties where they could do little harm. The clandestine distribution of communist leaflets failed to produce any agitation remotely comparable to the mutinies of 1917. Many communist activists had found the Nazi–Soviet Pact hard to stomach, and some seem to have developed greater loyalty to the men of their squad than to their party. On the home front communist propaganda advocated sabotage of the war effort, and police investigated suspected cases, but often it was difficult to tell whether faulty production of war materials was the result of negligence or of vandalism by workers who were disaffected rather than politically inspired. One proven case brought to light the sabotage of twenty aircraft engines at the Farman factory on the outskirts of Paris, leading to fatal accidents. The three communist perpetrators were shot in June. There were other incidents and, while the overall effect upon war production was apparently small, it was magnified by rumour.

German propaganda was more blatant, making use of loudspeakers and hoardings at the front and the broadcasts of the notorious Radio Stuttgart. Apparent German omniscience about the location and movements of French units was unsettling and greatly exaggerated by rumour, fuelling belief in a fifth column operating within France. In reality, the German intelligence service was greatly assisted by French casualness about ciphers, security and camouflage, and by communicative prisoners of war. When it came to propaganda and psychological warfare, the Germans seemed always to have the initiative. Both German and communist propaganda harped on the idea that peace was within easy reach if it weren't for the belligerent governments of Britain and France. Both fanned resentment of the British, who allegedly were getting the French to do their fighting for them while contributing only a tenth as many divisions as France from a larger population. The higher pay of British servicemen, greatly envied by the French, was a fertile theme for German attempts to divide the allies.

Not all the rumours circulating among French troops originated from enemy propaganda. Stories spread that the wine ration tasted bad because the authorities were adding bromide to it to curb the men's urges. In any case, the troops found no difficulty in supplementing their daily wine ration of between half-a-litre and a litre with drink from nearby bars. Alcohol consumption, traditionally high in France, had been growing in the 1930s, and heavy drinking was endemic in the army, aggravating its problems of morale, discipline and health. The scale of abuse was such that in April Reynaud attempted to limit the sale of alcohol, but even these partial measures were strenuously opposed by the wine trade, which wielded powerful influence in the National Assembly. The alcohol problem was but one manifestation of the slack discipline which prevailed in too many units. There were reports of soldiers installing their wives or girlfriends near their billets. In the evacuated districts around Sarreguemines, troops had 'smashed everything, crapped in the beds, broken into the cupboards with axes'. Here and elsewhere they 'made haste to loot, thinking that the first artillery bombardment would wipe out all trace of looting, along with the very existence of the looted houses'. Sometimes their officers set the example.[16]

Such instances were not typical of the whole army. As ever, the quality of unit commanders and NCOs was paramount in maintaining discipline and morale. There were few problems in elite units, any more than in the navy or air force, which were actively engaged in operations. (Between September 1939 and the end of April 1940 French aircrew flew 11,264 sorties, losing 57 planes to enemy action at a cost of 85 French dead, 30 wounded and 25 captured, but accounting for 72 German aircraft.)[17] Discipline remained generally sound, too, among the fortress troops of the Maginot Line, where the men lived like sailors on shipboard, with strict routines and fewer temptations than those billeted in villages or barns. Life in the dank, fetid tunnels of the great subterranean fortresses was certainly monotonous, and men were offered sun-ray lamp treatment against the disorienting effects of living by the glare of artificial light for weeks on end. Yet they remained ready to do their duty. Generally discipline tended to be better in regular army units than in reserve formations, and morale held up better at the front than in rear areas, where officers were more likely to be dug-outs from the last war, well past their best and resentful at having been recalled to fight all over again.

Official attempts to address the morale problem, such as the issue of footballs and 10,000 radio sets, visits by dignitaries, entertainment shows, the rotation of units and regular leave, had limited impact. The generous granting of leave may even have backfired, for it strengthened the troops' impression that life in Paris was carrying on as normal, increasing their sense of isolation at the front. Daladier's Scandinavian projects owed something to the need to show that France was fighting, but the Norwegian campaign proved to be only another demonstration of German military power and efficiency.

At the heart of the morale problems during the months known as *la drôle de guerre* (which, as Daladier commented, was no joke for those who experienced it)[18] lay the failure to motivate the troops with clearly defined war aims. France supposedly had gone to war to protect Poland, yet the Poles had been annihilated, condemning French soldiers to an apparently limitless period of waiting that exacted a heavier psychological toll than the high command had imagined. If there were few signs of outright defeatism, men were bound to ask why they had been mobilized. How long would they have to remain on a war footing? As one put it: 'We aren't at war, since we aren't fighting. I'm beginning to get fed up with it. I'd prefer a scrap, as I'd know why I was here and would have less time to think.'[19]

In a memorandum circulated to his superiors in January 1940 Colonel de Gaulle observed that 'many men are weighing the benefits of being with their unit against the inconveniences of their having been taken away from home'. Arguing that the combustion engine was revolutionizing warfare, his strongly held view was that, 'In the present war, as in all those that have preceded it, to remain inactive is to be beaten.'[20]

Nevertheless, on paper France appeared to be in a strong position if the Germans attacked. Including non-combatants, on 1 May she had 2.6 million men with the armies,[21] supported by nearly 400,000 men of the British Expeditionary Force.[22] Only after defeat did the Vichy regime insist that a 'decadent' republic had left the army hopelessly weak and outgunned, making defeat inevitable: an orthodoxy that was discredited long ago.[23] By contrast, in recent decades 'revisionist' histories have pointed to elements of French strength and German weakness. When an authoritative German account of the campaign appeared in 1996 it emphasized that the balance of forces looks rather different when the British, Belgian and Dutch armies are counted in the scales. It portrayed a German army greatly outnumbered by the allies, 135 divisions against 151, and purportedly 'inferior' in the quality and quantity of its weapons. Thus Germany had only 7,378 artillery pieces to the French 10,700 within an allied total of nearly 14,000; Germany had 2,439 tanks to the French 3,254 within an allied total of 4,204; Germany had 3,578 aircraft against the allied 4,469 (3,097 of which were French). The French had what was in some respects the best tank on either side, the Char B, whose 60mm armour was impervious to the guns of German tanks but whose 75mm gun could pierce the hull of any enemy tank. Even the cliché of an old-fashioned French army relying on horsepower versus a highly modernized and mechanized German army was debunked, for the images deliberately fostered in Nazi propaganda films distorted reality. The German army in 1940 employed as many horses as the French and twice as many as it had in 1914. Even the term Blitzkrieg – lightning war – apparently was more in vogue among English tabloid journalists than with German commanders. Thus the 'Blitzkrieg legend' appeared to have been turned on its head.[24]

Such headline figures appear to justify both the French government propaganda slogan 'We will win because we are the strongest' and the confidence of French generals in 1940 that they could withstand a German attack. But do they give an adequate picture of the relative strengths and weaknesses of the opposing forces? After all, there is more to military effectiveness than nominal strength.

In reality, the German Reich in 1940 was very far from being a David facing the allied Goliath. By dint of her rearmament efforts and her recent conquests in Central and Eastern Europe, she had reasserted her position as the single most powerful military nation in Europe. The Nazi–Soviet Pact and her rapid conquest of Poland ensured that she would have no eastern front to distract her high command and divide her forces as in 1914. She had no overseas empire to defend, and even after detaching 18 divisions to Scandinavia and the interior her 135 divisions in the West outnumbered France and Britain, her two principal enemies, combined. France had to detach 8 of her 105 divisions to watch the Alpine frontier, while Britain had only 11 divisions available when fighting began, not the 15 attributed to them by the German tally. Thus France and Britain could bring only 108 divisions to bear on the north-eastern front.[25] Moreover, Germany had far greater numbers than the French of soldiers aged between 20 and 27: that is, at the peak of their strength.[26] Belgium with her 22 divisions and Holland with her 10 hardly constituted a decisive counterweight, nor were they integrated into the allied order of battle. They were, after all, small neutral countries whose territory Germany chose to violate without a declaration of war. There was no unity of command over the 140 'allied' divisions. Learning the lessons of 1918, the British had agreed to accept French command of their land forces on the continent, but the Belgian and Dutch forces fought under their own command. Indeed, Belgium's reluctance to compromise her neutrality by fully co-ordinating her defence preparations with the French and British was to prove an Achilles heel to the allies. Nor, except in valour, was there any equivalence between the under-trained, under-equipped and unprepared Dutch forces with their 40 tanks and 124 combat aircraft and the Wehrmacht divisions that attacked them. In all, the margin of allied superiority in strength was nowhere near as great as the German figures might suggest, and was largely offset by the German advantage of unity of command and language.

Yet manpower was not to be the decisive factor in the campaign, during which the Germans needed to engage only ninety-three of their divisions. The key to their superiority lay elsewhere. Their preparation and planning maximized their advantages, which were further magnified by certain French failings. In terms of aircraft 'operational' on 10 May, the day when the German offensive began, they enjoyed a clear superiority of 2,589 aircraft to 1,453 allied.[27] The fastest French fighter, the Dewoitine D520, was slower than the Messerschmitt Bf 109E and, although it had a greater range, was less heavily armed and was anyway in short supply. The French had chosen not to produce dive-bombers in quantity, while the German Stuka was to wreak havoc on their columns; likewise they lagged behind in developing airborne troops, which the Germans were to employ so effectively. With regard to tanks, too, allied 'superiority' was more apparent than real. The number of tanks operational with units when the offensive began was nearly equal: 2,287 German to 2,270 French.[28] The Char B was heavy because it was designed for infantry support, not for speed. It had a small petrol tank and was prone to mechanical breakdown. Far from being a sign of inferiority, the lighter armour of the German tanks represented a deliberate option for greater speed and range over protection, a design better adapted to the kind of offensive warfare Germany had prepared to wage. Only the French SOMUA[29] tank could match the 40kph speed and 200km range of the Panzer Mk IV, but it was less heavily armed.

French tanks were inferior in other important respects. Their small turrets, allowing space for only the tank commander, made for a rate of fire four times slower than that of the German tanks, which had their main gun in their rotating turrets and could therefore more easily and quickly take aim and fire. Crucially, too, the majority of French tanks had no radios at all, partly because of fears of interception, and relied on the display of pennants by the tank commander, who had to communicate with his crew by applying pressure with his foot on the shoulders of the crewman below him. Such radios as were installed in French tanks were poor for communication both between crew members and between tanks.[30] One of the most significant advantages to the Germans in the coming battle would be the superiority of their radio communications between tanks and their commanders, between aircraft and aircraft, and between aircraft and ground control, while the French, relying on telephone calls between unit headquarters, were unable to respond to threats promptly.

Nor does the counting of conventional artillery pieces convey the importance of German superiority in the number and quality of their anti-aircraft and anti-tank weapons. They had 11,200 anti-tank (Pak) guns against the French 4,354, many of the latter incapable of piercing German armour and with inadequate ammunition stocks.[31] Similarly, the Germans had 9,300 anti-aircraft (Flak) guns, including 2,600 of the excellent rapid-firing 88mm gun, which doubled effectively as an anti-tank weapon. Even the most generous estimate of French anti-aircraft guns gives them fewer than 6,000 of all types, many with rudimentary sights. As with anti-tank guns, the French had too few and, in contrast to the German practice, they were drawn mostly by horses, or at best by converted tractors, and relied on telephone communication between batteries. That the French had too few horses was another problem largely of their own making, since poor care accounted for the deaths of nearly 10,000 per month over the winter of 1939/40.[32] These questions of relative weapon quality as well as quantity were often to decide tactical victory or defeat, life or death, on the battlefield.

Yet undoubtedly the greatest German advantage lay in their superior organization and application of the principle of concentration of force. This was true of their use of aircraft, as well as of tanks, motorized troops and artillery, and of their devastating combination of all arms to achieve overwhelming superiority of fire at the point of contact with the enemy. Allied passivity allowed them to choose the time and place of their attack, and Manstein's plan made best use of that advantage. While three of Germany's ten Panzer divisions (each with over 200 tanks),[33] plus fully motorized supporting infantry and artillery would accompany Army Group B in the northern offensive, the other seven were assigned to Army Group A for the thrust through the Ardennes. Morale among the young men of the elite Panzer units was high. Many were veterans of the Polish campaign. All were buoyed up by victory there and by news of the success in Norway. Coming to manhood in the Nazi era, they were eager to avenge the shame of Versailles and believed in their ability to defeat France. The Panzer divisions were formed in autonomous groups. Having faced effective tank attacks in 1918, and being forced to create their army anew, the Germans had organized a formidable and cohesive armoured force whose effectiveness was about to be put to the test. Confident in the readiness of his forces, Hitler believed that in the test of battle, 'our superiority in leadership, training and material' would prevail. He predicted that the French would find it difficult to replace their manpower losses after initial reverses, and judged that, 'Never since 1870 has there been such a favourable balance of political and military strength.'[34]

By contrast, there remains much truth in Air Minister Guy La Chambre's harsh verdict on the French general staff, which 'in 1914 was prepared for the war of 1870, and in 1940 for the war of 1914'.[35] Not that they had set their faces against all modernization, but they had channelled their ingenuity and much of their funding into the defences of the Maginot Line, making it by far the most sophisticated system of fixed defences in the world and forcing German strategists to think of ways of bypassing it. Nor, as we have seen, did France lack tanks. The question of forming armoured divisions had been studied and argued as earnestly among the French military as the Germans, conservative critics pointing out the dependence of tanks on fuel, their vulnerability without infantry support, and their heavy losses during the Spanish Civil War. In Germany, too, there were generals who thought and planned using the formulae of 1914–18, including those who opposed Manstein's apparently reckless gamble. Yet in Germany the modernizers prevailed, while the French formed only three light mechanized divisions. Belatedly, in response to German success in Poland, the French high command did hasten the creation of three armoured divisions in January 1940, and a fourth under de Gaulle would follow. But each was significantly smaller than a German Panzer division, all save one having 160 tanks. All three were barely formed and incompletely trained and equipped when the campaign opened in May.

Part of the explanation of the German lead in armour is that France had no dictator to cut through the debate, to say of a tank force, 'That's what I need!' as Hitler did in Germany.[36] His support was as important to the creation of the Panzer divisions as it was to the adoption of the Manstein plan. Yet a more deep-seated reason was that since the Briand era France had been politically and militarily committed to a defensive policy in which an armoured striking force seemed to have little place. The French army also carried the intellectual burden of victory, which elevated the successful tactics of 1918 into dogma and discouraged innovation.[37] The lessons of that year seemed to teach that there would be time to bring up troops to seal any breach in the line and contain the enemy onslaught by a properly prepared 'methodical battle'. The costliness of the offensive would make it an uninviting proposition for the aggressor. That was the argument of Marshal Pétain's foreword to a 1939 book by the fortifications expert General Chauvineau entitled *Is an Invasion Still Possible?*[38] French doctrine insisted that tanks should remain in close support of infantry units, and in May 1940 990 of France's 2,270 tanks remained dispersed in 'penny packets' among her nine field armies. For in French thinking her masses of conscript infantry remained the 'Queen of Battles'. The same thinking tied a portion of French air strength to close support of the army, with a complicated division of command between the air force and the army that would prove a recipe for delay and dispersal of effort.

The same lack of clarity hovered over the division of responsibilities within the high command itself. General Gamelin, who had his headquarters in a casemate in the Château de Vincennes outside Paris, was commander-in-chief of all land forces. In January 1940 he made his deputy, General Alphonse Georges, whose headquarters were at La Ferté-sous-Jouarre, responsible for the north-eastern front, while the general staff were based at Montry, midway between the two. The resulting confusion of responsibilities and duplication of reports were unlikely to facilitate rapid and clear decision-making in a crisis.

General Gamelin's general battle plan was well prepared, nevertheless, and would have served to parry the German offensive as it had been originally conceived in the autumn of 1939. Although he worried that the Germans might attempt to outflank the Maginot Line by a surprise attack through Switzerland, he believed it more likely that they would attack the north-eastern end of the allied line, where the open plains best suited tanks. That they would do so seemed to be confirmed by an incident on 10 January when a German light aircraft made a forced landing in fog near Mechelen in Belgium. The German staff officer on board tried to burn the papers he was carrying, but the fragments retrieved by the Belgian military confirmed allied suspicions about German intentions – they would come through Belgium as in 1914, but would attack Holland as well. This time Gamelin did not intend to wait for allied forces to be outflanked. He would send a strong force of his best troops to meet the Germans on Belgian soil, for it was in both French and British interests to gain space and to halt the German forces as far as possible from their own frontiers. Three options for defensive lines in Belgium had been marked on French maps, but Belgian neutrality prevented the allies from actively preparing them. Believing the German offensive imminent, the allies moved their forces up to the Belgian frontier following the Mechelen incident. By doing so they alerted the Germans to their likely reaction to an offensive through the Low Countries. 'That plane accident has made everything clear to the enemy,' Hitler told his generals on 20 January, lecturing them on the importance of secrecy.[39] Ironically for the allies, their intelligence windfall had strengthened the case at German headquarters for adopting the Manstein plan.

The chances of a successful German assault in the Sedan sector were enormously aided by the complacency of the French high command about the possibility of an enemy advance through the Ardennes. Although in 1938 some junior officers had carried out a map exercise which envisaged a German offensive in that sector, the French high command remained too inclined to assume that the rugged, forested terrain of the Ardennes made it unsuitable for a large-scale offensive involving tanks. Moreover, while the French had informed themselves about German tactics in Poland, they had concluded that what would work in the open spaces of the east could not be repeated against France. Gamelin had noted on 9 October 1939 that each Polish division had to defend 30 to 40 kilometres of territory, whereas the French on the other hand could deploy one division for every 10 kilometres.[40] Yet that was not true for the armies in his centre. For instance, at Sedan one division had a front of 17 kilometres. Worse, that particular division, the 55th, was a 'Series B' unit, that is to say it was composed mostly of reservists in their 30s and 40s and largely officered by reservists. One of their officers thought them little better than militia.[41] The 55th was a third-rate unit safely tucked away in a quiet sector where the defences were still unfinished.

At the beginning of March two Deputies on a tour of the Sedan front, Pierre Taittinger and Ernest de Framond, were alarmed at the sight of unfinished and un-camouflaged pill-boxes, for which the armoured doors had not yet arrived, noting the ease with which the Germans might cross the Meuse at this town whose name was one 'of ill omen for our arms'. When their report was forwarded to General Huntziger, commanding Second Army, he replied loftily that the gentlemen were mistaken: 'I judge that no urgent measure need be taken to reinforce the Sedan sector ...'[42] His superior, General Billotte, commanding the north-eastern army group, came to a different conclusion, and ordered a new line of stronger defences to be constructed further south along the line of hills overlooking the Meuse. This work had barely begun in early May, but it was assumed that there would be months in which to complete it.

On 8 May intelligence decrypts indicating German preparations caused General Vuillemin to put the air force on alert, but in the army the next day life carried on as normal. At least 15 per cent of French troops were on leave on 9 May, and several units had been moved to the rear for training manoeuvres. The general staff had become inured to alerts followed by stand-downs. In the west it was a day of political crises as in London Neville Chamberlain prepared to resign the following day and in Paris Paul Reynaud privately announced his intention to do so after Daladier opposed his wish to dismiss Gamelin. But the life of the Third Republic was about to be terminally disrupted. On the night of 9/10 May reports came in that German forces were crossing the frontiers of The Netherlands, Belgium and Luxembourg. By dawn on Friday, 10 May, even before the alert had reached French army units, German bombs were raining down on allied targets.

Chapter 16

Breakthrough on the Meuse

'On the morning of 10 May I was woken by the sound of bombs, as was most of the French Army,' recalled Captain André Beaufre, a staff officer attached to the French General Headquarters. All along the front, the drone of waves of German bombers passing overhead announced to French troops that the real war had at last begun. The wail of sirens heralded raids on Paris, Calais, Dunkirk and a score of other towns with railway yards, command centres or supply depots. Nearly fifty airfields and bases in eastern France were targeted. German bulletins claimed some 400 allied aircraft destroyed that first day. The French share of that loss was in reality nearer sixty, many of which could be repaired as quickly as the damaged airfields themselves. The blow to French air strength was serious, but by no means crippling.[2] The mood in Paris was at first one of curiosity and excitement rather than alarm.

The brunt of the German onslaught that Friday morning fell upon the Netherlands. With the aid of deception, including German soldiers dressed in Dutch uniforms, they seized the first bridge over the Dutch border at Gennep before it could be demolished. Further ahead, the crucial river crossings at Moerdijk, Dordrecht and Rotterdam were seized by paratroopers and airborne troops, who held them until ground forces could reach them. Although a simultaneous attempted coup against the airfields around The Hague failed with heavy losses, the boldness, speed and ingenuity of German airborne tactics succeeded in penetrating deep behind Dutch defensive lines before the defenders could react effectively. Such special operations, so much to Hitler's taste, paid a double dividend in the wave of fear and suspicion they spread throughout allied countries, where rumours of ubiquitous Nazi paratroopers and fifth columnists in an array of unlikely disguises gnawed at civilian nerves.

In the southern appendix of the Netherlands General Erich Höpner's XVI Panzer Corps dashed for Maastricht and its bridges over the Maas (the Dutch name for the river known to the French as the Meuse). Ahead of them, just over the Belgian frontier, airborne troops trained in the utmost secrecy pulled off the most spectacular coup of the campaign by landing gliders on the grassy surface of the huge subterranean fortress of Eben Emael. As the allies had never conceived of such a novel form of attack, there were no obstacles to hinder the silent German descent at dawn. Within minutes, as the startled Belgian garrison struggled to realize that

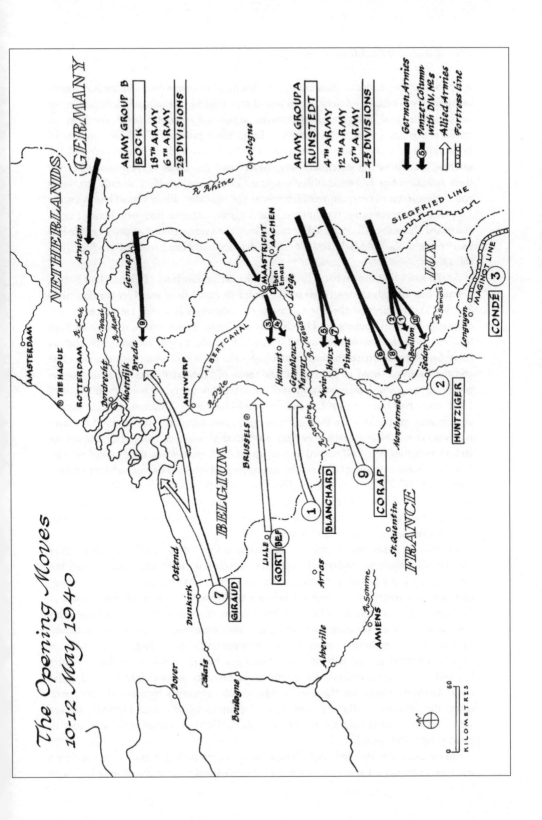

The Opening Moves
10-12 May 1940

GERMANY

NETHERLANDS

BELGIUM

FRANCE

LUX.

ARMY GROUP B
BOCK
18TH ARMY
6TH ARMY
= 29 DIVISIONS

ARMY GROUP A
RUNSTEDT
4TH ARMY
12TH ARMY
6TH ARMY
= 45 DIVISIONS

German Armies
Panzer Column
with Div. Nºs
Allied Armies
Fortress line

SIEGFRIED LINE

MAGINOT LINE

AMSTERDAM
THE HAGUE
ROTTERDAM
Dordrecht
Moerdijk
Arnhem
R. Lek
R. Waal
R. Maas
Breda
Gennep

Cologne
R. Rhine

ANTWERP
ALBERT CANAL
Maastricht
Eben Emael
Aachen
Liège
R. Dyle

BRUSSELS

LILLE
BEF
GORT

Arras

Ostend
Dunkirk
Calais
Dover
Boulogne
Abbeville
AMIENS
R. Somme

GIRAUD
7

Hannut
Gembloux
R. Sambre
Namur
R. Meuse
Yvoir
Houx
Dinant
St. Quentin
Monthermé
R. Semois
Bouillon
Sedan
Longuyon

BLANCHARD
1
CORAP
9

HUNTZIGER
2
CONDÉ
3

3 4
5 7
2 1 10
6 8

9

KILOMETRES
0   50

it was under attack, fewer than eighty elite German troopers disabled the fort's guns using another unheard-of device – hollow-charge explosives that could kill men inside steel cupolas and concrete emplacements supposedly proof against the heaviest artillery. Trapped within the darkened, fume-filled galleries of the fort, rocked by huge explosions and uncertain whether the Germans had already penetrated the interior, the surviving defenders were more than ten times more numerous than their attackers but lacked infantry training. They were in effect already prisoners and surrendered to German reinforcements the next day. Eben Emael had been the supposedly impregnable lynchpin of the Belgian defence line which ran north-westward along the Albert Canal, across which the Germans had already established two bridgeheads. The Belgian first line of defence had been breached as speedily as the Dutch.

At the news that the German invasion of the Netherlands and Belgium had begun, French and British troops received the order to enter Belgium. General Giraud's Seventh Army, nearest the coast, was to pass through Belgium via Antwerp and cross into Holland, joining the Dutch Army at Breda. To his south, the British were to advance to the line of the River Dyle, while on their right General Blanchard's First Army was to guard the Gembloux gap – the plain extending between the Dyle and the Meuse. Ahead of Blanchard, the tanks of General Prioux's Cavalry Corps would advance until they encountered the Germans to try to hold them off until First Army had time to establish itself around Gembloux. Officious Belgian border guards and mistrustful Belgian officers apart, the allied troops received a warm welcome from the population as they advanced at a steady pace. For fear of air attacks, some units at first moved only by night. Yet, even when they moved by day, air attacks were infrequent despite the fine spring weather. Daladier, who on 12 May came to attend a meeting on inter-allied co-ordination, was uneasy. That evening, he later recalled, he felt 'a sort of intuition ... that perhaps our general staff had fallen into a trap'.[3] The allied advance was viewed with satisfaction by the German high command for exactly that reason.[4]

On that 12 May the motorized vanguard troops of Giraud's Seventh Army crossed into Holland and reached Breda. Beyond it, they encountered not the Dutch army but a hostile reception from 9th Panzer Division en route to reinforce German paratroops at the Moerdijk bridges and then to reduce Dutch resistance at Rotterdam. Giraud was one of several French generals who did not share Gamelin's optimism about an advance deep into the Low Countries, believing that it would have been wiser to hold a shortened line in western Belgium. Rather than attempt to press forward against stiff opposition and risk being cut off, he pulled his units back into defensive positions. The speed of the German advance had forestalled the allied attempt to succour the Dutch. Meanwhile, attempts by allied air forces to check the progress of the German Army Group B by low-level bombing strikes were decimated by the startlingly ferocious and effective curtains of flak that rose to greet their every attack.

On the same day in southern Belgium General Prioux, too, had met the Germans head on – Höpner's Panzers advancing westwards from Maastricht. Prioux had been aghast to discover that the defensive positions supposedly prepared by the Belgians consisted not of trenches and barbed wire but of little more than an incomplete line of tank barriers.[5] He joined battle with the Germans around Hannut, east of Gembloux, with 415 tanks of his two light mechanized divisions against 623 tanks of two Panzer divisions. However, many of the German tanks were the light Panzer Mks I and II, and in two days of battle the French gave as good as they got, losing 105 tanks to the Germans' 160. Yet the poor communication between French tanks and their preference for linear defence eventually allowed the German tanks to pierce their line and push them back on the small industrial town of Gembloux. But Prioux had bought enough time for Blanchard's infantry to arrive and, for want of prepared defensive positions, to establish themselves behind the line of the Brussels-Namur railway. In a further two days of intense fighting in and around Gembloux the advancing Germans again had the advantage of air support, but the French had their artillery in play and inflicted further heavy losses on them. Then the French defensive battle in Belgium had to be abruptly cut short when on 15 May Blanchard's men received orders to pull back. The cause was the disturbing news that General Corap's Ninth Army on their right had apparently disintegrated, allowing German armoured divisions to pour through the gap in the French line like water through a broken dam. Confident until then of holding their own, the French and British armies in Belgium were suddenly in danger of being cut off from the rear.

While the attention of the French high command had been fixed on events in the Low Countries during the opening days of the campaign, it completely failed to appreciate the extent of the danger about to burst from the Ardennes. After the event it could be demonstrated that French intelligence services were in possession of several pieces of information indicating that the main German effort would be made in the centre, and that Sedan was their primary target. That there was a failure to present and analyse such intelligence systematically is doubtless true, even bearing in mind that recognizing which are the significant reports among hundreds of others is notoriously difficult without the benefit of hindsight, and that German intelligence services were using every subterfuge to convince the French that the real threat was an imminent surprise attack through Switzerland.[6] At bottom, however, growing evidence before 10 May of German intentions was disregarded or rejected by the French high command because it did not fit with their preconceptions of where the main battle would be fought. The Germans knew that this blindness could not last long once the campaign opened, and that their chances of achieving surprise depended on reaching and crossing the Meuse as rapidly as possible.

On the eve of the offensive small parties of German 'tourists' had arrived in Luxembourg tasked with preventing the demolition of bridges and disrupting communications. At dawn on 10 May motorized troops sped through the little duchy in a matter of hours and entered Belgium. There Belgian sappers had felled trees as roadblocks and blown deep craters in some roads, but few of these obstacles were defended, allowing German sappers to clear them rapidly. In the few places where the Germans met determined resistance they employed both frontal assaults and infiltration tactics to eliminate opposition as quickly as possible. Soon the few Belgian defenders disappeared northwards to meet what was considered the more pressing German threat, and the advancing Germans found themselves opposed instead by French cavalry units that had moved forward into Belgium. Mounted French troops found that their horses became terrified in the face of tanks firing machine guns. Finding themselves heavily outnumbered, French units proved equally skittish and were inclined to withdraw at the first suggestion that their flanks had been turned and that they had lost contact with neighbouring units.

By the morning of 12 May the vanguard of the Panzer columns had already reached the pretty town of Bouillon close to the French border, and during the day forced their way across the River Semois. At Bouillon they experienced for the first time an allied air attack, and one blast narrowly missed seriously injuring General Guderian, the guiding spirit of the Panzer operation, as he sat in his headquarters at the Hotel Panorama. It proved to be only a passing inconvenience. Mostly the skies over the Ardennes remained empty of allied planes while the immense German columns passed through the forest. The four Panzer divisions of Panzer Group Kleist presented the most inviting target, with over 41,000 vehicles (including 1,222 tanks) stretching out for mile after mile back to the Rhine on only four major routes, often snarled in immense traffic jams as infantry and Panzers jostled each other for right of way. Overhead German fighters pounced on any allied reconnaissance planes, a few of which nevertheless managed to take photographs and bring back reports of the avalanche of armour heading westwards. These reports were written off as exaggerated, alarmist or simply untrue. At most, the French command conceded that these might be secondary or diversionary attacks, like those being mounted by the German Army Group C opposite the northern end of the Maginot Line. Thus Guderian's leading units had surprise on their side as they crossed the French border. While some dealt with resistance from blockhouses, others drove on into a deserted Sedan on the evening of 12 May on the heels of the last French troops, who retreated to the south bank, blowing the bridges behind them. The Panzers had reached the Meuse in less than 60 hours since crossing the German frontier.

Some 70 kilometres to the north Panzer Group Hoth, comprising 5th and 7th Panzer Divisions, had also reached the Meuse – where it flows through Belgian territory. Their attempts to cross the river immediately were thwarted, both at Dinant, where the bridges were demolished, and at Yvoir to the north, where German scout cars drove onto the bridge just as a brave Belgian lieutenant named de Wispelaere succeeded in setting off the charges manually before being killed. Reconnaissance by a motor-cycle patrol between Yvoir and Dinant discovered a weir at the village of Houx which had been left intact by engineers for fear of lowering the level of the Meuse to the point where it would become fordable. A single file of men could pass over a footbridge to a small island in mid-river, and thence across the weir to the west bank. Under cover of darkness and mist German troops crept across and established themselves despite harassing fire coming from the hills to the west.

The defenders were men of Corap's Ninth Army, which had advanced into Belgium in conformity with First Army to their north. Exhausted by their march, they failed to follow orders to defend the Meuse crossings at the river's edge, remaining on the high ground above. During the day of 13 May the Germans forced two more crossing points between Dinant and Houx, urged on under galling fire by the hard-driving commander of 7th Panzer Division, General Erwin Rommel, a glory-hunter who refused to let any obstacle stand in his way. Like Guderian, he was in favour with Hitler, led from the front and believed in wrong-footing the enemy by always taking and holding the initiative. Unlike Guderian, who had devoted his career to the development of a Panzer army as a war-winning weapon, Rommel was an infantryman who had come lately to tanks. He brought with him the talent for daring infiltration tactics that had won him distinction in the Great War, and believed in forcing the enemy to keep his head down by driving at, over or around him with all guns blazing. Ordering nearby houses to be burned to provide a smokescreen for the crossing operation, he had his engineers build pontoon ferries so that the first tanks could be got across the Meuse. That night they completed a bridge so that more could follow. Rommel had kicked open the door leading to France while at Sedan Guderian was forcing it off its hinges.

Midway between these two, 6th Panzer Division, part of General Reinhardt's corps, had less success in trying to force a passage of the Meuse at Monthermé, where it arrived on the 12th. A picturesque tourist spot in peacetime, Monthermé lies within a loop of the Meuse at the foot of cliffs, and here the left bank was defended with determination by French colonial troops familiar with the ground. The German assault was also hindered when the Luftwaffe dive-bombed their own artillery. By nightfall the Germans had established themselves in the town, but as the French still held the base of the loop they were unable for the moment to exploit their small bridgehead. Further progress at Monthermé would have to await the outcome of Guderian's major assault at Sedan.

That assault came on the afternoon of 13 May. Guderian had planned it carefully, and obstinately carried through his own conception of the operation over that of his superior, General von Kleist. Kleist wanted the main crossing to be shifted well to the west of Sedan, but Guderian pointed out that that would necessitate a day's delay and would involve a crossing without the cover provided by the buildings of the town. Kleist also wanted the French defenders on the south bank softened up by one massive air raid, whereas Guderian had planned a continuous aerial bombardment by waves of forty aircraft targeting the French defences more accurately. Although Kleist insisted on his plan, Guderian had a collaborator in Luftwaffe general Bruno Lörzer, who professed to have received Kleist's order too late to change Guderian's plan.

The bombing began at 8 a.m. that fateful Whit Monday. The defenders on the south bank were, as we have seen, the reservists of 55th Infantry Division of General Huntziger's Second Army. They had been reinforced overnight by 71st Infantry Division, like them a 'Series B' division whose men were called upon to occupy ground unfamiliar to them. Moreover, both divisions lacked any sense of *esprit de corps* thanks to the practice adopted by the French of frequently reassigning companies, battalions and individuals between units according to local convenience. Thus the line opposite Sedan was defended by a hotchpotch of troops unfamiliar with each other rather than by cohesive units. Nothing in their training or experience prepared them for what came next. From midday the bombardment intensified, hardly troubled by any allied aircraft or by the few French anti-aircraft guns. Down shrieked the Stuka dive-bombers, pounding the defenders for what seemed an eternity. The crescendo was reached in the twenty minutes before 4 p.m. From the north bank German troops preparing to assault could feel the continuous blast waves and watched as a wall of sulphurous, yellowish-grey smoke billowed upwards from the seething cauldron of the French positions. No aerial bombardment of this concentrated fury had yet been seen in warfare, with German bombers flying more than 1,200 sorties over Sedan that day.

The French defenders were blinded by dust and deafened by noise, and had to keep their mouths open to stop their eardrums from bursting. The sound of the explosions, wrote Lieutenant Michard of 147th Fortress Regiment, 'merged together in one continuous thunderclap,' whilst the sinister whistling of every falling bomb, growing louder and louder as it descended, made each man freeze, believing himself personally targeted.[7] Weapons were damaged or dislodged, pill-boxes shaken to their foundations and telephone cables severed. Fewer than sixty men appear to have been killed but, as the Deputy Chief of Staff of Second Army, General Edmond Ruby, recalled:

> The moral effect was greater still. The gunners ceased firing and went to ground. The infantry, cowering in their trenches, dazed by the crash of the bombs and the howl of the descending dive-bombers, lacked the instinctive reaction to fire back at the enemy aircraft and to keep firing, if only to steady themselves. Their only concern was to keep their heads down, not daring to move. Five hours of this torture shattered their nerves, and they became incapable of reacting to the enemy infantry.[8]

At 4 p.m. the aerial bombardment temporarily shifted to the second line of French bunkers, giving the signal for the assault to begin. German pioneer troops launched their inflated rubber dinghies and began paddling across the 70m-wide Meuse. For all that has been said of the quality of the French units facing them, they were met with a hail of machine-gun fire from the defenders, so much so that attempts to cross by 2nd Panzer Division at Donchery west of Sedan and by 10th Panzer Division opposite Wadelincourt east of the town were thwarted for some while. Many of their inflatable dinghies were perforated by French fire. After several failed attempts it was a company from the Gross Deutschland Regiment of the elite 1st Panzer Division that first got across the river just west of Sedan. It was no coincidence that it was in support of 1st Panzer that Guderian had concentrated most of his available artillery, supplemented by fire from his tanks. Much of the German artillery was still making its way forward along the roads through the Ardennes.

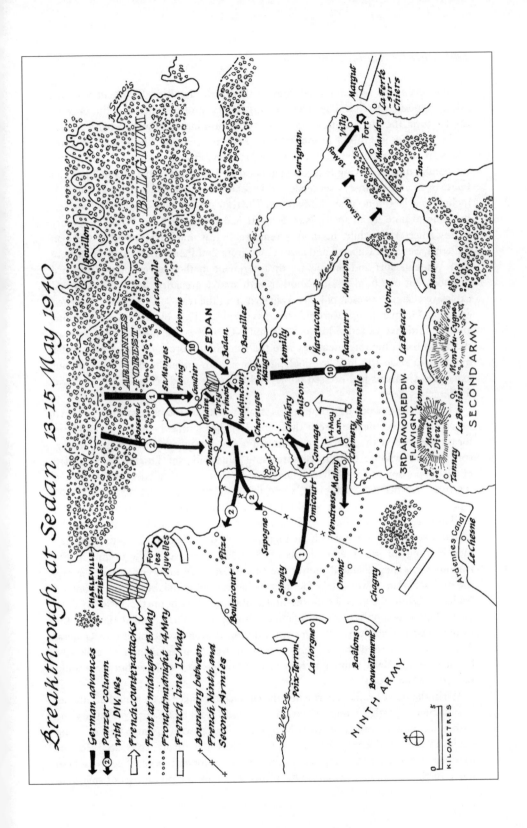

Breakthrough at Sedan 13-15 May 1940

Legend:
- � German advances
- (2) Panzer-column with DIV. Nos
- ⬆ French counter-attacks
- ····· Front at midnight 13 May
- ∘∘∘∘ Front at midnight 14 May
- ▭ French line 15 May
- +×+× Boundary between French Ninth and Second Armies

KILOMETRES 0 — 5

Labels on map:

BELGIUM

R. Semois

Bouillon

Lachapelle

Givonne

ARDENNES FOREST

St. Menges

Floing

Gaulier

Glaire

Torcy

Frénois

Donchery

Wadelincourt

Cheveuges

Pont Maugis

Balan

Bazeilles

SEDAN

Remilly

Chéhéry

Bulson

R. Chiers

R. Meuse

Carignan

Mouzon

Haraucourt

Raucourt

La Besace

Yoncq

Beaumont

Villy

Fort

Margut

La Ferté-sur-Chiers

Malandry

Inor

18 May

15 May

SECOND ARMY

3RD ARMOURED DIV.
FLAVIGNY

Mont-du-Cygne

Stonne

Mont-Dieu

La Bertière

Tannay

Le Chesne

Ardennes Canal

Chémery-Maisoncelle

Chémery

Connage

14 May a.m.

Vendresse Malmy

Omicourt

Singly

Omont

Chagny

Sapogne

Bulson

Pize

Boulzicourt

Fort les Ayvelles

CHARLEVILLE MÉZIÈRES

Poix-Terron

R. Vence

La Horgne

Badon

Bouvellemont

NINTH ARMY

Reinforcements soon followed, and to their right 1st Rifle Regiment got men ashore opposite Gaulier. The river crossing had been often rehearsed, but once on the far bank the German infantry improvised, pushing southward wherever they could, using dead ground to infiltrate the French defences. The French infantry who were supposed to defend the intervals between pill-boxes had decamped during the bombardment, leaving their occupants isolated and vulnerable. A small party of German assault engineers succeeded in knocking out several French blockhouses, including a large one near the battered Château de Bellevue where (had anyone the time to note it) a captive Napoleon III had met with King Wilhelm seventy years earlier. Meanwhile, in another remarkable feat much trumpeted in German bulletins, Sergeant Rubarth and eleven men from 2nd Panzer eventually got ashore near Wadelincourt and proved worth a regiment in themselves, edging forward to knock out one bunker after another with smoke grenades, hand grenades and explosive charges. As each pill-box was taken from the rear, so French fire slackened and more German troops were able to cross the river. Thus by platoon-scale actions and the initiative of individual officers and NCOs, they established possession of the south bank, fighting their way into the suburb of Torcy and pressing on after nightfall to seize the hills overlooking Frénois. By midnight the victorious but exhausted Germans had pressed on beyond Cheveuges and occupied a bridgehead 5 kilometres deep.

French defeat turned into rout. It was small wonder that some men so ill-prepared for combat, overcome and utterly disoriented by the German bombing, should head for the rear, where the Luftwaffe continued to cause mayhem. But it was a rumour, spreading like wildfire, that turned retreat into panic, and panic into the disintegration of a large portion of 55th Infantry Division. At about 6 p.m. a crowd of maddened fugitives was fleeing southwards, some firing wildly, others having already cast away their weapons. The cry went up that 'The Panzers are at Bulson!' – a village 8 kilometres south of Sedan – and the rumour infected the heavy artillery and the rear area services through which the fugitives passed, adding to the flood of terrified men heading for safety with shouts of 'Run for your lives!' The origins of the rumour were later disputed, but at the time there were no German tanks across the river at Sedan. It would take German engineers until midnight to build a pontoon bridge at Gaulier, across which the first tanks passed early on the 14th. At dusk on 13 May it was only German infantry pushing southwards, and at the time the rumour began French troops were still offering resistance. According to General Ruby, who witnessed it, the Bulson rumour was 'a phenomenon of collective hallucination'.[9] Many claimed to have received orders to withdraw, but none could say from whom exactly.

When the tide of runaways reached the command bunker of General Lafontaine, commander of 55th Infantry Division, at Fond-Dagot just south of Bulson, he rushed out and attempted to stem it, trying to reason with his men and ordering lorries to be parked across the road. It was useless. Eventually, convinced that his headquarters was at risk of capture, Lafontaine asked for and received permission to move further south to Chémery. One of his staff took the precaution of smashing the telephone switchboard, with the result that communication and command broke down. The panic eventually affected perhaps 20,000 men, whose flight delayed reinforcements advancing up the darkened roads. Some fugitives did not stop until they reached Rheims, 80 kilometres away. Some were rounded up the next day at Vouziers, which they pillaged, until an air raid started another stampede. Perhaps the worst effect of the rumour was that the French abandoned eighty artillery pieces at Sedan, allowing the Germans to consolidate their bridgehead overnight with little inconvenience or loss. When the colonel of heavy artillery who had given credence to the rumour realized the consequences of having ordered the abandonment of his post, he committed suicide.

It was imperative for the French to eliminate the German bridgeheads at Sedan and Houx in the first hours before they could be reinforced and expanded:

> *A little fire is quickly trodden out,*
> *Which, being suffer'd, rivers cannot quench.*[10]

In the small hours of the anxious, chaotic night of 13/14 May the reserve of 10 Corps slowly made its way to its start line south of Sedan, where Lafontaine was to lead it in an attempt to recover the lost ground. But there were delays caused by thousands of fleeing soldiers and civilians on the roads and by muddle and painfully slow communications and, in sum, the two-pronged counterattack that should have started at dawn did not make contact with the Germans until after 8.30 a.m. By that time there really were Panzers at Bulson, and at Connage further west. They had hurried forward without having to encounter any French minefields that might have slowed them. The French began their attack promisingly enough, destroying two German tanks and disabling a third, but 1st Panzer Division struck back hard. Within two hours the French withdrew, having lost thirty out of their forty tanks. News of this disaster, and a sense of having been abandoned, hastened the disintegration of 71st Infantry Division, which melted away without fighting. A pattern of abortive French counterattacks had been set, with the chances of success diminishing daily.

With every hour that passed more German tanks, guns, vehicles and men were funnelled across the pontoon bridge over the Meuse at Gaulier. General Billotte, the French army group commander, grasping that victory or defeat hung on destroying that bridge, asked the air force to launch a raid. When French pilots were briefed for their mission the spirit of General Margueritte's sacrificial cavalry charge in 1870 down the slopes above the bridge was evoked.[11] But those slopes were now sown with some of the more than 300 anti-aircraft guns that Guderian had deployed to protect the bridge that was his lifeline. Throughout the day allied bombers ran a gauntlet of flak. They appeared in small groups, giving German gunners plenty of time to aim, while above them German fighters sought their opportunities. The British provided 109 of the 152 bombers employed, but they were all obsolete Fairey Battles or Blenheims, which made easy targets. They lost forty-seven bombers. The French, flying at greater height and aiming at several targets within the bridgehead, lost three out of forty-three bombers and two more seriously damaged.[12] The allies also lost some fifty fighters between them. Yet after all the bravery and sacrifice, when the explosions died away and the dust cleared, the bridge at Gaulier was still standing. Guderian himself began to feel that the success of the German operations so far was 'almost a miracle'.[13]

The French had one more card to play: perhaps their strongest. The 3rd Armoured Division and 3rd Motorized Infantry Division had been ordered up to counterattack. These were among the army's best troops, and the tank crews 'were champing at the bit in their eagerness'.[14] They were ordered to attack at midday on the 14th, but once again there were delays getting into position caused by breakdowns, the need to refuel – a lengthy business in the French army – and bomb-cratered roads. The 3rd Armoured was so newly constituted that its supply, maintenance, staff and support services were not yet fully functional. The division had not yet mastered the techniques of moving efficiently as a fighting unit. At 3.30 p.m. the exasperated corps commander, General Flavigny, called off the attack, claiming later that he felt it was 'doomed to failure'.[15] Although a tank specialist, in the crisis he reacted in the way instinctive to most French generals schooled in the lessons of the First World War, giving priority to forming a defensive line to 'contain' the German offensive. He broke 3rd Armoured Division into small groups of tanks guarding every road leading south from Sedan. When word of this got back to General Georges he reminded Huntziger, commanding Second Army, that 'The 3rd Armoured Division was put at your disposal to counterattack towards Sedan,' ordering him to try again.[16]

Huntziger was reputedly a brilliant man, tipped as a future commander-in-chief. When the Germans first crossed the Meuse he had spoken confidently of making them prisoners.[17] He passed on Georges's orders, but seems to have been giving as much attention to moving his headquarters far to the rear, to Verdun. At any rate, Georges's orders were not executed. Reassembling the scattered tanks took far longer than dispersing them, and as the hours of 15 May ticked away no counterattack took place. Postponed until 5.30 p.m., it was eventually cancelled by Flavigny. Sixteen tanks that had not received the cancellation order advanced a kilometre, only to find themselves without support and the target of every German gun in the vicinity. They withdrew after losing four tanks. An evasive explanation of the failure was sent to Georges, and Huntziger sacked the commander of 3rd Armoured Division. Whether the full counterattack could have succeeded in throwing the Germans back into the Meuse remains a matter of speculation: but it is certain that the French never had a better opportunity than on 14 May, and that they did not take it. Had the roles been reversed, the Germans would not have hesitated.

While the French shied away from risk, Guderian again played for high stakes. After beating off the first French attack on the morning of 14 May he acted upon his motto of 'Whack them, don't tickle them!' and swung 1st and 2nd Panzer Divisions westwards to force a passage across the Ardennes Canal. They met stubborn, but localized, opposition from French cavalry units guarding the southern flank of Corap's Ninth Army, but the French defence was hardly helped by the nearest available infantry division being marched back and forth by a series of counter-orders until it was a spent force. By nightfall the Panzers had advanced 10 kilometres beyond the canal. Guderian left only 10th Panzer Division and the infantry of the Gross Deutschland Regiment to hold the southern flank of the Sedan bridgehead, where they became involved in heavy, seesaw fighting in and around the hilltop village of Stonne. French timidity in launching an armoured counterstroke justified his gamble. While the French were trying to restore a First World War style continuous front, Guderian knew that he had to forestall them by maintaining his forward momentum. He was favoured by the French high command misreading his intentions, plausibly but wrongly supposing that he was aiming to turn the northern end of the Maginot Line. Judging enemy plans by their own practice, they assumed that the Germans would need several days to bring forward their heavy artillery before attempting a breakout. Instead, Guderian struck while the front remained fluid. On 15 May he continued his push westwards.

On the French side General Touchon, long a prominent doubter of the value of armoured divisions, was sent to plug the gap that was opening up between the left of Second Army and the right of the Ninth. But he had too few troops within immediate reach to succeed. Those who found themselves in the path of the Panzers fought hard to halt them. At Bouvellemont it took all the formidable leadership skills of the indefatigable Lieutenant Colonel Hermann Balck – to whom German success at Sedan owed so much – to galvanize the exhausted men of his 1st Rifle Regiment to stir from their slit trenches to take the burning ruins of the village, fiercely defended by the French 152nd Infantry Regiment. At La Horgne further north the Algerian and Moroccan troops of 3rd Spahi Brigade paid a terrible price for resisting all day, losing a third of their officers and men, but in the end were overcome. While 1st Panzer Division was dealing with this resistance the 2nd to its north was bypassing the French positions. By the morning of 16 May Guderian's force had broken through into open country. Before French troops could take up the defensive line designated by Touchon, the Germans were already past it.

Meanwhile further north the centre and left of Ninth Army were also reeling from simultaneous blows. French attempts to resist the German onrush from Houx and Dinant were as ineffectual as those at Sedan. Many a French infantry unit found itself isolated and struggling with woefully inferior firepower to beat off aggressive German frontal attacks, only to be suddenly forced to surrender to enemy infantry who had infiltrated around their rear. Whereas the Germans proved adept at combining all arms for the assault – infantry, artillery, armour and aviation – the French army in a crisis once again showed itself incapable of carrying out orders to mount a rapid and effective counterattack. Small local French successes, like that of French tanks at Haut-le-Wastia, west of Houx, on 14 May, went unsupported and unexploited. On that day Rommel's forces captured Onhaye, 5 kilometres west of the Meuse, firmly consolidating the German bridgehead. The French here were paying part of the price of Munich, for many of Rommel's tanks now spreading panic among them were the excellent Czech T-38s.

Finding their improvised positions everywhere breached and their flanks turned, disorganized and demoralized by harassing air attacks, the troops of Corap's Ninth Army gave way. Different halt lines designated on maps by its generals as rallying points only added to the confusion as units streamed back towards the French frontier. Thousands of French prisoners were already falling into German hands. On the morning of 15 May Rommel, setting out westwards with his 7th Panzer Division, collided near Flavion with the French 1st Armoured Division under General Bruneau, which had been sent forward to stabilize the French position. The surprise was mutual. After a short engagement, Rommel led his tanks around the southern flank of the French force and continued westwards, leaving 5th Panzer Division following in his wake to take them on. Bruneau's leather-jacketed crews had been caught at a disadvantage, not having completed their refuelling – those supply tankers that had survived aerial attack being at the rear of his columns. The 1st Armoured inflicted significant losses on the Germans during the course of the day, but their cumbersome Char Bs, out of radio contact with one another, floundered in isolation, picked off by German tanks hunting in packs and manned by gunners who had learned their opponent's weak spot – a radiator grill on the side of the hull. The Luftwaffe again provided the air support that the French signally lacked. French crews who were not incinerated in their tanks and tried to escape from them risked being cut down by fire from supporting German infantry. Some set their own tanks ablaze and abandoned them when they ran out of fuel. Other tanks broke down during the retreat. The next morning, when Bruneau rallied the remnant of his division, he had only seventeen tanks left – a mere tenth of his force. The 1st Armoured Division had been all but annihilated at Flavion without stemming the French retreat.

Some remnants of Ninth Army tried to rally at the French frontier, where a line of pill-boxes offered temporary security: except that the last troops to man them had left them locked and had entrusted the keys to civilian mayors who sometimes had already fled. General Corap, an old colonial soldier who was not part of the inner circle of the French military hierarchy, was made the scapegoat for the débâcle and was sacked on 15 May, his repeated warnings about the weaknesses of his front and vain requests for more weapons being conveniently forgotten. General Giraud, considered to be more dynamic, was brought down from Seventh Army to replace him, but he could do little to restore the situation and within four days was captured as the Germans overran what until recently had been the French rear areas.

The third German breakout on 15 May came at Monthermé, where Reinhardt's Panzers overwhelmed the French defenders who had just received orders to withdraw. To recover time, Reinhardt's leading units raced ahead and by evening reached Montcornet, 66 kilometres to the south-west, rounding up dazed French prisoners before they could grasp what was happening. Their swift advance also disrupted the assembly of the French 2nd Armoured Division. While its tanks were still being unloaded from railway flatcars at Hirson, its support vehicles which had gone ahead by road found themselves cut off by German columns. Amid the confusion of finding enemies all around, 2nd Armoured was dispersed before getting the chance to concentrate and fight. In just six days from the opening of hostilities the Germans had punched an 80-kilometre hole through the centre of the French line, scattering organized opposition in that sector. That day, too, the Dutch formally capitulated, following the end of resistance and the bombing of Rotterdam the previous day. Victory in Holland released more combat troops for the next phase of operations against the allies in Belgium.

Already at 7.30 a.m. on the 15th the British prime minister, Winston Churchill, who had taken office only on the 10th, had been awoken by a telephone call from Paris. Speaking in English, Paul Reynaud told him, 'We have been defeated ... We are beaten; we have lost the battle.' The next afternoon Churchill flew to Paris to confer with the French cabinet. In a room at the Quai d'Orsay occurred a scene he was to immortalize: his question to the despondent French, 'Where is the strategic reserve?', Gamelin's reply with a hopeless shrug of the shoulders that there was none left, and the long ensuing pause during which Churchill gazed out of the window at elderly officials busily trundling out wheelbarrows full of documents which they cast on bonfires they had lit in the gardens in preparation for the evacuation of Paris. The French asked for more RAF fighter squadrons to be sent to France. Churchill already had authority to send another four, and by telegram that evening asked the cabinet to approve the despatch of six more, stressing the gravity of the French situation and that, 'It would not be good historically if their requests were denied and their ruin resulted.' Churchill stayed up late until the cabinet's agreement arrived and he was able to tell Reynaud and Daladier that they would have the ten additional squadrons. Daladier shook his hand in silent thanks.[18]

The seemingly endless Panzer columns had meanwhile left behind the hills of the Meuse region and were advancing into the open plains of north-eastern France. There were few organized French units in a position to challenge them, and fuel supply was no impediment. In the years of building up the Panzer force Guderian had involved himself in the minutiae of every technical problem affecting the fighting capability of his tanks – radios, armament and refuelling – and the Polish campaign had shown the way to further improvements. In contrast to French practice, where each tank had to wait its turn for a petrol tanker, German tanks could be refuelled rapidly because of the well-organized continuous delivery of 'jerrycans' full of petrol at points along the route, and the collection of empties. Thus with only occasional requisitions from abandoned French garages, the Germans were able to keep moving without depending on air drops. The only brake on the Panzers' rate of advance came not from the enemy but from their own high command, which had grown nervous about their exposed left flank. That anxiety was rooted in common military prudence, but also in the haunting memory of the Marne in 1914. Then too the French had seemed to be in headlong retreat just prior to the counterattack that had halted an apparently irresistible German offensive.

Guderian was mindful of the parallel, but he drew a different lesson. When Kleist ordered him to halt, he accused him of playing the part of Hentsch, who in German legend had been solely responsible for robbing Germany of victory. Kleist flew to see Guderian at Montcornet on the morning of 17 May and, without congratulating him on his achievements, gave him a dressing-down for repeated disobedience and ordered him definitively to halt. Guderian became equally enraged and asked to be relieved. Kleist unhesitatingly obliged him. General List, commander of Twelfth Army, was sent out to calm things down and agreed a compromise that enforced the letter of Kleist's orders by requiring Guderian's headquarters to remain fixed. At the same time Guderian, who was to remain in command, was allowed to send forward a 'reconnaissance in force', which was all the leeway he needed to carry on his advance under another name.

Meanwhile to his north Rommel paid even less heed to orders from above. On the night of 16/17 May he crossed the border from Belgium into France, breaking through the French frontier defences near Solre-le-Château in a matter of hours before shooting his way through the middle of a dumbfounded French motorized infantry division as its soldiers lay sleeping, and pushing on through Avesnes, where the few remaining tanks of the French 1st Armoured Division met their destruction, then onward to the Sambre at Landrecies and across it to Le Cateau soon after dawn. The speed at which Rommel's 7th Panzer advanced was earning it a reputation among the French as 'the phantom division', but it could not move fast enough for its commander. Driving back down the road to hurry forward the rest of his tanks, Rommel ordered the French troops he passed to throw down their weapons and to march southwards and surrender themselves. On a dozen occasions any determined Frenchman might have shot Rommel dead, for at this point he had no infantry escort; but such was the authority of his commands and the psychological dominance established by the Panzer advance that he was obeyed. The French were surrendering in droves.

Both Rommel on the right flank and Guderian on the left sensed that the way to keep the French guessing and deny them time to organize a counterattack was to keep moving forward. That was not how the situation appeared to Runstedt, commanding Army Group A, whose caution was shared by Hitler. They thought it imperative to bring up infantry to line the western flank of the Panzer corridor before the spearheads advanced further. Kleist had been merely the messenger of the halt order, not its author. Hitler had long insisted, over the caution of his generals, that France was weaker than it appeared and could be defeated quickly. Once the French suffered heavy losses, he told General Halder on 10 October 1939, defeatism and pacifism would do their work. During his confrontation with Brauchitsch on 5 November Hitler again insisted that the French were not what they had been in 1914. Weakened by parliamentary strife, the French only wanted to live in peace and comfort. Their army, being a reflection of its people, had little will to fight: it would fold after the first defeats.[19] Yet now that his forecast seemed about to be vindicated, Hitler feared that even a small setback might break the spell of German invincibility and encourage the allies. There were unpleasant scenes with his senior generals, at whom he ranted and raged, accusing them of putting victory at risk. Halder, who had started as a critic of the Manstein plan, had become convinced of its operational viability and its leading champion. On 17 May he noted that Hitler seemed 'frightened by his own success'.[20] Only late on the 18th did he obtain grudging formal permission for the advance to continue.

Guderian was forging ahead anyway, his passage announced by heavy air-raids on the towns in his path. The Panzers reached Saint Quentin on the 18th. The

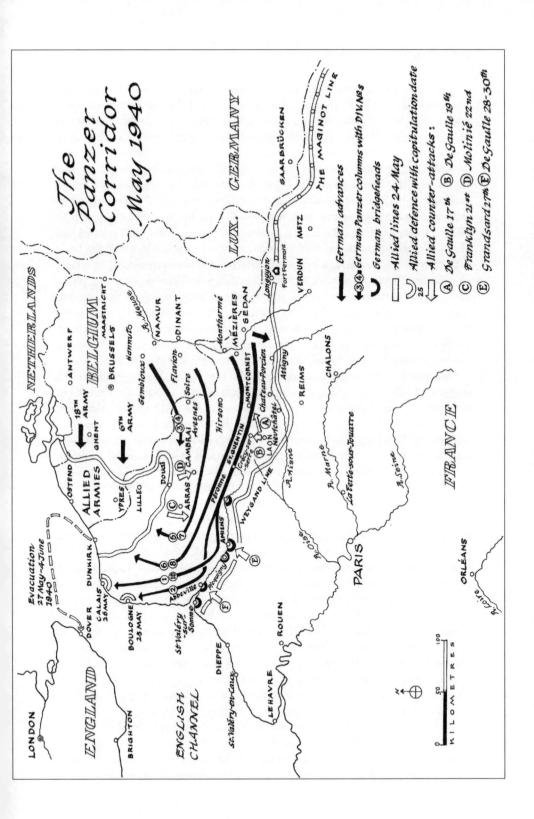

The Panzer Corridor May 1940

LONDON
ENGLAND
BRIGHTON
ENGLISH CHANNEL

NETHERLANDS
BELGIUM
GERMANY
LUX.

Evacuation 27 May–4 June 1940
DOVER
CALAIS 26 May
DUNKIRK
OSTEND
ALLIED ARMIES
YPRES
LILLE O
BOULOGNE 25 May
St.Valéry-sur-Somme
Abbeville
DIEPPE
St.Valéry-en-Caux
LE HAVRE
ROUEN

ANTWERP O
18TH ARMY
GHENT
BRUSSELS O
Hannut O
MAASTRICHT
R. Meuse
6TH ARMY
Gembloux O
NAMUR O
R. Meuse
DINANT O
Flavion
Soire
Avesnes
CAMBRAI
Douai
ARRAS
Péronne
AMIENS
Picquigny
ST.QUENTIN
Hirson O
Montcornet
Château-Porcien
MONTCORNET
Crécy-sur-Serre
LAON
Neufchâtel
Attigny
R. Aisne
R. Aisne
R. Oise
MÉZIÈRES
Monthermé
SEDAN
Longuyon
Fort Fermont
VERDUN
METZ
SAARBRÜCKEN
THE MAGINOT LINE
REIMS O
CHALONS O
R. Marne
La Ferté-sous-Jouarre
R. Seine

WEYGAND LINE

PARIS
FRANCE
ORLÉANS
R. Loire

N
50   100
KILOMETRES

German advances
3 4 German Panzer columns with DIVNes
German bridgeheads
Allied lines 24 May
25 Allied defence with capitulation date
Allied counter-attacks:
(A) De Gaulle 17th (B) De Gaulle 19th
(C) Franklyn 21st   (D) Molinié 22nd
(E) Grandsard 27th (F) De Gaulle 28–30th

next day Péronne was taken, and with it a group of French officers who had arrived for a conference. The Panzers rolled on across the old Somme battlefields, where huge armies had struggled for years. On 20 May Amiens, which the Germans had failed to take in 1918, was captured, and bridgeheads were established south of the Somme as a precaution against any French counterattack. Another column moved on Abbeville, or rather what was left of it after German bombers turned the town centre with its many medieval and seventeenth-century buildings into a brazier, causing hundreds of civilian casualties.[21] A battalion from 2nd Panzer Division was the first to reach the Channel coast near Noyelles on the Somme estuary. Despite Hitler's interference and Runstedt's caution, the Panzer leaders had reached their objective, fully aware that if they hesitated or failed they would suffer the fate of their French counterparts in being subordinated to conservative-minded infantry commanders. They had completed what Churchill would later describe as a 'scythe-cut'[22] across north-eastern France, cutting off the allied armies in Belgium from their bases, their supplies and the rest of their forces, in effect penning them against the sea. Seeing the trap closing around the northern armies, on 17 May Billotte predicted to General Prioux amid the burning buildings of Douai that, 'We are headed towards another Sedan, and one more terrible still than in 1870.'[23]

Guderian had been right in counting on the slowness of French reactions. The surprise and shock of the German breakthrough seemed to send the French high command reeling. General Georges, in command of the north-eastern front, over-worked, deprived of sleep and still suffering from a wound he had received at Marseille in 1934 when King Alexander of Yugoslavia was assassinated, collapsed in tears at news of the breakthrough at Sedan. His chief of staff, General Doumenc, kept his head and tried to organize counterattacks, but the information flooding into headquarters was always out of date and the units to which orders were sent had often disintegrated or fallen back under German attacks. *Les Bondons* was like bedlam, with files and papers spread out as if for a jumble sale, staff working amid the competing noises of clacking typewriters, ringing telephones and the comings and goings of motorcycle despatch riders in the yard, while cloying odours from cooking or blocked lavatories wafted through the cluttered rooms.[24] Captain Beaufre recalled that, 'Orders were given for various cutting-off operations, for stands "to the death"; nothing happened; nothing could slow up the advance.' Trying to convey the mood at headquarters, he recalled disbelief 'that this was real, that France was dying and that something would not happen to save us at the last moment'. They were living through 'a bad dream': yet the word 'nightmare' was not strong enough to describe the pervasive sense of impotence.[25] At least by the 17th it appeared that the Panzers would not, after all, advance straight on Paris, where rumour and alarm were taking hold. Efforts were made to patch together a defensive front along the line of the Rivers Somme and Aisne.

To buy time for these efforts to succeed, Georges ordered Colonel de Gaulle to launch an offensive with the forces he had to hand. His 4th Armoured Division had existed only since 11 May and was incomplete. Among the many essentials it lacked were sufficient supporting artillery and infantry. Nevertheless, appalled by the chaos he saw around him, the aloof and autocratic de Gaulle was determined to strike a blow. On 17 May he led his tanks north-eastward from Laon towards Montcornet and shot up some German convoys, but found himself blocked at the River Serre, where hastily summoned German artillery and dive-bombers forced him to retreat at a cost of 23 out of 85 tanks, though with 130 prisoners in tow.

Two days later, on 19 May, de Gaulle tried again, this time with 150 tanks, advancing directly north from Laon, only to be beaten back in an action at Crécy-sur-Serre. Once again the harpy-like Stukas forced a withdrawal. The German counterattack, said medical officer Bernard Lafay, was 'unimaginable': 'They attacked in waves,' bombarding 'everything that moved, everything that lived.' During a lull he and his medical team ran out to try to save tank crewmen who were rolling on the ground in blazing clothing screaming in agony. Amid flame and smoke the medics clambered into tanks seeking anyone alive among the corpses, but suffered casualties themselves as 'the burning tanks blew up with terrific explosions, shells went off like fireworks and chunks of armour fell back to earth'. Having brought away the surviving wounded, Lafay confessed that he didn't know how any of them had got out alive – 'It was Hell. Sheer Hell.'[26] De Gaulle lost thirty-eight tanks. Although his supporters subsequently exaggerated the effect of his attack to boost his political career, he had at least demonstrated that even inexperienced French troops could take the offensive under an enterprising leader, and the Paris press made the most of it. But, save perhaps for causing Guderian 'a few uncomfortable hours',[27] de Gaulle lacked the strength to achieve more. More important for the future was the resolution he made to himself before going into action: 'If I live, I will fight, wherever I must, as long as I must, until the enemy is defeated and the national stain washed clean.'[28]

While the Panzers were racing unchecked to the sea, the French high command remained reluctant to pull divisions out of the Maginot Line to form a reserve, and not only because many of those thirty-six divisions were fortress troops untrained for mobile warfare. Beginning with attacks around Longwy from the very start of the offensive, there were increasing signs that the Germans were preparing to launch a major assault on the Maginot Line, or even around its southern end through Switzerland. These appearances were the result of clever deception work and of demonstrations by the nineteen divisions of General von Leeb's Army Group C. For their part, the Germans were anxious to keep French divisions pinned down to prevent any possibility of a counterattack to pinch off the base of the Panzer corridor. The remnant of General Huntziger's Second Army was still holding the 'shoulder' of the broken French line south of Sedan. The little village of Stonne changed hands no fewer than seventeen times in bloody fighting between 15 and 17 May, and in the course of this struggle Huntziger pulled troops back from the area between the Rivers Chiers and Meuse.

This withdrawal presented the Germans with the opportunity to attack a small fort at the westernmost end of the Maginot Line at La Ferté-sur-Chiers, 20 kilometres east of Stonne. They brought the fort under heavy artillery and aerial bombardment from 16 May while infantry worked their way around it. Pre-war budget cuts had left flaws in La Ferté's defences, and by the evening of 18 May German combat pioneers had worked their way up to it, managing eventually to blow open a gun embrasure in a steel turret, enabling them to lob in more charges. The resultant fire spread to an ammunition store, causing a large explosion. The garrison under Lieutenant Maurice Bourguignon was forced to seek shelter in a gallery 35 metres below ground. Choking on fumes in the pitch darkness, they managed to telephone their commander early the next morning to ask permission to surrender as the fort was now useless. It was refused, and all 107 men perished of asphyxiation like miners in a pit fire. Coming only a week after the fall of Eben Emael, this successful German assault on a fort further shook French confidence in the invulnerability of their defences, and seemed to presage the turning of the Maginot Line.

On 19 May Reynaud finally sacked Gamelin who, for all his intellectual gifts, had presided over an unrelieved disaster. The exasperated premier saw Gamelin as a man more suited to be a Prefect or a bishop than an army commander. 'I've had enough of this,' he had confided at the time of the invasion of Norway: 'I would be a criminal to leave this man without nerve, this philosopher, at the head of the French army.'[29] Reynaud had moved to oust Gamelin on 9 May, but when the Germans attacked the next day he concluded that it was inopportune to change commanders. So Gamelin was reprieved, but his performance only confirmed Armaments Minister Raoul Dautry's judgement that Gamelin was 'incapable of any act of will, or of giving an order. His fear of responsibility is evident.'[30] Gamelin remained serenely above the fray, occasionally offering 'advice' or 'suggestions' to Georges, who was buckling under the pressure of trying to control the battle – which did not deter Gamelin from proposing, on 16 May, to offload responsibility for the Alpine front onto him as well,[31] just as he had already delegated liaison with the Belgians. Gamelin had a certain contempt for Georges, writing later that 'his character never matched his intelligence ... He had the makings of a chief of staff, not of a wartime commander.'[32] Besides being an unwitting self-portrait, this judgement raises the question of why Gamelin left Georges in command. Indeed, on 18 May General Doumenc suggested that Gamelin might wish to take direct command himself. 'Of course,' was Gamelin's characteristic reply, 'Let me know the most suitable time and opportunity.'[33]

In a fifteen-page memorandum to the Defence Minister explaining what had gone wrong, Gamelin spread responsibility all around. The document set the tone for his post-war memoirs, in which he frequently expressed 'surprise', 'astonishment' or 'regret' at the lamentable failings of his subordinates, or showed that unfortunate developments were all down to the derelictions of duty of the reservists, the politicians, the Belgians, the British or whomever. To Churchill he had encapsulated his view of the reasons for French failure with a laconic, 'inferiority of numbers, inferiority of equipment, inferiority of method'.[34]

The irony was that a general so criticized for his passivity had exposed France to catastrophe by his one bold strategic decision, taken against the advice of his subordinates, namely to send his best troops, including the cream of his armour and motorized infantry, far into Belgium, leaving no powerful reserve to deal with an emergency elsewhere. This disposition had, however, been approved by both the British and French governments. Like his former master Joffre (who had died in 1931), Gamelin's opening gambit had failed but, unlike Joffre, he proved unable to recover the situation. It should be said that, unlike Joffre, Gamelin had to keep divisions on the Italian front, for an attack by Mussolini seemed imminent. Nor, in moving up troops for a counterattack, did Joffre have to cope with the incessant aerial bombardment of the railway system. Tracks were broken in 300 places between 10 and 20 May 1940, though repair crews worked wonders in trying to keep the system functioning. In 1914 Joffre had time to organize a counterattack because the German army was advancing at walking pace while he could move up reserves faster by rail. In 1940 the German spearheads advanced at the speed of motorized vehicles, much faster than the French could organize a riposte. This fact would have confronted any French commander: but what the French government and army craved was someone with Joffre's will to fight and ability to take command. Gamelin could imitate only the calm, as if it were an end in itself rather than merely a requisite for directing the battle. He was very critical of the lack of calm at Georges's headquarters, but his own calm was simply that of detachment and resignation. If the ultimate test of a commander-in-chief is his judgement in knowing where and when to commit the strategic reserve, Gamelin failed the test.

On the evening of 16 May Reynaud had cabled General Weygand in Beirut to return to France to take command. At the same time he sought to strengthen his cabinet by bringing in the revered authority figure of Marshal Pétain, who was asked to return from Spain. For balance, the strong-willed republican Georges Mandel, once Clemenceau's right-hand man, was given the Interior Ministry.

Sensing his imminent replacement, Gamelin travelled to Georges's headquarters on 19 May, sat in a side room and penned a memorandum to him beginning, 'Without wishing to intervene in the conduct of the battle ...' It pointed to the opportunity for a blow against the communications of the Panzers in the direction of Mézières, invoking the need for 'extreme audacity', and concluded that it must be executed 'in a matter of hours'. Gamelin marked it as a 'Personal and Secret Instruction' and slipped it onto Georges's desk, telling him to read it later.[35] Then he left. When an astonished Georges read it he understandably viewed this last-minute offering from Gamelin as merely for the historical record. Amid Gamelin's typical prescriptions for what 'must be done', there was no measuring of means to ends, no hint of where the reserves to attack with were to come from, and no specific orders. As Gamelin well knew, having told Churchill previously, there was no strategic reserve. That afternoon at Vincennes he received Reynaud's letter dismissing him.

In Paris that Sunday the entire government joined a large congregation at a special service at Notre-Dame to implore the saints to intervene to save France.

Chapter 17

French Exodus and British Exit

On a map, the German advance almost resembles a bold chess gambit – a surprise checkmate in four swift moves against an opponent who had imagined himself at only the beginning of a long, evenly matched contest. Viewing the theatre of war from the air, pilot Antoine de Saint-Exupéry, flying a reconnaissance mission from Meaux towards Arras in a Bloch 174 aircraft on 23 May, could feel a certain detachment from the turmoil beneath him. At 33,000ft time and motion seemed suspended, and he could make out only a layer of dirty-white smoke blanketing the landscape of north-eastern France. Yet beneath it, he knew, was a chaos of destruction of towns, of villages, of crackling flames, crashing beams and swirling black smoke.[1]

If heavy artillery in 1914–18 had caused more concentrated destruction in certain areas, German bombing raids in 1940 caused widespread dislocation and fear across a much deeper swathe of territory in which familiar town centres were reduced to flame and rubble.[2] The disruption of rear areas created havoc as the bombardment forced commanders to move their headquarters repeatedly, leaving units without orders as they tried to fight off German columns that attacked from what had been their rear.

Adding to the chaos, from the start of the fighting hundreds of thousands of civilians left their homes and headed south and west in search of safety. On the outbreak of war there had been an organized evacuation of civilians from the eastern frontier zones of Alsace and Lorraine to southern France. A quarter of a million people had left Strasbourg at the beginning of September 1939, leaving it a virtual ghost town, and tens of thousands of schoolchildren had been sent away from Paris for safety. But the exodus of May and June 1940 was of a different order altogether. It was as if a giant foot had kicked an ant-hill, thought Saint-Exupéry, and the ants were swarming out.[3] For the most part people did not wait for instructions. First across the French frontier came Dutch refugees, followed closely by Belgians. At first they were kindly received, though the welcome wore thin as their numbers swelled and communities found their resources drained. Then, as it became clear that the Germans were advancing, the French too began to migrate. Sometimes families took the decision very quickly, on the first report or rumour that the Germans were close. In many places the exodus was triggered by the arrival of crowds of refugees in otherwise peaceful villages. Families left meals uneaten on the table and their unmilked cows bellowing in the fields, setting out with no idea of where they were going or what they would do when they got there. 'In 1814,' lamented Jacques Minart on 16 May, 'the cry was "The Cossacks are coming!"; in 1870, "Here come the Uhlans!"; in 1940, "Here come the Panzers!", and everyone flees.'[4]

The contagion of rumour has been likened to the 'Great Fear' that swept the countryside in 1789. Yet this mass migration, however ill-prepared, was an essentially rational response to danger – even if reports that the Germans were using poison gas like the Italians in Abyssinia proved unfounded. To seek to escape the bombing was only natural, but families soon discovered that what had been safe areas in 1914–18 were now within the reach of the Luftwaffe, which machine-gunned and bombed the endless columns crowding the roads. In this war civilians found themselves deliberately rather than incidentally targeted, though in their midst were retreating soldiers who 'moved along like blind men, like shabby wraiths'.[5] In Belgium and north-eastern France stories of German atrocities in 1914 and memories of the subsequent occupation spurred people's desire to escape their clutches, as did more recent newsreels of the fate of civilians during the Spanish Civil War. Reports of systematic brutality by German troops in Poland had also filtered westwards, adding a further incentive to flight, and some Jewish families had a sound instinct for what Nazi conquest might bode for them.[6]

Typically, the better-off refugees – those with motor cars and the means to buy petrol, food and lodging en route – formed the vanguard of the exodus. However, petrol was often unavailable and cars had to be abandoned, adding to the congestion. Behind the motorists came a bizarre variety of horse-drawn vehicles piled high with family possessions and heirlooms, many of which were soon abandoned by the wayside. In the rear came poorer people on foot or on bicycles, carrying what they could in suitcases, wheelbarrows or prams, some pushing along elderly relatives or small children in the broiling sun. Some 90,000 children became separated from their parents – sometimes for months – often following lifts being accepted without any clear arrangements for a rendezvous. The journey posed other hazards, too. Belgians with their unfamiliar accents and carrying their characteristic bright red blankets aroused French suspicions of fifth columnists signalling to enemy aircraft. On the roads the sound of approaching planes might give only a few seconds' warning to dive for shelter behind a tree or into a ditch before a terrifying burst of fire left its trail of wrecked vehicles and dead horses and people littering the roadside.

In the towns vast traffic jams formed as vehicles queued to cross bridges over major rivers. Mattresses strapped to car roofs provided no protection against bombs. A resident of Abbeville, Madame Cardenne, described a long line of vehicles caught by bombers as they attempted to leave the town: 'It was horrible – I shall never forget it. I can still see all those burnt-out wrecks. In one of them was a woman carbonized with a baby in her arms.' Like many of the passengers killed by a raid on the railway station, many victims were Dutch or Belgian refugees far from home who never could be identified from their charred remains. Another group of foreign refugees, seeking safety by crossing the unfamiliar Somme estuary near Saint-Valéry in the early hours of 21 May, were engulfed by the incoming tide, their cries freezing the blood of local people helpless to save them from their misadventure.[7]

The disorder was compounded because many of the staff essential to running local services – mayors, administrators, policemen, firemen and medical staff, as well as bakers and butchers – joined the exodus. Unmanned telephone exchanges aggravated the chaos. Among the evacuees thronging the roads were the inmates not only of religious houses, but of prisons and mental asylums as well. Misguided orders for the gendarmerie to withdraw opened the gate to mayhem, as traffic went undirected and pillage ran unchecked. The French state seemed to have abdicated in many districts, which were left without any civil authority at all.[8] With frightening speed, one of the most civilized countries in Europe was falling into anarchy. Such conditions severely hampered allied military operations, though they were a consequence of military defeat rather than its cause.

Amid this maelstrom, could the new French commander-in-chief, General Maxime Weygand, impose his will? A spry cavalryman with high cheek-bones and the energy of a man less than half his seventy-three years, at first he inspired confidence. Reynaud had brought him in as a strong man with an abundance of fighting spirit. Weygand carried with him all the prestige of having been the faithful second of Marshal Foch throughout the ordeal of 1914–18, and of having read out the peace terms to the Germans at the armistice of Rethondes. He seemed the antithesis of Gamelin, whose predecessor as Army Chief of Staff he had been in 1930–5. In that role Weygand had been instrumental in promoting the motorization of the infantry and in equipping the cavalry with tanks. Authoritarian, irascible and opinionated, he was not the man to shelter at Vincennes offering 'suggestions'. On 20 May he told a shaken Billotte over the telephone that, 'It is by attacking and fighting like dogs that we shall beat the Panzers, which must be at the end of their tether ... Attack southwards.'[9] Churchill was impressed when on 22 May he heard Weygand expound his plan for a pincer attack from north and south to cut the Panzer spearheads off from the German forces advancing to support them.

However, the 'Weygand Plan' was stillborn. On 21 May Weygand had risked a hazardous flight to the isolated northern armies to co-ordinate a counterattack. Although he met King Leopold of the Belgians at Ypres, Lord Gort, commander of the British Expeditionary Force, failed to appear. Weygand interpreted this as a deliberate snub, whereas actually Gort did not learn about the rendezvous until too late. Billotte, to whom Weygand explained his plans, was fatally injured in a car crash that evening – one of many deaths on the overcrowded, unlit roads during those weeks – and it was three days before Weygand appointed Blanchard as his successor, just at a time when strong co-ordination was vital. The British had in fact counterattacked southwards near Arras on 21 May with a force of seventy-four tanks (sixteen of them the heavily armoured Mark II Matildas), administering the sharpest blow yet to the advancing Germans until Rommel rallied his panicky troops and halted the attack with his 88mm artillery. With no air support, the British lost nearly two-thirds of their tanks and were beaten back. A smaller force of French tanks had participated, but at one point during the confusion French and

British forces mistakenly opened fire on each other. The episode was an ominous symbol of the poor co-ordination, misunderstandings and recriminations that were beginning to pull the alliance apart under the strain of defeat. Indeed, for the next stage of the campaign French and British narratives diverge markedly.

In the widely accepted French view, drawing on residual popular mistrust of 'perfidious Albion' and deliberately fostered under the Vichy regime, the counter-attack to pinch off the Panzer corridor failed because the British refused to take part. For decades after the war some commentators insisted that, as in 1914, the only thought of the British was to re-embark for home as quickly as possible, and that they behaved, in Pétain's words, 'in a totally callous and selfish manner while demanding the sacrifice of every able-bodied Frenchman'.[10] After all, Britain had a larger population and industrial capacity than France, yet she had fielded an army smaller than Belgium's and refused to commit her air force fully. Not only had she pursued a pre-war policy that had encouraged the revival of Germany, but she was now abandoning France with indecent haste. British troops evacuated Boulogne on 23 May without notifying the French commandant, who was continuing resistance, just as they pulled back from Arras that night without notifying the French, jeopardizing the whole allied line in the north. At Dunkirk they destroyed large quantities of weapons that could have been used by the French defenders, and occasionally there were ugly scuffles and threats exchanged between British and French soldiers on the beaches. French troops who attempted to board British ships in the early stages of the evacuation were forcefully rebuffed, in the spirit of Gort's remark that 'every Frenchman embarked is at [the] cost of one Englishman'.[11] Meanwhile French troops under General Fagalde were fighting on the western perimeter at Dunkirk while the British escaped.

Marc Bloch, whom we last met as a sergeant in 1914 and who, after a distinguished career as a professor of medieval history, was now serving as an officer on Blanchard's staff, had many British friends and connections and was critical of French liaison failures. Yet in such circumstances, he pointed out, French troops would have needed a superhuman degree of charity not to feel bitter as they watched one ship after another carrying their comrades in arms to freedom.[12] Mistrust deepened when Gort's assurance to the French Admiral Abrial on 31 May that British troops would form part of the rearguard covering the final evacuation was overtaken by events, and a somewhat embarrassed General Alexander had to inform Abrial the next day that his latest orders from London were to embark all remaining British troops the following night, while there was still time. Thus, while the British regarded the evacuation of Dunkirk as a 'miracle', probably a more typical French attitude was embodied in the acid riposte of Commander de Lapérouse of the French navy who, on hearing Alexander tell Abrial that everything that could be saved had been saved, retorted, 'Except honour, General.'[13]

The British perspective on these events is naturally very different, and under-lines the extent to which, in losing the battle on the Meuse, France had also lost the confidence of her allies. British disillusion was the greater because of the exaggerated faith her leaders had reposed in the French army and its high command. Having placed themselves under French command, the British were dismayed to have received virtually no orders during the crucial days of the campaign, and then to find themselves trapped through no fault of their own. An exasperated General 'Tiny' Ironside, Chief of the Imperial General Staff, noted, 'God help the B.E.F. Brought to this state by the incompetence of the French Command.'[14] On 20 May Ironside found Blanchard and Billotte 'in a state of complete depression. No plan, no thought of a plan. Ready to be slaughtered ... I lost my temper and shook Billotte by the button of his tunic. The man is completely beaten.'[15] At Blanchard's headquarters Marc Bloch watched his general staring fixedly at a map 'as though hoping to find on it the decision that eluded him', while one of his corps commanders told Blanchard to 'Do anything you like, sir, but at least do something!' Blanchard and other French commanders were already talking about capitulation.[16]

The British had chosen to attack at Arras on the 21st without waiting for some French units that were not ready. The next day a fraction of those French units under General Molinié launched its own attack in the direction of Cambrai. Like the British effort, the French blow lacked sufficient strength to cause the Germans lasting damage, and was broken up by air attacks. The British could claim that their attack at least had an important effect on the more cautious spirits in the German high command, particularly Runstedt, delaying the Panzer advance on the Channel ports and Dunkirk and contributing to the notorious 'Halt Order' of 24 May which made a gift to the allies of precious time for establishing a perimeter to protect their evacuation. As for the 'Weygand Plan', Churchill's enthusiasm notwithstanding, Gort thought it unworkable. It took too little account of strong and mounting German pressure on the allied pocket, nor of the inevitability of that line being broken if the BEF were shifted southwards as Weygand proposed. With his communications cut and his ammunition limited, Gort felt in no position to mount a major counterattack.[17] With some justification, the British suspected that they were being set up as scapegoats by the French, whose counterattack from the south did not materialize until 27 May, and then on a small scale. By that time the Germans were too strong to be dislodged. Weygand's assertion on 23 May that the French had already retaken Amiens was unfounded, and he seemed not to grasp the scale and speed of the German operations.

If Weygand had been Foch's understudy, it was becoming evident that he lacked both his late mentor's ability to match means to ends and his talent for managing allies. Although even a hostile critic like de Gaulle conceded that the battle was already lost by the time Weygand took command,[18] the British official history dryly observed that exhortations to 'fight like dogs' were no substitute for definite and practical orders.[19]

Gort's straightforward character hardly fitted that of the Machiavellian schemer of French legend. The British withdrew from Arras on 23 May to avoid being cut off by Rommel's forces. By 25 May Gort had come to the view that the Battle of France was lost; that French ideas that the northern armies could maintain themselves where they stood were wholly unrealistic, and that his duty was to save as much of the BEF as he could. When the Belgian army capitulated on 28 May –

also to fierce French indignation and accusations of betrayal – Gort was able to plug the resulting gap in the allied line, so preventing the Germans from breaking through and stopping the Dunkirk evacuation in its tracks. He would have been unable to do so had he committed the BEF to a counterattack southwards as Weygand, and indeed Churchill, had wished.

As for the evacuation, it was true that Gort was inclined to leave the French to fend for themselves. But if very few French troops were evacuated at first it was also partly because Weygand, having been sceptical about evacuation, did not give the order to his forces until 29 May. Despite many frictions on the Dunkirk beaches, aggravated by the language barrier, exhausted Royal Navy crews continued to risk their lives to bring French troops away after the BEF had been evacuated. Regarding the vexed issue of committing the remaining strength of the Royal Air Force to France, given their alarming loss rate in May, the British held to the view that they must keep back their remaining fighters and pilots for the defence of the British Isles. French arguments that that battle could better have been fought over France than England were unconvincing to British leaders facing their own battle for national survival. During the Battle of Britain the RAF enjoyed the key advantages that its planes did not have to face German anti-aircraft fire and its Spitfires and Hurricanes operating with full tanks and early warning of the enemy approach could take on Messerschmitts nearing the limit of their range. The reverse had often been true in the fighting over France. Meanwhile, British fighters bore the brunt of trying to defend the skies over Dunkirk.

Defeat envenomed such Anglo-French quarrels, yet the unexpected success of the evacuation was a joint achievement with momentous consequences. With hindsight the British could argue that it proved to be in the best long-term interest of both countries, for had the British army been forced to lay down its arms, could the West have resumed the fight with any hope of success? At the very least the prospect of eventual French liberation would have become more fragile and distant. Between 26 and 28 May 58,583 British troops were evacuated but, after Reynaud and Weygand pressed Churchill to intervene to ensure equal treatment, the final week of Operation Dynamo saw 139,732 British and 139,097 allied (123,095 of them French) troops disembarked at British ports.[20] Some 44,500 of these were carried by the 263 French vessels of all descriptions that took an active part in the evacuation, and which in addition shipped nearly 4,000 French troops directly to French ports.[21] After a brief transit through southern England, where they received a hospitable welcome, most of the rescued French troops were quickly shipped back to Cherbourg and Brest.[22]

As the British official history acknowledged, the part played by French soldiers and sailors in making the evacuation possible should be neither forgotten nor undervalued.[23] In the final days of the evacuation French troops had taken over the entire responsibility for defence of the shrinking perimeter and fought hard to hold their ground as long as they could, despite the hopelessness of their position. They fought 'like maniacs', wrote the French Major Daniel Barlone, 'to try to delay, for an hour or two, the closing of the infernal circle' beneath 'a ghastly sky, rent unceasingly by the explosions of the whining shells', while 'immense columns of grim black smoke from the flaming oil tanks' radiated heat that seemed like 'the suffocating breath of the last judgement'.[24] Among the 6,000 French casualties was the capable and respected General Louis Janssen of 12th Motorized Infantry Division, commanding the eastern perimeter, who was killed on 2 June when his command post amid the sand dunes received a direct hit from a dive-bomber. That night botched communications and mismanagement led to his men being among the 10,000 troops left behind when the rescue ships had to sail. The next, and final, night's operation was much more successful in terms of numbers, but thousands of French troops who scrambled aboard were stragglers or non-combatants who had been sheltering in the cellars of Dunkirk. They emerged in a horde to fill the places intended for the disciplined rearguard, who thus found themselves among the 40,000 prisoners taken by the Germans when they entered Dunkirk on 4 June.[25] Nearly 3,000 civilians had been killed or wounded during the fighting around the ruined town.

The Germans had also finally overcome French resistance at Lille, where the remnants of five divisions of Blanchard's First Army had held out for four days from 28 May after being cut off. The fighting in the Lille suburbs was desperate and house to house, as German troops infiltrated between pockets of French soldiers motivated by sheer angry determination not to go down without a fight. Many civilian refugees were trapped in the combat zone. Finally, with food and ammunition dwindling, resistance ended on the night of 31 May.[26] The German commander, General Waeger, was sufficiently impressed that next day he accorded the surrendering French under General Molinié the honours of war, allowing them to parade through the Grand Place of Lille with their arms while his own men stood to attention. Waeger was reprimanded by his superiors for this chivalric gesture, all too rare in a campaign in which SS units were already carrying out sporadic massacres of civilians and captured allied troops.[27] About 35,000 French troops were captured in the Lille pocket, but their fight had tied down the best part of seven German divisions at a crucial time during the Dunkirk evacuation. Although there was a certain irony in a compliment from the British, whom some French captives were inclined to blame for having withdrawn, Churchill paid just tribute to their 'splendid contribution to the escape of their more fortunate comrades and of the BEF'.[28]

While fighting raged at Lille and Dunkirk, as the Germans tightened the noose around the allied northern armies, they continued to bring up reinforcements to line the western edge of the 'Panzer corridor' facing the French front that had been established along the Rivers Somme and Aisne – the 'Weygand Line'. For their part, the allies made several attempts to eliminate the bridgeheads that the Germans had established south of the Somme. On 27 May General Grandsard threw two colonial infantry divisions at the Amiens bridgehead, while the British 1st Armoured Division took part in a French offensive on the lower Somme towards Abbeville. Both attacks were repelled with heavy losses, the British losing to enemy action 65 out of 180 tanks engaged. Next evening the French 4th Armoured Division under de Gaulle launched a fresh offensive against the Abbeville bridgehead and achieved initial success, creating panic in the German ranks and maintaining momentum when the attack resumed on the morning of the 29th. Both sides suffered severe losses but the Germans eventually rallied while the French were plagued by the usual problems with communications and the supply of fuel and ammunition. When the obstinate de Gaulle attempted a frontal assault on Mont de Caubert overlooking Abbeville on 30 May it proved suicidal for his crews: 'The enemy artillery fired incessantly, destroying tank after tank,' reported an observer.[29] The British 51st (Highland) Division relieved his men, but were similarly unable to exploit their initial success in their attack of 4 June.

By that date the Germans were massing for the next phase of the campaign: 'Case Red', the operation to envelop and destroy the remaining French armies. While German infantry were mopping up at Dunkirk, all ten Panzer divisions began rolling southwards. Hitler's 'Halt Order' had at least enabled them to carry out necessary repairs, and they had been regrouped for the coming offensive. There was little doubt about the outcome, for German forces now outnumbered the French two to one. Weygand could muster scarcely fifty divisions to defend the 360-kilometre stretch of territory between the Maginot Line and the Channel. Recognizing that he did not have the strength to hold a continuous line, he adopted a chequerboard system of defence in depth, with his troops holding strong-points – or 'hedgehogs' – at strategic points. Remarkably, the morale of French troops had revived after the defeats of May, and soldiers' letters suggest a renewed determination to make a stand. A captain wrote to his wife that 'the defeatists and bad Frenchmen should be taken out and shot'. Nor were such opinions confined to officers; soldiers, too, spoke of being in good spirits despite heavy losses. Troops from the north were particularly keen to take vengeance on the Germans for the destruction they had wrought, and were confident of being able to hold their own. Expressing a common sentiment, one soldier assured a friend that 'we shall have that pig Hitler'.[30]

The impending German offensive was preceded on Monday, 3 June by a 200-bomber air-raid on Paris. André Maurois recalled one of his children saying, 'Look, a swarm of bees!' as at lunchtime the sky suddenly filled with small, buzzing specks.[31] The targets of Operation Paula were in the suburbs rather than the city centre and included the Air Ministry, airfields and the Citroen and Renault factories which had been turned over to war production. The damage to production was considerable, and there were over 900 casualties, 254 of them killed.[32]

At dawn on 5 June a heavy air and artillery bombardment announced the opening of the German offensive on the Somme. Weygand exhorted his men to defend their positions with no thought of retreat: 'The fate of our country, the preservation of its freedoms and the future of our children depend on your holding fast.'[33] His men fought obstinately, and the air attacks produced little of the panic seen in May. As the Germans pushed out of their bridgeheads at Amiens and Péronne they found the going hard. French 75mm guns – still in service but firing modern armour-piercing shells – inflicted heavy losses. The 10th Panzer Division had two-thirds of its 180 tanks out of action by the end of the battle, while at the village of Marchélepot south of Péronne, defended by a unit of foreign anti-fascist volunteers, furious close-quarter fighting continued for hours on 6 June in scenes more reminiscent of 1870 than 1940. As at Lille, there were instances of French officers committing suicide rather than be taken. French colonial troops proved particularly effective in combat, though when captured both they and their white officers risked falling victim to Nazi racial bigotry. Alleging mutilation of their wounded by 'savages', some German units singled out French Senegalese prisoners for brutal treatment. There were several documented cases of massacres during the campaign. The high numbers of Senegalese combat deaths – 17,000 out of 40,000 engaged – owed something to the tacit no-quarter policy pursued by German soldiers towards black troops, and a study has suggested that 'at least 1,500 to 3,000' of these were murdered after surrender.[34]

The French were too thinly stretched to resist everywhere along the Somme, and had no reserves to repel the Germans who penetrated between their strong-points. Within three days the Weygand Line had been outflanked. Characteristically, it was Rommel, crossing the Somme near Picquigny north-west of Amiens, who first broke through with his Panzers, weaving his way around the French defenders and striking out for the Seine, entering a heavily bombed Rouen on 9 June. That city's bridges were briefly defended by three tanks, which destroyed some German tanks before being knocked out. Enraged by this resistance, the Germans at first forbade the fire brigade access to the district of the ancient Norman capital adjacent to the bridges, leaving much of the old quarter to be reduced to ashes.

On that same Sunday the Germans launched an all-out assault on the Aisne front. The valley of the Aisne was obscured by smoke as a thunderous bombardment covered attempts by German infantry to cross the river between Neufchâtel and Attigny. The fighting was intense and on the first day the French held their ground. They were engaged, Weygand told them, in the final struggle.[35] French liaison officer Lieutenant Robert Felsenhard described how men of his 57th Infantry Regiment, fighting near Voncq, were giving way under the pressure of numbers when they were suddenly re-inspirited by the arrival of a few tanks to support them and launched a counterattack: 'The surprised Germans stopped, then turned about, demoralized, pursued by a yelling horde of our men with fixed bayonets.' The 36th Infantry Division, to which his regiment belonged, took some 500 German prisoners that day.[36] By nightfall the Germans had made little progress apart from establishing a bridgehead at Château-Porcien. But from there the next day they managed to break out, beating off French counterattacks from the east. Guderian, now commanding a Panzer group of two corps, committed his armour to exploit the success, and German air support was again overwhelming. By nightfall the French line on the Aisne had been pierced, and on 11 June German troops took Rheims and pressed on towards the Marne. To avoid capture, French General Headquarters had withdrawn on 9 June from La Ferté-sous-Jouarre as far as Briare on the Loire.

News that the Germans were within two days' march of Paris accelerated the exodus from the capital that had gathered momentum after the air-raid of 3 June and the closure of the schools on the 8th. Parisians assumed that their city would be defended street by street, with all that would entail in bloodshed and destruction. Troops were preparing defences on the outskirts of the city and engineers were placing obstacles against glider or parachute landings in the major public spaces and preparing demolition charges for the bridges over the Seine. Faced with conflicting or uncertain official advice, hundreds of thousands of Parisians left the capital, making their way southwards as best they could. The railway stations were besieged as people struggled to get aboard the last trains.[37]

Despite earlier protestations that it would not abandon the capital, on 10 June the government recognized that the imminent arrival of the Germans made it time to depart. Before setting off on the road south that night, Paul Reynaud broadcast the news that Italy had chosen this day to 'stab us in the back' by declaring war. 'How shall we judge this act?' he asked his listeners: 'France has nothing to say. The watching world will judge.'[38] Alarmed that the war might end without his participation, Mussolini had said, 'I need a few thousand dead so as to be able to attend the peace conference as a belligerent.'[39] He declared war on France and Britain at the same time, for the moment seemed ripe for Italy to expand her Mediterranean empire at their expense.

It was a dark hour for the democracies – quite literally so in Paris, where on 11 June the decision to ignite oil refineries to deny petrol reserves to the Germans created a pall of oily smoke that obscured the sun and coated everything in soot. Only the next day did Weygand give formal instructions that Paris was designated an open city and would not be defended. The police remained to keep order, while retreating troops were directed around the capital rather than through it. Amid the prevailing confusion it was decided to smash the radio transmitting equipment at the base of the Eiffel Tower, but plans to demolish the tower itself were abandoned. Crucially, the multi-national team working with Polish-built replicas of the German 'Enigma' encoding machine had succeeded on their own initiative in getting them safely to the south of France. A German change of code had made their messages unreadable for three vital weeks from 2 May, but the future of allied decoding had been safeguarded by preventing the Germans from discovering how much the allies knew about their system.[40]

Once the French lines had been broken on the Somme and Aisne, the Panzer divisions advanced through northern and eastern France at astounding speed. Large parts of the retreating French army had been reduced to a disorganized mass. During these agonizing days the French cabinet was divided over what course to take. Reynaud was for continued resistance. Those supporting him in his desire to continue the fight, either from French North Africa or by forming a 'redoubt' in the Brittany peninsula, included prominently Interior Minister Georges Mandel, in whom something of the old Jacobin fire still burned, and the newly appointed Under-Secretary of State for Defence, the freshly promoted General de Gaulle. But Reynaud's appointment in May of men whom he assumed to be symbols of national resistance had actually entrenched a powerful group in favour of an armistice.

Within a week of taking command, Weygand had concluded that an armistice was imperative once the army had made a stand to redeem its 'honour'. Whatever Gamelin's failings or private views, his fidelity to the Republic had never been questioned. Weygand on the other hand, a strong Catholic, monarchist and former anti-Dreyfusard, had from the outset displayed a virulent animus against the despised Republic and its politicians, on whose shoulders he was determined to lay the responsibility for the defeat. In July 1939 he had declared publicly, 'I believe that the French Army is better than at any other period of its history; it has first rate equipment, fortifications of the highest order, excellent *morale* and a remarkable high command.'[41] Yet on 25 May he lectured Reynaud that 'this war is sheer madness, we have gone to war with a 1918 army against a German army of 1939. It is sheer madness.'[42] Weygand violently rejected Reynaud's proposal that the army might capitulate in the field, leaving the government free to continue the conflict elsewhere. Reynaud, who did not enjoy the support of a majority party and whose own political base was narrow, lacked the authority or strength of will to overrule or dismiss him. Weygand viewed notions of continuing the struggle in Brittany or North Africa as fantasies. It would take weeks to reorganize and re-equip French troops brought back from Dunkirk, he did not have enough men or anti-aircraft guns to improvise a defence of the Breton peninsula, and German air power would make supply difficult.[43] After losing her major industrial centres, France would be heavily dependent for her war materials on her Anglo-Saxon allies.

More influential still than Weygand was the 84-year-old Marshal Pétain, revered as the defender of Verdun in 1916 and the most respected and popular soldier in France. A pre-war right-wing press campaign had argued that *Pétain is the man we need* to lead the country out of political chaos.[44] Frail though it was, his voice as vice-premier commanded great authority, and he used it to urge an immediate armistice. Like Weygand, he had no love for the parliamentary Republic, and his conservatism made him see surrender to the Germans as a lesser evil than communism and the threat of internal disorder. The army must be preserved as the instrument of the moral regeneration of the nation, therefore preserving its 'honour' by an armistice was paramount over other considerations. Like Weygand, Pétain was a bitter Anglophobe, disposed to blame all France's troubles on the British alliance. Pétain's mistrust of the British seems to have been nurtured during his service in Lanrezac's Fifth Army in 1914, and he was convinced of their determination to fight 'until the last available drop of French blood should have been shed'.[45] Also in favour of the armistice was Under-Secretary of State for Foreign Affairs Paul Baudouin, a conservative banker who admired Mussolini and had opposed France's entering the war. Baudouin was a protégé of Reynaud's partner, Hélène de Portes, who behaved as if she were a member of the cabinet and gave the premier no rest night or day from her hectoring insistence that he make peace.

Harsh choices now confronted both parties to the Anglo-French alliance. At Reynaud's invitation, Churchill flew to France on 11 June to attend a war council at Briare. The British prime minister encouraged the French to defend Paris and to wage guerrilla warfare. Pétain countered that making Paris a ruin would not affect the final outcome. When Churchill tried evoking the spirit of 1918, Pétain, who had been little touched by it, pointedly reminded him that in 1918, when he had had to send help to Haig, Britain had many more divisions in line: divisions that were now conspicuous by their absence. Weygand again asked for every last fighter squadron to be thrown into the decisive battle: but for the British the Battle of France had ceased to be the decisive battle. That would come, Churchill insisted, 'when Hitler hurls his Luftwaffe against Britain'. It was essential that Britain hold back her last reserves to meet that imminent challenge. Privately, the British were convinced that sending more squadrons to France would be to squander them. As he sat dining with the French that evening, Churchill was informed that British bombers attempting to take off from airfields near Marseille to bomb Turin and Milan had been prevented from doing so by local people who blocked the runways with vehicles, fearing that an attack on Italy would bring reprisals on the south of France.[46] For their part Pétain and Weygand were unconvinced by Churchill's repeated insistence that Britain would fight on come what may. Weygand had already told de Gaulle that once France had been defeated, 'England won't wait a week before negotiating with the Reich.'[47]

On Churchill's final visit to France on 13 June he encouraged the French to fight on, but the British hand was weak. All he could offer was a few more divisions if the French could hold out until 1941. But the best British division remaining in France, the 51st (Highland), had just retreated to the Channel coast and become trapped at Saint-Valéry-en-Caux, where the bulk of it – 10,000 men – had to surrender to Rommel on 12 June. Churchill blamed the French high command's slowness in giving the order to withdraw, but at home he was later criticized for ignoring military advice and sacrificing a division much needed for home defence in a vain gesture of political solidarity with the French.[48] Otherwise Churchill could only urge Reynaud to appeal to President Roosevelt for support, with predictable results. Roosevelt offered the materials of war, humanitarian aid, personal sympathy and encouragement, but he had neither the constitutional power nor a political mandate to go further.[49]

On 28 March Britain and France had agreed not to make a separate peace, but at their meeting in Tours Reynaud felt obliged to ask Churchill what Britain's stance would be were France compelled to accept one. Churchill could not formally agree to a separate peace, but promised that if Britain won the war, 'France would be restored in her dignity and her greatness.' The British delegation then left, nobody having told them that they were expected at a meeting of the French cabinet at the Château of Cangé that evening.[50] Their absence further strengthened the hand of those urging an armistice. Weygand, obsessed by the spectre of the Commune of 1871, sought to heighten the sense of urgency by relaying a report that the Communists had seized power in Paris. Mandel refuted this dramatic claim by telephoning Roger Langeron, the capital's Prefect of Police, who reported that on the contrary everything was calm there. Next day the cabinet continued its flight to Bordeaux, where the local authorities were strongly against any continuation of the war.

Power in Paris was seized on 14 June not by the Communists but by the Germans, who marched into the city in the early hours and paraded through it all day, hoisting the swastika flag on the Arc de Triomphe and the Eiffel Tower. News of this epochal event flashed around the world, where it was widely lamented as the snuffing out of the light of western civilization by a new barbarism[51] – though it elicited a congratulatory telegram to Hitler from the deposed Kaiser Wilhelm II from his exile in Holland. That night British troops remaining in France were formally removed from French command and marched to Cherbourg and the Breton ports for re-embarkation to England. About 136,000 British (many of them rear-area troops) and 20,000 Polish soldiers were brought away, though not all safely: nearly 3,000 men were lost when the liner *Lancastria* was sunk by German bombers on 17 June.

Chapter 18

'Combat must cease'

The situation of the French armies had become hopeless as German forces surged through the French interior in an expanding torrent. Where they met opposition they simply drove around it, leaving the roads and going across country if necessary, finding their way with the excellent Michelin maps with which they were better provided than the French. Following the Panzers and their motorized infantry down the highways came columns of infantrymen chanting their marching songs. By 16 June Guderian's men had taken Langres. Next day they reached Pontarlier on the Swiss border, Guderian having to reassure an incredulous Hitler poring over his maps that there was no mistake about the place name. On the 18th Guderian occupied Belfort, so in a sense achieving the objective of the 1914 Schlieffen strategy by cutting off the French forces in Alsace and Lorraine from the rear. The Panzers had completed the strategic encirclement of the Maginot Line which, besides being isolated, was weakened by the belated withdrawal of many of the interval troops defending it to fight elsewhere.

Even so, German infantry and artillery supported by the Luftwaffe had a hard task reducing its forts in this little noted final phase of the campaign. The German army had several days of bitter fighting after it launched Operation Tiger on 14 June to bludgeon its way through the Saar Gap in the centre of the Maginot Line, while on 15 June Seventh Army crossed the Rhine into Upper Alsace to begin a series of assaults that penetrated the French defences around Colmar. Sixteenth Army turned the western end of the Maginot Line, capturing Metz on 17 June, but by no means all French defenders were ready to give up easily, as a costly and vain assault on the Fortress of Fermont on 21 June demonstrated. By that date the Germans had reduced about a fifth of the fortified works of the Maginot Line, but there was no escape for the remaining garrisons.

Far to the west, German forces raced into Brittany. An air-raid on Rennes on 17 June hit an ammunition train, killing 550 people. German troops marched in next day, while another column took Cherbourg. In central France Lyon, the country's second city, fell on the 19th. The government had reached Bordeaux on 15 June, where there were angry clashes between Reynaud and Weygand, who insisted on an armistice. Pétain made it clear that he would never leave the country, and the next day threatened to resign unless an armistice were requested. The need to end

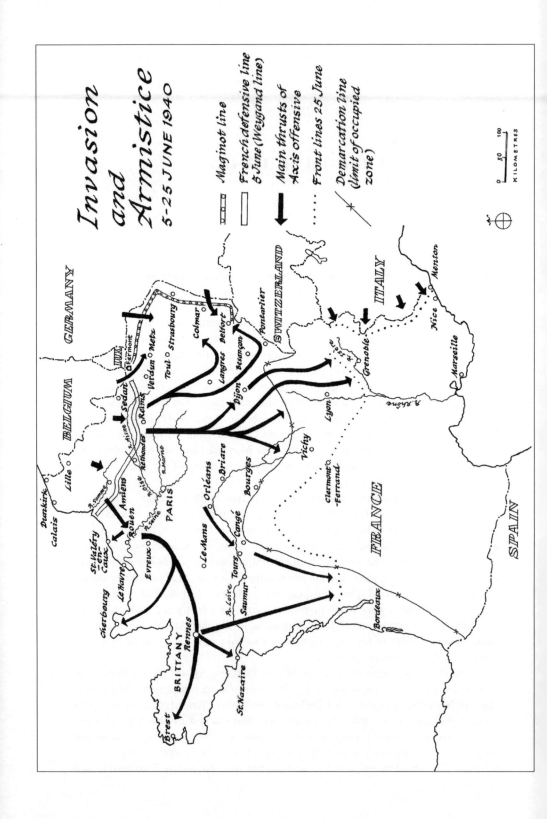

Invasion
and
Armistice
5–25 JUNE 1940

Maginot line

French defensive line
5 June (Weygand line)

Main thrusts of
Axis offensive

Front lines 25 June

Demarcation line
(limit of occupied
zone)

0   50   100
KILOMETRES

GERMANY

BELGIUM

Dunkirk
Calais
Lille
St.Valéry-en-Caux
Cherbourg
Le Havre
Rouen
Evreux
R.Somme
Amiens
R.Oise
R.Seine
PARIS
R.Marne
Le Mans
Orléans
Briare
Bourges
Tours
Cangé
Saumur
R.Loire
BRITTANY
Rennes
Brest
St.Nazaire
Bordeaux

Sedan
R.Aisne
Rethondes
Reims
Verdun
Metz
Toul
Strasbourg
Clermont
Colmar
Langres
Belfort
Besançon
Dijon
Pontarlier
SWITZERLAND
Vichy
Clermont-
Ferrand
Lyon
R.Rhône
Grenoble

ITALY
Nice
Menton
Marseille

FRANCE

SPAIN

hostilities as a prerequisite for 'restoring order' had become the preoccupation of the military men. As Marc Bloch put it, 'the spirit of Bazaine triumphed'.[1] Although the pernicious political divisions of pre-war France were not the direct cause of military defeat, they underlay the eagerness of the Right to seek an armistice as a prelude to the creation of a 'new order' in France.

While the cabinet argued, apparently on the brink of a split, France seemed to be descending into chaos under the impact of military defeat. Georges Sadoul, a conscripted journalist, found himself on 16 June amid crowds of refugees at Sully, a crossing point on the Loire. He was accosted by an angry, tearful woman who demanded, 'What are you soldiers waiting for to stop this war? It's got to end. Do you want them to slaughter us all with our kids? ... Why are you still fighting? Oh, if I could get my hands on that scum-bag Reynaud!' Around him soldiers were throwing away their ammunition and asking the same question: 'Why continue, why let these poor people be massacred, when it's all gone to hell? What are they waiting for to make peace?' An air-raid on overcrowded Sully that afternoon created more horrific scenes of slaughter among soldiers and civilians alike.[2] Southern France was thronged with 8 million refugees, including 1.8 million Belgians and 150,000 from Holland and Luxembourg.[3] The 6.2 million French refugees constituted one-sixth of the country's civilian population uprooted from their homes, with all the attendant problems of feeding them and finding them shelter. Many southern towns were full to overflowing. In some areas groups of disbanded soldiers were resorting to pillage to feed themselves and were helping themselves to whatever else they wanted. In occupied Paris there was even a sense of relief that German forces appeared to be behaving well, more like tourists than conquerors. This was part of a deliberate policy, and German propaganda leaflets and radio broadcasts reiterated the message that surrender was the quickest way to end France's agony.

Paul Reynaud had warned Weygand that nineteenth-century notions of honourable armistice were naïve: 'You are taking Hitler for Wilhelm I, the old gentleman who took Alsace-Lorraine from us and that was that. But Hitler is Genghis Khan.'[4] A last-minute attempt from London to strengthen Reynaud's hand by a proposal for Anglo-French political union backfired. The plan had been drafted by a Frenchman, Jean Monnet, and forwarded by de Gaulle to a receptive Churchill, but was dismissed by the French cabinet. Former premier and appeaser Camille Chautemps thought it a scheme to reduce France to a British dominion. Weygand condemned it as a step to French vassalage. Chautemps, who had just heard of the bombing of Blois, insisted that the cabinet must decide 'whether we want to stop the killing or not'.[5] The cabinet agreed to Chautemps' proposal that they should enquire what armistice terms Germany would offer. Feeling himself defeated, but not putting the armistice issue to a vote, a physically and emotionally exhausted Reynaud gave up the struggle and resigned on the night of 16 June.[6]

When President Lebrun invited Pétain to form a government, the marshal accepted with alacrity, using his Spanish contacts to open communication with the Germans. The next day, without waiting to learn what terms the Germans might offer, he addressed the nation in a radio broadcast, stressing his compassion and concern for the refugees and saying, 'It is with a heavy heart that I tell you today that combat must cease.'[7] These words sowed confusion. Many French troops still resisting interpreted them as an order to lay down their arms, or at least as a signal that further sacrifice was futile. A million men docilely surrendered over the following days, encouraged by the Germans to believe that their detention would be brief. Other units or small groups fought on in isolated actions, like the encircled troops who defended the Marne-to-Rhine Canal around Toul at heavy cost, or the cavalry cadets at Saumur who fought to defend bridges over the Loire on 19–20 June.[8] Civilians often assumed that Pétain's announcement meant that the danger was past, but until the armistice was signed the Germans kept up unrelenting pressure. Towns continued to be bombed and columns of refugees to be machine-gunned. The French government's designation of all towns of over 20,000 inhabitants as open towns on 18 June was an attempt to limit the damage, but it hamstrung attempts at orderly retreat by their own forces, drawing a strong protest from General Georges.[9] There were clashes between military commanders and civilians who wanted to prevent further destruction of their towns. In central France mayors hastened to put out white flags, one even going so far as to inform the Germans of French defensive positions around his town.[10] Captain Beaufre reported that a tank officer who tried to defend Vierzon was killed by local people.[11] In one well-documented case in Lorraine on 20 June the colonel of the surrounded 153rd Artillery Regiment threatened to shoot a man if he did not obey a clearly suicidal order to advance towards enemy lines. Weighing his options, the soldier shot his colonel dead.

Whatever their inner reservations, a majority of French people apparently greeted the prospect of peace with intense relief. Pétain was widely trusted as a reassuring grandfather figure. Anything that promised an end to fear, suffering and destruction and offered a return to some semblance of normality was to be embraced. Georges Sadoul had noticed that refugees had turned to him for help simply because his uniform made him an authority figure[12]: France as a whole did much the same thing in looking to Pétain for salvation. Sometimes reactions to news of the armistice went far beyond simple relief. A veteran of the Great War who had been recalled in 1939 witnessed scenes of rejoicing at Bordeaux rivalling the celebrations on its boulevards in November 1918. The sight was enough, he confessed, to make him want to weep tears of shame and rage.[13] At the other end of the spectrum a few people, including a leading Paris surgeon, chose suicide rather than submit to German rule.

Amongst those who refused to accept defeat was General de Gaulle, a man imbued to an exceptional degree with a sense of his own destiny. Upon learning of Reynaud's resignation he flew to London on 17 June. He had been an admirer and protégé of Pétain until the two quarrelled in 1938,[14] but he now viewed him and Weygand as men of the past whose military policies had brought France to this state. In Pétain, he judged, there had once dwelt a very great man who 'had died sometime around 1925',[15] leaving only the aged defeatist fixated on the enemy within and seeing it as his mission to call his countrymen to repentance for their sins. Pétain thought only in terms of the battle for Metropolitan France, where his government lacked the organized troops, space and will to continue the struggle. De Gaulle insisted that the loss of the Battle of France was an episode in a wider struggle to be fought in alliance with Britain and her Empire, which ruled the seas. From boyhood he had been deeply moved by the spirit of the National Defence in 1870–71: his father had been wounded during the Siege of Paris and his mother had conjured up the despair her family had felt at the news of Bazaine's capitulation.[16] Safe in London, with Churchill's support on 18 June at the BBC he broadcast an appeal to French soldiers. It was the same day that Churchill delivered his 'Finest Hour' speech in the House of Commons, and de Gaulle's message to his country-men had no less significance for the future course of the conflict:

> This war has not been decided by the Battle of France. This war is a world war. . . . [T]he wider world holds all the means necessary one day to crush our enemies. Struck down today by mechanized force, we can win in the future with superior mechanized force . . . Whatever happens, the flame of French resistance must not and will not be snuffed out.[17]

The general was not a well-known figure and was unpopular in the army. Few Frenchmen seem to have heard his broadcast, which at first attracted disappointing numbers of recruits. The great majority of French officers still felt that their first loyalty was to the existing military hierarchy, whose orders they would obey. Nevertheless, the word 'resistance' had been thrown down like a gage in defiance of Pétain.

De Gaulle was beyond the reach of Pétain's spite, though Weygand as Defence Minister later insisted that de Gaulle be sentenced to death after being found guilty of treason in his absence. The Pétain regime propagated the widely accepted view that those who left France were cowards and deserters. A party of Left-wing Deputies and former ministers, including Daladier and Mandel, sailed from Bordeaux for North Africa on 20 June on the liner *Massilia*, but were arrested on reaching Casablanca. British hopes of a French government carrying on the war from North Africa were disappointed. The man who might have been its guiding spirit, Georges Mandel, a Jew, was murdered by Vichy thugs in 1944.

It was to avoid pushing the French to the last extremity of resistance that Hitler left them a portion of the south of France, their empire and their fleet. His troops already occupied the French northern and western coasts, so important for his ongoing war against Britain, and controlled the greater part of French industrial and agricultural resources. It was convenient to him to keep a compliant French government in being, and for the moment he needed no more. In the justificatory declaration that he had Keitel read at the armistice proceedings, he was content to include a polite acknowledgement of French bravery and of their 'heroic resistance' in an uninterrupted sequence of bloody battles.[18] The terms were otherwise harsh, reflecting Hitler's desire for a very public reversal of Germany's humiliation at Versailles. As for the French in 1919, the place chosen for the signature was of the highest symbolic importance and the ceremony was played out in front of the cameras. General Huntziger, leading the French armistice delegation, was summoned to

Rethondes, where on 21 June he faced Hitler in the very railway carriage in which Foch and Weygand had dictated terms to the German delegation on 11 November 1918. This time it was the French who were not allowed to discuss the main points of the surrender terms, France whose army was limited to 100,000 men and whose fleet must be disarmed under Axis supervision at designated ports. Germany was to occupy three-fifths of French territory, with France bearing the entire costs of the occupation.[19] To meet the needs of the war against Britain, France north of the Somme became a forbidden military zone, much of it administered from Brussels – an arrangement recalling Pan-Germanist aims of 1914 and a first step in the administrative fragmentation of France. Going beyond the armistice terms, Germany shortly re-annexed Alsace-Lorraine and began a programme of forced re-Germanization. Instead of being allowed home, the immense haul of 1,850,000 French prisoners of war were to be detained in Germany pending a final peace settlement. Although tens of thousands of men took the opportunity to slip away in the early weeks of detention, 1,580,000 were sent to prisoner of war camps in Germany and were put to work in fields, factories, mines and construction sites. Some 37,700 of them died in captivity and the negotiated release of certain categories of prisoner was slow. Nearly a million men were still being held in 1945, and received little honour on their return to their own country.[20]

Pétain might declare that under the armistice terms, signed on 22 June, 'honour is safe'.[21] Yet the French had agreed to hand over foreign opponents of the Nazi regime who had taken refuge in France. The British request to send 400 captured Luftwaffe pilots to Britain before the armistice was ignored. They were returned to the Germans – meaning, Churchill complained, that 'we had to shoot them down a second time'.[22]

The coming into force of the armistice was conditional upon France also agreeing a cease-fire with Italy, whose ill-prepared troops had begun their offensive on 21 June. They achieved little against strong French defences and suffered significant losses at the hands of the heavily outnumbered French Army of the Alps under General Olry. In five days of fighting Olry succeeded not only in keeping the Italians in check, but in fending off the Panzer columns that had advanced down the Rhône valley and were attacking his rear along the River Isère. The Italians gained only a little territory where the French made tactical withdrawals, mainly along the coast around Menton. Agreement with Italy was reached quickly, and the armistice came into force on 25 June. Here and there along the Maginot Line, on both the German and Italian fronts, indignant French fortress commanders refused to surrender until ordered to do so by their own government. The last forts were surrendered in the first week of July.

What had this disastrous campaign, the worst defeat in her history, cost France? Gaps in the record have made the exact figure for French losses in May–June 1940 a subject of debate. Although totals of 100,000 or 120,000 deaths were cited in the post-war decades, an official estimate of 92,000 dead and 200,000 wounded was widely accepted by many historians[23] until research published in 2001 suggested a lower figure of 55,500 military deaths between 10 May and 30 June 1940, a further

9,000 who either died from their wounds or were otherwise unaccounted for, and 123,000 wounded.[24] These figures represent a minimum, and we should not forget that possibly 20,000 civilians also died during the campaign,[25] meaning that a total figure of over 80,000 deaths in seven weeks is not improbable. These losses compare to 49,000 German dead or missing and 111,000 wounded,[26] the Germans suffering more heavily in June than in May. They had lost 714 tanks, over a quarter of those operational on 10 May. British losses totalled 68,111 in killed, wounded and missing, plus 599 deaths from injury or disease.[27]

It was a frequent complaint of French troops that the sky was empty of their own aircraft, but French aircrew paid a heavy toll during the battle: 541 dead, 105 missing and 364 wounded. Of roughly 900 French aircraft lost, 230 had been destroyed on the ground by enemy action.[28] In aerial combat French airmen had too often found themselves outnumbered wherever they met the enemy. Their fighters, tied to the protection of bombers or observation aircraft, had fallen prey to faster German fighters. Defective organization and delays in communication had led to French squadrons wasting much effort in vain attempts to intercept German raiders who had already dropped their bombs and left. By the end of the campaign French aircrew, exhausted and dangerously reduced after seven weeks of intense combat, were nearing the end of their tether. After the war much was made of figures purporting to show that meanwhile hundreds of aircraft had been turned out of French factories, more than enough to make up for combat losses. Yet, in reality, most of the aircraft 'produced' and parked in their hundreds on southern airfields were not yet armed, finished and combat-ready. Few were actually delivered to combat units, which had difficulties even maintaining existing machines because of the inadequate supply and distribution of spare parts. As the armistice loomed, General Vuillemin gave orders to save as many airworthy machines as possible by flying them to North Africa. The French air force in 1940 was overwhelmed by superior force, organization and tactics, but it had fought hard. It should be added that, French myths of British lack of commitment notwithstanding, the RAF lost 931 aircraft in the Battle of France, and suffered 1,526 casualties.[29] The Luftwaffe's losses were also severe – around 1,300 aircraft lost, 1,355 aircrew killed and 1,226 wounded.

The French might congratulate themselves on having retained their fleet at the armistice, but that satisfaction was short-lived. Churchill's request that the French fleet sail to British ports before the armistice was unacceptable to the new French government, but to Britain (and behind her the United States) even the slightest risk that it might fall into Hitler's hands was an intolerable threat to her survival. Giving notice that Britain had no intention of having 'her neck wrung like a chicken' (a phrase coined by Weygand),[30] Churchill took the 'hateful decision, the most unnatural and painful in which I have ever been concerned'[31] to open fire on French battleships moored at Mers-el-Kébir west of Oran. Following the rejection of an ultimatum, on 3 July French ships were sunk or crippled by British fire, and the blood of 1,297 dead French sailors widened the rift between Britain and the

Pétain regime.[32] The wave of Anglophobia that swept France helped bury another major casualty of the defeat, the Third French Republic.

As in 1870, the regime that had presided over a catastrophic defeat took the blame for failing to protect the country from invasion and was overthrown without regrets and with minimal resistance. In September 1870 the overthrow came in the form of a Left-wing revolution, in 1940 that of a parliamentary vote. From his prison cell, the former socialist minister Jean Zay lamented, 'The Republic often feared a dictatorship of victorious generals. It did not think to beware of one by defeated generals.'[33]

Leaving Bordeaux because of the German occupation, the National Assembly convened at the small spa town of Vichy in the unoccupied zone. There on 10 July, in a vote orchestrated by Pierre Laval, Marshal Pétain was empowered by 569 votes to 80 to remake the constitution. Next day Pétain became Head of the French State, displacing President Lebrun and the Republic created in 1875. The new regime appealed to all enemies of the Republic and many who were dissatisfied with it – right-wing ideologues, fascist fellow travellers, anti-communists and anti-Semites, political opportunists, the higher clergy and conservatives inspired by the slogan of 'Work, Family, Fatherland' which replaced the republican 'Liberty, Equality, Fraternity'. It also attracted pacifists, technocrats disillusioned by the inefficiencies of the parliamentary regime who saw authoritarian government as a means of modernizing France, and those who believed that France's future lay in partnership with Germany. The mass of French people at first acquiesced because they trusted Pétain and wanted to pick up the pieces of their lives after an unimaginable disaster. He seemed to offer a guarantee that some remnant of French identity and sovereignty could be saved from the wreck.

Only with the passage of time did the full cost to France of military defeat in 1940 become apparent. The 'partnership' with Germany in a new European order dreamed of by the minority of collaborationists was revealed as a sham as Hitler exploited French resources to feed his ever-expanding ambitions. With brutal frankness he estimated that by policing France the Pétain regime saved him at least fifteen infantry divisions which he would otherwise have had to deploy.[34] The puppet status of Vichy was exposed when Hitler occupied the rest of France on 11 November 1942 in response to the American invasion of North Africa, and ordered the remnant of the French army to be disbanded. Around the world, France's prestige as a major power had suffered a blow from which it never wholly recovered, whetting the appetite of those with designs on her empire.[35]

In 1940 France lost her liberty, with all the miseries that flowed from that loss. Oppression manifested itself not only through the arrests, internments and executions that became the constant accompaniment of life under occupation, but also in the numberless privations, anxieties and humiliations suffered by the occupied. The bleak balance sheet of four years of German rule included 650,000 civilian Frenchmen compelled to work in Germany for Hitler's war effort and tens of thousands of French citizens deported and murdered, their fate doubly tainted by the willing complicity of the Vichy authorities who operated their own apparatus of state repression. The victims included 67,000 resisters and other 'undesirables' sent to concentration camps where almost half died, together with 76,000 Jews rounded up in France, four-fifths of them by the Vichy authorities, of whom only 2,500 survived to bear witness to their suffering.[36] Liberation, too, had its price: 70,000 French civilians were killed in the allied air war against Germany, France was once again turned into a battleground and the divisions between resisters and collaborators spilt over into the vicious bloodshed characteristic of civil wars. France was to agonize for decades over the choices and deeds of her divided citizens in wartime – far longer than over the responsibilities and events of the military defeat itself.

What of the victor? A week after the armistice, in the early hours of 28 June 1940, those Parisians who were about were astounded to see Adolf Hitler make a brief unannounced tour of the architectural highlights of the capital he had conquered. Hitler was basking in having at last avenged the shame of defeat in 1918 which had propelled him into political life. In these days he also made a nostalgic trip to the battlefields where he had fought in the Great War. He had come to Paris not for a triumphal victory parade – that took place in Berlin on 6 July – but for inspiration for his proposed remodelling of Berlin. He told Albert Speer that he had considered destroying Paris, but had not done so because it was doomed to be eclipsed by the German capital. To see Paris, he said, had been 'the dream of my life. I cannot say how happy I am to have that dream fulfilled today.'[37]

Yet Hitler had other dreams that went far beyond the settling of scores with France – dreams that would consume the lives of millions. The spectacular success of the campaign against France gave him the aura of a military genius who could do no wrong, both in his own eyes and in those of the German people. As so often, military victory contained the seeds of the next defeat. One year after the armistice with France he attacked the Soviet Union, confident of a similar lightning victory.

During the final allied campaign against Germany in 1944–5 there occurred what seemed for a few days like a replay of 1940. In December 1944 Hitler, as he had in May 1940, gambled everything on a surprise offensive through the Ardennes against an overconfident enemy who had left himself weak in that sector. Once again the Germans achieved surprise, once again thousands of dazed prisoners – Americans this time – were sent marching off to Germany while the Panzers rolled forward to exploit the breach achieved by concentrated German firepower. Once again startled allied commanders worked frantically to plug the hole in their line amid unsettling rumours of fifth columnists operating in their rear. But there the parallels ended. The Panzers were not half as strong as they had been in 1940, and their fuel supplies were limited. There were no longer large German forces available to mount diversionary attacks, and this time the allies had sufficient mobile reserves to contain the danger and used them more adeptly than the French high command in 1940. While battle-hardened and motorized American troops were able to hold up the German advance, armoured troops bore down from north and south against its flanks: just the response the German high command had feared in 1940. Most of all, the balance of air power had been completely reversed. Whereas in 1940 fine weather had enabled the Luftwaffe to exploit its 2 to 1 superiority fully, in December 1944 the Germans could achieve surprise only under cover of fog and low cloud when allied aircraft could not fly. Once the weather cleared, allied air forces reasserted their dominance, and the last German offensive in the west was broken.

In the allied invasion and occupation of Germany that followed, Free French forces played an honourable part, as they had in North Africa, Italy and elsewhere. But by that time the Franco-German duel had ceased to be one of the mainsprings of European or world politics. Defeated and diminished, both countries had to redefine their relationship amid the ruins of a Europe now dominated by the superpowers of East and West which had combined to destroy Hitler.

Conclusion

Three times in seventy years France chose war with Germany rather than accept her further expansion. Each war was preceded by a compromise (Luxembourg in 1867, Agadir in 1911 and Munich in 1938) which for France represented a maximum concession to Germany and made a peaceful outcome of the next crisis less likely. Each compromise was followed in due course by what France regarded as an intolerable German provocation that threatened her continued existence as a Great Power: the Hohenzollern Candidature for the Spanish throne in 1870, the German ultimatums of August 1914, and the invasion of Poland in 1939. This account has sought to provide a compact narrative of the resulting military campaigns of 1870, 1914 and 1940.

Any interpretation of these events, and the patterns that may be discerned in them, will depend not only upon the standpoint of the reader in space and time, but also upon their temperament. Thus a cynic might dismiss the details of these bygone battles between quarrelsome neighbours as being of no more significance than those of a fight between two dogs in a pit who savage each other until the stronger mortally wounds the weaker, and then in its turn is devoured by even bigger dogs. Some might conclude that if these disastrous conflicts teach anything, it is that wars beget wars; that blood feuds will continue until both sides are reduced to a state of mutually ruinous exhaustion; and that the consequences of wars are nearly always worse than the evils they are intended to combat. An optimist, on the other hand, might insist that these intermittent encounters are anomalies best forgotten, and that the most significant developments in French and German society over the past century and a half have been their remarkable achievements in the fields of science and the arts, spurred on in part by their competition. The wars were thus only brief interruptions, or even stimulants, to the general technical advances of civilization and to the supposed long-term continuities of cultural and economic history. In this reassuring view of the past, encouraged by successive decades of peace and relative security, conflict has come to be viewed as exceptional, and the details of military campaigns are seen increasingly as the province of technical specialists, with no place these days in the syllabus of 'serious' history taught in colleges. An idealist might add that the Franco-German wars belong to a past age of tribal nationalism; a necessary stage in the progression from the nineteenth-century ideal of the nation–state towards European unity. In this perspective, the wars of the past have supposedly taught the unacceptable price of resorting to inter-state violence, and their memorials serve only as a sort of Gothic *memento mori* – the skeleton under the high altar of modern European peace and progress. From any of these viewpoints, the way that these historical events actually unfolded, what the combatants themselves believed they were fighting for, and the choices that confronted statesmen, commanders and citizens, often in circumstances of the gravest difficulty, uncertainty and danger, have little interest.

More prosaically, a determinist might take a long view of the rivalry between France and Germany as merely an inevitable period of friction during which France adjusted itself to the new reality of German growth in industry and population as her own declined in relative terms. Much as the subterranean pressure of tectonic plates grinding against each other periodically causes earthquakes, so the power relationship between France and Germany was recalibrated by occasional wars. France, it is true, won a victory in 1918, but only at a cost that accelerated her relative decline. A materialist, invoking John Maynard Keynes's dictum that German unity was 'built more truly on coal and iron than on blood and iron',[1] might suggest that the outcome of the military contest hung on which side had the biggest battalions and the most effective weapons.

The historian seeking the reasons for victory and defeat, while remaining wary of any general explanation that assumes the inevitability of a particular outcome, or one that leans too heavily on a single cause, must certainly give prominence to questions of relative military strength and firepower. In 1870 Germany's numerical superiority and Krupp guns overpowered France, whose trust in the Chassepot and the *mitrailleuse* proved misplaced. France and Germany were approximately equal in population in 1870, but France's inferior military showing lost her the chance to reverse all Prussia's gains of the previous six years. French defeat opened the way to German unity, and thereafter the balance of strength swung heavily against France, compelling her to put a higher percentage of her young men into uniform to keep pace with Germany.

In 1914 the French army's first assaults were broken by heavy artillery and machine guns, but in the open field it was the technical excellence of its 75mm gun that enabled it to survive. Meanwhile, the co-ordinated intervention of the Russian army caused the Germans to detach troops eastwards, tipping the balance of strength in the west in the allies' favour and making possible the 'Miracle of the Marne'. In 1940 that eastern counterweight was missing: nor did France have the compensating force of American troops and a fully mobilized British army as she had during the German offensives of 1918. The likely consequences had been predicted by Marshal Foch in 1919. Once Germany had rearmed, he warned, 'a German general, counting on the effectives available to him but not to us, could judge that he was in a position to knock out the French army before the British had made their appearance, and the British army before the arrival of the Americans'.[2] When the concentrated armoured spearhead of German elite forces, supported by massive air power, struck the weak centre of the extended French Army in

May 1940, it broke through, creating shock waves that multiplied its force. The combination of the Stuka and the 88mm gun had an even more shattering psychological impact than German artillery in 1870, whose accuracy and rapidity of fire had astounded the French. In both cases surprise, speed and concentration of destructive power enabled the Germans to keep the initiative from start to finish. In explaining the suddenness of the defeat of June 1940, the British ambassador wrote that he would 'describe France as a man who, stunned by an unexpected blow, was unable to rise to his feet before his opponent delivered the *coup de grâce*'.[3]

The importance of shock tactics as an element in German success can hardly be overemphasized, and we should be in no hurry to discard the term Blitzkrieg, of which the 1940 campaign remains the classic example. That not everything went to plan on the German side, that their generals squabbled and Hitler hesitated, while success owed much to the initiative and improvisations of dynamic subordinates like Guderian and Rommel, should not tempt us to underestimate the devastating impact of the German offensive. 'Blitzkrieg', after all, was the term used by those on the receiving end of the assault to describe the overwhelming experience of being pulverized, disoriented, outmanoeuvred and defeated, about which there was nothing at all mythical. Recent analyses of the French defeat have tended to focus on the achievements of French rearmament after 1936 and the few areas where the French army had parity or superiority over the Wehrmacht. It is therefore important to keep in mind that in 1940 the French army on its eastern frontier remained significantly weaker than the German, and that her air force was less than half the size of the Luftwaffe. Moreover, administrative delays, lack of co-ordination and a sometimes misplaced search for perfection meant that the French had taken too long in developing too many kinds of new weapon. Crucially, when the invasion came they were inferior to the Germans in key weapons: notably modern motorized anti-aircraft guns that would have enabled her to blunt the force of the Luftwaffe's attack, anti-tank mines and anti-tank guns that would have done the same against the Panzers. Of these, noted one analyst, France was 'appallingly short'.[4] The German Mauser machine gun was also markedly superior to French models. And, for all that has been written of the supposed 'superiority' of certain models of French tank, in battle the Germans had the advantage in that they had more tanks that were faster, more manoeuvrable, had a greater range and could fire more quickly and accurately than their cumbersome opponents. Each German division packed significantly more firepower than its French counterpart. In these respects, the modern legend of Germany's 'strange victory' in 1940 has been somewhat overdrawn.

Thus production figures alone cannot provide a sufficient explanation of combat effectiveness. Similarly, if population figures alone determined victory, Austria should have beaten Prussia in 1866, and then our story would have turned out very differently indeed. Any comparative reckoning of German and French forces necessarily leads into a consideration of the use each side made of the military potential available to it. The quality of political and military leadership, of military institutions, doctrine and tactics, affected the outcome of each confrontation. Napoleon III's ill-starred attempts to pose as the patron of Prussia, then as mediator between Prussia and Austria, were subverted by Prussia's startling military success of 1866. In 1870 Napoleon's hopes that Austria, Italy and Denmark would join him in putting an end to Prussia's ambitions proved as insubstantial as Le Bœuf's belief that France's army of long-service soldiers could deal with Germany's short-service conscripts before Germany adopted a new rifle that might rival the Chassepot. In the event, French tactics forfeited many of the advantages that might have been reaped from their superior infantry weapon, and their chaotic mobilization contributed to the strategic mistakes that cost them the war. The German decision for war in 1870 was more soundly based on an assessment of their own potential compared to the known weaknesses of the French army, which could not achieve the enlargement envisaged by the Niel reforms until the mid-1870s. When Crown Prince Friedrich Wilhelm joined Bismarck and Moltke on 15 July 1870, the day the excited French Chamber voted war credits, they confided to him that the strength and condition of the French army were 'in reality far less imposing than was hitherto imagined, making our prospects more favourable than has been supposed'.[5] The military machine built by Wilhelm I, Roon and Moltke and intelligently directed by the latter took pitiless advantage of the faulty dispositions and mistakes of the French high command, who allowed themselves to be encircled and were forced to capitulate.

Compared to the military virtuosity displayed by Moltke in 1870, the generals and statesmen of the Great War have been generally condemned as a singularly inept and unimaginative generation. The 'butchers and bunglers' school of British writers had precedents in France, where critics pointed to the clumsy tactics and obdurate persistence in failure displayed in both the 1914 frontier battles and Joffre's repeated and costly frontal assaults throughout 1915. Yet this judgement confronts us with a paradox, in that the French generals of 1914 succeeded in turning back the tide of German invasion where their predecessors in 1870 and their successors in 1940 so catastrophically failed. Just as French diplomacy had succeeded in securing the support of both Russia and Great Britain, so the French held their line during the retreat of August 1914 and mounted an effective counteroffensive. This ability to recover from a false start argues underlying military competence rather than its opposite, and even suggests that Joffre's much criticized propensity for the offensive was a key ingredient of victory. Admittedly, the younger Moltke showed little of the calm judgement and consistency of purpose of his uncle, but Joffre's achievement at the Marne cannot be dismissed as simply a consequence of German mistakes. Since the alarm bell of Agadir in 1911 France had provided herself with an expanded army and had regained her confidence, resolved to submit to no more German threats. As it happened, she hardly had to make a decision on whether to join the war as Russia's ally – Germany's war plan made it for her. Despite being deficient in heavy artillery and suffering a bloody repulse at the frontier, Joffre shifted his forces intelligently to produce a victory that had seemed impossible only a few days before. It was a limited victory, certainly, in that it did not expel the invader from French or Belgian soil, but one which undeniably saved France, prevented Germany from imposing her will and made eventual allied victory possible.[6]

As several historians of the fall of France in 1940 have observed, had France lost the Battle of the Marne (as she might so easily have done), there would have been no shortage of books demonstrating that the event and the fall of the Third Republic were 'inevitable'.[7]

The contrasting failures of 1940 can be explained in military terms without resorting either to conspiracy theories or to generalizations about the 'decadence' of French society in the 1930s: but that does not preclude taking into consideration defects in French military institutions and doctrines long before 1939. French victory in 1918 and the consequent German disarmament provided welcome relief from the heavy military burden France had borne for her own defence since the army reforms of 1872. The massive debt incurred to fight the Great War, and the defensive posture adopted by France in the heyday of the League of Nations in the late 1920s, encouraged reductions in the term of military service, which stood at just one year between 1928 and 1936. Just as in 1870, many of the men recalled to service in 1939 were inadequately trained, with no knowledge of the latest weapons. The officer corps was too small, having been weakened by poor pay and conditions that failed to attract the brightest candidates, as well as by the slaughter in 1914–18 of many promising junior officers whose leadership potential was lost to the next generation. The pacifism of the inter-war years, in itself a reaction to the brutalities of the trenches, also played a part in deterring some young men from taking up officer training. Observers sometimes noted that the ethos among junior officers in 1940 was very different from 1914, and that their men were less ready to obey them. Even so, as its performance in early June 1940 suggests, this army might well have evolved into an effective instrument, given time to harden itself to the experience of campaigning. That had happened to the army of 1914. But time was denied the army of 1940 by the overwhelmingly effective German offensive, and by the failure of the French high command to have devised an effective combination of strategy, weaponry and tactics to counter it.

Parts of the French army in 1940 fought very well indeed when they got the opportunity, whether in Belgium, along the Somme and the Aisne, in the Maginot Line or in the Alps. But, as Hitler observed to Mussolini, the components of the French army were of very uneven quality,[8] and that proved a fatal flaw. There is general agreement that the reservists who faced the Panzer onslaught across the Meuse in May 1940 were poorly trained, equipped and led. General Corap of the French Ninth Army voiced concerns before the event that his troops were slovenly, ill-disciplined and insubordinate.[9] The opportunities for more intensive weapons and tactical training offered by the tedious months of the phoney war were not used as productively as they should have been. Nevertheless, we should pause to reflect that we do not know how well regular troops with higher morale and better unit cohesion would have stood up to the sheer weight of explosive dropped on those hapless reservists caught in the inferno around Sedan on 13 May. Doubtless Gamelin would have done well to have replaced them with better troops from the overmanned Maginot Line. Be that as it may, had it not been for the scale of French losses in the Great War, reservists of that age group would not have been on the front line at all. They were only there, wrote one historian of the pre-war French army, 'to make up numbers'.[10]

British troops apparently stood up better to Stuka attacks, having been trained to dig slit trenches to protect themselves against aerial attack, and 'were encouraged to fire at attacking aircraft with whatever weapons they had, an exercise highly beneficial to morale'.[11] But in Britain, too, extreme reluctance to face another hideously costly land war in Europe had resulted in an army too small and too ill-equipped to play the part it had in 1918, increasing the vulnerability of the allies to a surprise attack.

Marc Bloch went straight to the heart of matters when he described Germany's triumph in 1940 as 'essentially a victory of the intellect'[12] – a remark equally applicable to 1870. It was also a triumph of preparation and training. It is idle to pretend that four hastily assembled, incomplete and inexperienced French armoured divisions fighting in isolation were any match for the concentrated Panzer divisions, which were fully functional before the war, had the experience of the Polish campaign behind them and were masters of their weapons and their logistical arrangements. The allies were also completely outmatched by the German practice of close co-operation between ground and air forces. While the Luftwaffe cleared the way for the Panzers, the allied air effort was hampered by flawed command arrangements, inter-service rivalry and too many obsolete aircraft types.

Although the 1940 campaign has been analysed by many commentators, it is worth reiterating the part played in German victory by superior radio communications at all levels of command. In 1914 German communications functioned very imperfectly, while Joffre kept control of his army both through a trusted team of liaison officers and by staying in constant touch with his army commanders. In 1940 the Germans were always one step ahead while allied commanders floundered to react. Images of Guderian controlling the battle from the front from his radio-equipped armoured command vehicle contrast tellingly with those of distraught French generals, far in the rear, vainly struggling to control the battle with maps showing outdated information, sending and receiving despatches or telephoning orders that had been outmoded by events. Bloch observed that, 'from the beginning of the war to its end, the metronome at [French] headquarters was always set several beats too slow'.[13] The same had been true in 1870.

A French historian of the defeat of the Franco-Prussian War invoked the saying that a day of misfortune teaches more lessons than a decade of prosperity.[14] In war the lessons of failure come at a terrible price and focus the minds of the defeated as nothing else can, as was true of the Germans after their defeats of 1806 and 1918, and of the French after theirs of 1870–71. Both emerged from their ordeal with a stronger sense of national identity and unity and learned from harsh experience how to turn the tables on the victor. In 1914 France had both the will to resist and a commander-in-chief who had stamped his authority on the army, possessed the will to win and proved capable of parrying the German blow. But victory brings with it the risk of complacency, and a forgetfulness of the full extent of the organization, effort and sacrifice required to achieve success. The French high command in 1940 proved unequal to its task, though it was unlucky in that had Hitler launched his offensive between November and January, as he intended, French plans would have stood a much better chance of thwarting him. Speculation over the role of chance, of personality, of military and political misjudgements, and such variables as the weather will always entice historians to pursue different explanations of what one called 'the phantom of that defeat'.[15]

The enquiry and speculation may continue, but the traces of the wars are being reclaimed by nature. All the combatants of 1870 and 1914 have gone, and the ranks of those who remember 1940 are melting away like snow. Their surviving weapons and uniforms are safely confined within museums, while only fragments of their experiences and arguments are recorded in libraries and archives. The towns and villages ruined by the fighting have mostly been painstakingly rebuilt, though not without losing something of their past. As Henri de Wailly wrote in 1980 of his native Abbeville, 'The town where I was born has disappeared, destroyed by the war. In its place there is another that bears the same name, but which its former inhabitants have difficulty in recognizing.'[16]

There remains the deceptively placid and cultivated landscape of France's north-eastern frontier, pathway of invading armies down the ages, memorably described by Charles de Gaulle in 1934 as 'this fatal avenue' in which 'we have just buried one third of our youth'.[17] For the most part it is sparsely populated, only the occasional military cemetery, memorial or overgrown pill-box betraying its lugubrious significance for Frenchmen and Germans. At the scenes of so much mutual slaughter, of so much fear, violence, suffering and sacrifice the physical evidence of those titanic struggles lies rotting and rusting beneath the soil, to be disturbed only when a ploughshare, building development or heavy rain unearths some metal relic or fragment of human bone or tooth. Like the first-century poet Lucan brooding over the accursed and haunted plains of Thessaly, steeped in so much Roman blood, the latter-day traveller to those ill-fated regions may ponder,

> *What rolling years, what ages, can repay*
> *The multitudes thy wars have swept away!*[18]

Notes

The Background

Epigraph: Anatole Prévost-Paradol, *La France nouvelle*, Paris, 1868, pp. 377–8.

Chapter 1

1. Maximilien Robespierre, 'Sur le parti que l'Assemblée nationale doit prendre relativement à la proposition de guerre annoncée par le pouvoir exécutif', speech of 18 December 1791, and 'Sur la guerre', speech of 2 January 1792, *Œuvres*, vol. 8, Paris, 1953, pp. 61, 81.
2. Joseph von Sonnenfels, quoted in T.C.W. Blanning, *The French Revolutionary Wars 1787–1802*, London, 1996, p. 247.
3. Robespierre, 'Sur le parti ...' (etc), speech of 18 December 1791, *Œuvres*, vol. 8, p. 49.
4. Letter of 24 August 1845, Renan, *Souvenirs d'enfance et de jeunesse*, vol. 2, p. 915, quoted in Claude Digeon, *La crise allemande de la pensée française (1870–1914)*, Paris, 1959, p. 40.
5. Lamartine, Manifesto of 4 March 1848, quoted in Raymond Poidevin & Jacques Bariéty, *Les relations franco-allemandes 1815–1975*, Paris, 1977, p. 26.
6. Jules Claretie, *La France envahie*, Paris, 1871, p. 313.

Part I

Epigraph: Prévost-Paradol, p. 389.

Chapter 2

1. Queen Victoria to the king of the Belgians, 12 November 1863, in George E. Buckle ed., *The Letters of Queen Victoria* (Second Series), London, 1926, vol. 1, p. 114.
2. Quoted in Otto Pflanze, *Bismarck and the Development of Germany*, Princeton, 1990, vol. 1, p. 259.
3. Metternich to Mensdorff, 26 July 1866, quoted in Nancy Nichols Barker, *Distaff Diplomacy: the Empress Eugénie and the Foreign Policy of the Second Empire*, Austin, Texas, 1967, p. 153.
4. Léonce Patry, *La guerre telle qu'elle est*, Paris, 1896, p. 2.
5. Napoleon III to Marshal Niel, 19 February 1869, [France], Ministère des Affaires Étrangères, *Les Origines diplomatiques de la guerre de 1870–1871*, 29 vols., Paris, 1910–32, vol. 23, No. 7249, pp. 280–1.
6. Oubril to Gorchakov, 12/24 February 1869, and Bismarck to Reuss, 9 March 1869, in Chester W. Clark, 'Bismarck, Russia and the War of 1870', *Journal of Modern History*, vol. 14 (1942), pp. 197–9.
7. Karl Anton to Prince Karl of Romania, before 9 December 1868, quoted in Lawrence D. Steefel, *Bismarck, the Hohenzollern Candidacy, and the Origins of the Franco-German War of 1870*, Cambridge, Mass., 1962, pp. 27–8.

8. Quoted in Pierre Lehautcourt, *La Candidature Hohenzollern, 1868–70*, Paris, 1912, p. 199.
9. Max von Versen, diary entry for 19 June 1870, in Georges Bonnin ed., *Bismarck and the Hohenzollern Candidature for the Spanish Throne: The Documents in the German Diplomatic Archives*, London, 1957, p. 278.
10. Alfred Darimon, *Notes pour servir à l'histoire de la guerre de 1870*, Paris, 1888, p. 98.
11. Quoted in Steefel, p. 114.
12. Quoted in Robert H. Lord, *The Origins of the War of 1870*, Cambridge, Mass., 1924, pp. 45–6.
13. C.P. Beauchamp Walker, quoted in Josef Becker ed., *Bismarcks spanische 'Diversion' 1870 und der preußisch-deutsche Reichsgründungskrieg*, 3 vols., Munich, 2003, vol. 3, p. 24. On Bismarck's possible conflation of the events of 12 and 13 July see William L. Langer, 'Bismarck as a Dramatist', in A.O. Sarkissian ed., *Studies in Diplomatic History and Historiography*, London, 1961, pp. 199–216.
14. Loftus to Granville, 13 July 1870, quoted in Steefel, p. 177.
15. Report from Berlin dated 14 July, *The Times*, 18 July 1870, p. 9, column 5.
16. Émile Ollivier, *Histoire et philosophie d'une guerre*, reprint, Paris 1970, pp. 170–1.

Chapter 3

1. Quoted in Aimé Dupuy, *1870–1871, La Guerre, La Commune et la presse*, Paris, 1959, p. 36.
2. [France] Assemblée Nationale, *Enquête parlementaire sur les actes du Gouvernement de la Défense Nationale*, 18 vols., Versailles, 1872–5: *Dépositions des témoins*, vol. 1, p. 11; and see Émile Ollivier, *L'Empire libéral*, 18 vols., Paris, 1895–1918, vol. 14, pp. 98–100. Le Bœuf was later reported in the press to have told a Deputy that 'if the war were to last a year, we would not have to purchase even a gaiter button' – see Henri Guillemin, *Cette curieuse guerre de 70: Thiers-Trochu-Bazaine*, Paris. 1956, p. 42 n., quoting *L'Illustration* of 27 August 1870. General François Charles du Barail, *Mes Souvenirs*, 3 vols., Paris, 1894–6, vol. 3, p. 148, gives a slightly different version. State Councillor Évariste Bavoux, in his memoir, *Chislehurst-Tuileries: Souvenirs intimes sur l'Empereur*, Paris, 1873, p. 70, insisted that Le Bœuf had incessantly repeated that 'the soldier's equipment lacked not a single gaiter button.'
3. Germain Bapst, *Le Maréchal Canrobert: Souvenirs d'un siècle*, 6 vols., Paris, 1904–13, vol. 4, p. 87.
4. Du Barail, vol. 3, p. 140.
5. Figures from Fernand Giraudeau, *La Vérité sur la campagne de 1870*, Marseille, 1871, p. 120.
6. A.R. Allinson ed., *The War Diary of the Emperor Frederick III, 1870–1871*, London, 1927, p. 6, entry for 15 July 1870.
7. German General Staff, *The Franco-German War, 1870–1871* (cited hereafter as GGS), 5 vols., 1874, reprinted Nashville, 1995, vol. 1, p. 39.
8. Helmuth von Moltke, *The Franco-German War, 1870–71* (Introduction by Michael Howard), London, 1992, p. 7.
9. Darimon, p. 73.
10. Quoted in Adrien Dansette, *Du 2 décembre au 4 septembre: Le Second Empire*, Paris, 1972, p. 291.
11. Bapst, vol. 4, p. 71. This exchange took place in the Chamber at about 5 p.m. on 2 January 1868. Bapst explains the circumstances in which it was omitted from the parliamentary record.
12. Charles Antoine Thoumas, *Les Transformations de l'Armée française*, 2 vols., Paris, 1887, vol. 2, p. 637.
13. Henri Ortholan, *L'Armée du Second Empire 1852–1870*, Paris, 2009, pp. 62–3, 70.
14. Darimon, p. vi.
15. Ollivier, *L'Empire libéral*, vol. 14, pp. 451–2; Lehautcourt, *La Candidature Hohenzollern*, p. 574.
16. Eugène Georges Stoffel, *Rapports militaires écrits de Berlin 1866–1870*, Paris, 1871, Report of 23 April 1868, p. 106.
17. GGS, vol. 1, Appendix I, p. 83; Appendix V, p. 111.
18. Thoumas, vol. 2, p. 129; Barthélémy Louis Joseph Lebrun, *Souvenirs militaires 1866–1870*, Paris, 1895, pp. 258–9.
19. Stoffel, p. 112.
20. Charles Sarazin, *Récits sur la dernière guerre franco-allemande*, Paris, 1887, p. 11.

21. Victor Derrécagaix, *La Guerre moderne*, 2 vols., Paris, 1885, vol. 1, pp. 404–12.
22. Trochu to War Minister, quoted in Louis Le Gillou, *La Campagne d'Été 1870*, Paris, 1938, p. 42.
23. Thoumas, vol. 2, p. 638.

Chapter 4

1. Émile Alexandre Gavoy, *Étude de faits de guerre: Le Service de Santé Militaire en 1870*, Paris, 1894, pp. 14, 23.
2. Quoted in Jean François Lecaillon, *Été 1870: La guerre racontée par les soldats*, Paris, 2002, p. 75.
3. GGS, vol. 1, p. 250.
4. Ducrot to MacMahon, 4 a.m., 3 August 1870, quoted in Ernest Picard, *1870: La perte de l'Alsace*, Paris, 1907, p. 145.
5. GGS, vol. 1, p. 136; and on varying calculations of French losses see Pierre Lehautourt, *Histoire de la Guerre de 1870–1871*, 7 vols., Paris, 1900–8, vol. 3, Annexe 6, p. 547.
6. Sarazin, *Récits*, p. 22.
7. Picard, *La perte de l'Alsace*, pp. 276–80.
8. Extraits du journal du Commandant David, reprinted in Charles Fay, *Journal d'un Officier de l'Armée du Rhin*, 5th edn, Paris, 1889, pp. 366–7. David was killed on 31 August in fighting around Sedan.
9. Sarazin, *Récits*, pp. 48–9.
10. GGS, vol. 1, p. 197; Lehautcourt, *Histoire de la Guerre*, vol. 3, pp. 329–30 and Annexe 7.
11. Fay, *Journal*, p. 54.
12. Léonce Rousset, *Histoire générale de la guerre franco-allemande (1870–71)*, Paris, 6 vols., 1896, vol. 1, p. 331.
13. Léonce Rousset, *Le 4e corps de l'Armée de Metz: 19 juillet–27 octobre 1870*, Paris, 1899, p. 50.
14. Ollivier, *L'Empire libéral*, vol. 15, p. 504.
15. Gramont to La Tour d'Auvergne, 25 July 1870, in Ollivier, *L'Empire libéral*, vol. 15, p. 483.
16. Quoted in Lehautcourt, *Histoire de la Guerre*, vol. 1, pp. 376–80.

Chapter 5

1. Emperor Napoleon to Marshal Bazaine, 13 August 1870, in Bazaine, *L'Armée du Rhin*, Paris, 1872, p. 50.
2. Rousset, *Le 4e corps*, pp. 67–8.
3. Lehautcourt, *Histoire de la Guerre de 1870–1871*, vol. 4, p. 307.
4. Lecaillon, *Été 1870*, pp. 100, 105.
5. GGS, vol. 1, Appendix XV, p. 118; Picard, *La Guerre en Lorraine*, vol. 1, p. 260.
6. Notably GGS, vol. 1, pp. 337–8.
7. F. A. Bazaine, *Épisodes de la guerre de 1870 et le blocus de Metz*, Madrid, 1883, pp. 70–1, 77.
8. Order of 6.30 p.m., 15 August 1870, GGS, vol. 1, p. 351.
9. Quoted in Picard, *La Guerre en Lorraine*, vol. 2, p. 9.
10. Gustave Marchal, *Le Drame de Metz*, Paris, 1894, pp. 141–3.
11. GGS, vol. 1, p. 373.
12. GGS, vol. 1, p. 378.
13. Quoted in Picard, *La Guerre en Lorraine*, vol. 2, p. 72.
14. Alexandre Farinet, *L'Agonie d'une Armée (Metz 1870): Journal de guerre d'un porte étendard de l'Armée du Rhin*, Paris 1914, pp. 137–57.
15. Quoted in François Roth, *La Lorraine dans la guerre de 1870*, Nancy, 1984, pp. 31–2.
16. GGS, vol. 1, p. 412 fn.
17. Patry, *La guerre telle qu'elle est*, pp. 86–7.
18. Picard, *La Guerre en Lorraine*, vol. 2, p. 134; GGS, vol. 1, Appendix XXI, p. 142.
19. Patry, *La guerre telle qu'elle est*, p. 83.

20. Picard, vol. 2, p. 29 n. By contrast, for the war as a whole Edmond Delorme, *Traité de chirurgie de guerre*, 2 vols., Paris, 1888, vol. 2, p. 978, calculated that only 6 per cent of German wounds were caused by French artillery.
21. Patry, *La guerre telle qu'elle est*, p. 84.
22. Quoted in Picard, vol. 2, p. 45.
23. GGS, vol. 2, Appendix XXVI, p. 26; Picard, vol. 2, p. 134 fn.
24. Testimony of Major Fix in *Le Procès du Maréchal Bazaine*, Paris, 1873, part 3, p. 425; N. Théodore Fix, *Souvenirs d'un officier d'état-major: deuxième série (1870–1894)*, Paris, [n.d., circa 1900], p. 36; Hugues Louis Jarras, *Souvenirs*, Paris, 1892, pp. 111–18.
25. Joseph d'Andlau, *Metz: Campagne et Négotiations*, Paris, 1872, p. 83; Dr Ferdinand Quesnoy, *Armée du Rhin*, 2nd edn, Paris, 1872, pp. 67–8.
26. Jarras, *Souvenirs*, pp. 118, 122, 125–6, 130–1.
27. GGS, vol. 2, pp. 23–4.
28. Fritz Hoenig, *Twenty-Four Hours of Moltke's Strategy* (translated by N.L. Walford), Woolwich, 1895, p. 113.
29. GGS, vol. 2, p. 116.
30. Prince zu Hohenlohe-Ingelfingen, *Letters on Infantry* (translated by N.L. Walford), 2nd edn, London, 1892, pp. 51–2, 102, 131–3.
31. Gavoy, pp. 31–3.
32. Letter of Colonel Donau, 5 October 1900, quoted in Lehautcourt, *Histoire de la Guerre de 1870–1871*, vol. 5, p. 611.
33. Jarras, *Souvenirs*, p. 126; Fay, pp. 114–15.
34. Charles H.R. de La Tour du Pin, *Feuillets de la vie militaire sous le Second Empire, 1855–1870*, Paris, 1912, pp. 164–5; Rousset, *Le 4e corps*, pp. 257–8, sets the context and gives a slightly variant form of words.
35. Notebook of Lieutenant d'Astier de la Vigerie, quoted in Bapst, vol. 6, p. 510.
36. Gavoy, pp. 19–20.
37. GGS, vol. 2, Appendix XXIV, pp. 8, 23.
38. Picard, *La Guerre en Lorraine*, vol. 2, p. 357.

Chapter 6

1. Moltke, *The Franco-German War of 1870–71*, London, 1992, p. 64.
2. GGS, vol. 2, Appendix XXXI, p. 35.
3. A. Flamarion, *Le Livret du docteur: Souvenirs de la campagne contre l'Allemagne et contre la Commune de Paris 1870–1871*, Paris, 1872, p. 16.
4. *Histoire de l'Armée de Châlons par un volontaire de l'Armée du Rhin*, Brussels, 1871, p. 73.
5. Louis de Narcy, *Journal d'un officier de Turcos, 1870*, Paris, 1902, pp. 325–7.
6. *Histoire de l'Armée de Châlons par un volontaire de l'Armée du Rhin*, p. 74.
7. Sarazin, p. 74.
8. Charles Antoine Thoumas, *Souvenirs de la guerre 1870–1871: Paris, Tours, Bordeaux*, Paris, 1893, p. 29.
9. Eugène Stoffel, *La Dépêche du 20 août 1870*, Paris, 1874, p. 20.
10. [France] Assemblée Nationale, *Enquête parlementaire sur les actes du Gouvernement de la Défense Nationale: Dépositions des témoins*, vol. 1, p. 239 (Rouher).
11. Ernest Picard, *Sedan*, 2 vols., Paris, 1912, vol. 1, pp. 75–6.
12. Jarras, *Souvenirs*, pp. 131–3.
13. War Minister to emperor, 11 p.m., 27 August, and War Minister to MacMahon, 1.30 p.m., 28 August 1870, in A.Poulet-Malassis ed., *Papiers secrets et correspondance du Second Empire*, 10th edn, Paris, 1877, pp. 242–3.
14. Narrative of Lieutenant Gérard in Albert Verly, *Les Étapes douloureuses (L'Empereur de Metz à Sedan)*, Paris, 1908, pp. 63–4. The soldier in question, identified as D..., a former Zouave who had served in the Crimea, was killed at Sedan four days later.

15. Gabriel Monod, *Allemands et Français: Souvenirs de campagne*, Paris, 1872, pp. 21–2. In his 1892 novel *La Débâcle*, Émile Zola, apparently drawing on Monod's observation, portrayed Napoleon as heavily made up: see the 1984 Gallimard edition edited by Henri Mitterand, p. 214, and ibid. pp. 644–5, note 68, on the subsequent controversy.

16. Napoleon III to Sir John Burgoyne, 29 October 1870, quoted in Darimon, p. 257; and similarly to Eugénie, 3 September 1870, in Paul Guériot, *La Captivité de Napoléon III en Allemagne*, Paris, 1926, pp. 63–4.

17. Hugo Helvig, *Operations of the I Bavarian Army Corps under General von der Tann*, 2 vols., London, 1874, vol. 1, p. 57.

18. Pierre Guillaume Defourny, *L'Armée de MacMahon et la bataille de Beaumont*, 2nd edn, Brussels, 1872, pp. 98–9.

19. GGS, vol. 2, Appendix XL, p. 62.

20. *Histoire de l'Armée de Châlons par un volontaire de l'Armée du Rhin*, p. 135.

21. *Journals of Field-Marshal Count von Blumenthal for 1866 and 1870–71*, London, 1903, p. 110.

22. Lieutenant E.S. Buisson d'Armandy, 4th Marine Regiment, Revue d'Histoire, *La Guerre de 1870–1871, rédigé à la Section historique de l'État-major de l'Armée*, 48 vols., Paris, 1901–13: *Armée de Châlons*, vol. 3, p. 30.

23. Charles E. Ryan, *With an Ambulance during the Franco-German War*, London, 1896, pp. 55–6. The allegation was taken up by Bismarck: see Moritz Busch, *Bismarck; Some Secret Pages from His History*, 3 vols., London, 1898, vol. 1, pp. 198–200.

24. Letter of Dr Frank, *Pall Mall Gazette*, 30 September 1870, p. 11; Pierre Gabriel François-Franquet, *Sedan en 1870: La bataille et la capitulation par un Sedanais*, Paris, 1872, p. 143; André Gollnisch, *Quelques documents sur Sedan pendant la guerre et l'occupation, 1870–1873*, Sedan, 1889, pp. 20–3; Barthelémy Louis Joseph Lebrun, *Bazeilles-Sedan*, 6th edn, Paris, 1884, Note vii, pp. 323–8.

25. Auguste Ducrot, *La Journée de Sedan*, Paris, 1871, p. 23; Lebrun's report in E.F. de Wimpffen, *Sedan*, Paris, 1871, p. 211.

26. Ducrot, *Journée*, p. 31.

27. Henri Pierre Castelnau, 'Sedan et Wilhelmshöhe', *La Revue de Paris*, 15 October 1929, p. 852.

28. William Howard Russell, *My Diary During the Last Great War*, London, 1874, pp. 187–99.

29. Russell, p. 203.

30. Castelnau, p. 861.

31. Sarazin, p. 115.

32. Sarazin, p. 119.

33. GGS, vol. 2, Appendix XLVIII, p. 84.

34. Walter Littlefield ed., *Bismarck's Letters to his Wife from the Seat of War 1870–1871*, New York, 1903, p. 43; Moritz Busch, *Bismarck in the Franco-German War, 1870–1871*, 2 vols., London, 1879, vol. 1, pp. 103–10; Archibald Forbes, *My Experiences of the War between France and Germany*, 2 vols., London, 1871, vol. 1, pp. 243–6.

35. King Wilhelm to Queen Augusta, Vendresse, 3 September 1870, *Pall Mall Gazette*, 9 September, p. 8.

36. GGS, vol. 2, p. 408 and Appendix XL, pp. 85–100.

Chapter 7

1. Francisque Sarcey, *Le Siège de Paris: impressions et souvenirs*, 21st edn, Paris, 1871, pp. 48–9.

2. Circular of 6 September 1870, in Favre, *Gouvernement de la Défense Nationale*, 3 vols., Paris, 1875, vol. 1, p. 385.

3. Goncourt, *Journal: Mémoires de la vie littéraire*, ed. Robert Laffont, Paris, 1956, vol. 2, p. 369.

4. Bapst, *Le Maréchal Canrobert: Souvenirs d'un siècle*, 6 vols., Paris, 1904–13, vol. 4, pp. 34–5.

5. Arthur Chuquet, *La Guerre 1870–71*, Paris, 1895, p. 362.

6. Patry, *La guerre telle qu'elle est*, pp. 299–301.

7. Maurice d'Hérisson, *Journal d'un officier d'ordonnance, juillet 1870–février 1871*, Paris, 1885, p. 22.

8. Sarazin, p. 294.

Part II

Epigraph: André Tardieu, Speech to alumni of the École des Sciences politiques, May 1913, quoted in Rudolph Binion, *Defeated Leaders: The Political Fate of Caillaux, Jouvenel, and Tardieu*, New York, 1960, p. 240.

Chapter 8

1. GGS, vol. 5, pp. 174–8. Franco-German relations during the occupation can be traced in *Occupation et Libération du Territoire: Correspondances*, 2 vols., Paris, 1903.
2. Allan Mitchell, *The German Influence in France after 1870*, Chapel Hill, 1979, pp. 99–104, 127.
3. Quoted in A.J.P. Taylor, *The Struggle for Mastery in Europe, 1848–1918*, Oxford, 1954, p. 226.
4. Mitchell, *The German Influence*, p. 54, quoting Alfred de Falloux.
5. Speech of 10 August 1880 at Cherbourg, quoted in Jean-Marie Mayeur, *Léon Gambetta: La Patrie et la République*, Paris, 2008, pp. 302–4.
6. Quoted in G.P. Gooch, *Franco-German Relations 1871–1914*, London, 1923, p. 21.
7. Ferry himself used this phrase several times, for instance, when addressing schoolchildren of his native Saint-Dié on 30 July 1889 (see Paul Robiquet ed., *Discours et opinions de Jules Ferry*, Paris, 1898, vol. 7, p. 366). Defending his colonial policy, he replied to his critics, the 'Tartufes of patriotism', by asking, 'must we, in the name of a fevered but short-sighted chauvinism, confine French foreign policy in a straitjacket and, our eyes fixed on the blue line of the Vosges, allow everything to be decided and carried through without us and around us?' (*Le Tonkin et la Mère-patrie*, 12th edn, Paris, 1890, p. 51.) Finally, in his testament, he asked to be buried 'facing that blue line of the Vosges, whence the lament of the vanquished rises to my faithful heart'.
8. Bertrand Joly, *Déroulède: l'inventeur du nationalisme français*, Paris, 1998, p. 66.
9. Poidevin & Bariéty, p. 120; Jean-Michel Gaillard, *Jules Ferry*, Paris, 1989, p. 575.
10. Adrien Dansette, *Le Boulangisme*, Paris, 1946, pp. 72–7.
11. Henri Rochefort, quoted in Philippe Levillain, *Boulanger: fossoyeur de la monarchie*, Paris, 1982, p. 32.
12. Quoted in Edgar Feuchtwanger, *Bismarck*, London, 2002, p. 254; Gooch, p. 32.
13. Poidevin & Bariéty, pp. 113–15.
14. 'Le Joujou patriotisme', *Le Mercure de France*, April, 1891, quoted in Digeon, pp. 360–1.
15. The phrase 'Ni guerre, ni renoncement' was used by Jean Jaurès in *La Dépêche de Toulouse*, 31 December 1887, quoted in Bertrand Joly, 'La France et La Revanche (1871–1914)', *Revue d'histoire moderne et contemporaine*, vol. 46 (2), 1999, p. 335.
16. Full text in William L. Langer, *The Franco-Russian Alliance, 1890–1894*, Cambridge, Mass., 1929, p. 260.
17. *Lyon Républicaine*, 20 August 1891, quoted in E. Malcolm Carroll, *French Public Opinion and Foreign Affairs 1870–1914*, New York, 1931, p. 155.
18. Quoted in Taylor, pp. 466–7.
19. Mansion House speech, 21 July 1911, in *War Memoirs of David Lloyd George*, 2 vols., London, 1933, vol. 1, p. 44.
20. Lloyd George, *War Memoirs*, vol. 1, p. 42.

Chapter 9

1. Taylor, pp. xxiv–xxxi; John H. Clapham, *The Economic Development of France and Germany 1815– 1914*, 2nd edn, Cambridge, 1923, pp. 5, 278.
2. Quoted in Paul-Marie La Gorce, *The French Army: A Political–Military History*, London, 1963, p. 8.
3. Marquis de Chasseloup-Laubat, 12 March 1872, quoted in Richard D. Challener, *The French Theory of the Nation in Arms 1866–1939*, New York, 1965, p. 33.
4. Quoted in Allan Mitchell, *Victors and Vanquished: The German Influence on Army and Church in France after 1870*, Chapel Hill, 1994, p. 26.
5. Quoted in André Bourachot, *De Sedan à Sedan; une histoire de l'armée française*, vol. 1, 1870–1918, Paris, 2011, p. 96.

6. Adapted from Joseph Revol, *Histoire de l'Armée française*, Paris, 1929, p. 204.
7. Henry Contamine, *La Revanche, 1871–1914*, Paris, 1957, p. 150. Bourachot, *De Sedan à Sedan*, vol. 1, p. 89, gives different figures but showing the same pattern.
8. Joly, *Déroulède*, p. 292.
9. Captain Mangin d'Ouince, quoted in William Serman & J-P. Bertaud, *Nouvelle histoire militaire de la France 1789–1919*, Paris, 1998, p. 603.
10. See Raoul Girardet, *La Société militaire dans la France contemporaine, 1815–1939*, Paris, 1953, pp. 214–20.
11. General Langlois, quoted in Charles de Gaulle, *La France et son armée*, Paris, 1938, p. 222.
12. *Mémoires du Maréchal Joffre*, 2 vols., Paris, 1932, vol. 1, pp. 15–16.
13. De Gaulle, p. 230.
14. Rousset, *Histoire générale de la guerre franco-allemande (1870–71)*, vol. 2, p. 149.
15. See Michael Howard, 'Men Against Fire: The Doctrine of the Offensive in 1914', in Peter Paret ed., *Makers of Modern Strategy from Machiavelli to the Nuclear Age*, Oxford, 1986, pp. 510–26. On German tactics and training, see Terence Zuber, *The Battle of the Frontiers: Ardennes 1914*, Stroud, 2007, pp. 12–79.
16. Quoted in Henri Ortholan & Jean-Pierre Verney, *L'Armée française de l'été 1914*, Paris, 2004, p. 49.
17. Quoted in Jean-Raymond Tournoux, *Pétain et de Gaulle*, Paris, 1964, p. 51.
18. Palat, 'Les manoeuvres de Languedoc', *Revue des deux mondes*, 15 October 1913, quoted in André Bourachot, *Joffre: de la préparation de la guerre à la disgrâce, 1911–1916*, Paris, 2010, p. 53.
19. See S.R. Williamson, 'Joffre Reshapes French Strategy, 1911–1913', in Paul M. Kennedy ed., *The War Plans of the Great Powers 1880–1914*, London, 1985, pp. 133–54, especially pp. 137–9.
20. Quoted in Gerd Krumeich, *Armaments and Politics in France on the Eve of the First World War,*. Leamington Spa, 1984, p. 27.
21. Challener, pp. 71–4; David B. Ralston, *The Army of the Republic: The Place of the Military in the Political Evolution of France, 1871–1914*, Cambridge, Mass., 1967, p. 364.
22. See Douglas Porch, *The March to the Marne: The French Army 1871–1914*, Cambridge, 1981, pp. 184–5.
23. Jean-Charles Jauffret, 'L'Épée', in André Corvisier ed., *Histoire militaire de la France*, vol. 3 (sous la direction de Guy Pedroncini): *De 1871 à 1940*, Paris, 1992, p. 21.
24. Tournoux, *Pétain et de Gaulle*, p. 53, quoting a speech by Paul Reynaud to the Chamber in January 1937.

Chapter 10

1. Péguy to Maurice Reclus, 3 January 1912, quoted in Digeon, p. 513 n.
2. Quoted in Poidevin & Bariéty, p. 199.
3. Eugen Weber, *The Nationalist Revival in France, 1905–1914*, Berkeley, 1959, pp. 122–3; and on Franco-German antagonism see Michael E. Nolan, *The Inverted Mirror: Mythologizing the Enemy in France and Germany, 1898–1914*, New York, 2005.
4. Conversation of 6 November 1913: see Hubert Beyens, *Deux années à Berlin, 1912–1914*, 2 vols., Paris, 1931, vol. 2, pp. 39–40, and Jean Stengers, 'Guillaume II et le Roi Albert à Potsdam en novembre 1913', in Académie Royale de Belgique, *Bulletin de la Classe des Lettres et des Sciences Morales et Politiques*, 1993, pp. 227–53.
5. As reported by the Belgian minister to Berlin, 20 February 1914, quoted in Weber, p. 159.
6. Baron Guillaume's report to his government, 8 May 1914, quoted in Weber, p. 159.
7. Jean-Jacques Becker, *1914: Comment les Français sont entrés dans la guerre*, Paris, 1977, pp. 51–2; and see Jean-Jacques Becker & Gerd Krumeich, *La Grande Guerre: Une histoire franco-allemande*, Paris, 2012, pp. 51–60.
8. Raymond Poincaré, *Comment fut declarée la Guerre de 1914*, Paris, 1939, p. 5.
9. Christopher M. Andrew, 'France and the German Menace', in Ernest R. May ed., *Knowing One's Enemies: Intelligence Assessment before the Two World Wars*, Princeton, 1984, pp. 130, 143–5.
10. Quoted in Annika Mombauer, *Helmuth von Moltke and the Origins of the First World War*, Cambridge, 2001, p. 220.

11. Remarks to Kurt Riezler on 7 July 1914, quoted in Holger H. Herwig, 'Imperial Germany', in May, *Knowing One's Enemies*, p. 63.

12. See John F.V. Keiger, 'France', in Keith Wilson ed., *Decisions for War, 1914*, London, 1995, pp. 121–49.

13. John F.V. Keiger, *France and the Origins of the First World War*, London, 1983, pp. 150–2, 160.

14. Keiger, 'France', in Wilson, pp. 141–2.

15. Text of the German declaration of war in Poincaré, p. 149.

16. C.E. Callwell ed., *Field Marshal Sir Henry Wilson: His Life and Diaries*, 2 vols., London, 1927, vol. 1, pp. 78–9.

17. Harold Nicolson, *Lord Carnock: A Study in the Old Diplomacy*, London, 1930, p. 419.

18. Edward Spears, *Liaison 1914*, London, 2000, p. 12; Robert & Isabelle Tombs, *That Sweet Enemy: The French and the British from the Sun King to the Present*, London, 2006, p. 464.

19. Poincaré, p. 130.

20. *L'Humanité*, 18 July 1914.

21. Quoted in Jean-Jacques Becker, *L'Année 14*, Paris, 2004, p. 112.

22. Poincaré, pp. 156–8.

23. Becker, *1914*, pp. 379–400.

24. Péguy to Madame Péguy, 3 p.m., 3 August 1914, in Victor Boudon, *Avec Charles Péguy de la Lorraine à la Marne, août–septembre 1914*, Paris, 1916, p. 163.

25. Becker, *1914*, p. 295.

26. Charles de Gaulle, *La France et son armée*, p. 239.

27. See Becker, *1914*, pp. 344–63; Jules Maurin & Jean-Charles Jauffret, 'Les Combattants face à l'épreuve de 1914 à 1918', in Guy Pedroncini ed., *Histoire militaire de la France, vol. 3, de 1871 à 1940*, Paris, 1992, pp. 272–5; and Richard Cobb, 'France and the Coming of War', in R.J.W. Evans & Hartmut Pogge von Strandmann, *The Coming of the First World War*, Oxford, 1990, pp. 142–3.

28. See Jean Galtier-Boissière, *La Fleur au fusil* (Préface de Jean-Claude Lamy), Paris, 1980, (original edn 1921), pp. 62–3.

29. André Maginot, *Carnets de patrouille*, Paris, 1964, p. 19.

30. Pierre Miquel, *La Grande Guerre*, Paris, 1983, p. 29.

31. Spears, pp. 12–13.

32. Allan Mitchell, *Victors and Vanquished*, pp. 63–4, contends that 'the true author of the miracle of the Marne ... was not Joffre but Freycinet'.

33. René de Thomasson, *Le Revers de 1914 et ses causes*, Paris, 1919, p. 81.

34. Marc Bloch, *Souvenirs de Guerre, 1914–1915*, Paris, 1969, p. 9.

35. [France], Ministère de la Guerre: État-Major de l'Armée – Service historique, *Les Armées Françaises dans la Grande Guerre*, Paris, 1936, (cited hereafter as *AFGG*) Tome 1, vol. 1, pp. 54–5; Contamine, *La Revanche (1871–1914)*, p. 203; and the same author's *La Victoire de la Marne*, Paris, 1970, pp. 95–6.

36. J.E. Edmonds, *Military Operations: France and Belgium, 1914*, London, 1937, vol. 1, pp. 6–7, 19, 486–7. For reckonings of relative strengths by numbers of divisions see Jean Doise & Maurice Vaïsse, *Politique étrangère de la France: Diplomatie et outil militaire 1871–1991*, Paris, 1992, pp. 240–3; and Contamine, *La Revanche*, pp. 200–7.

37. Contamine, *La Victoire de la Marne*, pp. 86–9.

38. Fernand Gambiez & Marcel Suire, *Histoire de la Première Guerre mondiale*, 2 vols., Paris, 1968–71, vol. 1, *Crépuscule sur l'Europe*, pp. 107–9.

Chapter 11

1. *AFGG*, Tome 1, vol. 1, p. 224 fn. 5; and see Jean-Paul Claudel, *La Bataille des frontières: Vosges 1914–1915*, Nancy, 1999, pp. 41–56.

2. David Stevenson, *French War Aims Against Germany 1914–1919*, Oxford, 1982, p. 12.

3. Becker, *1914*, pp. 519–23.

4. Instruction générale No. 1, GQG, 7 a.m., 8 August 1914, *AFGG*, Tome 1, vol. 1, Annexes, No. 103, pp. 124–6.

5. A derogatory comparison used by Commandant Driant, quoted in Bourachot, *Joffre*, p. 18.

6. Contamine, *La Victoire de la Marne*, p. 131.

7. Sewell Tyng, *The Campaign of the Marne*, London, 1935, p. 66.

8. René Christian-Frogé, *Morhange et les Marsouins en Lorraine*, Paris, 1917, pp. 60–4.

9. Diary quoted in Holger H. Herwig, *The Marne 1914: The Opening of World War 1 and the Battle that Changed the World*, New York, 2009, p. 97.

10. John Horne & Alan Kramer, *German Atrocities 1914: A History of Denial*, London, 2001, p. 74; Claudel, pp. 91–3.

11. Boudon, *Avec Charles Péguy*, pp. 71–2.

12. Henri Desagneaux, *A French Soldier's War Diary 1914–1918*, Morley, Yorks, 1975, p. 4 (entry for 2 August); John Charteris, *At G.H.Q.*, London, 1931, p. 33. On the French *crise espionnite* and *l'Affaire du bouillon Kub* see Becker, *1914*, pp. 505–13.

13. Jan Karl Tannenbaum, 'French Estimates of Germany's Operational War Plans', in May ed., *Knowing One's Enemies*, pp. 150–71.

14. Joffre, *Mémoires*, vol. 1, pp. 135–6.

15. General Charles Lanrezac, *Le Plan de campagne français et le premier mois de la guerre (2 août–3 septembre 1914)*, Paris, 1929, p. 75.

16. Joffre, *Mémoires*, vol. 1, p. 282.

17. Berthelot to Messimy by telephone, 18/19 August 1914, quoted in Fernand Engerand, *La Bataille de la Frontière (août 1914): Briey*, 2nd edn, Paris, 1920, pp. 113–14 & fn.

18. Albert Tanant, *La Troisième Armée dans la bataille: souvenirs d'un chef d'état-major*, Paris, 1922, p. 58.

19. For a detailed analysis of the battle drawing on German after-action reports see Zuber, *The Battle of the Frontiers*.

20. Letter quoted in Jean-Pierre Guéno & Yves Laplume, *Paroles de Poilus: Lettres et carnets du front (1914–1918)*, Paris, 1998, pp. 26–31.

21. Horne & Kramer, pp. 54–61.

22. Fernand Engerand, *Le Secret de la Frontière, 1815–1871–1914: Charleroi*, Paris, 1918, p. 537. The French slang for large shells, *marmites*, meant literally 'cooking-pots'.

23. Contamine, *La Revanche 1871–1914*, pp. 242–3.

24. Contamine, *La Revanche*, p. 240.

25. Lanrezac, p. 171.

26. Contamine, *La Revanche*, p. 276; and his *La Victoire de la Marne*, p. 120.

27. Galtier-Boissière, pp. 80–109.

28. See David Stevenson, 'French Strategy on the Western Front, 1914–1918', in Roger Chickering & Stig Förster eds, *Great War, Total War: Combat and Mobilization on the Western Front, 1914–1918*, Cambridge, 2000, pp. 297–326; David Stevenson, *French War Aims Against Germany*, pp. 216–18; and Robert A. Doughty, *Pyrrhic Victory: French Strategy and Operations in the Great War*, Cambridge, Mass., p. 35.

29. Joffre to Messimy, 24 August 1914, *AFGG*, Tome 1, vol. 2, Annexes vol. 1, No. 149, pp. 124–5.

30. Notes pour toutes les armées, GQG, 24 August 1914, *AFGG*, Tome 1, vol. 2, Annexes vol. 1, No. 158, pp. 128–9; and see No. 821, pp. 547–8, for instructions to the artillery dated 27 August.

31. See Jonathan M. House, 'The Decisive Attack: A New Look at French Infantry Tactics on the Eve of World War I', *Military Affairs*, vol. 30 (1976), pp. 164–9.

32. Tanant, p. 6.

33. De Gaulle, *La France et son armée*, p. 243.

34. Niall Ferguson, *The Pity of War*, London, 1998, p. 96.

35. Contamine, *La Victoire de la Marne*, p. 239.

36. Jacques Bainville, *Journal inédit (1914)*, Paris, 1953, pp. 58, 62, entries for 29 & 30 August; Boudon, *Avec Charles Péguy*, pp. 109–10; Galtier-Boissière, p. 89; and see Becker, *1914*, pp. 551–2. On the ambivalent legacy of 1870 for the generation of 1914, see Jean-François Lecaillon, *Le Souvenir de 1870: Histoire d'une mémoire*, Paris, 2011, pp. 143 ff.

37. Spears, pp. 318–19.

38. Jean Charbonneau, *La Bataille des Frontières et la Bataille de la Marne vues par un chef de section (8 août–15 septembre 1914)*, Paris, 1928, pp. 74–5.
39. See Pierre Miquel, *Les Poilus: La France sacrifiée*, Paris, 2000, pp. 129–30.
40. 31 August 1914, quoted in Boudon, p. 102.
41. Quoted in Tyng, p. 181.
42. 'Instructions to Sir John French from Lord Kitchener, August 1914', in Edmonds, *Military Operations: France and Belgium, 1914*, vol. 1, Appendix 8, pp. 499–500.
43. Callwell, *Field-Marshal Sir Henry Wilson*, vol. 1, p. 103; Philip Magnus, *Kitchener: Portrait of an Imperialist*, London, 1958, pp. 8–9, 279.
44. Lanrezac, pp. 258–9.
45. Reproduced in both manuscript and printed versions in *Mémoires du Général Gallieni: Défense de Paris, 25 août–11 septembre 1914*, Paris, 1920, pp. 65, 72–3. On wartime Paris see Pierre Darmon, *Vivre à Paris pendant la Grande Guerre*, Paris, 2002.
46. D'Espérey to Joffre, Bray-sur-Seine, 1600 & 1645, 4 September 1914, *AFGG*, Tome 1, vol. 2, Annexes vol. 2, Nos. 2398 & 2399, pp. 704–5; English translation in Edmonds, vol. 1, p. 279.
47. Ordre général No. 6, GQG, 2200, 4 September 1914, *AFGG*, Tome 1, vol. 2, Annexes vol. 2, No. 2332, pp. 660–1.
48. Quoted in Alphonse Grasset, *La Bataille des Deux Morins: Franchet d'Espérey à la Marne, 6–9 septembre 1914*, Paris, 1934, p. 53.
49. Gallieni, *Mémoires*, pp. 123, 127–8, refutes the notion that the continuing British retirement was in conformity with French wishes.
50. Callwell, *Field-Marshal Sir Henry Wilson*, vol. 1, p. 174.
51. Joffre, *Mémoires*, vol. 1, pp. 392–4.
52. Spears, pp. 415–18.
53. Joffre to Millerand, 5 September 1914, *AFGG*, Tome 1, vol. 2, Annexes vol. 2, No. 2468, pp. 768–9.
54. Proclamation aux troupes, GQG, 8 a.m., 6 September 1914, *AFGG*, Tome 1, vol. 2, Annexes vol. 2, No. 2641, p. 889 (also in Joffre, *Mémoires*, vol. 1, pp. 394–5).

Chapter 12

1. Péguy to Madame G. Favre, 8 August 1914, in Boudon, p. 166.
2. Boudon, p. 147.
3. See L. Di Stefano ed., *L'Épopée des taxis de la Marne*, Jaignes, 1999; and Jean-Pascal Soudagne, *Les taxis de la Marne*, Rennes, 2008.
4. Orders to commanders of the French Third and Fourth Armies, 5 September 1914, in *AFGG*, Tome 1, vol. 2, Annexes vol. 2, Nos. 2470 & 2473, pp. 769, 771.
5. Gabriel Hanotaux, *La Bataille de la Marne*, 2 vols., Paris, 1922, vol. 1, p. 320. General Roques was commander of 10th Division, 5 Corps, Third Army.
6. Galtier-Boissière, pp. 167–8.
7. See Charles Le Goffic, *Les Marais de Saint-Gond (Histoire de l'Armée Foch)*, Paris, 1916, pp. 169–200; and Élie Chamard, *La Bataille de Mondement (septembre 1914)*, Paris, 1939.
8. See Maxime Weygand, *Mémoires*, Paris, 1953, vol. 1, *L'Idéal vecu*, p. 127, and André Tardieu, *Avec Foch (août–novembre 1914)*, Paris, 1939, pp. 51, 55.
9. Ferdinand Foch, *Mémoires*, Paris, 1931, vol. 1, p. 127.
10. Quoted in Henri Isselin, *La Bataille de la Marne*, Paris, 1964, p. 222. Both Germain Foch and Paul Bécourt had been killed near Longwy on 22 August – see Jean-Christophe Notin, *Foch*, Paris, 2008, p. 125.
11. Instruction personelle et secrète, 1700, 5 September 1914, *AFGG*, Tome 1, vol. 2, Annexes vol. 2, No. 2525, p. 803, translated in Spears, *Liaison 1914*, p. 541, Appendix XXXIV.
12. Stephen Ryan, *Pétain the Soldier*, New York, 1969, p. 56.
13. Hanotaux, *La Bataille de la Marne*, vol. 1, p. 176.
14. Charteris, p. 29.
15. See Herwig, *The Marne, 1914*, pp. 302–3.

16. Maurice Genevoix, 'Sous Verdun', in *Ceux de 14*, Omnibus edn, Paris, 1998, p. 66.

17. Interview with M. Christianson in *Le Matin*, 14 December 1918, quoted in Gabriel Hanotaux, *Histoire Illustrée de la Guerre de 1914*, 17 vols., Paris, 1919, vol. IX, p. 104.

18. Private conversation quoted in L.E. Muller, *Joffre et la Marne*, Paris, 1931, half-title page.

19. Quoted in Charles Bugnet, *Foch Talks* (translated by Russell Green), London, 1929, p. 154.

20. Order of the Day to Sixth Army, 10 September 1914, in Boudon, p. 149.

21. See Jean-Jacques Becker, 'La bataille de la Marne, ou la fin des illusions', in Antoine Prost ed., *14–18: Mourir pour la patrie*, Paris, 1992, pp. 123–36.

22. Moltke to Field Marshal Freiherr von der Goltz, 14 June 1915, quoted in John C.G. Röhl, 'Germany', in Keith Wilson ed., *Decisions for War, 1914*, London, 1995, p. 27.

23. Charteris, p. 34.

24. Pierre Miquel, *La Bataille de la Marne*, Paris, 2003, pp. 260–1, 329–32.

25. Galtier-Boissière, p. 187.

26. Lt. Col. Larcher, 'Données statistiques sur les forces françaises 1914–1918', *Revue militaire française* (Paris), vol. 52 (1934), pp. 198–223 (May) and 351–63 (June). Larcher's figures – 216,000 for August and 238,000 for September – are slightly higher than those in *AFGG*, but include the sick.

27. Broken down as: August, 20,253 killed, 78,468 wounded and 107,794 missing; September, 18,073 killed, 111,963 wounded, 83,409 missing, see *AFGG*, Tome 1, vol. 2 part 2, p. 825 for August and Tome 1, vol. 3, Annexes vol. 4, No. 5296, p. 845 for September. Pierre Guinard, Jean Claude Devos & Jean Nicot, *Inventaire sommaire des Archives de la Guerre, Série N 1872–1919*, Troyes, 1975, introduction, p. 213, gives the combined French total for dead, missing and prisoners (i.e. excluding the wounded) in August and September as 329,000.

28. Contamine, *La Victoire de la Marne*, p. 378.

29. Herwig, *The Marne*, p. 315.

30. Edmonds, *Military Operations*, vol. 1, p. 363 fn.

31. Charbonneau, pp. 99–102.

32. Galtier-Boissière, pp. 180–1.

33. Genevoix, 'Sous Verdun', in *Ceux de 14*, p. 66.

34. J-B. Duroselle, *Clemenceau*, Paris, 1988, p. 614.

35. Quoted in David Stevenson, *1914–1918: The History of the First World War*, London, 2004, p. 129.

36. Serman & Bertaud, pp. 728, 738; Guinard, Devos & Nicot, pp. 216–17, for quantities in service with the army; and de Gaulle, *La France et son Armée*, pp. 270–1.

37. Pierre Darmon, *Vivre à Paris pendant la Grande Guerre*, pp. 351–80.

38. Text of the armistice in Pierre Renouvin, *L'Armistice de Rethondes, 11 novembre 1918*, Paris, 1968, pp. 415–22.

39. Abbé Lissorgues, *Notes d'un aumônier militaire*, 1921, pp. 186–7, quoted in André Ducasse, ed., *La guerre racontée par les combattants*, 2 vols., Paris, 1932, vol. 1, p. 214.

40. Raymond Poincaré, *Au Service de la France*, 10 vols., Paris, 1926–33, vol. X, p. 413; and see Darmon, *Vivre à Paris*, pp. 411–15.

41. Quoted in Jean Autin, *L'Impératrice Eugénie ou l'empire d'une femme*, Paris, 1990, p. 364.

42. Desagneaux, p. 105, entry for 18 November 1918.

43. Poincaré, *Au Service de la France*, vol. X, pp. 441–50.

Part III

Epigraph: Georges Sadoul, *Journal de guerre (2 septembre 1939–20 juillet 1940)*, Paris, 1977, pp. 20–1.

Chapter 13

1. This figure includes 260,000 North African and 215,000 colonial troops – see Guinard, Devos & Nicot, Introduction, Annexe VII, pp. 204–9.

2. The total includes 36,600 army officers, 6,300 naval personnel, 28,600 men who died of their wounds between 11 November 1918 and 1 June 1919, and 258,000 listed as missing. See Michel Huber, *La*

Population de la France pendant la guerre, Paris & New Haven, 1931, pp. 414–15. Huber's figures are conveniently reproduced in Jean-Jacques Becker, *The Great War and the French People*, Providence, R.I., 1985, p. 330.

3. J-J. Becker & Stéphane Audoin-Rouzeau, *La France, la Nation, La Guerre: 1850–1920*, Paris, 1995, p. 286.

4. Ferguson, *The Pity of War*, p. 337.

5. Guinard, Devos & Nicot, p. 209.

6. Huber, pp. 447–8; and see Stéphane Audoin-Rouzeau & Annette Becker, *1914–1918: Understanding the Great War*, London, pp. 188, 202, 210.

7. Poidevin & Bariéty, p. 239; Serman & Bertaud, p. 777.

8. Jacques Binoche, *Histoire des relations franco-allemandes de 1789 à nos jours*, Paris, 1996, p. 112.

9. Henry Contamine, 'La France devant la victoire', *Revue d'histoire moderne et contemporaine*, vol. 16, 1969, pp. 131–41.

10. Renouvin, *L'Armistice de Rethondes*, pp. 262–7.

11. Huber, p. 891.

12. Georges Clemenceau, *Grandeurs et misères d'une victoire*, Paris, 1930, p. 168.

13. Maxime Weygand, *Foch*, Paris, 1947, p. 288.

14. 'Some Considerations For The Peace Conference Before They Finally Draft Their Terms' (The 'Fontainebleau Memorandum', 25 March 1919), in David Lloyd George, *The Truth About The Peace Treaties*, 2 vols., London, 1938, vol. 1, p. 408.

15. Speech of 25 September 1919, quoted in Duroselle, *Clemenceau*, p. 733.

16. Quoted in Weygand, *Foch*, pp. 296, 302.

17. The slogan was coined by Finance Minister Lucien Klotz: see Denise Artaud, 'Reparations and War Debts: The Restoration of French financial power, 1919–1929', in Robert Boyce ed., *French Foreign and Defence Policy, 1918–1940: The Decline and Fall of a Great Power*, London, 1998, pp. 86–106.

18. Quoted in Jacques Bariéty ed., *Aristide Briand, la Société des Nations et l'Europe 1919–1932*, Strasbourg, 2007, p. 85.

19. See Stanislas Jeanneson, *Poincaré, la France et la Ruhr (1922–1924): Histoire d'une occupation*, Strasbourg, 1998, p. 204. With family dependants, the number of people expelled approximated 140,000.

20. Poidevin & Bariéty, p. 280; and see Margaret MacMillan, *Paris 1919: Six Months that Changed the World*, NY, 2003, p. 480.

21. See Martin S. Alexander, 'In Defence of the Maginot Line: Security policy, domestic politics and the economic depression in France', in Boyce ed., *French Foreign and Defence Policy, 1918–1940*, pp. 164–94.

Chapter 14

1. Radio broadcast, 6 October 1933, in André François-Poncet, *Souvenirs d'une ambassade à Berlin: septembre 1931–octobre 1938*, Paris, 1946, p. 154.

2. Interview of 15 September 1933, François-Poncet, p. 151.

3. D.C. Watt ed., Adolf Hitler, *Mein Kampf* (translated by Ralph Manheim), London, 1992, pp. 569–70, 589, 607–9.

4. Conversation of 5 March 1934, quoted in Jean-Baptiste Duroselle, *France and the Nazi Threat: The Collapse of French Diplomacy 1932–1939*, English edn, NY, 2004, p. 57. On Hitler's attempt to block publication of *Mein Kampf* in France see Claude Quétel, *L'impardonnable défaite 1918–1940*, Paris, 2010, p. 90.

5. Quoted in Poidevin & Bariéty, p. 288.

6. Doise & Vaïsse, p. 402.

7. Quoted in Robert J. Young, *In Command of France: French Foreign Policy and Military Planning 1933–1940*, Cambridge, Mass., 1978, p. 73.

8. François-Poncet, p. 151; and similar comments quoted in Ian Kershaw, *Hitler 1889–1936: Hubris*, London, 1998, p. 547.

9. Pius XI to François Charles-Roux, 16 March 1936, quoted in Duroselle, *France and the Nazi Threat*, p. 136.

10. Hugh Trevor-Roper ed., *Hitler's Table-Talk 1941–1944*, Oxford, 1988, pp. 258–9 (27 January 1942).

11. Radio broadcast, 8 March 1936, François-Poncet, p. 253.

12. Quoted in Albert Speer, *Inside the Third Reich* (translated by Richard and Clara Winston), London, 1970, p. 170; and see Binoche, pp. 178–82.

13. See Stephen A. Schuker, 'France and The Remilitarization of the Rhineland, 1936', in *French Historical Studies*, vol. 14 (1986), pp. 299–338; and P.M.H. Bell, *The Origins of the Second World War in Europe*, 3rd edn, Harlow, 2007, pp. 239–43.

14. Quoted in Rod Kedward, *La Vie en bleu: France and the French since 1900*, London, 2006, p. 178.

15. Sportpalast speech, 26 September 1938, quoted in Alan Bullock, *Hitler: A Study in Tyranny*, Harmondsworth, 1962, p. 461.

16. See Martin S. Alexander, *The Republic in danger. General Maurice Gamelin and the politics of French defence, 1933–1940*, Cambridge, 1992, pp. 163–4, 167.

17. Quoted in Duroselle, *France and the Nazi Threat*, p. 274.

18. Remarks to the crowd outside 10 Downing Street, evening, 30 September 1938, quoted in R.A.C. Parker, *Chamberlain and Appeasement: British Policy and the Coming of the Second World War*, Basingstoke, 1993, p. 181.

19. Crouy Chanel, quoted in Élisabeth du Réau, *Édouard Daladier 1884–1970*, Paris, 1993, p. 285.

20. Gabriel Péri, quoted in Danielle Tartakowsky, *Le Front populaire: La vie est à nous*, Paris, 1996, p. 87.

21. *Le Populaire*, 1 October 1938.

22. Duroselle, *France and the Nazi Threat*, p. 299. Renouvin was later murdered by the Nazis for resistance activity.

23. 2 October 1938, quoted in Duroselle, *France and the Nazi Threat*, p. 293.

24. André François-Poncet, *Au Palais Farnèse: Souvenirs d'une ambassade à Rome 1938–1940*, Paris, 1961, pp. 22–3.

25. 13 & 19 December 1938, quoted in René Rémond & Janine Bourdin eds., *Édouard Daladier, chef de gouvernement avril 1938–septembre 1939*, Paris, 1977, p. 271.

26. 6 February 1939, quoted in Bell, p. 288.

27. Doise & Vaïsse, p. 366.

28. See Richard Overy, *1939: Countdown to War*, London, 2009, pp. 43, 111.

29. Christel Peyrefitte, 'Les premiers sondages d'opinion', in Rémond & Bourdin eds., *Édouard Daladier*, pp. 265–78.

30. See Peter Jackson, 'Intelligence and the End of Appeasement', in Boyce ed., *French Foreign and Defence Policy 1918–1940*, pp. 234–60.

31. See Réau, pp. 361–2.

32. Quoted in Bullock, p. 538.

33. Philippe Henriot ed., *Carnets secrets de Jean Zay, Ministre de l'éducation nationale dans les cabinets Blum et Daladier septembre 1938–septembre 1939*, Paris, 1942, pp. 80–1.

34. Robert Coulondre, *De Staline à Hitler: Souvenirs de deux ambassades 1936–1939*, Paris, 1950, p. 314.

35. François-Poncet, *Souvenirs d'une ambassade à Berlin*, p. 142.

36. See the accounts extracted in Robert J. Young, *France and the Origins of the Second World War*, Basingstoke, 1996, pp. 127–9.

37. Quoted in Jean-Louis Crémieux-Brilhac, *Les Français de l'an 40*, vol. 1, *La Guerre oui ou non?*, Paris, 1990, p. 59.

38. Wladimir d'Ormesson, *Carnets inédits*, quoted in Crémieux-Brilhac, vol. 1, p. 56.

39. Quotations from Young, *France and the Origins*, pp. 55, 127–8: compare P.J. Flood, *France 1914–18: Public Opinion and the War Effort*, pp. 10, 14, 16, and a similar conversation recorded in Marc Bloch, *L'Étrange défaite: témoignage écrit en 1940*, Paris, 1990, p. 170.

Chapter 15

1. Quoted in Ian Kershaw, *Hitler 1936–45: Nemesis*, London, 2000, pp. 223, 230.
2. Gamelin to War Minister, 6 April 1935, quoted in Pierre Le Goyet, *Le Mystère Gamelin*, Paris, 1975, p. 117; and see further Nicole Jordan, *The Popular Front and Central Europe: The Dilemmas of French Impotence, 1918–1940*, Cambridge, 1992, and her 'The Cut Price War on the Peripheries: The French General Staff, the Rhineland and Czechoslovakia', in Robert Boyce & Esmonde M. Robertson eds., *Paths to War: New Essays on the Origins of the Second World War*, NY, 1989, pp. 128–66.
3. Gamelin to Colonel Fyda, Polish military attaché in Paris in Maurice Gamelin, *Servir*, 3 vols., Paris, 1946–7, vol. 3, pp. 60–1.
4. André Bourachot, *De Sedan à Sedan: une histoire de l'armée française*, vol. 2, *1918–1940*, Paris, 2012, p. 323.
5. Gamelin, *Servir*, vol. 3, pp. 73–6.
6. Quoted in Crémieux-Brilhac, vol. 2, *Ouvriers et soldats*, p. 403.
7. Charles de Gaulle, *War Memoirs*, vol. 1, *The Call to Honour 1940–1942* (translated by Jonathan Griffin), London, 1955, p. 40.
8. Helmuth von Moltke, 'Thoughts on Command (1859–70)', in Daniel J. Hughes ed., *Moltke on the Art of War: Selected Writings*, Novato, CA, 1993, p. 77.
9. *Le Temps*, 3 March 1940, quoted in Crémieux-Brilhac, vol. 1, p. 229.
10. Quoted in Kershaw, *Nemesis*, p. 265.
11. See Karl-Heinz Frieser, *The Blitzkrieg Legend: The 1940 Campaign in the West*, Annapolis 2005, pp. 22–5.
12. Directive No. 6 for the Conduct of the War, 9 October 1939, in H.R. Trevor-Roper ed., *Hitler's War Directives 1939–1945*, London, 1964, p. 13.
13. Quoted in Frieser, p. 79.
14. On the genesis of the Manstein plan see Frieser, pp. 60–99; Heinz Guderian, *Panzer Leader* (translated by Constantine Fitzgibbon), London, 1952 (reissued in paperback 2009), pp. 89–98; and Mungo Melvin, *Manstein, Hitler's Greatest General*, London, 2010, pp. 132–55.
15. G. de V. to Loulou, quoted in Crémieux-Brilhac, vol. 2, p. 433.
16. Jean-Paul Sartre, *War Diaries: Notebooks from a Phoney War, November 1939–March 1940* (translated by Quintin Hoare), London, 1984, pp. 32, 153–4, entries for 23 November and 21 December 1939.
17. See François Cochet, *Les soldats de la drôle de guerre, septembre 1939–mai 1940*, Paris, 2004, pp. 170–3.
18. Quoted in Cochet, p. 51. The phrase *la drôle de guerre* was generally credited to the journalist and novelist Roland Dorgelès.
19. Quoted in Crémieux-Brilhac, vol. 2, p. 427.
20. 'Mémorandum ... aux généraux Gamelin, Weygand et Georges et à MM Daladier et Reynaud, le 26 January 1940', reprinted in Charles de Gaulle, *Trois études*, Paris, 1971, pp. 71–101 (quotations from pp. 88–90).
21. In total, France had 5,096,629 men 'with the colours' on that date, of whom three-quarters of a million were overseas, 181,000 in the air force and 176,000 in the navy. The remaining 3,985,320 were in Metropolitan France, of whom 2,651,802 were with the armies and the remainder on duty in the interior – P. Le Goyet, *La défaite, 10 mai–25 juin 1940*, Paris, 1990, pp. 142–3.
22. L.F. Ellis, *The War in France and Flanders 1939–40*, London, 1953, p. 19, gives the strength of the entire BEF on the continent (including RAF personnel) at the end of April 1940 as 394,165.
23. Notably by Colonel A. Goutard in his book *1940: La guerre des occasions perdues*, Paris, 1956, translated in abridged form as *The Battle of France, 1940*, London, 1958.
24. See Frieser, pp. 4–11, 28–54.
25. For comparative tables of French and German divisions on 10 May, see Bourachot, vol. 2, pp. 326–7.
26. Crémieux-Brilhac, vol. 2, p. 395.
27. These figures are Frieser's, who attributes 879 to the French in the north-eastern theatre. Patrick Facon, *L'Armée de l'Air dans la tourmente: La bataille de France 1939–40*, 2nd edn, Paris, 2005, pp. 167–70, discusses the difficulties in counting aircraft and reckons the number of modern French

combat aircraft operational in France on 10 May at 1,013, though he puts the German total somewhat higher than Frieser's. In all, Facon concludes, the allies were outnumbered in the air by at least two to one, and probably rather more.

28. Bourachot, vol. 2, pp. 292–5.
29. Société d'Outillage Mécanique et d'Usinage d'Artillerie.
30. On the comparative characteristics of French and German tanks, the excellent graphic charts in Frieser, pp. 40–1, should be supplemented with the tables in Bourachot, vol. 2, pp. 271–7.
31. Doise & Vaïsse, p. 418.
32. Cochet, p. 200.
33. See Bourachot, vol. 2, p. 294.
34. Führer conferences of 10 October 1939 and 26 March 1940, in Charles Burdick & Hans-Adolf Jacobsen eds., *The Halder War Diary 1939–1942*, Novato, CA, 1988, pp. 70–1, 109.
35. Quoted in William L. Shirer, *The Collapse of the Third Republic: An Inquiry into the Fall of France in 1940*, NY, 1969, p. 17.
36. Quoted in Guderian, p. 30.
37. See Robert Doughty, *The Seeds of Disaster: The Development of French Army Doctrine 1919–1939*, Hamden, Conn., 1985.
38. N.A.G. Louis Chauvineau, *Une Invasion est-elle encore possible?*, Paris, 1939, pp. v–xxi.
39. *The Halder War Diary*, p. 90.
40. Gamelin, *Journal*, quoted in Martin S. Alexander, 'Gamelin et les leçons de la campagne de Pologne', in Maurice Vaïsse ed., *Mai–juin 1940: Défaite française, victoire allemande, sous l'œil des historiens étrangers*, Paris, 2000, pp. 59–74, p. 63.
41. Crémieux-Brilhac, vol. 2, p. 571. On the 55th see also Robert A. Doughty, *The Breaking Point: Sedan and the Fall of France, 1940*, Hamden, Conn., 1990, pp. 112–20.
42. Taittinger to Daladier 21 March, Huntziger's reply 8 April 1940, quoted in Crémieux-Brilhac, vol. 2, pp. 569–70.

Chapter 16

1. André Beaufre, *1940: The Fall of France*, London, 1967, p. 179.
2. Patrick Facon, *Batailles dans le ciel de France, mai–juin 1940*, Saint-Malo, 2010, pp. 95–101.
3. Quoted in Crémieux-Brilhac, vol. 2, p. 548.
4. See Adolf Heusinger, *Hitler et l'O.K.H. 1923–1945*, Paris, 1952, p. 51.
5. René Jacques Adolphe Prioux, *Souvenirs de guerre 1939–43*, Paris, 1947, p. 62; and for scathing comments on the Belgian defences see Daniel Barlone, *A French Officer's Diary (23 August 1939–1 October 1940)*, (translated by L.V. Cass), Cambridge, 1942, p. 49 (entry for 15 May).
6. On the intelligence aspects of the campaign see particularly Ernest R. May, *Strange Victory*, London, 2009, pp. 347–70; and Frieser, pp. 140–4, 247–8.
7. Quoted in Jean-Pierre Richardot, *100,000 Morts oubliés: les 47 jours et 47 nuits de la bataille de France, 10 mai–25 juin 1940*, Paris 2009, pp. 121–4; and for a French narrative based on eye-witness accounts, see Claude Gounelle, *Sedan, mai 1940*, Paris, 1965, pp. 141–65.
8. Edmond Ruby, *Sedan, terre d'épreuve: avec la IIme Armée mai–juin 1940*, Paris, 1948, p. 127.
9. Ruby, p. 133.
10. Clarence in Shakespeare's *Henry VI, Part 3*, Act IV, scene viii, lines 7–8.
11. Frieser, p. 179.
12. French aircraft used included Amiot 143s, Breguet 693s, Potez 631s and LeOs [Loiré-et-Olivier] 451s. On losses see Facon, *Batailles dans le ciel de France*, p. 114.
13. Guderian, p. 106.
14. Ruby, p. 168.
15. Quoted in Doughty, *The Breaking Point*, p. 289.
16. Ordre particulier No. 91, cited in Gaston René Roton, *Années cruciales: La Campagne 1939–1940*, Paris, 1947, p. 172.
17. Ruby, p. 144.

18. Winston S. Churchill, *The Second World War*, 6 vols., London, 1948–54, vol. 2, *Their Finest Hour*, pp. 38–46.
19. *The Halder War Diary*, pp. 70–1; Heusinger, *l'O.K.H.*, pp. 44–5.
20. *The Halder War Diary*, p. 149. Similarly Guderian, p. 109, thought Hitler 'frightened by his own temerity'.
21. On events in the town in the context of the campaign see Henri de Wailly, *Le coup de faux – Assassinat d'une ville: Abbeville 1940*, Paris, 1980.
22. Churchill, *Finest Hour*, p. 74. Writing in 1949, Churchill appears to have been the first person to use this term. All subsequent references to the Germans having planned and executed something called 'Operation *Sichelschnitt*' therefore appear to be anachronistic – see Kershaw, *Nemesis*, pp. 291, 920 n. 43.
23. Prioux, p. 86.
24. Jacques Minart, *P.C. Vincennes, Secteur 4*, 2 vols., Paris, 1945, vol. 2, pp. 184–5.
25. Beaufre, pp. 179, 183, 188.
26. Quoted in André Soubiran, *J'étais médecin avec les chars: Journal de guerre*, Paris, 1963, pp. 139–42.
27. Guderian, p. 111. The French tanks whose foray disturbed Guderian were probably not de Gaulle's at all, but belonged to 2nd Armoured Division.
28. De Gaulle, *War Memoirs*, vol. 1, p. 44. For the actions around Montcornet and Laon see Paul Huard, *Le Colonel de Gaulle et ses blindés: Laon (15–20 mai 1940)*, Paris, 1980.
29. Paul Baudouin, *Neuf mois au gouvernement, avril–décembre 1940*, Paris, 1948, pp. 24–5.
30. Quoted in Le Goyet, *Le mystère Gamelin*, pp. 258–9.
31. Goutard, pp. 101–2.
32. Quoted in Robert J. Young, 'French Military Intelligence and Nazi Germany, 1938–9', in May, *Knowing One's Enemies*, p. 306.
33. Gamelin, *Servir*, vol. 3, p. 415.
34. Churchill, *Finest Hour*, p. 44.
35. *Instruction personelle at secrète* No. 2, 19 May 1940, in Le Goyet, *Le mystère Gamelin*, p. 339; and for Georges's reaction see Roton, pp. 206–7. Minart, vol. 2, pp. 190–1, has a facsimile of the original manuscript. For an exceedingly charitable view of Gamelin see Martin S. Alexander, 'Maurice Gamelin and the Defeat of France, 1939–40', in Brian Bond ed., *Fallen Stars: Eleven Studies of Twentieth Century Military Disasters*, London, 1991, pp. 107–40.

Chapter 17

1. Antoine de Saint-Exupéry, *Pilote de guerre*, Paris, 1942 (reprinted 2012), p. 80; and on the flight, from which three of the nine escorting French fighters failed to return, see Emmanuel Chadeau, *Saint-Exupéry*, Paris, 1994, pp. 341–2.
2. The extent of the destruction is impressively documented by the photographs assembled in Thibault Richard, *France mai–juin 1940: l'ampleur d'un désastre*, Prahecq, 2010.
3. Saint-Exupéry, p. 100.
4. Minart, vol. 2, p. 161.
5. Léon Werth, *33 jours*, Paris, 2002, p. 33.
6. See Horne & Kramer, pp. 401–3; Bloch, *L'Étrange défaite*, p. 162. A fine account of the exodus in English is Hanna Diamond, *Fleeing Hitler: France 1940*, Oxford, 2007, which can be supplemented by Chapter 1 of Richard Vinen, *The Unfree French: Life under the Occupation*, London, 2006, pp. 26–44.
7. De Wailly, *Le coup de faux*, pp. 26–7, 49, 60–2, 111–13.
8. Henri de Wailly, *1940: L'Effondrement*, Paris, 2000, pp. 331–47.
9. Weygand, *Mémoires*, vol. 2, *Rappelé au service*, Paris, 1950, p. 93: and see Sir John Dill's report to the prime minister, 20 May 1940, in Ellis, p. 105.
10. Pétain to U.S. Ambassador William C. Bullitt, 4 June 1940, quoted in Orville H. Bullitt ed., *For the President: Personal and Secret. Correspondence between Franklin D. Roosevelt and William C. Bullitt*, London, 1973, p. 451.

11. Gort to CIGS, 2.49 p.m., 29 May 1940, quoted in Eleanor M. Gates, *End of the Affair, The Collapse of the Anglo-French Alliance, 1939–40*, London, 1981, p. 112.
12. Bloch, *L'Étrange défaite*, p. 102.
13. Minutes of the meeting at Bastion 32, Abrial's headquarters, at 1.30 p.m., 1 June 1940, in Richardot, p. 304; and on Anglo-French difficulties see John C. Cairns, 'The French View of Dunkirk', in Brian Bond & Michael D. Taylor eds., *The Battle of France and Flanders 1940: Sixty Years On*, Barnsley, 2001, pp. 87–109.
14. Roderick Macleod & Denis Kelly eds., *The Ironside Diaries 1937–1940*, London, 1962, p. 327 (entry for 21 May).
15. *Ironside Diaries*, p. 321.
16. Bloch, *L'Étrange défaite*, pp. 58, 141–3.
17. See J.R. Colville, *Man of Valour: The Life of Field-Marshal the Viscount Gort, VC, GCB, DSO, MVO, MC*, London, 1972, pp. 206, 211–12.
18. De Gaulle, *War Memoirs*, vol. 1, pp. 56–7.
19. Ellis, p. 103.
20. Ellis, pp. 246–7; Jacques Mordal, *Dunkerque*, Paris, 1968, pp. 497–9.
21. See Richardot, p. 336.
22. Barlone, p. 62; Bloch, *L'Étrange défaite*, pp. 50–1.
23. Ellis, p. 247.
24. Barlone, pp. 55, 60 (entries for 29 & 30 May 1940).
25. Mordal, pp. 364–6, 445.
26. See Jean Delmas, Paul Devautour & Eric Lefèvre, *Mai–juin 40: Les Combattants de l'Honneur*, Paris, 1980, pp. 130–76, which is also a notable pictorial record of the campaign.
27. See Étienne Dejonghe & Yves Le Maner, *Le Nord-Pas-de-Calais dans la main allemande, 1940–1944*, Lille, 2002, p. 52.
28. Churchill, *Finest Hour*, p. 86.
29. Quoted in Henri de Wailly, *De Gaulle sous le casque: Abbeville 1940*, Paris, 1990, p. 272.
30. Extracts quoted from Crémieux-Brilhac, vol. 2, *Ouvriers et soldats*, pp. 637–44.
31. André Maurois, *The Battle of France* (translated by F.R. Ludman), London, 1940, p. 199.
32. Herbert Lottman, *The Fall of Paris, June 1940*, London, 1992, p. 178.
33. Order of 5 June in Weygand, *Rappelé au service*, p. 168.
34. Raffael Scheck, *Hitler's African Victims: The German Army Massacres of Black French Soldiers in 1940*, Cambridge, 2006, pp. 53–60, 165–6; and see Jean-François Mouragues, *Soldats de la République: Les Tirailleurs sénégalais dans la Tourmente, France mai–juin 1940*, Paris, 2010, pp. 135–58.
35. 'Nous sommes au dernier quart d'heure. Tenez bon.' – Order No. 1471, 10 a.m., 9 June 1940, in Weygand, *Rappelé au service*, pp. 186–7.
36. Quoted in Christophe Dutrône, *Ils se sont battus, mai–juin 1940: Les photos et témoignages inédits de la Bataille de France*, Paris, 2010, p. 170 – another remarkable pictorial history of the campaign.
37. Lottman, p. 293, notes that on 26 June 1940 only 983,718 people remained from a pre-war population of 2,829,746. The absentees, however, presumably included men in military service as well as those who had left in September 1939.
38. Paul Reynaud, *Au Cœur de la Mêlée*, Paris, 1951, p. 731.
39. Mussolini to Marshal Badoglio, 26 May 1940, quoted in Pietro Badoglio, *Italy and the Second World War: Memories and Documents* (translated by Muriel Currey), Cambridge, 1948, p. 15.
40. See Gustave Bertrand, *Enigma*, Paris, 1973, pp. 88–9, 99–102.
41. Speech at a horse show in Lille, 2 July 1939, quoted in Bernard Destremau, *Weygand*, Paris, 1989, p. 363.
42. Quoted in Edward L. Spears, *Assignment to Disaster*, vol. 1, *Prelude to Dunkirk*, London, 1954, p. 190.
43. See Baudouin, *Neuf mois*, pp. 151–2 (entry for 12 June).
44. Gustave Hervé, *C'est Pétain qu'il nous faut*. See further Julian Jackson, *France: The Dark Years 1940–1944*, Oxford, 2001, pp. 123–6, 278–81; and Nicholas Atkin, *Pétain*, Harlow, 1998, pp. 58–9.
45. Pétain to Bullitt, 4 June 1940, quoted in Bullitt, p. 451.

46. Churchill, *Finest Hour*, pp. 135–42.
47. Conversation of 8 June, quoted in de Gaulle, *War Memoirs*, vol. 1, p. 61. According to Reynaud, *Au Cœur de la Mêlée*, p. 777, Weygand expressed himself even more colourfully to Henri de Kerillis on 13 June that the British wouldn't last a week.
48. Churchill, *Finest Hour*, pp. 134–5; and see Saul David, *Churchill's Sacrifice of the Highland Division: France 1940*, London, 1994, pp. 238–41.
49. On the Franco–American relationship see William R. Keylor, 'France and the Illusion of American Support, 1919–1940', in Joel Blatt ed., *The French Defeat of 1940: Reassessments*, New York, 2006, pp. 204–44; and on American attitudes to the fall of France Julian G. Hurstfield, *America and the French Nation, 1939–1945*, Chapel Hill, 1986, pp. 12–13, 39–40.
50. Churchill, *Finest Hour*, pp. 157–67.
51. See Richardot, pp. 386–9, citing Robert Frank, 'Les incidences nationales et internationales de la défaite française', in Christine Levisse-Touzé ed., *La Campagne de 1940*, Paris, 2001, p. 523.

Chapter 18

1. Bloch, *L'Étrange défaite*, p. 144.
2. Sadoul, *Journal de guerre*, pp. 352–6.
3. Diamond, p. 150.
4. Cabinet discussion of 12 June 1940, in Reynaud, *Au Cœur de la Mêlée*, p. 760; and see Baudouin, p. 149.
5. Baudouin, p. 174.
6. It was not customary to call votes in French cabinet meetings. Given its fateful consequences, Reynaud's decision to resign has remained controversial. For analysis see Thibault Tellier, *Paul Reynaud: Un indépendant en politique, 1878–1966*, Paris, 2005, pp. 624–57, and Jean-Pierre Azéma, *1940: L'Année noire*, Paris, 2010, pp. 132–53.
7. Jacques Isorni ed., *Philippe Pétain: Actes et écrits*, Paris, 1974, pp. 448–9.
8. Details of the final combats may be traced in Roger Bruge, *Les Combattants du 18 juin*, 5 vols., Paris, 1982–9, and the same author's illustrated volume *Juin 1940: Le Mois maudit*, Paris, 1980.
9. See Roton, p. 293.
10. Crémieux-Brilhac, vol. 2, *Ouvriers et soldats*, pp. 687–94.
11. Beaufre, p. 210.
12. Sadoul, p. 351.
13. A. Ducasse, J. Meyer & G. Perreux, *Vie et mort des Français 1914–1918*, Paris, 1959, p. 455 fn. 4.
14. On their relationship see the appendix to Richard Griffiths, *Marshal Pétain*, London, 1970, pp. 345–50 and Jean Lacouture, *De Gaulle*, vol. 1, *Le rebelle*, Paris, 1984, pp. 273–84.
15. Quoted in Crémieux-Brilhac, *La France Libre*, Paris, 2001, vol. 1, p. 59.
16. De Gaulle, *War Memoirs*, vol. 1, p. 10.
17. Premier appel, 18 June 1940, in Charles de Gaulle, *Discours et messages pendant la guerre, juin 1940–janvier 1946*, Paris, 1970, pp. 3–4.
18. Weygand, *Rappelé au service*, p. 250.
19. For the text of the armistice see Weygand, *Rappelé au service*, pp. 252–7.
20. On prisoners of war see Yves Durand, *La vie quotidienne des prisonniers de guerre dans les Stalags, les Oflags et les Kommandos, 1939–1945*, Paris, 1987; and Christophe Lewin, *Le Retour des prisonniers de guerre français*, Paris, 1986.
21. Radio broadcast, 25 June 1940, in Pétain, *Actes et écrits*, p. 453.
22. Churchill, *Finest Hour*, p. 161.
23. See e.g. Le Goyet, *La défaite*, p. 143.
24. Jean-Jacques Arzalier, 'La Campagne de mai–juin 1940: Les pertes?', in Levisse-Touzé, pp. 427–47.
25. In 1940 22,000 civilians died violently as a result of the war, the greater part of them in May–June. See Jean-Luc Leleu et al., *La France pendant la Seconde Guerre Mondiale: Atlas historique*, Paris 2010, p. 263.
26. Frieser, pp. 318, 429 fn. 26.

27. Ellis, p. 326.
28. See Facon, *Batailles dans le ciel de France*, pp. 223–40.
29. Ellis, p. 325.
30. Spears, vol. 2, p. 272. Churchill recalled the phrase in his speech to the Canadian Parliament on 30 December 1941. See his *History of the Second World War*, vol. 3, *The Grand Alliance*, p. 602.
31. Churchill, *Finest Hour*, p. 205.
32. On Mers-el-Kébir see Colin Smith, *England's Last War Against France: Fighting Vichy 1940–1942*, London, 2009, pp. 57–88; and Peter Mangold, *Britain and the Defeated French: From Occupation to Liberation, 1940–1944*, London, 2012, pp. 33–44.
33. Jean Zay, *Souvenirs et solitude*, La Tour d'Aigues, 2004, p. 51 (entry for 17 January 1941). Zay became another Jewish victim of Vichy, murdered in 1944.
34. Hitler to the Russian general Vlassov, June 1943, quoted in de Wailly, *1940: L'Effondrement*, p. 351 fn.
35. The impact of France's defeat upon the course of the Second World War and the global balance of power is surveyed in David Reynolds, '1940: Fulcrum of the Twentieth Century?', *International Affairs*, vol. 66 (2), 1990, pp. 325–50; whilst the short- and long-term impact of defeat on France itself is considered in Andrew Shennan, *The Fall of France, 1940*, Harlow, 2000.
36. Statistics from Leleu, pp. 120, 205–6, 209; and see Henry Rousso, *Les années noires: vivre sous l'occupation*, Paris, 1992, pp. 83–101.
37. Quoted in Speer, *Inside the Third Reich*, p. 172.

Conclusion

1. *The Economic Consequences of the Peace*, reprinted as *The Collected Writings of John Maynard Keynes*, vol. 2, Cambridge, 1971, p. 51.
2. Foch's presentation to the Council of Four, 31 March 1919, in Paul Mantoux, *Les Délibérations du Conseil des Quatre*, Paris, 1955, vol. 1, p. 93.
3. Sir Ronald Campbell to Lord Halifax, 27 June 1940, quoted in John C. Cairns, 'Some Recent Historians and the "Strange Defeat" of 1940', *Journal of Modern History*, vol. 46 (1974), pp. 60–85, p. 84 fn. 89.
4. Bradford A. Lee, 'Strategy, arms and the collapse of France, 1930–40', in Richard Langhorne ed., *Diplomacy and Intelligence during the Second World War*, Cambridge, 1985, pp. 43–67, p. 66.
5. Entry for 15 July 1870 in A.R. Allinson ed., *The War Diary of the Emperor Frederick III, 1870–1871*, London, 1927, p. 6.
6. For an assessment of the strategic significance of the Marne see Patrick Garreau, *1914: Une Europe se joue sur la Marne*, Paris, 2004, pp. 186–91.
7. See Julian Jackson, *The Fall of France: The Nazi Invasion of 1940*, Oxford, 2003, pp. 197–9.
8. Hitler to Mussolini, 25 May 1940, cited in John C. Cairns, 'Along the Road Back to France 1940', *American Historical Review*, vol. 64:3 (1959), pp. 583–603, p. 596.
9. Jackson, p. 160.
10. Henry Dutailly, 'Une puissance militaire illusoire, 1930–1939', in Pedroncini ed., *Histoire militaire de la France*, vol. 3, p. 357.
11. Colville, p. 198; and see Spears, vol. 1, p. 226.
12. *L'Étrange défaite*, p. 66.
13. *L'Étrange défaite*, p. 73.
14. Pierre Lehautcourt, *Campagne de l'Est en 1870–1871: Nuits, Villersexel*, Paris, 1896, p. viii.
15. Cairns, 'Some Recent Historians', p. 84.
16. De Wailly, *Le Coup de faux*, p. 9.
17. De Gaulle, *Vers l'armée de métier*, Paris, 1934, p. 12.
18. Lucan, *The Civil War* (as translated by Nicholas Rowe, 1719), Everyman edn, London, 1998, 'Pharsalia', Book 7, p. 215, lines 1195–6.

Further Reading

French printed sources quoted in this work are referenced in the notes. These suggestions are confined to works in English.

On 1870

Adriance, Thomas J., *The Last Gaiter Button: A Study of the Mobilisation and Concentration of the French Army in the War of 1870*, Westport, Conn., 1987.

Ascoli, David, *A Day of Battle: Mars-la-Tour 16 August 1870*, London, 1987.

Badsey, Stephen, *The Franco-Prussian War* (Osprey Essential Histories), Oxford, 2003.

Baldick, Robert, *The Siege of Paris*, London, 1964.

Barker, Nancy Nichols, *Distaff Diplomacy: The Empress Eugénie and the Foreign Policy of the Second Empire*, Austin, Texas, 1967.

Barry, Quintin, *The Franco-Prussian War*, 2 vols., Solihull, 2007.

Bressler, Fenton, *Napoleon III: A Life*, London, 1999.

Breuilly, John, *The Formation of the First German Nation-State, 1800–1871*, Basingstoke, 1996.

Bury, J.P.T., *Gambetta and the National Defence: A Republican Dictatorship in France*, London, 1936.

——, *Gambetta and the Making of the Third Republic*, London, 1973.

Bury, J.P.T. & Tombs, R.P., *Thiers 1797–1877: A Political Life*, London, 1986.

Carr, William, *The Origins of the Wars of German Unification*, Harlow, 1991.

Case, Lynn M., *French Opinion on War and Diplomacy during the Second Empire*, reprint, New York, 1984.

Clark, Christopher, *Iron Kingdom: The Rise and Downfall of Prussia, 1600–1947*, London, 2006.

Elliot-Wright, Philipp, *Gravelotte-St. Privat 1870: End of the Second Empire*, London, 1993.

Fermer, Douglas, *Sedan 1870: The Eclipse of France*, Barnsley, 2008.

——, *France at Bay 1870–71: The Struggle for Paris*, Barnsley, 2011.

Feuchtwanger, Edgar, *Bismarck*, London, 2002.

Förster, Stig, & Nagler, Jörg, eds., *On the Road to Total War: The American Civil War and the German Wars of Unification, 1861–1871*, Cambridge, 1997.

Guedalla, Philip, *The Two Marshals: Bazaine & Pétain*, London, 1943.

Holmes, Richard, *Fatal Avenue*, London, 1992.

——, *The Road to Sedan*, London, 1984.

Hooper, George, *The Campaign of Sedan: The Downfall of the Second Empire*, reprint, Worley Publications, 1998.

Horne, Alistair, *The Fall of Paris: The Siege and the Commune 1870–71*, London, 1965.

——, *The Terrible Year: The Paris Commune, 1871*, London, 1971 (reprinted 2004).

Howard, Michael, *The Franco-Prussian War: The German Invasion of France, 1870–1871*, London, 1961. (The classic work on the conflict.)

Hughes, Daniel J., ed., *Moltke on the Art of War: Selected Writings*, Novato, 1993.

Lerman, Katherine Anne, *Bismarck*, London, 2004.

McMillan, James F., *Napoleon III*, Harlow, 1991.
Milner, John, *Art, War and Revolution in France 1870–1871*, Yale, 2000.
Mitchell, Allan, *Bismarck and the French Nation 1848–1890*, New York, 1971.
Moltke, Helmuth von, *The Franco-German War of 1870–71* (Introduction by Michael Howard), London, 1992.
Ollivier, Émile, *The Franco-Prussian War and its Hidden Causes* (translated by George Burnham Ives), New York, 1912, reprinted 1970.
Patry, Léonce, *The Reality of War*, London, 2001.
Price, Roger, *The French Second Empire: An Anatomy of Political Power*, Cambridge, 2001.
Shann, Stephen, & Delperier, Louis, *French Army 1870–71: Franco-Prussian War 1: Imperial Troops*, London, 1991.
——, *French Army 1870–71: Franco-Prussian War 2: Republican Troops*, London, 1991.
Showalter, Dennis, *The Wars of German Unification*, London, 2004.
Steefel, Lawrence D., *Bismarck, the Hohenzollern Candidacy, and the Origins of the Franco-German War of 1870*, Cambridge, Mass., 1962.
Steinberg, Jonathan, *Bismarck: A Life*, Oxford, 2011.
Stone, David, *'First Reich': Inside the German Army during the War with France, 1870–71*, London, 2002.
Tombs, Robert, *The Paris Commune 1871*, Harlow, 1999.
——, *The War Against Paris*, Cambridge, 1981.
Wawro, Geoffrey, *The Franco-Prussian War: The German Conquest of France in 1870–1871*, Cambridge, 2003.
Williams, Roger L., *The French Revolution of 1870–1871*, New York, 1969.

On 1914

Becker, Jean-Jacques, *The Great War and the French People*, Providence, 1993.
Blond, Georges, *The Marne* (reprint) London, 2002.
Bredin, Jean-Denis, *The Affair: The Case of Alfred Dreyfus*, New York, 1986.
Carroll, E. Malcolm, *French Public Opinion and Foreign Affairs 1870–1914*, New York, 1931.
Challener, Richard D., *The French Theory of the Nation in Arms 1866–1939*, New York, 1965.
Chickering, Roger, & Förster, Stig, *Great War, Total War: Combat and Mobilization on the Western Front, 1914–1918*, Cambridge, 2000.
Chrastil, Rachel, *Organizing for War: France 1870–1914*, Baton Rouge, 2010.
Clark, Christopher, *Kaiser Wilhelm II: A Life in Power*, London, 2009.
——, *The Sleepwalkers: How Europe Went to War in 1914*, London, 2012.
Clayton, Anthony, *Paths of Glory: The French Army 1914–18*, London, 2003.
Doughty, Robert A., *Pyrrhic Victory: French Strategy and Operations in the Great War*, Cambridge, Mass., 2005.
Evans, R.J.W. & Pogge von Strandmann, Hartmut, eds., *The Coming of the First World War*, Oxford, 1990.
Flood, P.J., *France 1914–18: Public Opinion and the War Effort*, Basingstoke, 1990.
Fromkin, David, *Europe's Last Summer: Why the World Went to War in 1914*, London, 2004.
Gildea, Robert, *Children of the Revolution: The French 1799–1914*, London, 2008.
Gooch, G.P., *Franco-German Relations 1871–1914*, London, 1923.
Hamilton, Richard F. & Herwig, Holger H., *Decisions for War 1914–1917*, Cambridge, 2004.
——, eds., *War Planning 1914*, Cambridge, 2010.
Harris, Ruth, *The Man on Devil's Island: Alfred Dreyfus and the Affair that Divided France*, London, 2010.
Herwig, Holger H., *The Marne, 1914: The Opening of World War I and the Battle that Changed the World*, New York, 2009.
Holmes, Richard, *The Little Field Marshal: A Life of Sir John French*, 2nd edn, 2005.
Horne, John & Kramer, Alan, *German Atrocities 1914: A History of Denial*, London, 2001.
Howard, Michael, 'Men Against Fire: The Doctrine of the Offensive in 1914', in Peter Paret ed., *Makers of Modern Strategy from Machiavelli to the Nuclear Age*, Oxford, 1986, pp. 510–26.

Isselin, Henri, *The Battle of the Marne*, London, 1964.

Keegan, John, *Opening Moves: August 1914*, London, 1973.

——, *The First World War*, London, 1998.

Keiger, John F.V., *France and the Origins of the First World War*, London, 1981.

——, *Raymond Poincaré*, Cambridge, 1997.

Kennedy, Paul M., ed., *The War Plans of the Great Powers 1880–1914*, London, 1985.

Krumeich, Gerd, *Armaments and Politics in France on the Eve of the First World War*, Leamington Spa, 1984.

La Gorce, Paul-Marie, *The French Army: A Political-Military History*, London, 1963.

May, Ernest R., *Knowing One's Enemies: Intelligence Assessment before the Two World Wars*, Princeton, 1984.

Mitchell, Allan, *Victors and Vanquished: The German Influence on Army and Church in France after 1870*, Chapel Hill, 1994.

——, *The German Influence in France After 1870*, Chapel Hill, 1979.

Mombauer, Annika, *Helmuth von Moltke and the Origins of The First World War*, Cambridge, 2001.

Nolan, Michael E., *The Inverted Mirror: Mythologizing the Enemy in France and Germany, 1898–1914*, New York, 2005.

Porch, Douglas, *The March to the Marne: The French Army 1871–1914*, Cambridge, 1981.

Ralston, David B., *The Army of the Republic: The Place of the Military in the Political Evolution of France, 1871–1914*, Cambridge, Mass., 1967.

Senior, Ian, *Home Before The Leaves Fall: A New History of the German Invasion of 1914*, Oxford, 2012.

Spears, Edward, *Liaison 1914*, London, 2000.

Stevenson, David, *Armaments and the Coming of War: Europe, 1904–1914*, Oxford, 1996.

——, *French War Aims Against Germany 1914–1919*, Oxford, 1982.

——, *1914–1918: The History of the First World War*, London, 2004.

Strachan, Hew, *The First World War: Volume 1: To Arms*, Oxford, 2001.

Sumner, Ian, *French Poilu 1914–18*, Oxford, 2009.

——, *The First Battle of the Marne 1914*, Oxford, 2010.

——, *The French Army 1914–18*, Oxford, 1995.

——, *They Shall Not Pass: The French Army on the Western Front 1914–1918*, Barnsley, 2012.

Taylor, A.J.P., *The Struggle for Mastery in Europe, 1848–1918*, Oxford, 1954.

Tombs, Robert & Isabelle, *That Sweet Enemy: The French and the British from the Sun King to the Present*, London, 2006.

Tuchman, Barbara, *August 1914*, London, 1962.

Tyng, Sewell, *The Campaign of the Marne 1914*, London, 1935 (reprinted 2007).

Uffindell, Andrew, *The Marne 1914: A Battlefield Guide*, Barnsley, 2013.

Weber, Eugen, *The Nationalist Revival in France, 1905–1914*, Berkeley, 1959.

Wilson, Keith, ed., *Decisions for War, 1914*, London, 1995.

Zuber, Terence, *The Battle of the Frontiers: Ardennes 1914*, Stroud, 2007.

On 1940

Adamthwaite, Anthony, *Grandeur and Misery: France's bid for power in Europe 1914–1940*, London, 1995.

Alexander, Martin S., *The Republic in Danger: General Maurice Gamelin and the politics of French defence, 1933–1940*, Cambridge, 1992.

——, ' "No taste for the fight"?: French Combat Performance in 1940 and the Politics of the Fall of France', in Paul Addison & Angus Calder eds., *Time To Kill: The Soldier's Experience of the War in the West 1939–1945*, London, 1997, pp. 161–76.

Allcorn, William, *The Maginot Line 1928–45*, Oxford, 2003.

Atkin, Nicholas, *Pétain*, Harlow, 1998.

Bankwitz, Philip, *Maxime Weygand and Civil-Military Relations in Modern France*, Cambridge, 1967.

Barlone, Daniel, *A French Officer's Diary (23 August 1939–1 October 1940)* (translated by L.V. Cass), Cambridge, 1942.

Bell, P.M.H., *A Certain Eventuality: Britain and the Fall of France*, Farnborough, 1974.

——, *The Origins of The Second World War in Europe*, (3rd edn), Harlow, 2007.

Blatt, Joel, ed., *The French Defeat of 1940: Reassessments*, NY, 1998.

Bloch, Marc, *Strange Defeat: A Statement of Evidence Written in 1940* (translated by Gerard Hopkins), NY, 1999.

Bond, Brian, *Britain, France and Belgium 1939–1940*, 2nd edn, London, 1990.

——, ed., *Fallen Stars: Eleven Studies of Twentieth Century Military Disasters*, London, 1991.

—— & Taylor, Michael D., *The Battle of France and Flanders 1940: Sixty Years On*, Barnsley, 2001.

Boyce, Robert, ed., *French Foreign and Defence Policy, 1918–1940: The Decline and Fall of a Great Power*, London, 1998.

Bury, J.P.T., *France: The Insecure Peace, From Versailles to the Great Depression*, London, 1972.

Chapman, Guy, *Why France Fell: The Defeat of the French Army in 1940*, NY, 1969.

Churchill, Sir Winston, *Their Finest Hour*, London, 1949 (vol. 2 of *The Second World War*, 6 vols., London, 1948–54).

Deighton, Len, *Blitzkrieg: From the Rise of Hitler to the Fall of Dunkirk*, London, 1979.

Diamond, Hanna, *Fleeing Hitler: France 1940*, Oxford, 2007.

Doughty, Robert Allan, *The Seeds of Disaster: The Development of French Army Doctrine 1919–1939*, Hamden, Conn., 1985.

——, *The Breaking Point: Sedan and the Fall of France, 1940*, Hamden, Conn., 1990.

Duroselle, Jean-Baptiste, *France and the Nazi Threat: The Collapse of French Diplomacy 1932–1939* (English edn translated by C.E. Dop & R.L. Miller), NY, 2004.

Frieser, Karl-Heinz, *The Blitzkrieg Legend: The 1940 Campaign in the West*, Annapolis, 2005.

Gates, Eleanor M., *End of the Affair: The Collapse of the Anglo-French Alliance, 1939–40*, London, 1981.

Gaulle, Charles de, *War Memoirs*, vol. 1, *The Call to Honour 1940–1942* (translated by Jonathan Griffin), London, 1955.

Goutard, Adolphe, *The Battle of France, 1940* (translated by A.R.P. Burgess), London, 1958.

Griffiths, Richard, *Marshal Pétain*, London, 1970.

Guderian, Heinz, *Panzer Leader* (translated by Constantine Fitzgibbon), London, 1952 (paperback reissue, 2009).

Gunsburg, Jeffery A., *Divided and Conquered: The French High Command and the Defeat of the West, 1940*, Westport, Conn., 1979.

Horne, Alistair, *To Lose a Battle: France 1940*, London & Boston, 1969.

Hughes, Judith M., *To the Maginot Line: The Politics of French Military Preparation in the 1920s*, Cambridge, Mass., 1971 (reprinted 2006).

Imlay, Talbot C., *Facing the Second World War: Strategy, Politics and Economics in Britain and France, 1938–1940*, Oxford, 2003.

Jackson, Julian, *France: The Dark Years 1940–1944*, Oxford, 2001.

——, *The Fall of France: The Nazi Invasion of 1940*, Oxford, 2003.

Jackson, Peter, *France and The Nazi Menace: Intelligence and Policy Making 1933–1939*, Oxford, 2000.

Kedward, Rod, *La Vie en Bleu: France and The French since 1900*, London, 2006.

Kershaw, Ian, *Hitler*, 2 vols., London, 1998–2000.

Kiesling, Eugenia, *Arming Against Hitler: France and the Limits of Military Planning*, Lawrence, Kansas, 1996.

Knapp, Wilfrid, *France: Partial Eclipse. From the Stavisky Riots to the Nazi Conquest*, London, 1972.

Lottman, Herbert R., *The Fall of Paris, June 1940*, London, 1992.

MacMillan, Margaret, *Paris 1919: Six Months that Changed the World*, NY, 2003 (Original edn, *Peacemakers*, London, 2001).

McNab, Chris, *The Fall of Eben Emael: Belgium 1940*, Oxford, 2013.

May, Ernest R., *Strange Victory: Hitler's Conquest of France*, London, 2009.

Overy, Richard & Wheatcroft, Andrew, *The Road To War*, London, 1989.

Pallud, Jean-Paul, *Blitzkrieg in the West: Then and Now*, London, 1991.

Romanych, Marc & Rupp, Martin, *Maginot Line 1940: Battles on the French Frontier*, Oxford, 2010.

Scheck, Raffael, *Hitler's African Victims: The German Army Massacres of Black French Soldiers in 1940*, Cambridge, 2006.

Sebag-Montefiore, Hugh, *Dunkirk: Fight to the Last Man*, London, 2006.

Shennan, Andrew, *The Fall of France, 1940*, Harlow, 2000.

Shepperd, Alan, *France 1940: Blitzkrieg in the West*, London, 1990.

Shirer, William L., *The Collapse of the Third Republic: An Inquiry into the Fall of France in 1940*, NY, 1969.

Singer, Barnett, *Maxime Weygand: A Biography of the French General in Two World Wars*, Jefferson, North Carolina, 2008.

Spears, Edward L., *Assignment to Catastrophe*, 2 vols., London, 1954.

Stewart, Geoffrey, *Dunkirk and the Fall of France*, Barnsley, 2008.

Tombs, Robert & Chabal, Emile eds., *Britain and France in Two World Wars: Truth, Myth and Memory*, London, 2013.

Vinen, Richard, *The Unfree French: Life under the Occupation*, London, 2006.

Warner, Philip, *The Battle of France 10 May-22 June 1940: Six Weeks Which Changed the World*, London, 1990.

Williams, John, *France: Summer 1940*, London, 1969.

——, *The Ides of May: The Defeat of France, May-June 1940*, London, 1968.

Young, Robert J., *France and the Origins of the Second World War*, Basingstoke, 1996.

——, *In Command of France: French Foreign Policy and Military Planning 1933–1940*, Cambridge, Mass., 1978.

Index